INTRODUCTION

Welcome to the world of digital publishing ~ the book you now hold in your hand, while unchanged from the original **1969** edition, was printed using the latest state of the art digital technology. The advent of print-on-demand has forever changed the publishing process, never has information been so accessible and it is our hope that this book serves your informational needs for years to come. If this is your first exposure to digital publishing, we hope that you are pleased with the results. Many more titles of interest to the classic automobile and motorcycle enthusiast, collector and restorer are available via our website at **www.VelocePress.com.** We hope that you find this title as interesting as we do.

NOTE FROM THE PUBLISHER

The information presented is true and complete to the best of our knowledge. All recommendations are made without any guarantees on the part of the author or the publisher, who also disclaim all liability incurred with the use of this information.

TRADEMARKS

We recognize that some words, model names and designations, for example, mentioned herein are the property of the trademark holder. We use them for identification purposes only. This is not an official publication.

INFORMATION ON THE USE OF THIS PUBLICATION

This manual is an invaluable resource for the classic **TRIUMPH TR** enthusiast and a "must have" for owners interested in performing their own maintenance. However, in today's information age we are constantly subject to changes in common practice, new technology, availability of improved materials and increased awareness of chemical toxicity. As such, it is advised that the user consult with an experienced professional prior to undertaking any procedure described herein. While every care has been taken to ensure correctness of information, it is obviously not possible to guarantee complete freedom from errors or omissions or to accept liability arising from such errors or omissions. Therefore, any individual that uses the information contained within, or elects to perform or participate in do-it-yourself repairs or modifications acknowledges that there is a risk factor involved and that the publisher or its associates cannot be held responsible for personal injury or property damage resulting from the use of the information or the outcome of such procedures.

It is important that the reader recognizes that any instructions may refer to either the right-hand or left-hand sides of the vehicle or the components and that the directions are followed carefully. One final word of advice, this publication is intended to be used as a reference guide, and when in doubt the reader should consult with a qualified technician.

TRIUMPH OWNERS HANDBOOK of Maintenance & Repair

By
Technical Editors of
Clymer Publications

Published by
FLOYD CLYMER PUBLICATIONS
World's Largest Publisher of Books Relating to
Automobile, Motorcycles, Motor Racing, and Americana
222 NO. VIRGIL AVENUE, LOS ANGELES, CALIF. 90004

CONTENTS

Topic	Page
Announcement	3
Tuning	4
Tuneup Specifications	41
The Engine	42
Fuel System	105
Cooling System	94
Electrical Equipment	127
Wiring Diagrams	146
The Clutch	166
The Gearbox	185
The Propeller Shaft	197
The Rear Axle	201
Front Suspension & Steering	216
Springs & Shock Absorbers	249
Wheels & Tires	257
Brakes	266
TR 2-3 Body	294
TR 4 Body	297
TR 2-3 General Data	300
TR 4 General Data	312
Stromberg Carburetors	323

ANNOUNCEMENT

The TR OWNERS HANDBOOK has been of special interest to me during its preparation inasmuch as this breed of sports car is, I think, very well turned out. TRs are rugged, fast and quite reliable. Their competition record is an enviable one. And, all the TR owners whom I know are extremely happy with the machine. We have had a lot of demand from TR people for a book which presents the facts and mechanical details on their cars in layman's terms — one which would enable them to understand and maintain the automobile without going into the formal, technical and dry shop manual. This Handbook is not, of course, a shop manual, and we strongly urge the TR owner to take his major problems to an authorized TR service garage where trained mechanics and correct shop equipment are available. However, the book is detailed so that in an emergency it can be handed to a mechanic who is, perhaps, unfamiliar with the TR, and he can effect the necessary repairs using it as a guide. All specifications and data, as well as procedures, are those as given in the latest factory service information, and it is as reliable a guide as we can make it by drawing on technical bulletins and the experience of TR specialists. The Handbook will thus enable the owner to maintain and repair his car in whatever manner his experience and tools dictate.

Since many owners who have no inclination to do no more than tuneups and minor jobs, we are presenting the tuneup process as the first section of the book. If you are familiar with the car, this may be as much as you need to get under way. If the TR is new to you, I would suggest an advance study of the chapters on the engine, ignition, and fuel system. They are interesting enough to make good armchair reading, anyway, and a better acquaintance with the car will result.

I am sure that you will find the service diagnosis pages most helpful. Here, various symptoms, probable causes and remedies are given in easy-to-read form and 90% of all automotive troubles can be located by such an anlysis if carefully studied.

For the TR owner who is interested in racing, I suggest that he contact the Competition Department, Standard Triumph Motor Co., 575 Madison Ave., New York 22, N.Y., and request the latest competition tuning bulletin because of the continually changing rules and new modifications being permitted. These bulletins are kept up to date in a manner not possible with a volume of this size, so we have not included such competition data. The TR Handbook will, naturally, be of great assistance in carrying out any of the suggested work on chassis or drive line.

Good luck and happy motoring.

Floyd Clymer

TUNING UP THE TR

How often should you tune your car? Factory recommendations for service maintenance center around the 6,000 mile mark. This would be on a twice-a-year basis for the average driver. If much of your driving is stop-and-go, especially in cold weather, you may find yourself doing a little extra spark plug cleaning. The dashpots of the SU carburetors should also be inspected and topped up more frequently, say at 3,000 mile intervals. Generally speaking, however, a get-ready-for-Winter and a Spring house cleaning type of tune up will keep the TR in good shape. Other routine maintenance and inspection should not be overlooked, of course.

There are few things in sports car motoring that are as depressing as the realization that your engine is no longer the high-revving, smooth-running, ready-to-go-machine that you once knew. Other distressing symptoms are reluctance to respond to the starter button, slow acceleration or response to the foot, rough idle, reduced performance at top speeds, and increased gasoline consumption. When these conditions have developed, it is safe to say that we have lost touch with the condition of the engine, and that the engine is out of tune. Fortunately, in the great majority of cases, performance can be restored by the investment of a small amount of time and effort. The big difference in performance, smoothness, and economy is well worth the small amount of work involved.

For those owners who have invested in a used sports car, there may well be a revelation in store for you in the form of horsepower that you have never realized before.

The tune up reveals many things about the condition of your engine. A good engine that is out of tune will respond remarkably to the tune up procedures and adjustments.

For the engine that is in tune, the tune up procedure verifies that all the adjustments are on the mark and that you have an engine that will give you driving confidence. Equally important is the fact that the tune up will, besides insuring that the adjustments are correct, show up engine defects that involve minor repairs or which indicate a more serious situation that is developing. In either case a frequent tune up reveals these troubles early in the game and before serious damage is done to the engine.

The Tune Up Sequence

It is not absolutely necessary that a definite sequence of events be followed in doing a tune up, except that there are certain components of the engine that must be in proper order before you can make satisfactory adjustments on the others. As an example, it does little good to make carburetor adjustments if the valve adjustments are off, or if the distributor is giving trouble.

The general tune up usually proceeds in the following way.

1. **Valve adjustments** (Every 6,000 miles) — Since the valve tappet clearances are specified with the engine cold the valve adjustments should be checked first. The importance of the correct clearance cannot be overstressed. Should the clearances be set too close, there is the danger that upon heating, the valve stem expansion would not permit the valve to close properly with the possibility that the valves can overheat, warp, and burn.

They would also open earlier and close later than was intended. Tappet clearances that are too open (excessive clearance) reduce engine efficiency by opening later and closing earlier than was intended.

2. **Compression Check** (6,000 miles, or as thought necessary) — A compression check is made to determine the condition of the cylinders and valves. Serious compression drop or a 10% variation between cylinders indicates poor cylinder sealing which much be corrected before it is possible to tune up the engine. The compression check should always be made with the engine warm.

3. **Spark Plug Checks** (3,000-6,000 miles) — Examine each plug critically for insulator cracks, fouling, and electrode erosion. Clean and gap the electrodes to the specified gap and replace the plugs with a new gasket.

4. **Ignition Timing** (6,000 miles) — Ignition timing follows naturally after the spark plug check as the HT leads to the plugs are part of the ignition system. Make a visual examination of all the ignition leads and connectors for deterioration, poor contact, corrosion, and for arcing. Check the point condition, dress the points if needed, and gap to 0.015 inches. Check the condition of the distributor cap, rotor, arm, and brush. A dynamic timing check should be made of distributor action by use of the timing light if available to verify proper operation of the advance mechanism.

5. **Carburetor Checks** (3,000 miles) — Included in the carburetor check is the servicing of the air cleaners. Carburetors are adjusted to give proper idle speed, proper synchronization, and mixture. Routine maintenance of the S.U.s is done at this time.

Finally, follow up the tune up with a road test to check the tune up results. Set up a few acceleration tests that you and a friend can conduct with no more equipment than a stop watch, paper, and a suitable section of road. The road test will verify that your engine's performance is as good or better than it was before the tune up.

One important point to remember is that only an engine that is in good mechanical condition will tune properly. A tune up will cause a good engine to run properly but it will not correct a faulty engine. On the other hand, an engine in good condition will respond to a tune up to give smoother running, quicker acceleration, and improved top end performance.

The Tools You Need

It is assumed that the reader is in possession of the standard tool kit that is supplied with the Triumph. These kits contain all the tools necessary to perform all the general maintenance work that is covered in the instruction manual. These tool kits may be ordered through your Triumph dealer, Part No. 301413, or from the Standard Motor Co. LTD, Spares Division, Fletchamstead Highway, Coventry, England. In addition to those tools supplied in the tool kit, you will need the items listed below:
1. Screwdriver set — a good assortment ranging from small to quite large, insulated handle type.
2. Phillips screwdrivers — set
3. Offset screwdriver
4. Feeler gauge set
5. Spark plug gauge & tool
6. Spark plug wrench — long shank
7. Ignition file
8. Compression gauge
9. Timing light
10. Uni-syn (Multiple carburetor synchronizer) or SU tool
11. Extension light — portable and with a long cord.

The above tools and testers can be obtained for a cost of just slightly more than one good professional tune up, but will pay for themselves many times over in service and savings. Yet these few tools and devices will provide the owner with the essential information that is needed to perform the tune up intelligently.

The Parts You Need

The owner should provide himself with certain frequently used parts that must be replaced from time to time during tune up operations. It is strongly recommended that the following items be at hand before attempting your first tune up. The cost is small and the tune up will proceed much more smoothly and without frequent and frustrating interruptions. These items also serve as an emergency kit in case of breakdowns on the road and should be kept conveniently in the car.

1. Box of 100 spark plug gaskets. These must be replaced each time a plug is removed for inspection, cleaning, or gapping.
2. A replacement breaker point and condenser kit.
3. Spare set of spark plugs cleaned and gapped.
4. Two spare tappet ball pins and ball pin locking nuts.
5. Valve cover gasket and cement.
6. A spare jet needle of the type in use.
7. A spare set of advance weight springs.

Since most readers do not have a garage or service station type of spark plug cleaner and tester, the spare spark plug set permits the reader to install the spare set during the tune up then at some convenient time, he can have the other set cleaned and tested at his neighborhood service station.

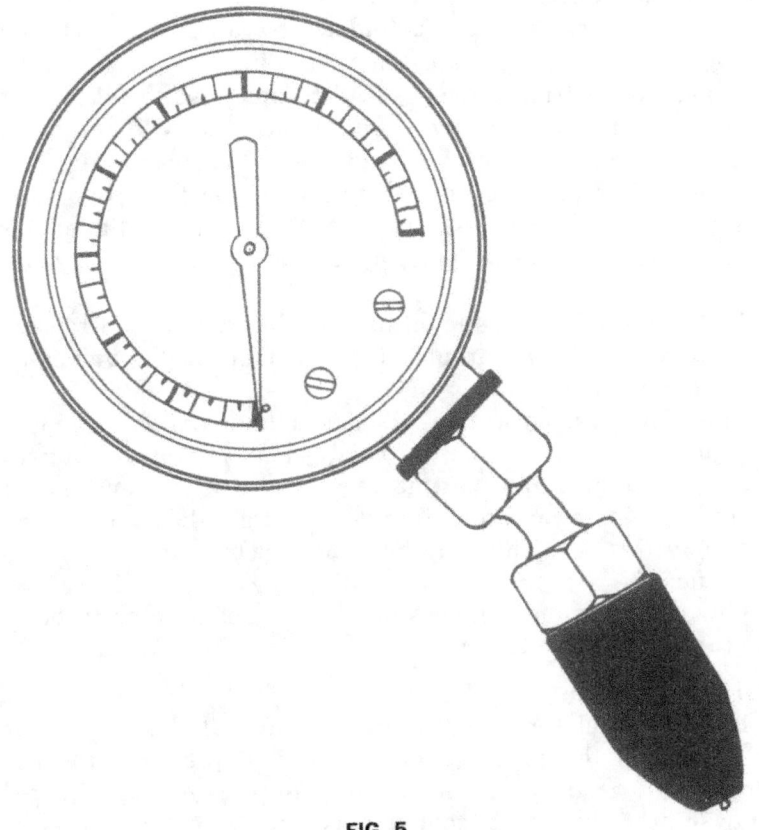

FIG. 5

The Compression Check

A compression check should be made a part of your major tune up procedure. The compression check gives you a good indication of the condition of your engine, for it tells you if rings are performing properly and whether or not valves are defective and giving you trouble.

The compression check should be done with the engine at operating temperature. Remove a spark plug and insert the compression gauge in the plug hole. Turn the engine over by use of the starter for a few revolutions to obtain a maximum reading on the gauge. Repeat the procedure for each cylinder, noting the readings. If the compression readings fall in around 120 - 125 and do not differ by more than 8 psi between cylinders, you have the assurance that your rings and valves are in good order. If all cylinders are uniformly low — or high — do not be alarmed. Compression gauges are not always accurate. **Differential** pressure is the important point.

Compression Defects

Low compression in one cylinder: If a low reading (10% or more) is obtained on one cylinder this indicates valve or ring trouble. To determine which, squirt some engine oil into the defective cylinder, turn the engine over once with the starter to clear some of the excess oil and insert the gauge again. If the compression returns to normal, this tells you that your valves are good but that the rings are defective on that cylinder. Low compression one one or more cylinders will give a rough running engine.

If the addition of engine oil to the cylinder does not raise the compression, then the trouble is most likely in the valves and a valve job is in order.

Low Compression in two adjacent cylinders: This condition may be an indication that the head gasket has blown between the two cylinders and that the gases are leaking from one cylinder to the other and therefore do not attain their normal compression pressure. This may be remedied by a head gasket replacement.

Low compression troubles must be corrected before proceeding further with the tune up.

Valve Adjustment

It is essential for a well tuned engine that the valves open and close in the proper sequence and at precisely the right moment in relation to the position of the pistons. Figure 7 shows the valve train components and how the valves are

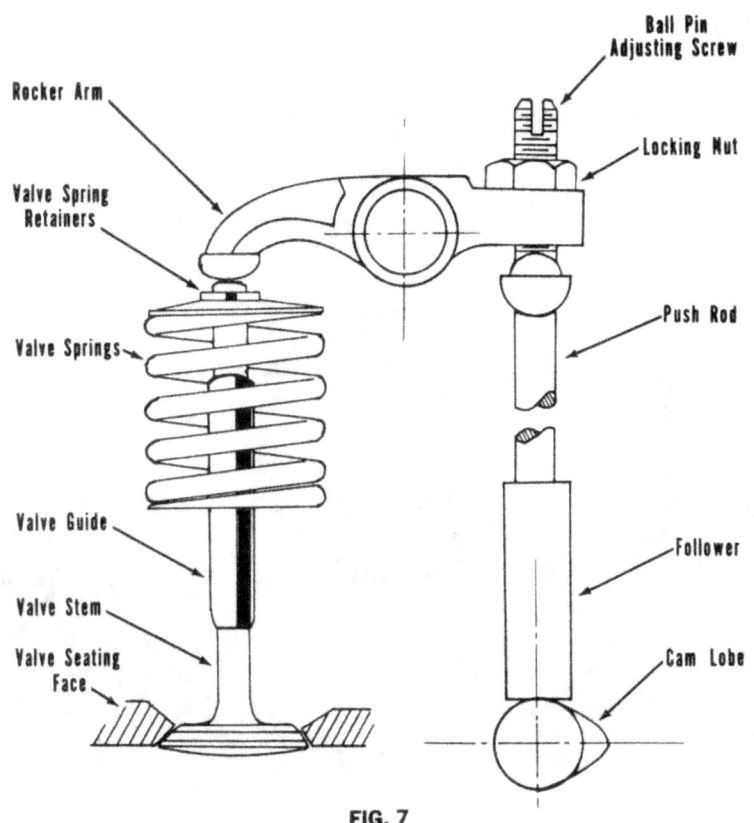

FIG. 7

actuated by the cam on the camshaft, through the lifter, the push rod, ball pin, rocker arm, and to the valve stem.

The camshaft is driven at one-half crankshaft speed and has cam lobes for each valve. The cam lobes are cut so that the valves open and close at the proper time and the proper amount in relation to the respective piston position in the cylinder. The valve train will do this provided the specified clearances are set.

Proper setting of the tappet clearances is one of the most important adjustments that is made during the tune up and the importance of setting the clearances precisely cannot be over emphasized. The clearances should be adjusted as accurately as your patience and ability to measure the gap will allow. Properly adjusted, the valves contribute to obtaining optimum performance by insuring that the cylinders receive their proper charge of fuel air mixture, by sealing off the cylinder for proper compression and combustion, and that the exhaust gases are expelled efficiently.

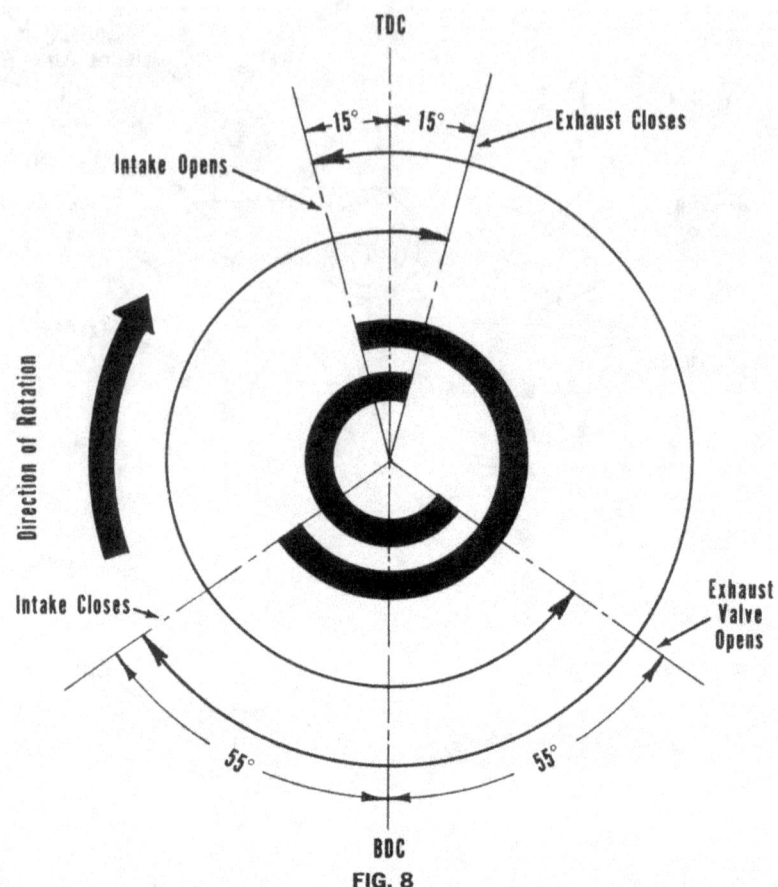
FIG. 8

Improper adjustment robs the engine of horsepower by not allowing the valves to open and close at the proper time in the cycle and may in some cases cause the valves to become damaged from overheating.

Adjustment of the valve tappet clearances is a mechanical procedure which can be done when the ignition or carburetion is out of adjustment, however, the valve tappet clearances must be properly set before it is possible to satisfactorily adjust the ignition system or the carburetors.

The following valve tappet clearances are recommended for the TR-2, TR-3 and TR-4 as listed below. **Measurements are made with the engine cold.**

	TR-2	TR-3-4
INTAKE	0.010 inches	0.010 inches
EXHAUST	0.012 inches	0.010 inches
HIGH SPEED	0.013 inches for both intake and exhaust. TR2/3/4	

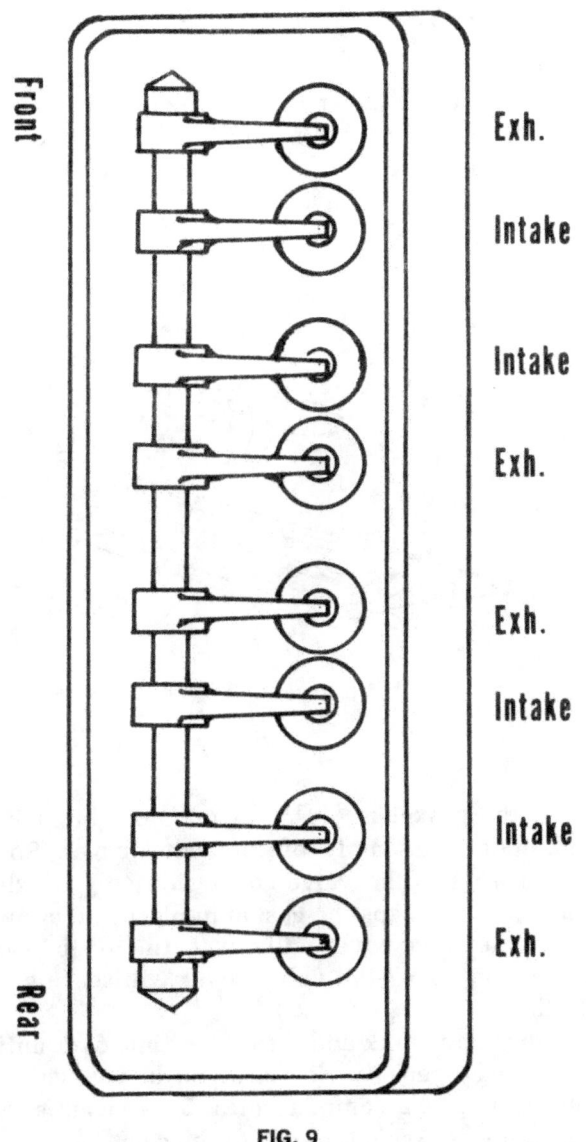
FIG. 9

The 0.013-inch clearance will give a noticeable increase in performance in most cases but is accompanied by considerable tappet noise. It then becomes a matter of personal choice. If the additional tappet noise is not annoying then the additional "snap" to be gained by the 0.013 clearance is there to be had.

Procedure

1. Remove the valve cover by unscrewing the two hold down nuts and lifting, taking care not to break the cork gasket. Have a cloth or paper laid out on which to place the valve cover and the gasket as it is removed.

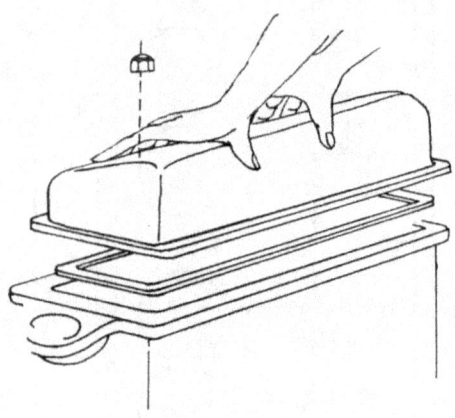

FIG. 10

NOTE: If the gasket is old or in poor condition it should be replaced upon reassembly of the valve cover. Some owners apply the gasket to the valve cover side only by glueing it on with cement. This keeps the gasket in place and allows frequent removal of the valve cover without tearing of the gasket. If the cork gasket is "alive" the valve cover will seat tightly without loss of oil.

2. Insert the hand crank and turn the engine over until the valve to be checked opens (rocker arm pushes valve down), then continue turning one complete turn. This ensures that the follower is on the backside (or heel) of the cam.

3. Place a thick bladed screw driver into the slot of the ball pin and wrench over the locking nut. See Figure 13.

4. Loosen the locking nut.

5. Keep pressure on the screw driver to remove any play in the valve train.

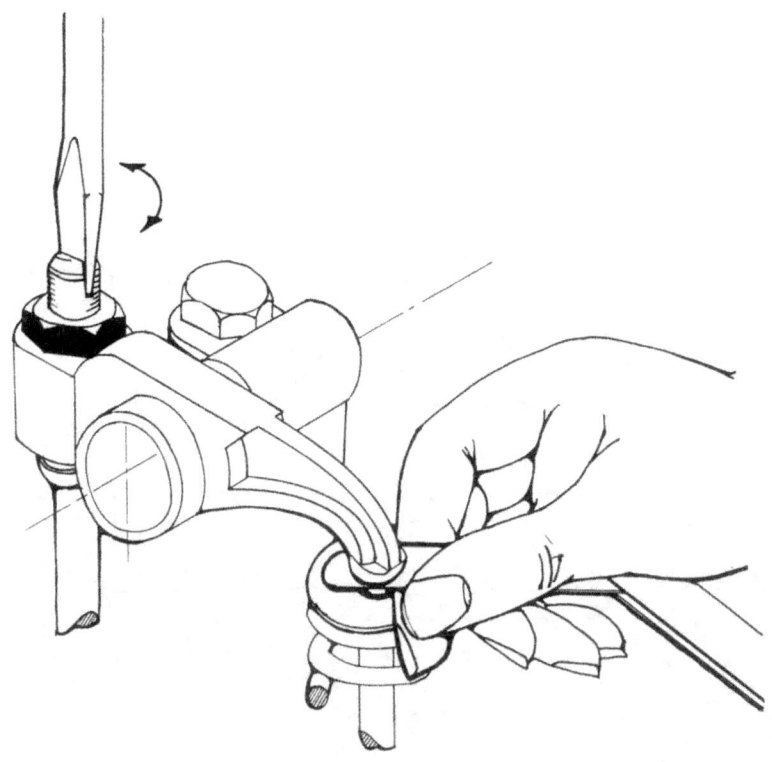

FIG. 11

6. Insert a feeler gauge of the proper thickness for the clearance to be measured and adjust the ball pin with the screw driver until the feeler gauge will pass between the rocker arm and the valve stem with a slight drag.
7. When satisfied with the clearance, hold the screwdriver in place and tighten down on the locking nut.
8. Keep the slack out of the valve train by pushing down on the ball pin and recheck the gap. If the gap is too close or loose, repeat the procedure.
9. Continue this procedure for each valve in turn.

NOTE: The faces of the tappet arm can become indented because of constantly being hammered against the tip of the valve stem. If you experience difficulty in adjusting the clearance correctly it may be from this cause. If this is determined to be the situation it will be necessary to replace the defective rocker arm with a new one. Another source of trouble is when the ball pin and locking nut have taken a set so that it becomes very difficult to adjust the ball pin and have it hold. In this case it will be necessary to replace the ball pin and set the clearance

as before.
10. Replace the valve cover and secure tightly to make a good oil seal.

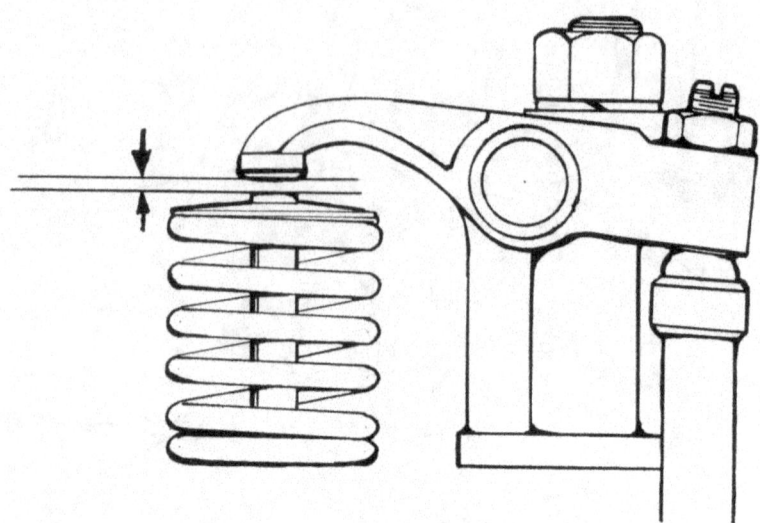

FIG. 12

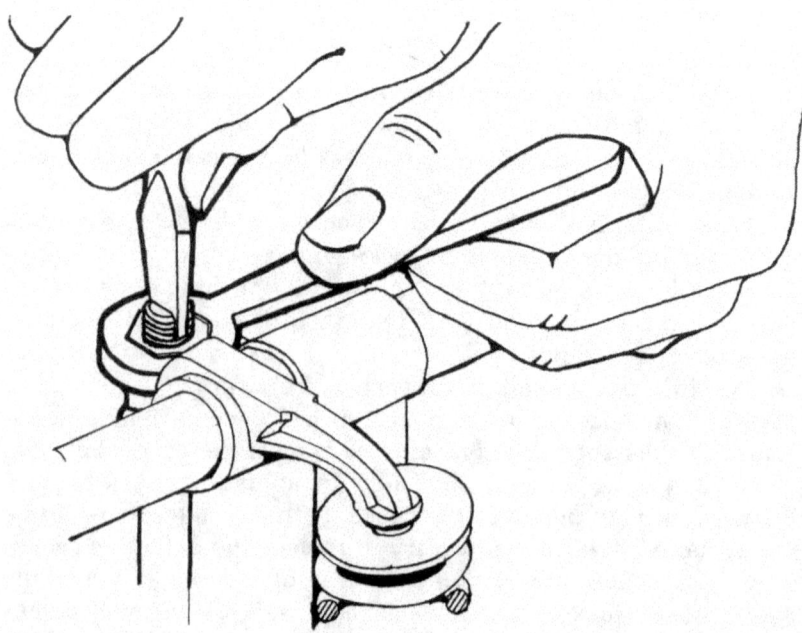

FIG. 13

FIG. 14

Plug Performance

The spark plug has a tremendous job to perform in its proper functioning in the ignition system and it can do this well or poorly depending on the care and attention it receives. Modern spark plugs must be capable of developing of in the neighborhood of from 12,000 - 16,000 volts across their gaps and to do this many times a second in an environment of extremely high temperatures and pressures. They must develop this voltage and discharge a spark of sufficiently intensity to ignite the compressed fuel air mixture which is considerably more difficult than merely discharging across an air gap.

At the same time there are processes and agents at work in the combustion chamber that tend to foul or erode the plug gaps. Certain driving conditions set up a plug for shorting and should be considered when analyzing plug troubles. Such a case is when the engine is running at slow speed with the engine still below operating temperature and lead deposits from the fuel deposit out on the spark plug insulator. Later, the engine is driven at highway speeds and the resultant increase in engine heat melts these deposits, making a lower resistance path between the electrodes which can cause misfire. Equally important to proper plug operation is the necessity for proper fuel/air mixture at all times. Proper ignition requires the use of a quality spark plug, properly gapped, in combination with proper carburetion and a well-functioning ignition system. If plug fouling becomes a frequent occurrence then it becomes necessary to check the ignition system, carburetion, and compression before assigning the blame to the plugs. Another area to consider is the heat range of the plugs you have in use. It

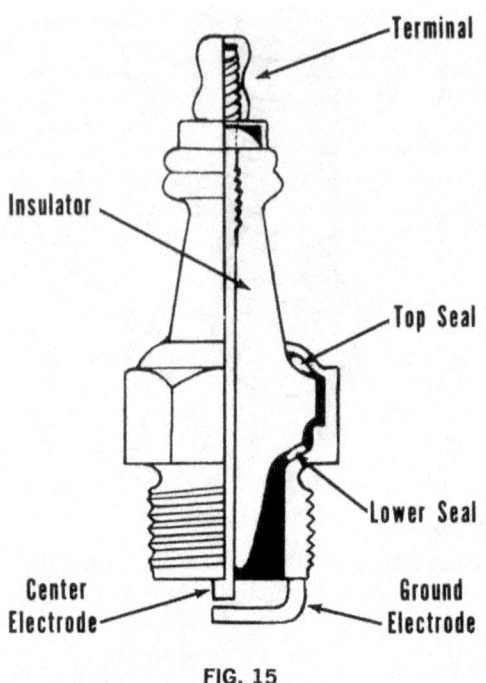

FIG. 15

may be that the heat range of the plugs is not compatible with the type of driving that predominates, in which case it may be well to shift to another type of plug.

In addition, it is important to have good spark plug gaskets, clean plug threads, and a good metal-to-metal contact. The spark plug must also form a reliable gas tight seal so that there is no loss of compression because of insulator cracks, poor seals, or because of a leaky gasket.

About Heat Range

The range of temperature in the combustion chamber is considerable and may vary from approximately 300 degrees C at 15 mph to 750 degrees C at high speeds. Plugs are made to operate effectively over specific bands of temperatures or are made for a particular Heat Range. The specific heat range for a plug is determined by the path the heat flow takes in travelling from the electrodes to the cylinder head. Figure 17 illustrates the difference in heat path for cold, medium, and hot, heat range plugs. Since most plugs may operate over a fairly wide range of temperature without harm or deterioration of performance, the best advice is to use the type of plugs supplied with your model Triumph unless the particular driving to which the car is put justifies going to another heat range.

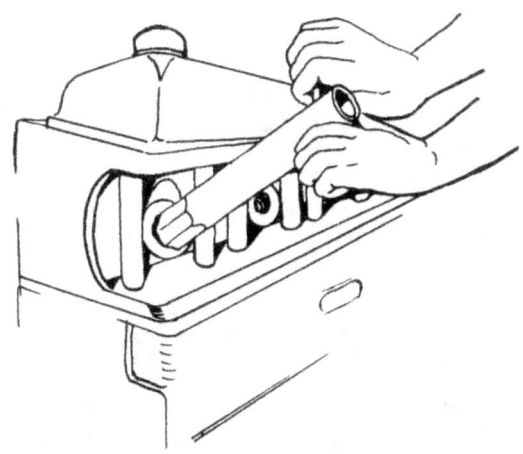

Plug Removal
1. Use a spark plug wrench and remove the spark plugs. Remove and throw away the old spark plug gaskets.
2. Keep the plugs in order so that they may be associated with their proper cylinder.

NOTE: Some owners use a small tray or rack type of plug holder such as shown in Figure 16. This keeps the plugs identified and permits a good visual inspection to be made. Spark plug holders are commercially available which mount under the hood and hold the spare set of plugs ready for convenient use.

3. Plug inspection. Note the condition of the plugs and look for the following conditions:

FIG. 16

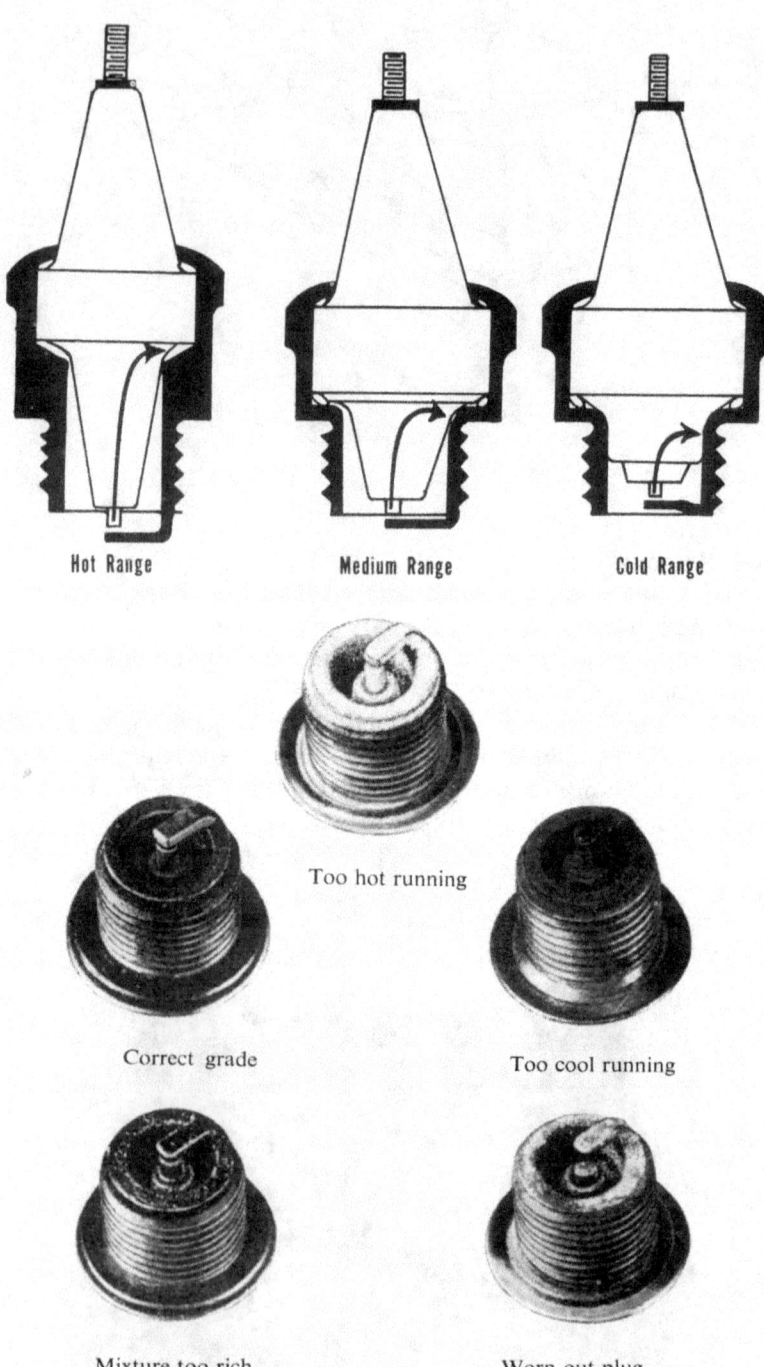

FIG. 17

a. **Oil Fouling:** This appears as a shiny black coating of carbon and in time will short out the plug and cause the firing to be erratic or to miss altogether. This condition indicates poor combustion is taking place or misfiring is occurring either because of a defective plug, faulty ignition, or poor compression.

b. **Lead Fouling:** This appears as a dry crusty formation and will cause the engine to miss at high speeds or under full load conditions.

c. **Insulator Chipped or Cracked:** Plug has failed because of rough handling or because of thermal or mechanical stress and requires plug replacement.

d. **Electrodes:** If the electrodes show signs of erosion or deterioration, the plugs should be replaced.

4. Clean the plugs by carefully wire-brushing or with a soft metal tool taking care not to damage the insulator or the electrodes. A preferred method of cleaning is by sandblasting the electrodes and lower insulator in a service station type of plug cleaner.

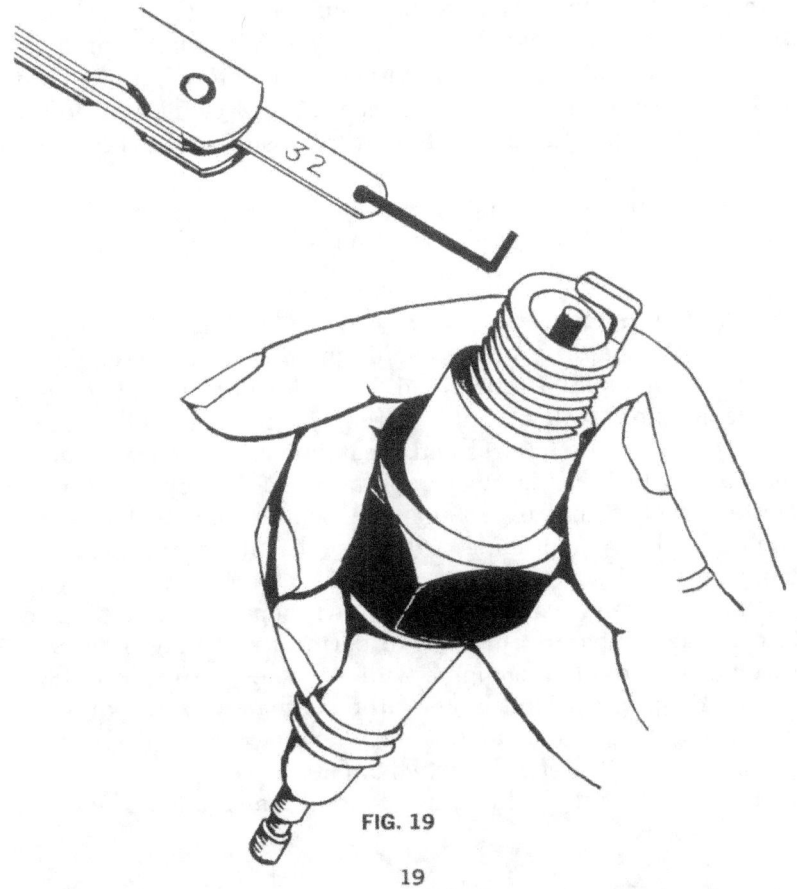

FIG. 19

5. Gap the plugs as shown in Figure 19 according to specifications in the table. If the gaps have eroded away considerably, it is best to replace such plugs with new ones. When adjusting the gap, never pry against the center electrode as this may damage the insulator and seal. Use a plug tool or long nose pliers to adjust the position of the ground electrode.

6. Clean the spark plug seats and install new gaskets. This is important and plugs should not be replaced with the old gaskets unless you have no other choice in the matter. Provide yourself with a liberal supply of these as they only cost a few pennies apiece.

Never use oil on the spark plug threads as this will interfere with proper heat transfer and may make the plug run too hot. If oil is used to clean the threads, make sure that the threads are wiped dry before installing.

7. Install the spark plugs in their respective cylinders using the spark plug wrench and the spanner furnished in the tool kit. Screw the plug in by hand until you feel the plug make contact with the gasket; then use the spark plug wrench to **hand** tighten the plug firmly against the gasket. When the plug is properly installed, the gasket is crushed but not completely flattened out.

Do not use a wrench with the spark plug socket and do not tighten with your full strength as it is possible to break off the plug in the cylinder head.

8. Connect the spark plug wires in the proper order, making certain that the connectors are clean and that they make good electrical contact.

The Ignition System

By far the majority of the conditions that cause an engine to be out of tune may be attributed to the development of troubles in the ignition system. This is true not only in tuning faults, but also for engine failures and breakdowns. However, frequent tune ups will keep the owner appraised of the condition of his ignition system and by frequent inspection of the wiring and cabling, can prevent some of the usual ignition troubles from happening.

The ignition system consists of two separate circuits. Each circuit has a separate function to perform and they both work together to provide the engine with a voltage sufficient to jump the spark plug gap and at the proper time so as to ignite the fuel air mixture in the combustion chamber at the instant when combustion is desired. These two circuits are:

1. **Primary Circuit** — The primary circuit has the job of increas-

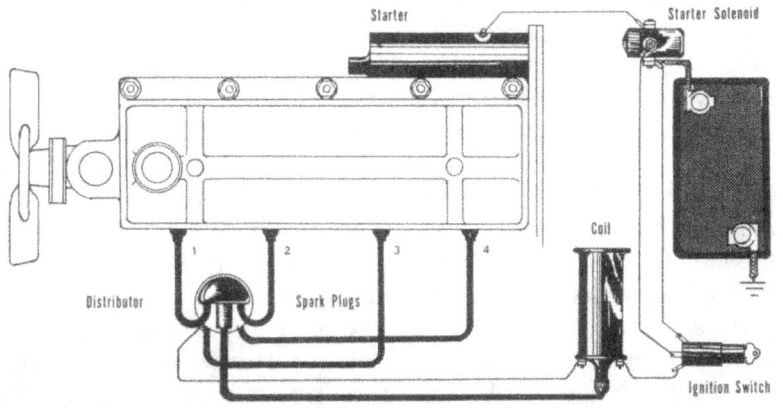

FIG. 20

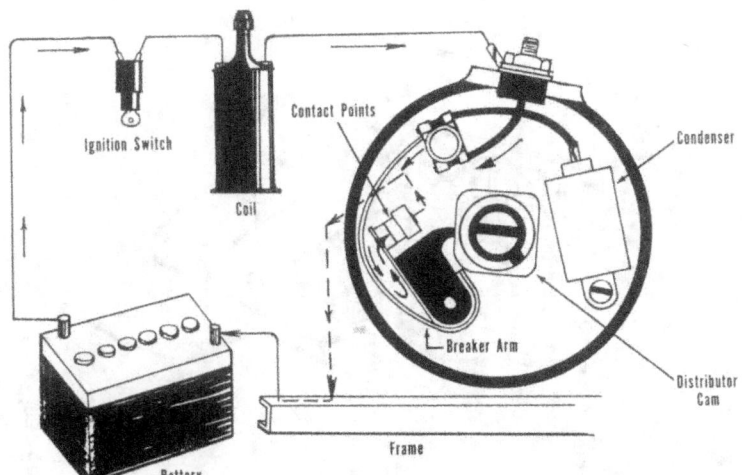

FIG. 21

ing the battery voltage to approximately 15,000 volts.

2. **Secondary Circuit** — The secondary has the function of distributing the high voltage generated in the primary circuit to the proper spark plug at the right time in the engine cycle.

The Primary Circuit

Figure 20 shows the major components of the primary circuit. The circuit is energized by turning on the ignition key. This connects the battery voltage to the primary side of the ignition coil from whence it goes to the distributor and finally to ground.

Figure 21 also shows the primary circuit and the primary path of current through the distributor. The current flowing through the primary side of the ignition coil (Figure 24) causes a strong magnetic field to be set up. By interrupting the primary circuit, the magnetic field is made to collapse — producing the high tension voltage necessary to jump the spark plug gap.

After the high tension voltage has been generated, the next task is to have a switch arrangement to carry the high voltage to the spark plugs in the firing order of the engine. This is the function of the components of the secondary circuit. The firing order for the TR is 1 3 4 2.

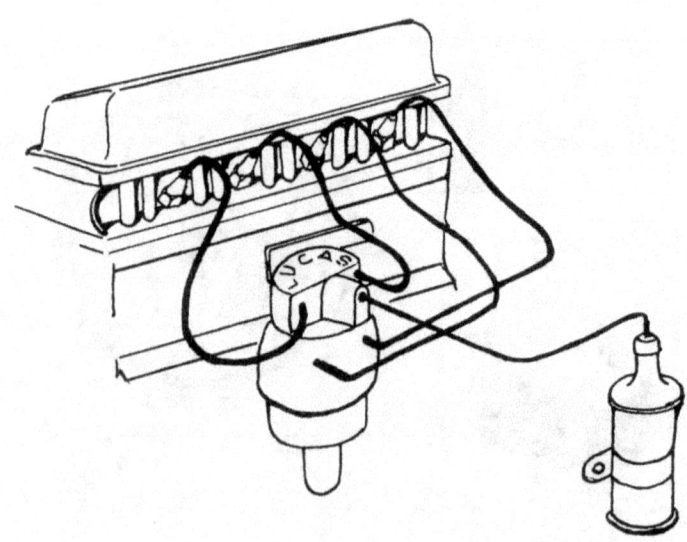

FIG. 22

The Secondary Circuit

The distributor provides the necessary switching to send the high voltage to the right spark plug according to firing order. Fastened to the top of the distributor shaft is a rotor which turns with the shaft. As the rotor rotates, it carries the high voltage to the four terminals located in the distributor cap. Each terminal in the cap supplies one of the plugs, so that, as the rotor turns, each spark plug is supplied with its high voltage spark when its turn comes up according to the firing order.

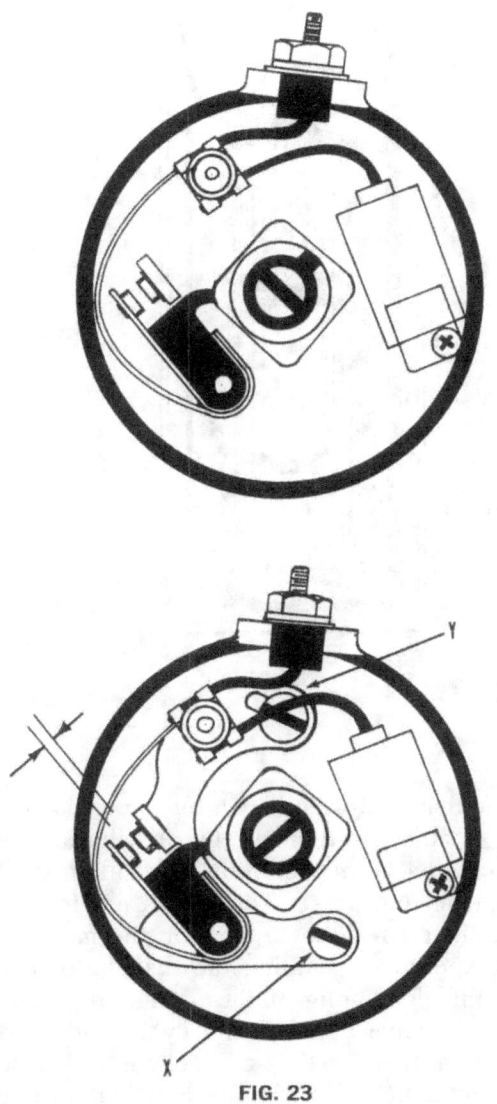

FIG. 23

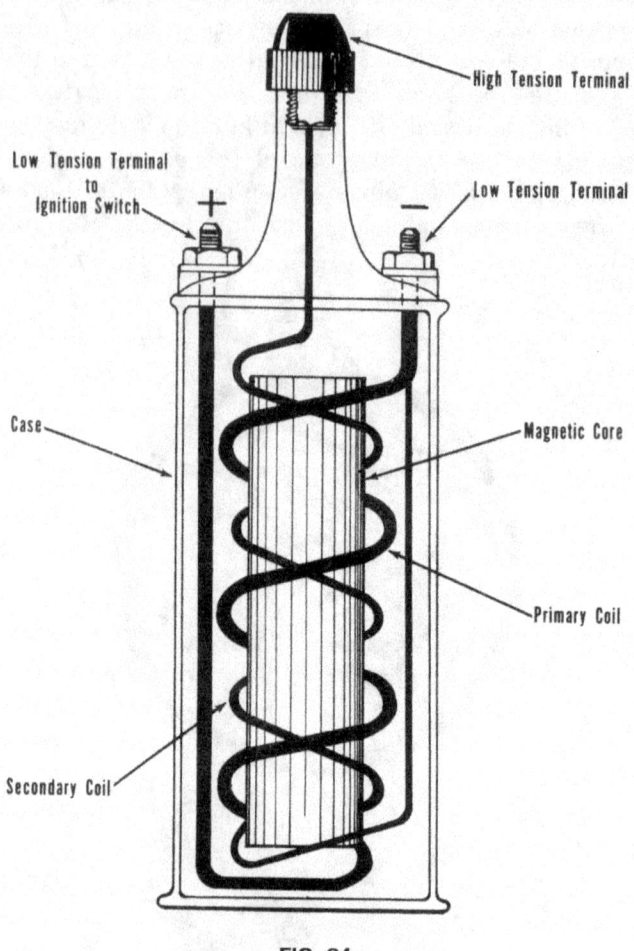

FIG. 24

Timing

The cam of the distributor is driven by the camshaft through suitable gearing so that rotation of the distributor cam makes and breaks the contact points; thereby controlling the development of the high tension pulse. The points are interrupted by the cam lobe in such a way as to develop the necessary spark regardless of engine speed. Timing the distributor consists of adjusting the point of opening of the points so that the spark is supplied at the proper time in the cycle and to close the points at the proper time so that a high voltage is developed for the next cylinder in order. Timing is accomplished by adjusting the distributor in such a way that the contact points open and close the proper amount and at the proper time in relation to the engine cycle.

Distributor Adjustments and Checks
1. Check the condition of the ignition wiring, particularly the spark plug leads. Look for loose connections and for signs of burning on the cabling where the wires come close or touch other parts of the engine.
2. Remove the distributor cap as shown in Figure 25. Clean the inside and outside of the cap with a dry cloth to remove all carbon or grease deposits.
3. Push the carbon brush in a few times to see that it moves freely in the cap.
4. Check the contact points for dirt or oil. If oil is present, clean the points carefully with a dry cloth.
5. If the points are clean and are worn even, proceed to check the point gap. If the contact points are pitted or burned or excessively worn, they must be dressed or replaced. Dressing and replacing the points is described later.
6. Use the hand crank and turn the engine over until the contact breaker arm is on the high point of the cam lobe. See Figure 23.
7. With a 0.015 inch feeler gauge, measure the point gap as shown in Figure 23. This should be 0.014 inch to 0.016.
8. **Adjusting Point Gap.** Loosen the two screws "X" and "Y" in Figure 23. This loosens the fixed contact plate so that its position can be moved to adjust the gap.
9. Move the fixed plate in the proper direction to give the correct gap.
10. Tighten the two screws that clamp the fixed contact plate exercising care so that the plate does not slip.
11. Re-check the gap spacing.

Dressing Contact Points
1. Remove the small nut, the insulation washer and the wire leads from the screw stud to which the spring of the breaker arm is secured.
2. Carefully remove the breaker arm.
3. Use a carborundum stone or fine ignition file and dress the points as shown in Figure 27. Dress the points until all pitting is removed and the point faces are smooth. Remove all abrasive material by carefully cleaning the points with a cloth dipped in solvent.
4. Reinstall the points making sure the insulating washers are properly placed on the pillar on the fixed breaker plate and on

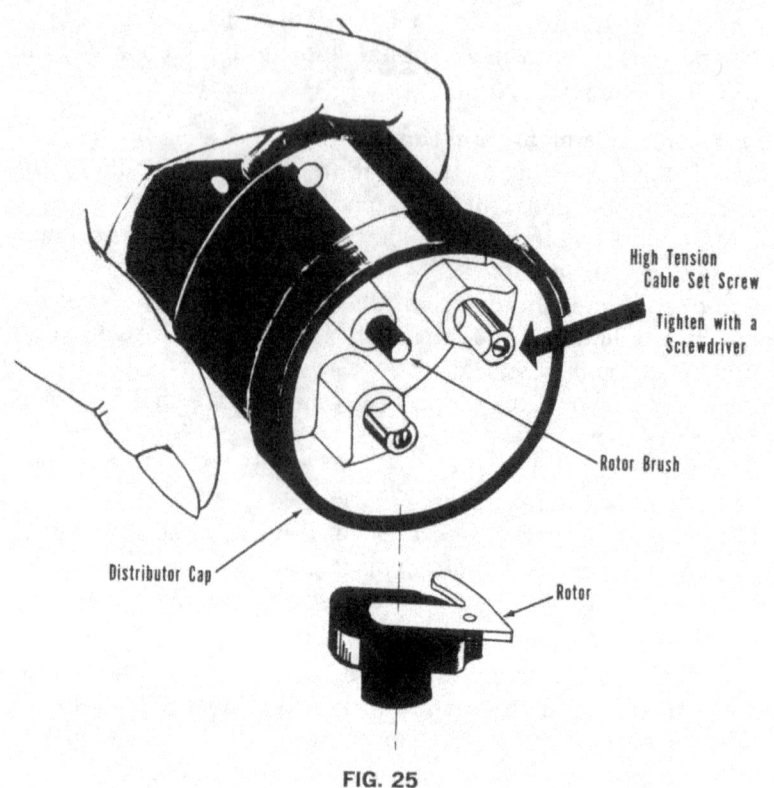

FIG. 25

the pivot post on the moving contact breaker plate.
5. Gap the points to 0.016 inches as before.

Timing Adjustment
1. Insert the hand crank and match up the hole in the fan pulley with the index marker on the timing chain cover. This is TDC. Now continue to turn the handcrank until a point of the flywheel $1/8$ inch from the hole counterclockwise is lined up with the index marker. This is 4 degrees before top dead center and is the static timing position.
2. Adjust the Advance-Retard knob on the distributor (Figure 26) until the contact points are just beginning to open. When this condition has been achieved, the ignition is then statically timed.
3. Remove the handcrank.
4. Install the rotor arm in the keyed slot in the distributor shaft.
5. Install the distributor cap and check the coil and spark plug leads.

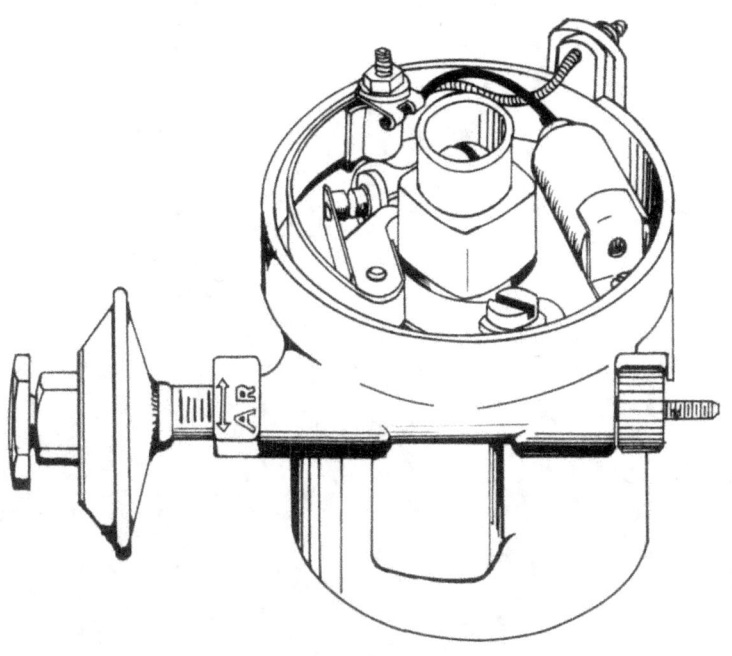

FIG. 26

Replacement of Contacts

If the points are so worn that they cannot be properly dressed, then the point set must be replaced as a pair. These may be obtained from TR dealers or most parts houses. Install the new fixed breaker plate loosely for the time being. Install the new breaker arm, again placing the insulating washers on the pillar and pivot posts. Now adjust the position of the fixed breaker plate to give the proper gap and clamp securely.

Recheck the gap and timing as before.

Using the Timing Light
Connecting the Timing Light (Engine Warm)
1. Shut off the ignition switch and remove #1 spark plug cable.
2. Connect the timing light leads as shown in Figure 32.
3. Start engine.

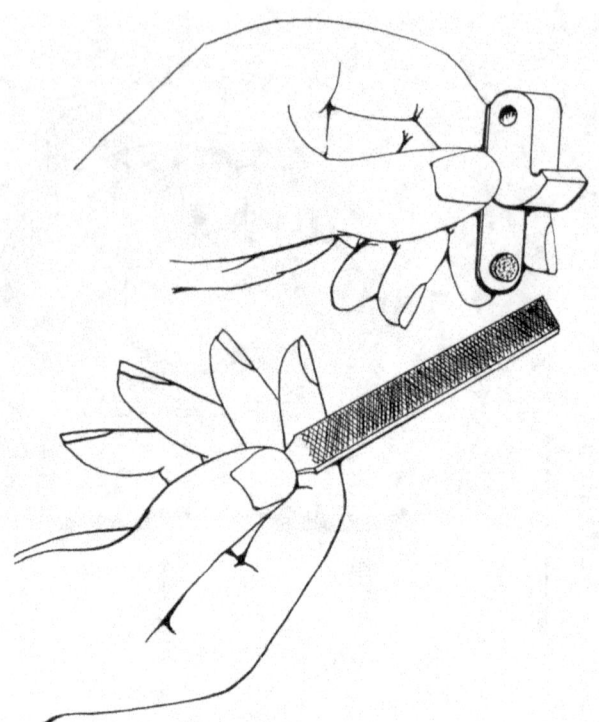

FIG. 27

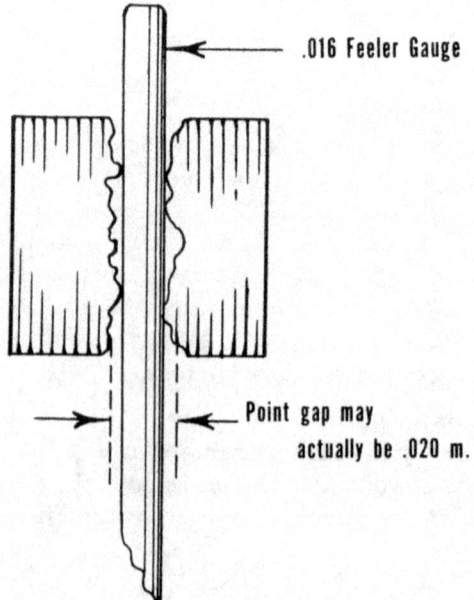

.016 Feeler Gauge

Point gap may actually be .020 m.

FIG. 28

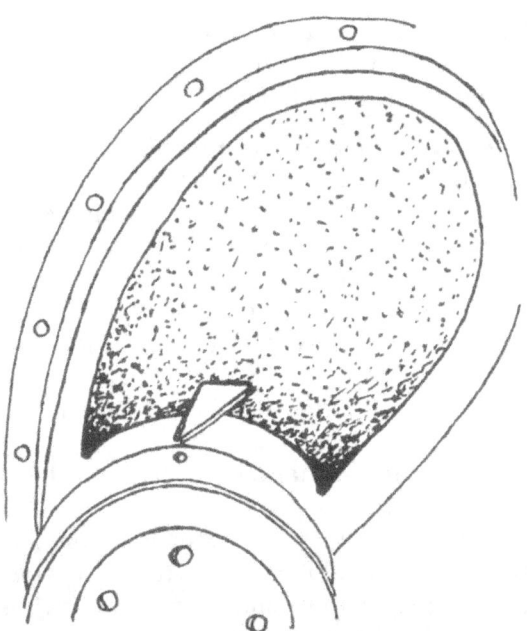

FIG. 29

CAUTION: Exercise extreme care to prevent the leads from getting caught in the fan or fan belt. Keep leads and hands well clear of the fan while using the light.

Checking the Timing With the Timing Light

1. Run the engine at idle speed (400-600) rpm and shine the light on the index pointer on the timing chain cover. Should the pointer and hole on the fan belt pulley be covered with dirt, it may not be possible to see them. For best results, clean off the pointer and hole and mark them with a strip of white paint.
2. The mark on the pulley and pointer should appear to be stationary with the hole appearing to be about $3/16$ inch counter-clockwise from the pointer on the circumference of the fan pulley.
3. Adjust the Advance-Retard knob to bring the timing mark $3/16$ inch from the pointer.
4. If the mark does not line up properly when the Advance-Retard knob is turned full scale, it will be necessary to loosen the distributor clamp screws and rotate the distributor until the mark moves to the proper position. Reclamp the distributor and repeat the above steps.

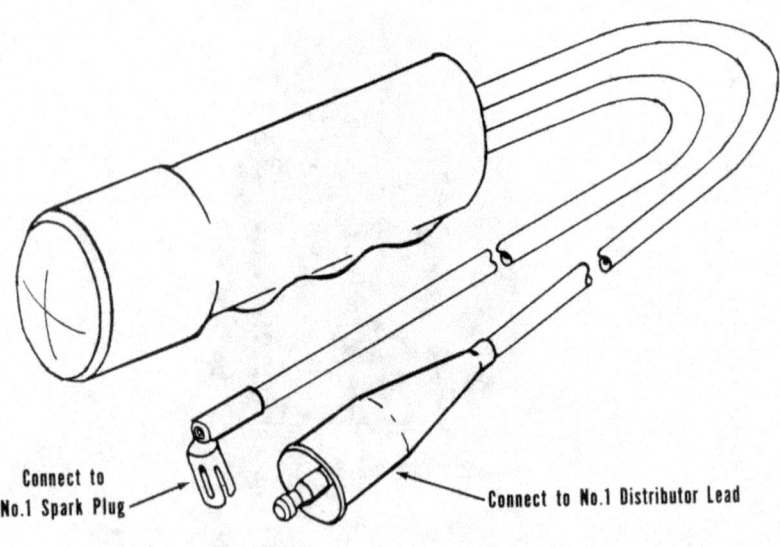

Connect to No.1 Spark Plug

Connect to No.1 Distributor Lead

FIG. 31

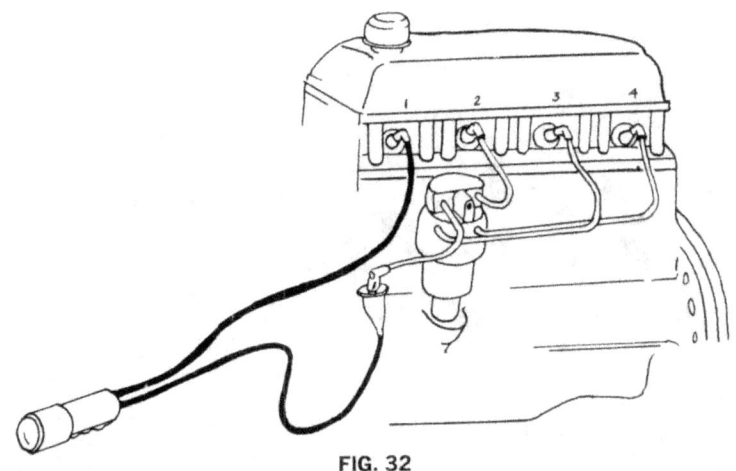

FIG. 32

Checking the Advance Mechanism
1. Increase engine rpms gradually by hand operation of the throttle linkage.
2. The timing mark should now move steadily and smoothly in a counterclockwise direction as the rpm is increased.
3. Reduce engine rpm gradually. The timing mark should now move steadily and smoothly to its idle position.

Any action of the timing mark that differs from the above indicates the advance control weights are binding or that the advance weights springs are loose or weak.

If trouble is indicated, remove the moving contact breaker plate, vacuum unit linkage, and the contact breaker base plate.

Then check the movement of the advance weights by hand. It may be that a few drops of oil will do the trick or that a spring has come loose. Try lubricating the weights and replace springs that appear weak or corroded. Reassemble the distributor and again set the timing.

S.U. Carburetor Adjustments
1. Remove the two air cleaners by removing the securing bolts that hold the air cleaners to the carburetor flange. Put aside for later servicing.
2. Disconnect the throttle linkage between the two carbs by loosening the nut on the folded clamp. See Figure 39. This permits individual adjustment of the carburetors to bring them into synchronization.
3. Disconnect the choke cable and the mixture control linkage between the carburetors, by removing the pin in the forked end of the jet control connecting rod.

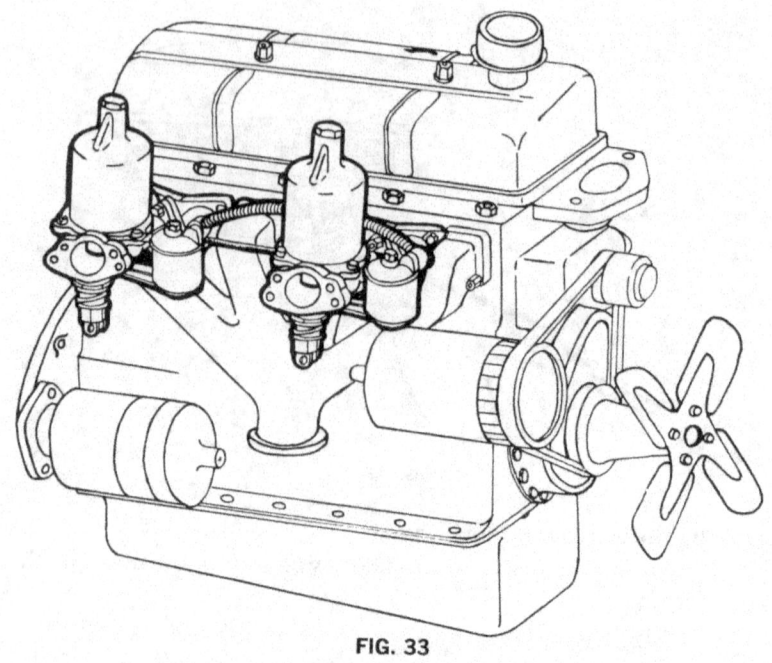

FIG. 33

4. Remove the damper piston by unscrewing the brass securing nut on top of the carburetor suction chamber.
5. Remove the suction chamber by removing the brass screws around the base. Move the arm that goes to the float bowl out of the way.
6. Remove the suction chamber and lift out the coil spring from the piston.

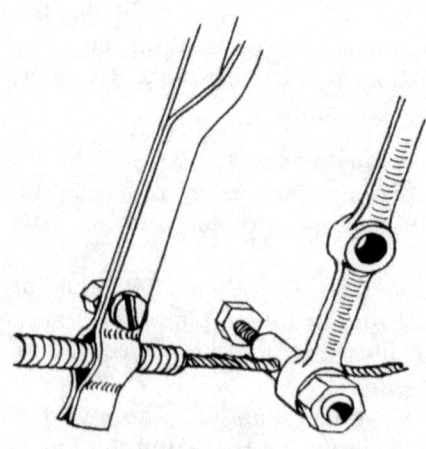

FIG. 34

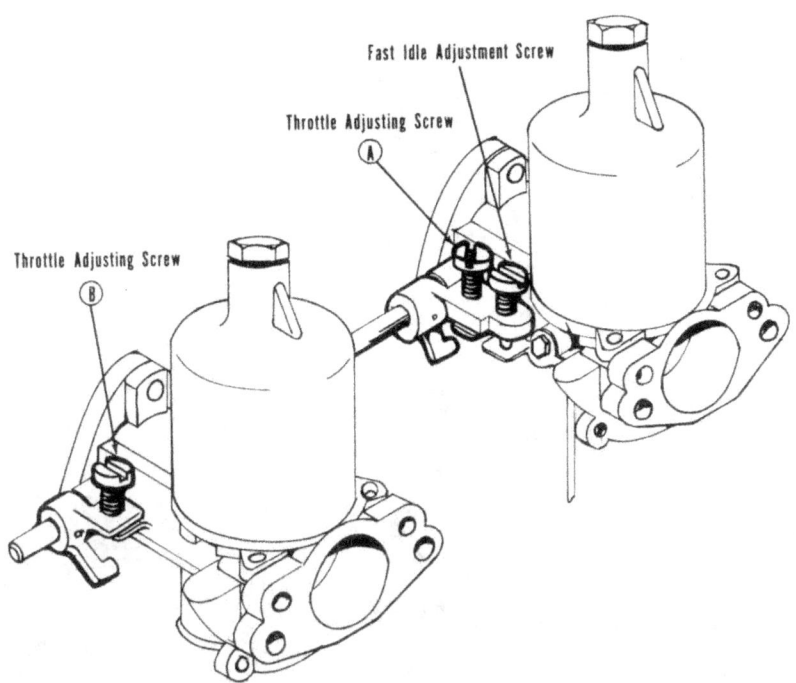

FIG. 36

7. Lift the piston straight up and pour out the oil in the reservoir. Check to see that the jet needle shoulder is flush with the bottom face of the piston. Examine the jet needle for wear that indicates the jet needle is not centered in the jet. Evidence of wear requires that the needle be replaced and checked for centering.

Regardless of the type of needle installed, it should set flush with the bottom face of the piston.

8. Slip the spring over the piston and slide the piston into position.
9. Replace the suction chamber, the support arm to the float bowl, and fasten in place with the brass screws.
10. Fill the hydraulic damper with oil and secure the damper piston washer and nut. Multi-grade (10-30) engine oil is excellent for this purpose.
11. Start the engine and allow it to warm up to operating temperature. Release the folded coupling on the throttle spindle connecting rod (Figure 39) preparatory to synchronization.
12. Adjust each throttle adjusting screw A and B in Figure 36 until the engine is turning over at approximately 500 rpm.

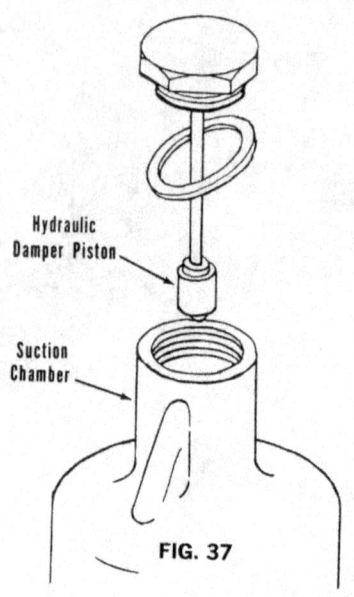

FIG. 37

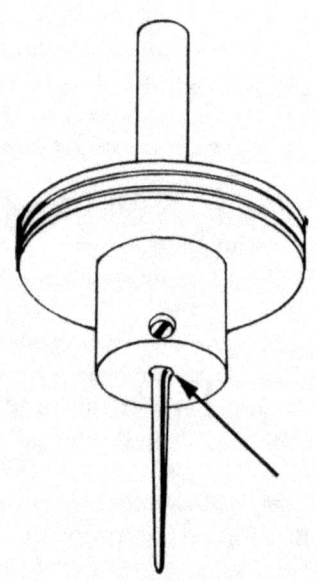

FIG. 38

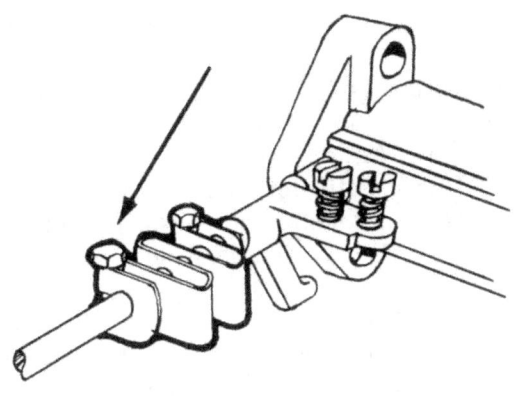

FIG. 39

13. **Adjusting by ear.** Listen to the hiss produced at each carburetor. If the intensity of the hiss is different, unscrew the throttle adjusting screw on the carburetor with the lower hiss and screw in on the adjusting screw of the other carburetor until the hiss from the two carburetors is the same. A short length of tubing can be used to isolate each carburetor — like a stethescope is used by a physician.

14. **Use of the UNI-SYN.** The UNI-SYN permits a much more accurate adjustment of the carburetor synchronization than is possible with the ears alone. The UNI-SYN is used in the following way:

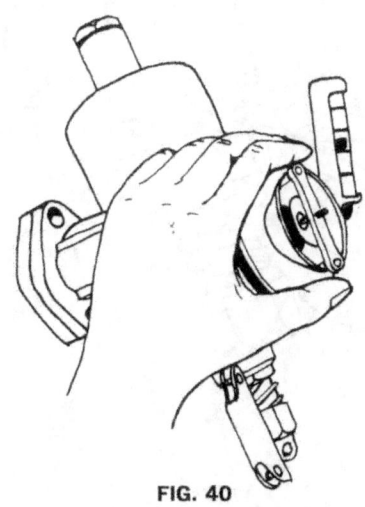

FIG. 40

a. Place the UNI-SYN over the throat of the right hand carburetor.

b. Adjust orofice screw on the UNI-SYN until the float rises to a graduation mark near the middle of the tube. Actually any of the marks may be used as a reference.

c. Place the UNI-SYN on the left hand carburetor.

d. Adjust the throttle adjusting screw on the left hand carburetor until the float rises to the same graduation as before in step (b).

e. Place the UNI-SYN over each carburetor throat in turn and re-check, noting the float level, and trim the throttle adjusting screws until the float rises to the same level for both carbs. When the indication is the same for the two carbs, the throttles are in sync. If idle speed has increased, it is only necessary to back off on the throttle screws an equal amount.

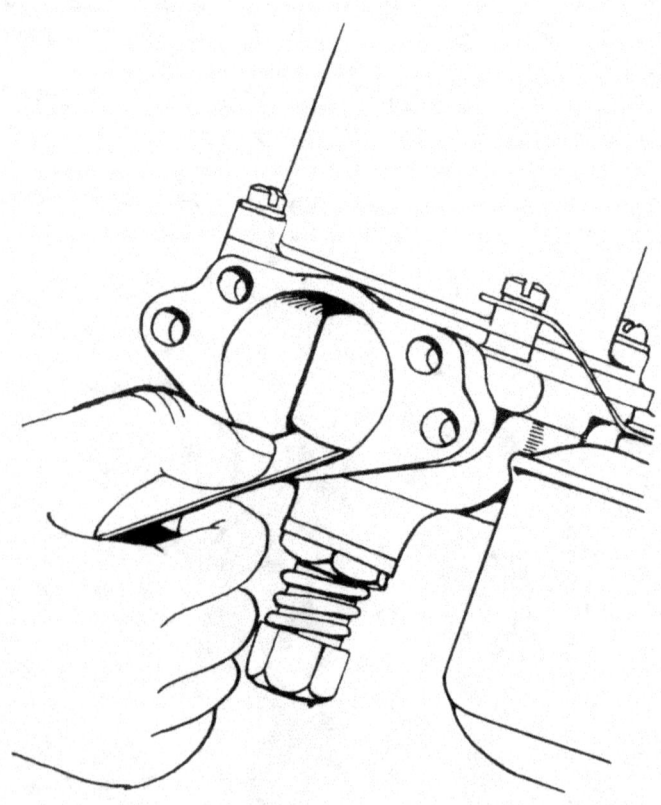

FIG. 41

15. **Mixture Adjustment.** Screw the adjusting nuts C in Figure 42 as far as they will go in a clockwise direction, looking from the bottom of the carburetor. Then back off the adjusting nuts about two and a half turns or about 16 flats of the adjusting nut. This serves as a starting point.

16. Using a small screw driver or a small piece of aluminum filed to the proper shape, lift the piston of each carburetor in turn no more than $\frac{1}{32}$ inch and carefully note if the engine speeds up or slows down.

a. Engine speeds up — Screw in on the adjusting screw until no engine rpm change is noticed when the piston is lifted.

b. Engine slows down — Back off on the adjusting nut a flat at a time until no change in engine speed occurs when the piston is lifted.

The fuel air mixture adjustment is correct when lifting of the piston causes no change in engine speed.

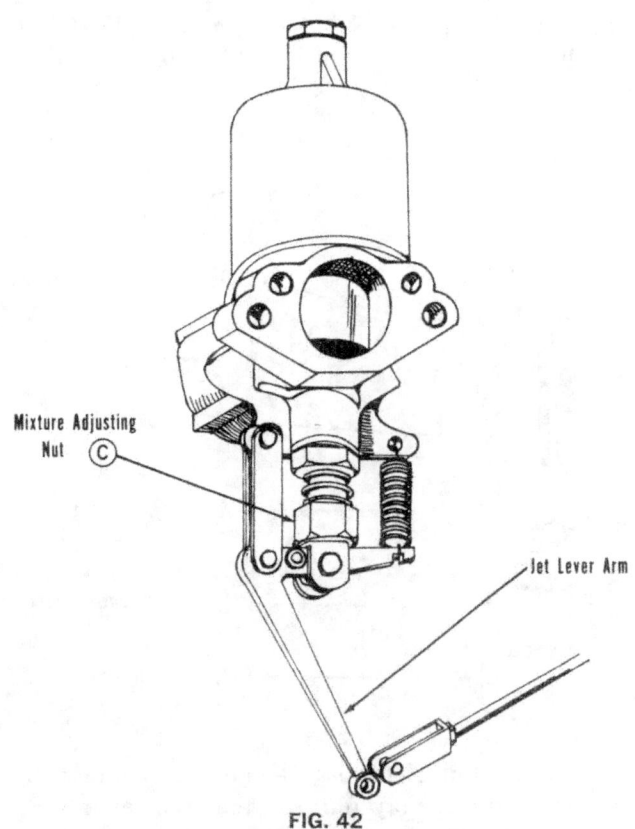

FIG. 42

17. **Check for Piston Hangup.** When you are satisfied that you have the mixture adjusted correctly, check the piston in each carburetor to see that it is free to move its full range without sticking or hanging up against the walls of the suction chamber. Do this by carefully lifting the piston about 1/2 inch, letting it fall and noting if it returns to the idle position smoothly. If there is any tendency to stick or hang up, check the following:
a. Check the hydraulic damper rod for a bend.
b. Check for rubbing of the piston against the suction chamber.
c. Check to see that the jet needle is not rubbing against the jet.

If the damper rod is bent, it may be possible to remove the bend by straightening. If it is determined that the piston is rubbing the suction chamber wall, try washing the piston and chamber walls and then apply a thin film of oil to the piston. This should remedy the trouble if the piston was sticking because of dirt. If the piston is sticking because the chamber is dented or out of round, it may be necessary to remove some metal from the high spot with emery cloth. If considerable metal has to be removed to relieve sticking, then it is best to get a new suction chamber to restore the carburetor to proper operation.

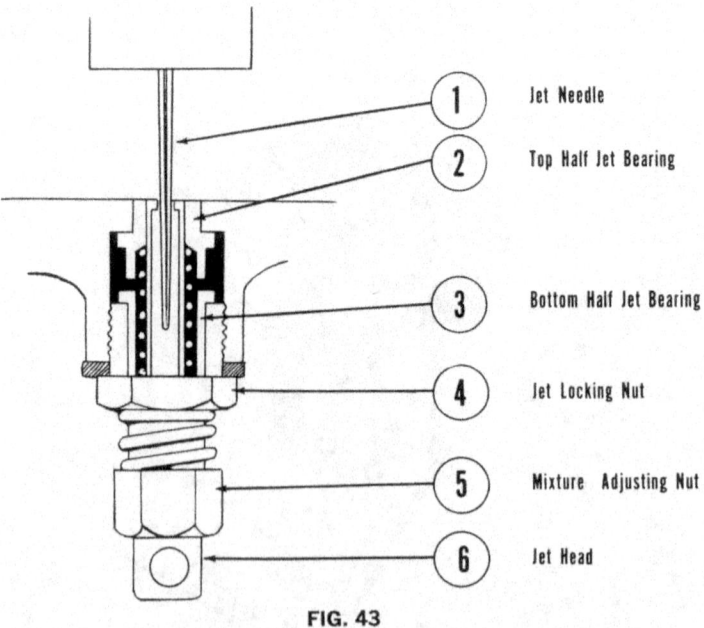

FIG. 43

1. Jet Needle
2. Top Half Jet Bearing
3. Bottom Half Jet Bearing
4. Jet Locking Nut
5. Mixture Adjusting Nut
6. Jet Head

The piston may stick if the jet needle rubs against the jet in which case the trouble may only be that the jet needle needs to be centered in the jet.

18. **To Center the Jet** (See Figure 43).
a. Remove the jet head (6), the adjusting nut (5) and spring. Replace the adjusting nut by screwing it up as far as it will go. Slide the jet head all the way until it rests against the bottom of the adjusting nut.
b. Loosen the jet locking nut (4).
c. Work the piston through its range, letting it fall each time until it is free.
d. When the piston action works freely, tighten the jet locking nut (4).
e. Replace the jet head assembly in the proper order and repeat the mixture adjustment procedure.

There may be an increase in engine rpm after the mixture adjustment has been made and as the engine approaches a tuned up condition. This is to be expected and it will be necessary to again adjust the throttle adjusting screw to reduce the hiss in each carburetor or to repeat the adjustment using the UNI-SYN.

19. Replace the mixture control linkage, making sure the jets are snug against the adjusting nuts. Adjust the end yoke in the linkage, if necessary, so that it matches the holes in the two jet levers.

20. Hold the throttle adjusting screws against their idling stops and tighten the screw on the folded clamp. This connects the throttle discs of the two carburetors together.

21. As a final check, note the exhaust at the tail pipe. It should be colorless and the exhaust note should have an even rhythm.

22. Install the choke cable and the carburetor tuning is complete.

23. **Air Filter Servicing.** The AC type air filters are of the oil wet metal gauze type and are secured to the carburetor flange by two stud bolts in the case of the TR 2. In the TR 3, equipped with an offset mounting, place the offset to the rear when replacing the air cleaners.
a. Remove the air cleaners and wash in fuel oil or solvent.
b. Wipe or allow to dry.
c. Coat the metal gauze with a coat of oil and mount the air cleaners to the carburetors.

Servicing of the air cleaners should be done as frequently as the owner may wish to go to the trouble and also clean them at least every 3000 miles. Do this oftener if the air is dusty. This service, if carried out religiously, will be rewarded by long engine life and many extra miles of driving before ring replacement becomes necessary.

The SU Tool

One of the best, least expensive non-mechanical aids to the performance of the carburetor tuning process is the "SU Tool" (in reality a kit of tools) which greatly speeds up the functions of checking piston free movement, synchronization of two or three carburetors, testing mixture strength, adjusting float level and centering the jet needle. The SU Tool is distributed by Messrs. MG Mitten Co., 1163 E. Green St., Pasadena, California, USA and inquiries should be directed to that firm relative to purchase.

In principle, the SU Tool achieves synchronization at any rpm from idling to top speed without the necessity for removing air cleaners by making it possible to visually check the height of the pistons in two or more carburetors simultaneously. The test rods of the tool kit allow the pistons to be lifted and dropped accurately to check free movement or mixture strength. The rods are also precision made for use as gauges for float level setting. A jet pin, which is used to replace the needle permits accurate centering without danger of bending the needle itself. The jet wrench included in the kit is made specifically for the jet adjusting nut and is conveniently short for easy manipulation.

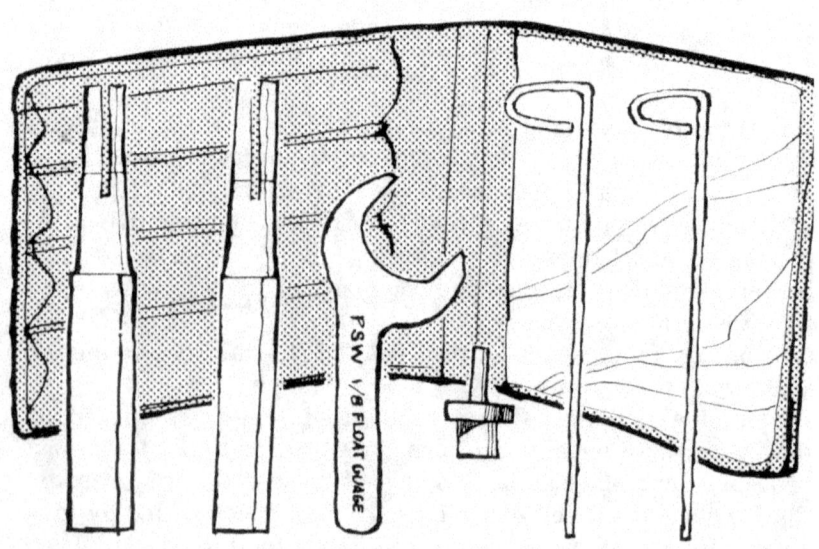

TUNE UP SPECIFICATIONS

	TR 2	TR 3	TR 4
BHP/RPM	90 @ 4800	95 @ 4800	105 @ 4600
Compression ratio	8.5 - 1	8.5 - 1	9 - 1
Tappet clearance Normal Running (Engine cold)	INTAKE 0.010 inch EXHAUST 0.012 inch	INTAKE 0.010 inch EXHAUST 0.010 inch	INTAKE 0.010 inch EXHAUST 0.010 inch
Tappet clearance for High Speed	INTAKE 0.013 inch EXHAUST 0.013 inch	INTAKE 0.013 inch EXHAUST 0.013 inch	INTAKE 0.013 inch EXHAUST 0.013 inch
Firing Order	1 3 4 2	1 3 4 2	1 3 4 2
Breaker Point Gap Setting	0.015 inch at high point on distributor cam	0.015 inch at high point on distributor cam	0.015 inch at high point on distributor cam
Ignition Timing Static	4 degrees BTDC	4 degrees BTDC	4 degrees BTDC
Ignition Timing Mark (TDC)* Top Dead Center	Hole in fan belt pulley and pointer index on timing chain cover	Hole in fan belt pulley and pointer index on timing chain cover	Hole in fan belt pulley and pointer index on timing chain cover
Spark Plugs Normal Cold Running Gap	Champion L 7 L 10 S Champion L 5 L 11 S 0.025 inch .032 inch	Champion L 7 Champion L 5 0.25 inch	Champion L 7 Champion L 5 0.25 inch
S.U. Needle	Normal FV High Speed GC	SM (Change Type TE or TD to SM)	SM
Compression Readings**	120-125 psi	120-125 psi	120-125 psi

*3/16 inch on the circumference of the crankshaft fan pulley is equivalent to 4 degrees from TDC.

**These readings will vary slightly depending on the type of gauge used.

THE ENGINE

The Standard Triumph engine as fitted to the TR 2-3-4 series is an overhead valve four. Only minor changes, such as increasing cylinder bore; cylinder head and carburetor alterations have been made since its introduction, so service procedures remain substantially identical from the earliest to the latest model. The cast iron cylinder block is of the wet-liner type. In engines prior to number 9095E, the cam bearings are integral with the block. Later blocks have bi-metal cam bearing inserts. These can be recognized at once by the three setscrews on the left side of the block which retain the rearmost cam bearings.

The cylinder sleeves are centrifugally-cast nickel-nickel iron and are graded and marked F G or H according to bore size to match similarly graded pistons. Sleeves are spigoted into the block and are located at the top by mating with the cylinder head. It will be noted that the sleeves stand above the block top surface by from .003 to .005 inches. Sealing at the bottom joint is accomplished by pairs of O rings, called figure eight joints, which seal two adjacent sleeves. These joints are plastic-coated steel and must be renewed when a sleeve is removed and replaced.

Pistons are of aluminum alloy, T-slotted and carry two compression rings and one oil ring. Pistons are graded, as mentioned, to allow selective assembly with sleeves of appropriate dimension, and the grade symbol F, G or H is stamped on the crown. The T-slot is on the non-pressure side (towards the cam).

The crankshaft is a manganese-molybdneum steel forging with integral counter balancing. It runs in three steel-backed plain metal bearings of the insert type. The main bearing caps are non-interchangeable since the bearing supports are align-bored during manufacture. Crankshaft thrust is taken at the center main with white-metal covered steel shims on either side of the bearing support.

Connecting rods are high-alloy steel forgings with offset caps. The piston pin hole is bronze-bushed and the piston pins are full-floating, being secured in the piston by circlips. The offset big end caps allow the piston-rod assembly to be pushed past the crank and up through the cylinder bores as well as reducing stresses on the securing bolts. With bearing caps removed it is possible to change the bearing shells without removing the piston assembly from the engine. The cap bolts are secured by locking plates.

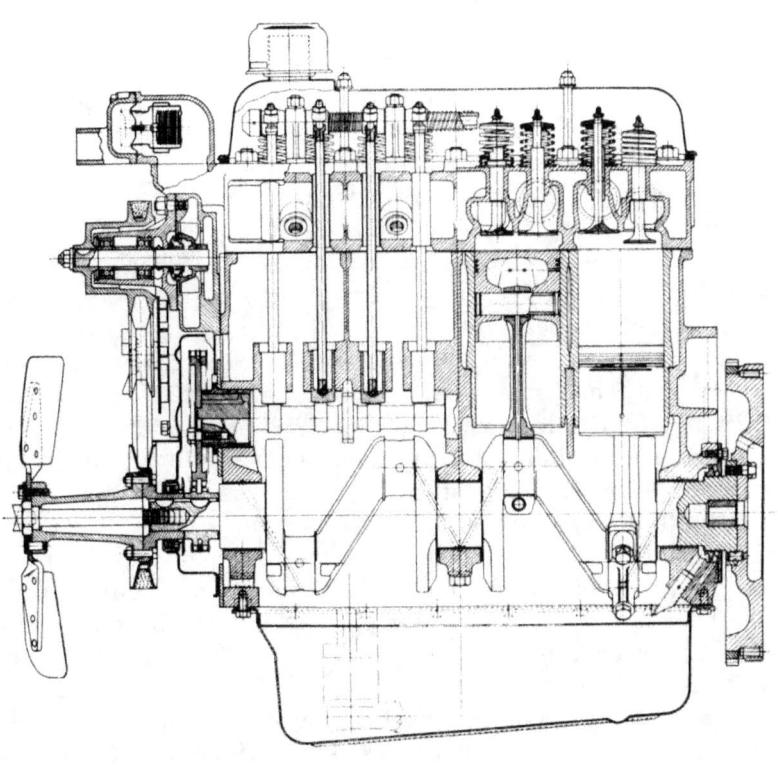

Valves are pushrod operated from a cam in the block. Pushrods are tubular and fitted with a ball at one end and a cup at the other. Interposed between pushrods and cam lobes are cylindrical chilled cast iron tappets which are hardened to increase wear resistance at the point where they engage the pushrod balls. Rocker arms are case hardened steel with phosphor bronze shaft bushings. The rocker shaft is hollow and carries oil to the rocker arms under pressure from the main supply. (See Lubrication)

Intake valves are made from chrome-nickel-silicon steel with a hardened stem tip. Exhaust valves (after engine No. TS 481 E) are high nickel-chromium-tungsten valve steel and stems are Stellite tipped. Intake valves are provided with two springs, exhaust valves with three springs. They are located by collars and retained by split, tapered keepers.

The cam is of iron alloy with hardened lobes, running in white metal insert bearings (after engine No. 9095E). Thrust is taken by the front bearing and end float is adjusted by varying the length of the bearing.

The cam is driven by a double roller silent chain from the crankshaft. The cam sprocket is secured to the shaft by two bolts but four holes are drilled in the sprocket. The holes are equally spaced but offset from a tooth center. Thus if the sprocket is fitted at a position 90° from its nominal location, a half-tooth timing adjustment is obtained. If the sprocket is turned back-to-front a ¹/₄-tooth change is made and if turned 90° in the reversed position ³/₄ of a tooth movement is made. The helical gear for distributor and tachometer drive is part of the cam as well as the eccentric lobe which operates the fuel pump.

Cam and crankshaft sprockets are aligned by means of shims placed behind the crankshaft sprocket. Scribed lines (as shown) are used to indicate the correct relative positions of cam and crank sprockets.

The Fuel System incorporates a shut off valve in the pipe line from the tank to the pump, this is situated on the left-hand chassis member adjacent to the engine. Fuel is supplied by an A.C. type UE Pump, to the twin carburetors. The vacuum pipe to the distributor is taken from the front carburetor.

The Hobourn-Eaton Double Rotor Oil Pump is of the submerged type and is self priming; oil is drawn from the engine sump through a gauze filter.

Coil Ignition is employed and the distributor has a vacuum and centrifugal automatic advance incorporated. It is sup-

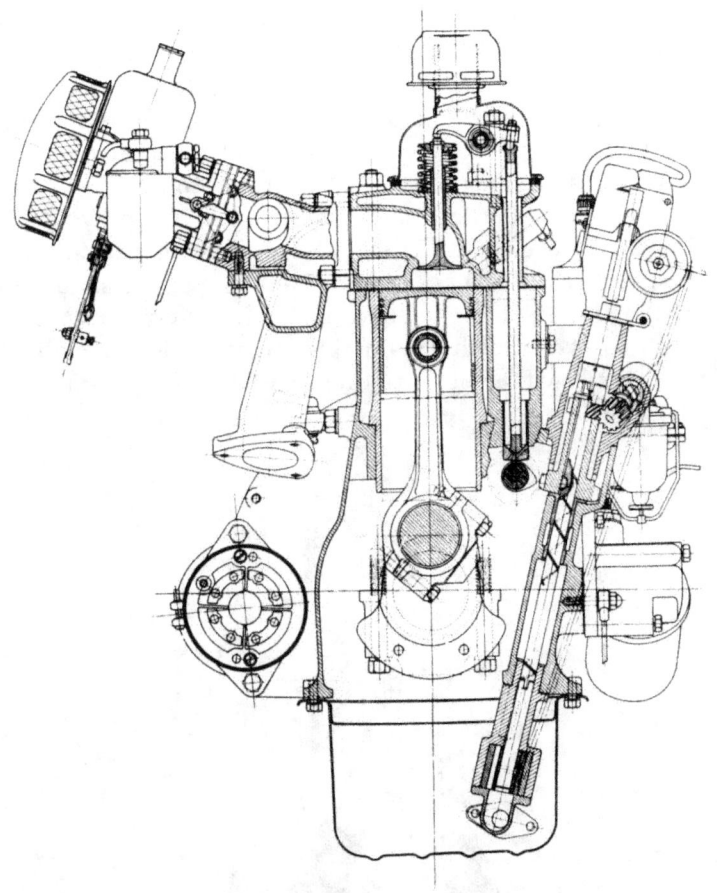

pressed for radio and television.

Engine mountains are of the flexible type, the front bearer being assembled on the rubber blocks on either side of the chassis frame, the gearbox itself being supported on a rubber pad secured to a cross member of the chassis frame.

The flywheel is manufactured from cast iron and is fitted with a shrunken starter ring of heat treated steel. It is located on the crankshaft by a dowel and secured by four bolts with lock plates. The flywheel is marked by an arrow which, when aligned with a scribe line on the cylinder block, sets Nos. 1 and 4 pistons at T.D.C. When fitting the flywheeel to the crankshaft ensure that both components are free from burrs. After fitting, the run-out should not be checked by a dial indicator to ensure the run-out does not exceed .003". Failure to observe this point may lead to clutch disorders and vibration. There are two dowel holes in the flywheel 90 degrees removed from one another; this will enable the flywheel to be turned 90 degrees should the teeth of the starter ring gear become increasingly worn and a replacement not be readily available. It must be remembered that the timing mark must be obliterated and a second stamped on the flywheel.

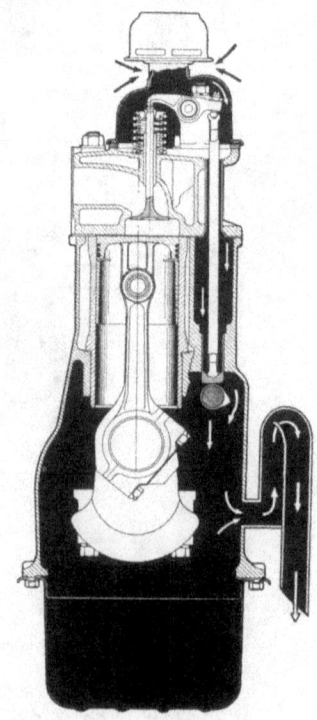

Crankcase Ventilation is effected by permitting air to be drawn out of the engine. To enable this ejection a large bore pipe in the form of an inverted "U" is fitted into the left-hand side of the cylinder block by means of an adapter welded to its end. The exposed end is cut away at an angle to provide a wider opening facing away from the slipstream.

The passage of air (the slipstream) created by the cooling fan or the movement of the car causes a depression at the angle opening of the inverted "U" pipe and air is drawn out of the cylinder block.

Fresh air is taken in through the rocker cover oil filler cap, circulating round the valve springs and rockers before passing down the push rod tubes into the cylinder block to replace air which is being drawn out. It is essential therefore that the filler cap is kept as clean as possible to allow free passage of air.

Engine Lubrication

Lubrication of the engine is by a Hobourn-Eaton pump. The pump is driven by a shaft which is mounted in a bush pressed into the cylinder block, and is provided with a helical gear which engages with a similar gear on the camshaft.

Oil is drawn into the pump through a primary gauze filter and passes through a channel in the pump casting to an annular space around the oil pump shaft. The annular space round the drive shaft is closed by the bush, and the oil thus forced through a hole in the cylinder block into the head of the external oil filter where some of this oil passes directly into the oil gallery which extends the length of the cylinder block; the remainder of the oil passes into the bowl of the oil filter under the pressure of the oil pump. When the oil pressure exceeds 70 to 80 lbs. per sq. inch it opens a spring loaded ball valve and passes into the sump. The oil on its way to the base of the filter is forced through the filtering media and passes up an annular space around the bowl holding bolt through a restrictor into the sump.

Full Flow Filter

In order to give the maximum protection to the engine when subjected to high speed or rally conditions, a filter of the full flow type was introduced on the TR3 models. This type of filter ensures that all the oil in circulation passes through the filtration system.

The full flow type of filter was introduced into normal manufacture at Engine No. TS.12650E., part numbers affected by this change being as follows:—

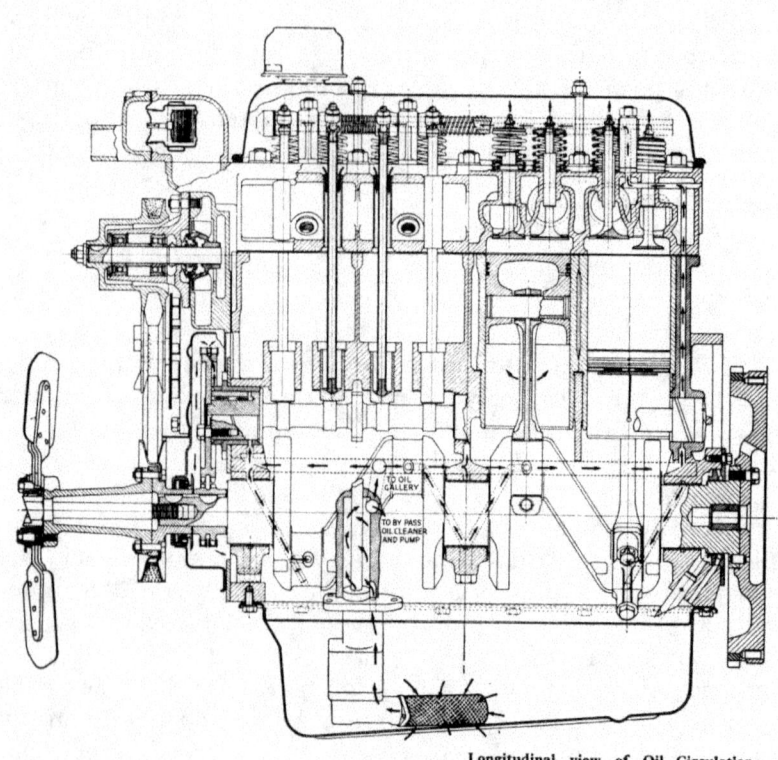

Longitudinal view of Oil Circulation.

Oil filter assembly, Part No. 301994, is replaced by Part No. 203271.

The replacement Element, Part No. 101963, remains the same for both types of filter.

The oil pressure on the full flow type of filter remains at 70 lbs. per sq. in. with an oil temperature of 70°C. at an engine speed of 2,000 r.p.m.

The new filter assembly can be fitted if desired to an engine prior to TS.12650E.

The oil passes from the gallery to the three main bearings, through drillings in the crankshaft to the big end bearing; then through further drillings in the connecting rods to the small end bushes and gudgeon pins. Splash lubrication is further assisted by a drilling into the oil passage between the small end and big end just below the piston skirt on each connecting rod.

By drillings from the channels leading to the main bearing oil is conveyed to the front, second and rear camshaft bearings. In the case of the third camshaft bearing this is fed direct from the oil gallery through a metering hole. A by-pass from the rear camshaft bearing conveys oil upwards through a drilling in the head and rearmost rocker pedestal to the rocker shaft. Oil passes along the hollow shaft and through radial holes to the rockers, leaving each rocker by a hole drilled vertically to each tappet ball pin.

The oil is prevented from escaping by the rocker cover and after lubricating the valve springs and ball pins, returns downwards through the push rod tubes lubricating the push rod tappets before entering the sump.

Oil from the front camshaft bearing lubricates the timing chain where four slots cut at 90° to each other on the face of the flange adjacent to the camshaft timing wheel allow oil to escape on to the timing wheel. The oil is thrown out by centrifugal force on to the underside of the flanged portion of the wheel on which the teeth are cut.

Six holes are drilled obliquely, alternately, from the back and the front of the wheel at equal intervals from the underside of the flange into the space between the two toothed rings. These holes allow the oil to be thrown on to the underside of the timing chain, ensuring its lubrication.

Oil Pump

The smaller center rotor is driven by a short shaft on which it is pressed and pegged in position. The two rotors are contained in a housing at the **base** of the oil pump casting, which

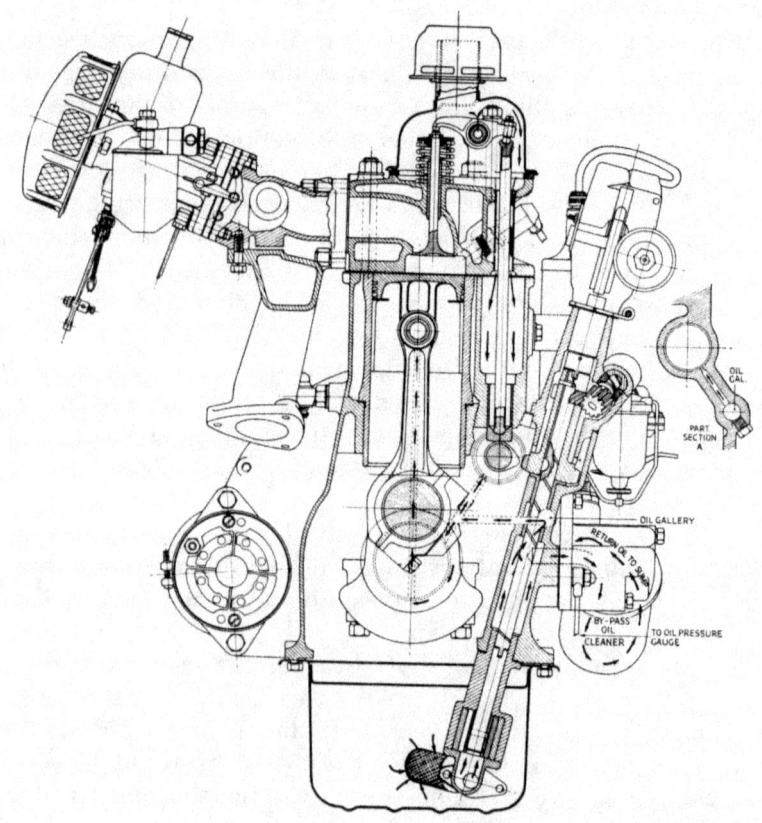

Cross section view of Oil Circulation.

is provided with a cover plate having a ground face, allowing only sufficient clearance on the two rotors to provide for lubrication. The centers of the rotors are offset.

The rotor shaft has at its upper extremity a recess which engages a tongue on the lower end of the drive shaft. The driving shaft is mounted in a phosphor bronze bush which is pressed into the cylinder block, and at its upper end a helical gear is secured by means of a Woodruff key. The helical gear on this shaft engages with a similar gear which is an integral part of the camshaft.

The center rotor, by its engagement with the outer rotor, drives the latter at a slightly lower speed owing to the difference in sizes.

Owing to the relative movement of the outer rotor around the inner rotor; and the close fit of the cover plate, oil is forced round between the lobes of the rotor and forced out of a hole in the top of the rotor casing and upward through a drilled passage to the annular space around the distributor drive shaft and to the oil filter and gallery.

To Remove Oil Pump from the Engine:
1. Drain the oil from the sump (preferable when the engine is warm) and jack up the car.
2. Remove the sump securing bolts and, lowering it at the front, first manouver the sump and try past the oil pump gauze filter as a unit.

To dismantle oil pump remove the two bolts securing the primary filter to the flange on the oil pump elbow. Take note of the position of the filter in relation to the elbow for re-assembly, i.e., the tube projecting inwards should be as near as possible to the bottom of the sump, thus ensuring clearance between the filter and the sump bottom.

To complete the dismantling it is only necessary to remove the four setscrews. The inner rotor and shaft and the outer rotor can now be removed and the dismantling is complete.

Servicing Oil Pump

As this pump provides a generous surplus of oil to that which is necessary for the engine lubrication, and owing to the design of the unit, very little wear is likely to occur in service, and little maintenance should be necessary to the unit during the life of the engine.

In actual practice, excepting the remote possibility of failures due to defective materials, no adjustments are likely to be required until approximately 200,000 miles have been covered, and then it is only likely to be limited to the elimination of end float in the rotors, and can be satisfactorily dealt with by lapping the joint faces of the pump body and cover. The clearance now between the rotors and cover plate should be from .0005" - .0025" and where a serious drop in oil delivery from the pump is associated with development of excessive end float, steps should be taken to lap the cover plate and body.

Engagement of Oil Pump and Distributor Driving Gear

This drive is taken from the helical gear on the camshaft through a similar gear unit mounted on the oil pump driving shaft.

The shaft has a tongue at the lower-most end which engages the oil pump mounted in the sump.

The helical gear unit is secured to the shaft by a Woodruff key. The upper gear of the unit drives the tachometer and the boss-like extension is fitted with a mills pin to prevent the gear and shaft from rising. The head has an offset recess into which the distributor shaft will seat.

When correctly engaged, the slot in the distributor driving boss, with No. 1 cylinder at T.D.C. on the compression stroke, should assume a position approximately "five minutes to five" with the offset towards the rear of the engine. In this position the slot will point directly towards the exhaust valve rod sealing tube for No. 1 cylinder, the distributor rotor will face No. 1 spark plug, and the keyway in the helical gear will be aligned with the oil dipstick when fitted.

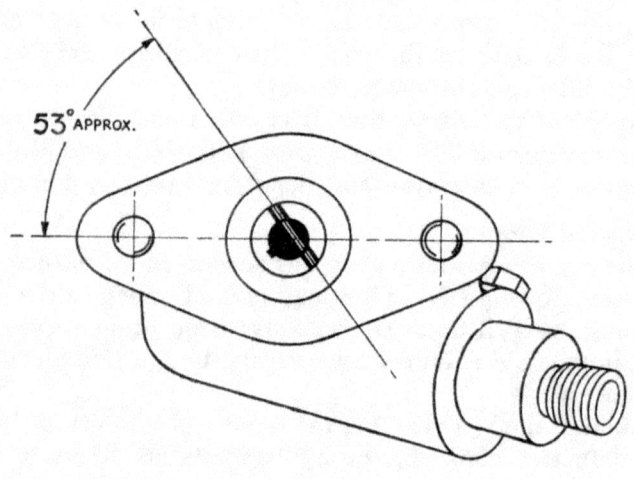

Crankshaft and Main Bearings

The crankshaft is a molybdenum manganese forging with ground journals and crankpins.

In addition to the servicing of accessories such as carburetors, generator, etc. plus routine maintenance and adjustments, all the following repairs or services listed prior to "Removing Engine and Gearbox" can be performed with the engine in the car. Others are best handled on the bench. It is possible of course, to remove the piston-connecting rod assemblies with the engine in place, and even the crankshaft main bearings can be handled from below in an emergency, but removal and refitting of the power unit is advised, wherever possible, in the interests of ease and thoroughness.

To Remove Camshaft

The camshaft may be removed from the engine while the unit is still in the chassis and the following procedure is used.

1. Remove the front cowl and radiator as described in "Removal of Engine."
2. Remove the cylinder head as described in "Decarbonizing." Immediately after removal of the cylinder head, sleeve retainers of local manufacture or Churchill Tool No. S.138 should be applied as shown.
In the event of sleeve movement, new figure eight washers should be fitted. Remove push rods and tappets.
3. Disconnect tachometer drive. Remove distributor assembly complete with pedestal by removing the two securing nuts at the crankcase. Do not slacken clamp bolt. Remove distributor and oil pump helical driving gear.
4. Check that the fuel has been turned off, remove pump and line. (See Fuel Section.)
5. Loosen off generator and remove fan and fan assembly by withdrawing four bolts and the extension bolt.
6. Remove the timing cover by withdrawing the seven setscrews, four bolts and one nut. Note the timing markings on the gear wheels and camshaft; this will assist in the reassembly.
7. Release the locking plate and withdraw the two setscrews. The timing chain can be lifted off the chain wheel and both components moved clear.
8. The front camshaft bearing is next removed by withdrawing the two setscrews and locking washers. The bearing can be lifted away.
9. The camshaft can now be drawn forward out of the cylinder block.

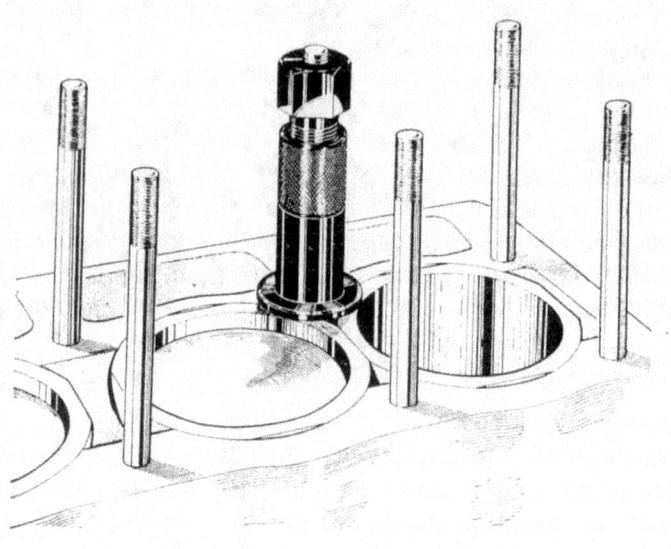

Refitting the Camshaft

Re-assembly is the reverse of removal. Special attention should be given to the following:

1. When resetting the valve timing, the engine should be set with Nos. 1 and 4 pistons at T.D.C. In this position the crankshaft timing wheel keyway is pointing vertically downwards.

Rest the camshaft chainwheel on the camshaft spigot and turn the chainwheel about the camshaft until the identification punch mark on the end of the camshaft can be seen through the punch marked hole in the chainwheel. Secure the chainwheel to the camshaft leaving the two bolts finger tight.

Turn the camshaft chainwheel until the scribe line thereon aligns with the scribe line on the crankshaft sprocket. **Without moving** the camshaft remove the camshaft chainwheel and when removed fit the timing chain to this wheel and the one on the crankshaft in such a manner that the scribe lines remain aligned. Reposition the camshaft chainwheel and check by simulating pressure on the chain tensioner that the timing marks have retained their positions and re-adjust if necessary. Tighten bolts to correct torque loading and turn over tabs of locking plates.

2. When refitting the oil pump and distributor driving helical gear, ensure that No. 1 piston is at T.D.C. on the compression stroke. In this position the correct engagement of the helical gear should allow the Woodruff key to be positioned towards

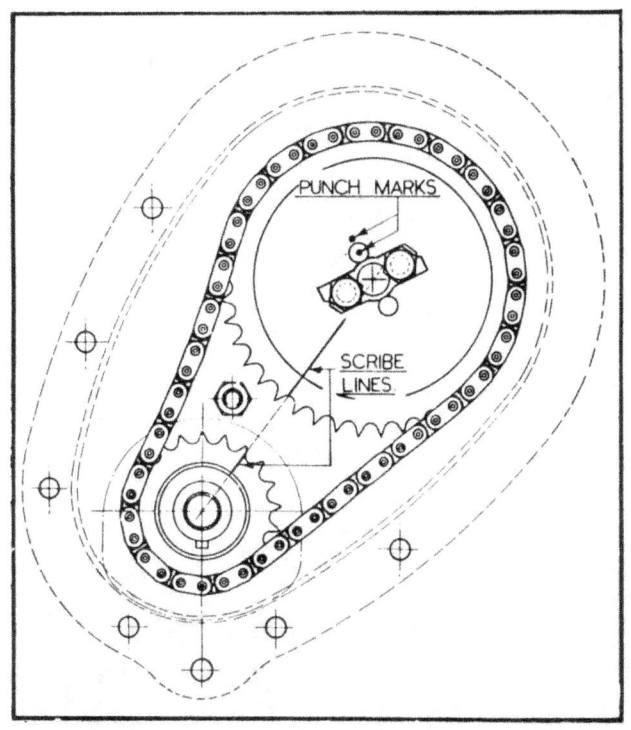

the front of the engine, pointing approximately towards the dipstick. It may be found that the oil pump shaft will not engage with the pump for the tongue and slot of these components are out of line. The engine will need to be turned over slowly until the shaft engages with the pump. Continue to turn the engine until the offset slot in the distributor drive boss attains the position as illustrated. Disengage the helical gear and remove it from the housing. Turn the engine over until No. 1 piston attains the T.D.C. position on the compression stroke and replace the helical gear when the shaft will engage with the oil pump.

3. Having refitted the cylinder head and rocker shaft it is advisable to apply oil to the ground surfaces where the rockers contact the valves, as these points do not immediately receive a supply of oil.

To Set Valve Timing in the Absence of Timing Wheel Markings

It is assumed that, for the purpose of this instruction, the cylinder head and valve gear are in position and the crankshaft sprocket is keyed to the crankshaft but the camshaft chainwheel has yet to be fitted. The following procedure is

recommended:
1. Set valve rocker clearances for Nos. 1 and 4 cylinders to .015" which is the valve timing clearances.
2. Turn crankshaft until Nos. 1 and 4 pistons are at T.D.C.

This position may be found by placing the keyway in the crankshaft vertically downwards.

3. Rotate the camshaft until the exhaust valve and inlet valve of No. 4 cylinder are at the point of balance. In this position the exhaust valve will just be about to close and the inlet just commencing to open. The inlet valve opens at 15° B.T.D.C. (TR 2-3) or 17° (TR 4) and the exhaust valve closes at 15° or (17°) A.T.D.C. 15° before or after T.D.C. is equivalent to .081" (2.06 mm.) piston travel or 1.5" (3.81 cm.) measured round the flywheel adjacent to the starter teeth.

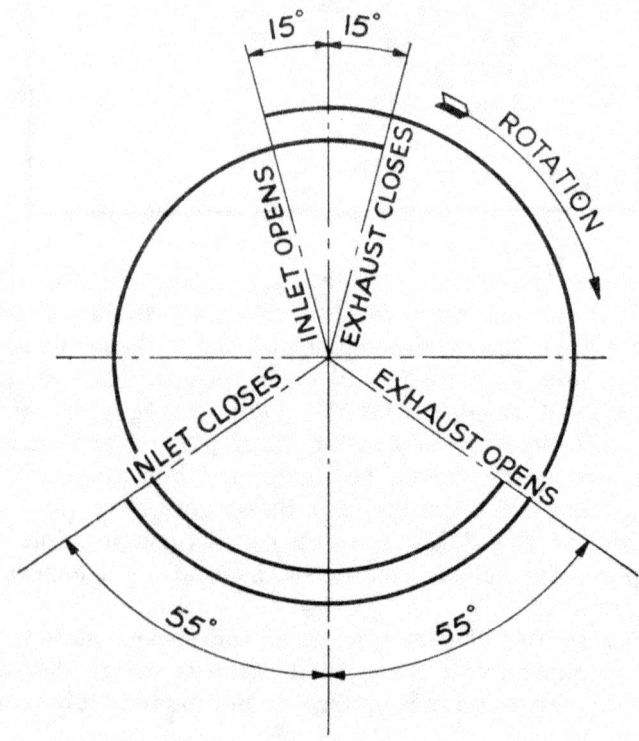

4. Offer up the camshaft chainwheel to the camshaft itself but without moving this shaft and adjust its engagement with the chain until a pair of holes in the chainwheel exactly match a pair in the shaft. It may be necessary to turn this wheel back to front to match these holes.

5. Having attained the correct position of the chainwheel relative to the shaft, encircle the wheel with the timing chain.
6. Without moving either crankshaft or camshaft, position the loop of the chain round the crankshaft sprocket in such a manner that the holes in the chainwheel match those in the camshaft.
7. The camshaft chainwheel is now secured to the camshaft by two bolts and locking plates, the bolts are not locked until a final check has been made.
8. A final check can be made when the engine is on a bench by marking the rear of the cylinder block opposite the T.D.C. mark on the flywheel with Nos. 1 and 4 cylinders at T.D.C. The flywheel is then moved a ¼ turn anti-clockwise (viewed from the front of the engine) and then turned slowly in a clockwise direction. As the flywheel is turned clockwise, insert a .010" feeler gauge between the valve stem and the rocker of No. 4 cylinder inlet valve until a slight resistance is felt, that is when the valve begins to open. At this stage the movement of the flywheel should be stopped; with a pencil mark the flywheel opposite the mark previously made on the cylinder block.

1 Valve
2 Rocker
3 Adjuster
4 Locknut
5 Push rod
6 Tappet
7 Camshaft

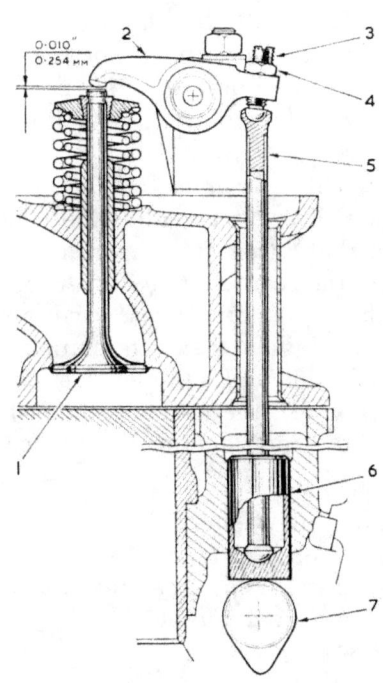

Remove the feeler gauge from the inlet valve.

Turn the flywheel clockwise until the feeler gauge can be inserted between the valve stem and the rocker of No. 4 cylinder exhaust valve, after which the flywheel is turned to T.D.C. Proceed to turn the flywheel slowly clockwise and at the same time putting a slight pull on the feeler gauge. The turning of the flywheel should be stopped at a point where the feeler gauge can be removed and this indicates that the exhaust valve has closed. A second mark of the pencil is now made on the flywheel opposite the mark on the cylinder block. With a rule measure the distance from the T.D.C. mark on the flywheel to each of the pencil marks.

If the timing is correct the two dimensions will be identical. Having finally proved the valve timing, the chainwheel locking tabs may be turned up.

9. The timing gears are now marked with a scribe line as shown.

10. Fit the timing chain tensioner and secure with plain washer and split pin. Replace timing cover.

The rocker clearances are now set to their working clearances.

Ignition and Distributor Timing

It is important that the "Distributor and Tachometer Gear Assembly" is fitted with an end float of .003" to .007".

This can be measured in the following manner:

1. Measure and note the thickness of a $1/2''$ washer and assemble it with the distributor-tachometer driven gear to the oil pump driving shaft.

2. Install this assembly in the cylinder block with the washer between the gear and the shaft bearing in the cylinder block. Ensure that the shaft is engaged in the oil pump.

3. Over the gear assembly fit the distributor adapter.

4. Utilizing feeler gauges, ascertain the distance between the distributor adapter and its mating face on the cylinder block.

5. When this measurement is compared with the thickness dimension of the washer the difference will represent the amount of "end float" or "interference."

Example

Thickness of washer .060"
Distance between faces .055"

The distance, being less than the washer, gives the gear assembly an "end float" of .005".

Conversely

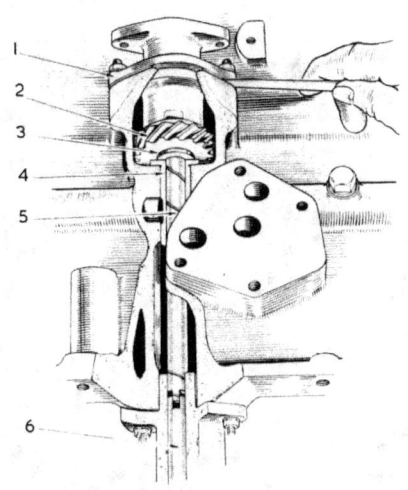

1 Distributor pedestal
2 Distributor drive gear
3 0·5″ (12·7 mm.) I.D. washer
4 Oil pump drive shaft bush
5 Oil pump drive shaft
6 Oil pump rotor shaft

Thickness of washer .060″
Distance between faces .065″

The distance being greater than the washer, gives the gear assembly an "interference" of .005″. It will be necessary to fit shims or packings under the distributor adapter to obtain the correct end float.

Assuming the first instance to be the case, it will be necessary to add one packing of .002″ thickness to bring the end float to top limit. For the second instance it will be first necessary to "zero" the interference, i.e., .005″ and add sufficient packings to obtain the correct end float. The packing necessary in this case is .011″ for a middle limit end float.

6. Remove the gear assembly, shaft and washer from the cylinder block.

7. Turn the engine until the piston No. 1 cylinder is at T.D.C. on compression stroke, in this position both valves will be closed.

8. Fit the Woodruff key to the oil pump driving shaft and insert the shaft in the block to engage the oil pump with its tongue. Rotate the shaft until the key is at right angles to the camshaft and points away from the engine.

9. Position and lower the distributor-tachometer driven gear on

the drive shaft until the keyway and the key engage. Continue a downward motion turning the gear clockwise to effect engagement with the driving gear on the camshaft. Caution must be exercised to prevent dislodging the Woodruff key.

10. When correctly engaged the offset slot in the gear assembly will be aligned with No. 1 pushrod sealing tube and the offset towards the rear of the engine.

11. Assemble the distributor adapter together with the necessary packings to obtain the correct end float. Secure with nuts and locking washers.

12. Fit the distributor body with the rotor arm pointing to No. 1 push rod tube.

13. Adjust the points to .015" and with the contact points just commencing to separate the vernier adjuster on the third marking of its scale, secure the body to the adapter bracket with the nut and lock washer with a plain washer, under the lock washer.

14. Advance the vernier a further 1 division, which is equivalent to advancing the ignition 4° on the flywheel B.T.D.C.

15. Fit the distributor cover, connect the plug leads to the correct plugs. The plugs having had their gaps set to .032". Fit the H.T. and L.T. leads to the ignition coil.

Decarbonizing

The factory recommends removal of the cylinder head for decarbonizing after the first 5,000 miles. Attention after this running period has the advantage of allowing the initial casting stresses to resolve themselves and permits the consequent valve seat distortion to be counteracted by valve grinding. Failure to carry out this initial valve grinding is a frequent cause of excessive fuel consumption of new cars. Subsequent attention will not normally be required until further considerable amount of running has been done — normally after about 15,000 miles.

The above mentioned figures only take into consideration a car which is used under normal conditions. If the car is being used for competition and high speed work valve grinding is done as and when necessary.

The procedure recommended for decarbonizing is a follows:
1. Disconnect the battery lead and plug leads from plugs.
2. Drain the cooling system.
3. Disconnect the fuel pipe clip, the top water and by-pass hoses and remove the thermo gauge bulb from the thermostat housing, then remove the latter from the cylinder head by withdrawing the two bolts.
4. Remove the two rocker cover securing nuts and lift off the rocker cover.
5. Remove the rocker shaft assembly by loosening off the four pedestal nuts progressively, allowing the assembly to rise as a unit.
6. Remove the heater hose from the water shut-off cock at the rear of the cylinder head. (Where heater is fitted.)

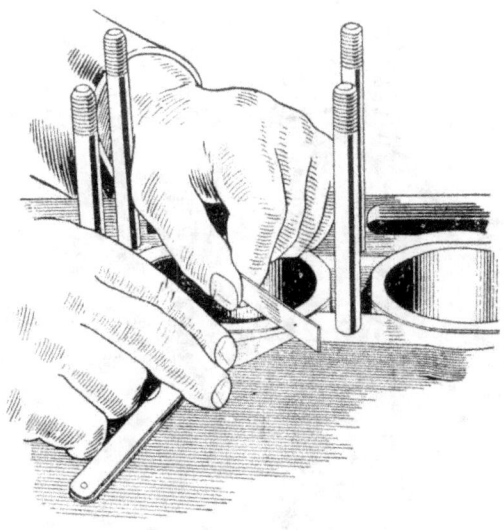

7. Disconnect the throttle and choke controls, the suction pipe and fuel feed pipe from the carburetors. While there is no need to remove the carburetors this can be effected at the carburetor and manifold joints. (See Fuel Section.)

8. Remove the ten cylinder head nuts and lift the head from the block. **Do not** attempt to break the seal of the cylinder head by turning the engine as this will disturb the cylinder sleeves.

9. Immediately after the head has been removed, place cylinder liner retainers in position and check the projection of the cylinder sleeves above the face of the cylinder block. The flange of the cylinder sleeves should stand proud by .003" minimum to .0055" maximum. If the cylinder sleeves have sunk below .003" new figure eight joints will need to be fitted.

Inspect also for cylinder sleeve movement and if any is suspected the cylinder sleeves and pistons will have to be removed and new figure of eight joints fitted.

Remove the push rods.

Lay the cylinder head on a bench so that the valve heads are supported, this will ensure that when pressure is exerted on the valve spring cap this spring will compress and the keepers easily removed.

The valves are numbered from the front of the engine and their positions should be kept. The carbon should be cleaned off with a solvent moistened rag.

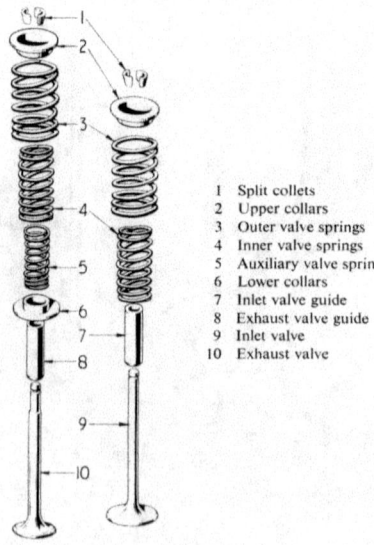

1 Split collets
2 Upper collars
3 Outer valve springs
4 Inner valve springs
5 Auxiliary valve spring
6 Lower collars
7 Inlet valve guide
8 Exhaust valve guide
9 Inlet valve
10 Exhaust valve

Grind the valves into their appropriate seating, where valve faces are badly pitted they should either be renewed or replaced. No attempt should be made to grind a badly pitted valve into its seating.

When the necessity of recutting a valve seat arises, it is important that the valve guides are concentric with the seats themselves. Where a valve guide is badly worn it should be replaced before the seat is recut.

While refacing valves, only remove sufficient metal to clean up the face, otherwise if too much is removed the edge will tend to curl up in service.

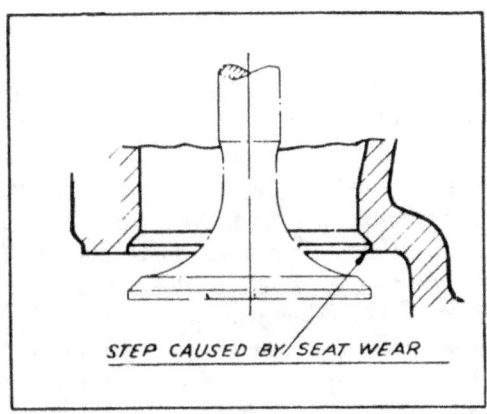

Where valve seats are badly worn or pitted they should be recut with an 89° cutter utilizing a pilot of the same diameter as the valve stem. Should the valve seating become embedded in the cylinder head as shown, it will first become necessary to employ at 15° cutter, to provide a clearance for the incoming or outgoing gases, following this with a cutter of $44^{1}/_{2}°$. This work should be carried out after the cylinder head has been cleaned.

Valve Guides

Check valve guide wear by inserting a new valve in the guide, lifting it $1/_8$" off the seat and rocking it sideways. Movement of more than .020" across the seat indicates that the guide needs replacing. Guides are pressed out and new ones fitted to stand .78" above the face of the cylinder head.

Removal of Carbon

Remove the spark plugs, clean, set and test ready for replacement. If for any reason such as badly burnt or broken electrodes, and damaged insulation the plug should be replaced.

Clean the carbon from the cylinder head, finally wipe the chambers clean. Scrape the valve ports clean, exercising great care not to damage the valve seats. When the head is clean of carbon blow out with a compressed air line and wipe with a rag moistened with solvent. Ensure that the contact face is perfectly clean and flat.

Before cleaning the carbon from the tops of the pistons, smear a little grease around the top of the two bores and raise the piston almost to the top. Fill the other two bores and tappet chambers with non-fluffy cloth; this will safeguard against any carbon chips entering the lower extremities of the engine. It is suggested that the piston crowns are cleaned, utilizing a stick of lead solder, which will not scratch the piston crown, in such a manner that the carbon deposit on the vertical wall of the piston and that deposit formed in each cylinder bore above the maximum travel point of the top piston ring is not disturbed. This carbon helps to insulate the piston rings from the heat generated during combustion and provides a secondary oil seal.

The use of emery cloth or other abrasive for polishing is not recommended as particles of such abrasive may enter the bores and engine after re-assembly, causing serious damage.

Having cleaned two pistons, brush and blow away the carbon chippings, taking care not to allow any to drop into the cylinder block. Lower the clean pistons in their bores and wipe away the grease, remove the cloth stuffing from the other two piston bores and grease the tops. After greasing the tops of the cylinder bore raise these pistons and fill the remaining two bores with the rag. Repeat the cleaning operation. On completion of the piston cleaning, wipe and blow away the carbon chips and clear the block face, particularly around the cylinder sleeves and the tops of these sleeves. Clean the grease from the cylinder bores and remove the cloth stuffing from the bores and tappet chambers.

The valve springs should be examined for damage and their length compared with new springs. If any doubt exists as to the condition they should be replaced. The exhaust valve is fitted with an auxiliary inner spring, making three springs in all. It should be noted that the close-coiled end of these springs is fitted nearest the cylinder head.

Ensure that the cylinder block and head faces are perfectly flat and clean, it should only be necessary then to apply a coating of grease to the cylinder gasket. Should it be decided to use a sealing compound, one of the non-setting type must be used for on future occasions when the head is removed, the cylinder sleeves may be disturbed because of their adherence to the gasket.

When refitting the cylinder head nuts, tighten them gradually in the sequence shown in order to produce an even pressure on the gasket and prevent undue strain in the cylinder block casting. It will be necessary to recheck the nut tightness when cold to 100—105 lbs./ft. Before tightening down the rocker shaft pedestals, screw back each adjusting screw and ensure that the ball ends of these screws engage correctly in the push rods. Failure to attend to this procedure can result in damage to the push rods. Smother the rocker gear with oil, particularly where the rockers bear on the valves.

Before replacing the rocker cover ensure that the cord joint is undamaged and shellaced to the cover, otherwise oil may leak through the joint.

After the first 500 miles the cylinder head nuts should be checked for tightness with the engine hot.

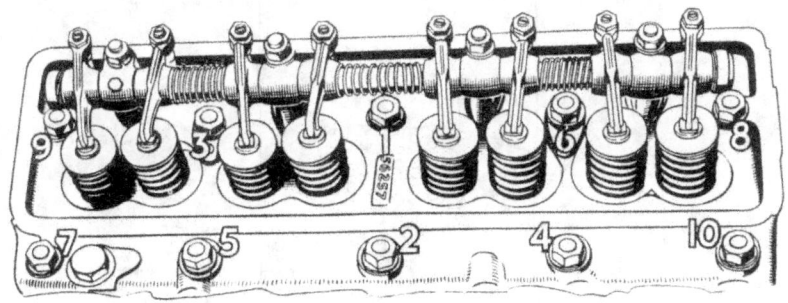

Cylinder head nut tightening sequence

The "Purolator Micronic" Oil Filter—Type 17F.5102

The Purolator Micronic filter consists of a plastic impregnated paper element which removes the finest particles of abrasive which invariably find their way into the engine. A filter of this type will stop not only the smaller microm sized particles of abrasive, but ensures a supply of clean oil to the engine at all times. The only attention which the filter needs is to see that the element is changed at periods not exceeding 8,000 miles. It is essential that this operation is carried out at specified periods to ensure maximum filtration. To renew the element proceed as follows:

1. Clean the outside of the filter casing.
2. Unscrew the center bolt and remove the filter casing and element.

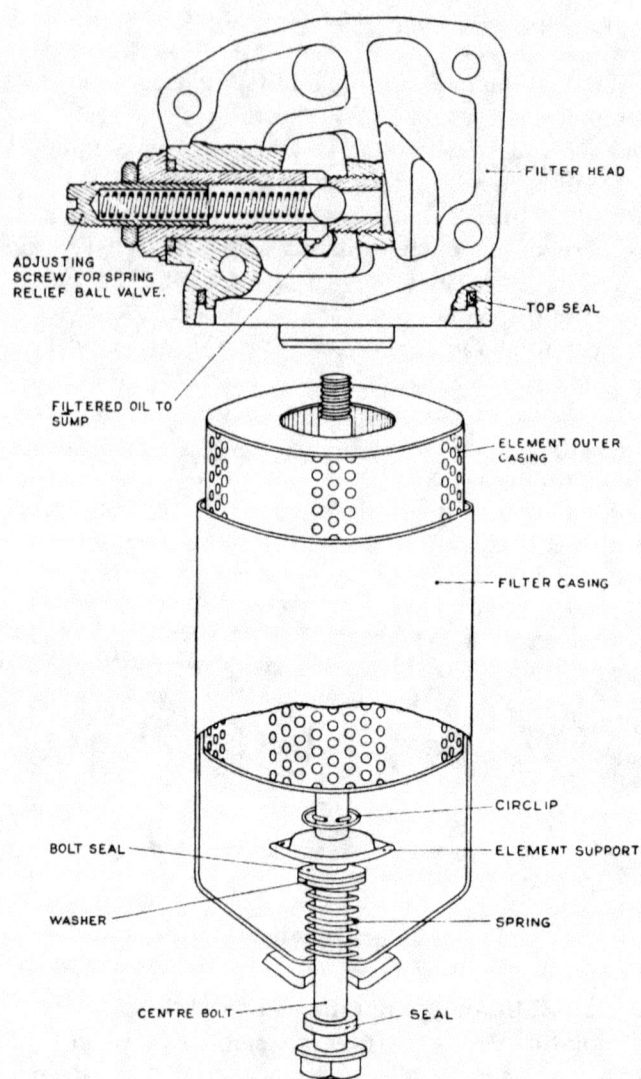

NOTE: The paper element, its perforated outer cover and element tube forms a complete element assembly. Ensure that the top seal is retained in position in the groove in the filter head.
3. Withdraw the element and clean the inside of the casing.
4. Insert a new element into the filter casing.
5. Fit the filter and new element to the filter head ensuring that the spigot formed on the head enters the center tube of the element squarely. Tighten the bolt sufficiently to ensure an oil-tight joint. (14-16 lbs. feet.)

6. Run the engine for a few minutes and inspect the filter for leaks. If leakage is noted between the filter casing and the head, the center bolt must be unscrewed and the casing and element withdrawn. A new top seal should then be fitted. If leakage occurs at the bottom of the filter, remove the circlip from the center bolt and withdraw the bolt from the casing; collect the element support, bolt seal, washer and spring. Ease the remaining seal out of the bottom of the casing and fit a new seal in its place. Insert the center bolt and fit the spring, the washer, a new bolt seal and the element support on to the part, fit circlip into its groove in the bolt. Place the element inside the casing and offer up the assembly to the filter head, screw the center bolt home. A certain quantity of oil will be lost due to the removal of the filter casing, and the sump should be topped up after assembly of the filter.

The filter casing should not be disturbed until element renewal is required. To do this invites the hazard that the accumulated dirt on the outside of the filter may be allowed to contaminate the inside; thus being carried into the bearings when the engine is re-started.

Do not attempt to reset the pressure relief valve which is incorporated in the filter head. This is the main engine pressure relief valve and is set at the factory to a predetermined figure.

Pressure Relief Valve (Full Flow Filter)

To check the relief valve operation, run the engine until normal operating temperature is reached. Slowly increase engine speed. At 2,000 rpm the oil pressure gauge should read 75 psi. then fall off to 70 psi. If necessary to adjust pressure, back off the locknut, rotate the screw clockwise to increase pressure, counterclockwise to reduce it. Retighten locknut when correct pressure is obtained.

Removal of TR 2-3 Engine and Gearbox

1. Disconnect the battery. Turn off fuel at shut-off cock.
2. The hood is removed by removing four hinge nuts, two at each hinge.
3. Drain off the cooling fluid by opening the taps, one at the base of the radiator and the second situated below the inlet and exhaust manifold in the cylinder block.
4. Drain off the oil from the engine and gearbox.
5. Disconnect the head and side light cables at their snap connectors. Remove the bolts from the top brackets and the bolt in the center of the cowling, this holds the hood lock connecting cable, release cable control at one side. Remove the twelve

setscrews (six per side) situated under the wheel arches. Remove the starting handle bracket and the steady rods from under the cowling and finally the nut and bolt from the steady plate.

6. To remove radiator disconnect top and bottom hoses, release the tie rods at the top and the bolts one either side at the base of the unit.

7. Disconnect the lever linkages at the foremost carburetor; disconnect the inner and outer cables of the choke control and the fuel feed pipes at their banjo unions. Remove the carburetors from the manifold.

8. Remove the horns from their brackets by first removing the four fixing bolts (two to each horn). There is no need to disconnect the horns from their cables. Disconnect generator leads and remove generator from its bracket and remove fan belt.

9. Remove front chassis cross tube by removal of three nuts and bolts at each flange.

10. Remove the three nuts and washers at the exhaust flange and break the joint.

11. Disconnect the flexible fuel pipe at the tap, the oil pressure gauge pipe, starter motor cable, L.T. lead at the coil, the tachometer drive at distributor pedestal and withdraw the water temperature gauge bulb.

12. To remove the seats, first remove the cushions and unscrew the sixteen nuts (eight to each seat) thus releasing the frame from the runners; it can then be lifted out.

13. Free the rubber gear lever grommet by the removal of three self-tapping screws from the gearbox cover pressing and remove the latter by unscrewing the thirteen setscrews, hidden by the trim and floor covering.

14. Remove the gear lever with grommet by loosening the locknut and unscrewing the lever.

15. Remove the speedometer drive, the overdrive cable at the snap connector and the starter motor by removing two nuts and bolts.

16. Drain the clutch hydraulic system. Disconnect the bundy tubing at the flexible hose at the left-hand side chassis member while holding the hexagon on the hose. Still holding the hexagon remove the hose securing nut and shakeproof washer; the flexible hose can now be withdrawn from its bracket.

17. Uncouple the propeller shaft by removing the four nuts and bolts securing the two flanges. Remove the two nuts holding the gearbox to the chassis frame.

18. Remove the four nuts and bolts (two each side) securing the

engine mountings to the chassis.
19. Fit slings to engine and lift out in a nose-up position.

Removal of TR 4 Engine and Gearbox
1. Remove battery, drain cooling system, engine oil and gearbox oil.
2. Disconnect fuel line to pump and from pump to carburetors and oil pressure tube.
3. Disconnect tachometer drive cable and distributor vacuum pipe.
4. Disconnect coil-to-switch wire and temperature sender wire.
5. Remove fan belt and disconnect engine ground strap.
6. Disconnect horns.

On the right hand side of the engine:
1. Disconnect heater valve control wire and heater hoses.
2. Disconnect mixture control cable and throttle rod.
3. Remove carburetors if desired (as a precaution against damage) and unbolt exhaust header pipe.

At the front of the car:
1. Release the U-bolt which supports the steering cross shaft housing.
2. Remove the steering shaft-to-box coupling bolt and move steering unit as far forward as possible.
3. Remove the front cross tube.
4. Remove hood and air deflector.
5. Remove radiator and the torque reaction brace.

Under the car:
1. Remove clutch slave cylinder and allow it to hang by hose.

Inside the car:
1. Remove cushions and carpets.
2. Remove the facia support which bridges the tunnel and the tunnel. Note that there are two screws at the top front of the tunnel which are easy to overlook.
3. Remove the speedometer cable, overdrive control cables (if fitted) and unbolt front end of propeller shaft.
4. Remove the gearbox top cover. It is a good idea to make a temporary cover from cardboard to prevent the entry of dirt or other foreign matter.

Attach a hoist to the engine lifting eye, or to whatever device is used to support the engine. Then:
1. Unbolt the front engine mounts.
2. Unbolt the rear engine mounts (adjacent to the handbrake) and the crossmember.
3. Lift the engine up and out, tilting the nose up to clear.

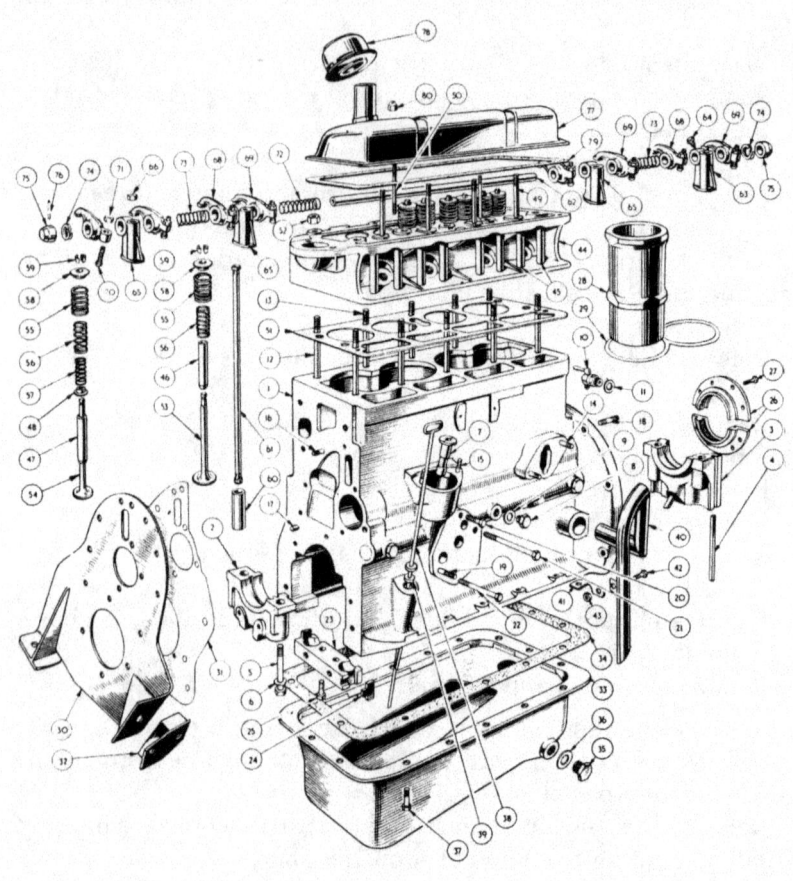

Exploded view of Cylinder Block Details

Ref. No.	Description	Ref. No.	Description
1	Cylinder Block.	40	Breather Pipe.
2	Front Bearing Cap.	41	Breather Pipe Clip.
3	Rear Bearing Cap.	42	Breather Pipe Clip Bolt.
4	Rear Bearing Cap Felt Packing.	43	Nut for Pipe Clip Bolt.
5	Bearing Cap Bolts.	44	Combustion Head.
6	Spring Washer for Bearing Cap Bolts.	45	Push Rod Sealing Tubes.
7	Oil Pump Drive Bush.	46	Inlet Valve Guide.
8	Oil Gallery Blanking Screw.	47	Exhaust Valve Guide.
9	Washer for Blanking Screws.	48	Exhaust Valve Guide Collar.
10	Drain Tap.	49	Rocker Pedestal Stud.
11	Washer for Drain Tap.	50	Rocker Cover Stud.
12, 13	Combustion Head Studs.	51	Combustion Head Gasket.
14	Petrol Pump Studs.	52	Combustion Head Securing Nut.
15	Distributor Studs.	53	Inlet Valve.
16	Front Engine Plate Stud.	54	Exhaust Valve.
17	Front Engine Plate Locating Dowel.	55	Outer Valve Spring.
18	Gearbox Stud.	56	Inner Valve Spring.
19	Oil Filter Stud.	57	Auxiliary Exhaust Valve Spring.
20, 21, 22	Oil Filter Attachment Bolts.	58	Valve Spring Collars.
		59	Split Cones.
		60	Valve Tappet.
		61	Push Rod.
23	Front Bearing Sealing Block.	62	Rocker Shaft.
24	Sealing Block Pads.	63	Rocker Pedestal (with oil passage drilled).
25	Screw for Sealing Block.	64	Rocker Pedestal Screw.
26	Rear Oil Seal (always a mated pair).	65	Rocker Pedestal.
27	Setscrews for Rear Oil Seal.	66	Rocker Pedestal Attachment Nut.
28	Cylinder Sleeve.	68	No. 1 Rocker.
29	Figure of Eight Joint.	69	No. 2 Rocker.
30	Front Engine Plate.	70	Ball Pin.
31	Engine Plate Joint Washer.	71	Ball Pin Locking Nut.
32	Engine Front Mounting.	72	Rocker Centre Spring (coil).
33	Oil Sump.	73	Rocker Intermediate Spring (coil).
34	Joint Washer for Oil Pump.	74	Rocker Outer Spring (flat coil).
35	Oil Drain Plug.	75	Shaft End Collars.
36	Washer for Drain Plug.	76	Mills Pins for Shaft End Collars.
37	Oil Sump Bolts.	77	Rocker Cover.
38	Dipstick.	78	Oil Filler Cap.
39	Felt Washer for Dipstick.	79	Rocker Cover Joint.
		80	Nyloc Nuts.

Dismantling Engine

It is sound policy to clean the exterior of the engine and gearbox before commencing to dismantle.
1. Detach gearbox by removing the nine nuts and bolts from the clutch bell housing.
2. Remove the clutch from the flywheel by withdrawing the six securing bolts.
3. Remove the flywheel by unlocking the tab washers and withdrawing the four bolts.
4. To remove the fuel pump, first disconnect the pipe to the carburetors and then remove the nuts and lock washers from the studs. It will be noticed that the rearmost stud accommodates the oil pressure gauge pipe clip.
5. Remove rocker cover, together with oil filler cap.
6. Remove vacuum pipe from distributor and spark plug leads, H.T. and L.T. leads at the ignition coil. Avoid loosening clamping bolt and remove distributor from pedestal, secured by two nuts with locking and plain washers. Lift out distributor and tachometer driving shaft assembly.
7. Remove the ignition coil.
8. From the front of thermostat housing remove the nut holding the clip for the fuel and vacuum pipes; these two pipes are strapped together and can be lifted away. Remove the by-pass hose from the thermostat housing to the water pump housing after undoing the two hose clamps. Withdraw thermostat housing as a unit following the removal of the two bolts and lock washers securing it to the combustion head.
9. Remove water pump impeller after withdrawing one bolt and two nuts.
10. Remove the water pump housing which is held by two bolts and spring washers.
11. Proceed to remove oil filter assembly by first removing the cap nut holding the oil pressure pipe banjo to the filter. This pipe can now be detached. The remaining three bolts can then be removed and the filter assembly taken away.
12. Remove generator bracket and pedestal.
13. Remove fan assembly by withdrawing four bolts, followed by the extension bolt; the hub and hub extension can now be withdrawn from the crankshaft.
14. Remove timing cover and packing, remove chain tensioner after withdrawal of split pin and washer. Observe the markings on the camshaft chainwheel and crankshaft sprocket.
15. Release the tabs of the locking plate and withdraw the two bolts to release camshaft chainwheel, the chain can now be

freed from the crankshaft sprocket. Camshaft chainwheel and chain can now be lifted away and the crankshaft sprocket and Woodruff key removed from the crankshaft, followed by the shims.

16. Lift rocker shaft assembly by removal of the four pedestal nuts.

17. Remove the inlet and exhaust manifolds by removing eight nuts and six clamps.

18. Remove cylinder head by removal of ten nuts and washers and lift out the push rods and tappets.

19. The camshaft can be withdrawn by first removing two bolts securing the front bearing, then the bearing and finally the camshaft.

20. Remove the nineteen sump bolts and remove the sump. Care should be taken not to damage the oil pump filter.

21. Remove oil pump from inside cylinder block by unscrewing the three nuts and washers.

22. Remove the front engine plate from the block by removing the five attachment bolts, and discard the packing.

23. Remove the bearing caps, bottom halves of the shell bearings and thrust washers by releasing the tables of the locking plates and withdrawing the bolts. Remove also the big end bearing caps and bottom halves of the shell bearings by releasing the locking plates and withdrawing the bolts.

24. Lift out the crankshaft and collect the upper halves of the shell bearings.

25. Collect the upper halves of the big end shell bearings and withdraw the connecting rods and pistons from cylinder block. The cylinder sleeves may be tapped out gently from below.

Re-assembly of Engine

When the engine is completely dismantled the following procedure is suggested for re-assembly.

The cylinder block and head should be examined for leakage at the various core plugs. If these do show signs of leakage they must be renewed, their seatings thoroughly cleaned and new plugs fitted with jointing compound.

The main and big end journals of the crankshaft should be checked for wear against standard dimensions.

Wear in excess of .0025″ on the crank pins and the journals should be met by regrinding, but where the bearing alone is seriously worn (in excess of .003″) its replacement should suffice.

The bores of the sleeves should be measured and if more

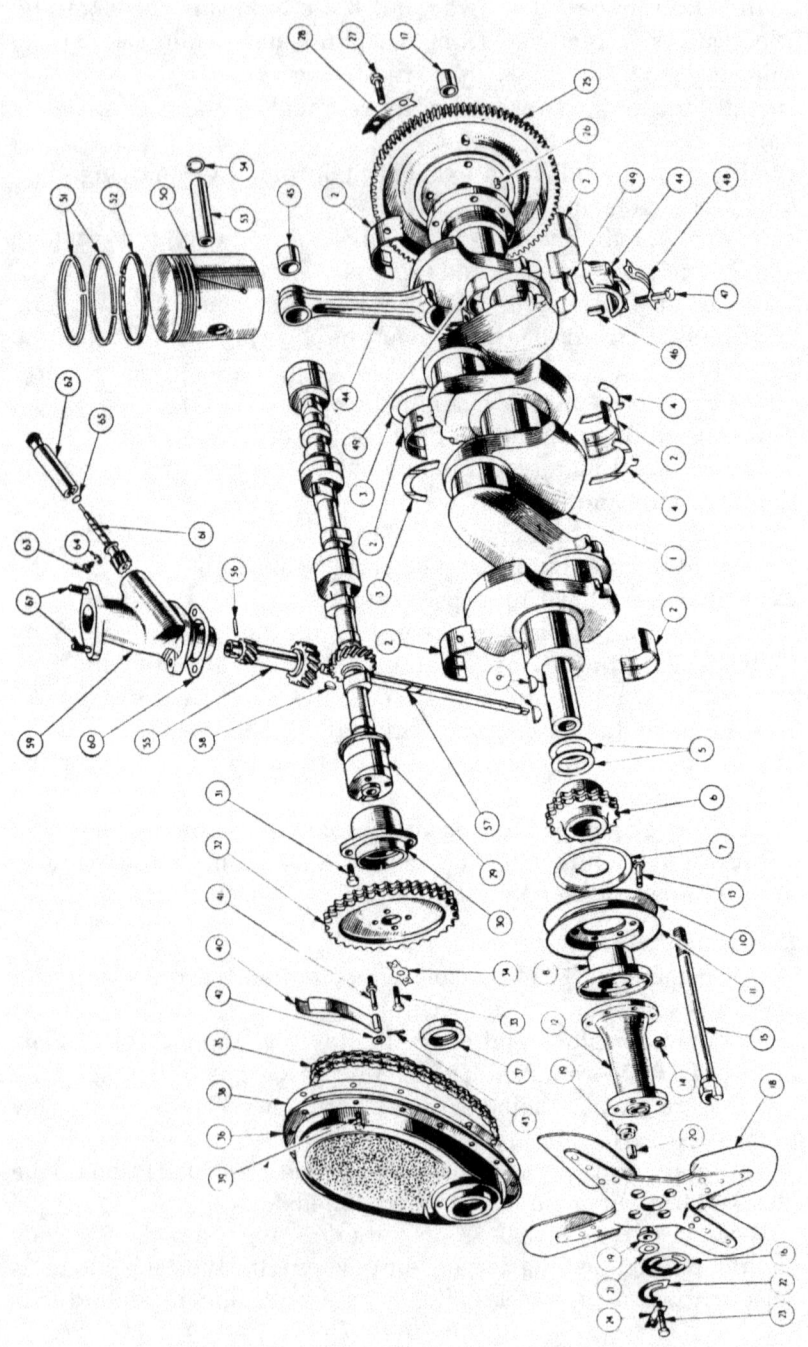

Key to Crankshaft Assembly

1. Crankshaft.
2. Crankshaft Main Bearings.
3. Top Thrust Washer.
4. Lower Thrust Washers.
5. Sprocket Locating Shims.
6. Crankshaft Sprocket.
7. Oil Deflector.
8. Fan Pulley Hub.
9. Woodruff Keys.
10. Rear Half of Fan Pulley.
11. Front Half of Fan Pulley.
12. Fan Pulley Hub Extension.
13. Fan Pulley Bolt.
14. Nyloc Nut for Fan Pulley Bolt.
15. Extension Bolt with Starter Dog Head.
16. Lock Washer for Extension Bolt.
17. Constant Pinion Pilot Bush.
18. Cooling Fan Assembly.
19. Rubber Bushes.
20. Metal Sleeves for Rubber Bushes.
21. Plain Washer.
22. Balance Piece.
23. Fan Attachment Bolt.
24. Locking Plate for Fan Attachment Bolts.
25. Flywheel.
26. Flywheel Locating Dowel.
27. Flywheel Attachment Bolt.
28. Flywheel Bolt Locking Plate.
29. Camshaft.
30. Front Camshaft Bearing.
31. Camshaft Bearing Attachment Bolt.
32. Camshaft Chain Wheel.
33. Chain Wheel Securing Bolt.
34. Chain Wheel Bolt Locking Plate.
35. Timing Chain.
36. Timing Cover.
37. Crankshaft Oil Seal.
38. Timing Cover Joint Washer.
39. Timing Cover Attachment Bolt.
40. Chain Tensioner.
41. Chain Tensioner Fulcrum Pin.
42. Washer for Chain Tensioner Pin.
43. Split Pin for Chain Tensioner Pin.
44. Connecting Rod.
45. Small End Bearing.
46. Hollow Dowel.
47. Connecting Rod Bolt.
48. Lock Plate for Connecting Rod Bolts.
49. Connecting Rod Bearing.
50. Piston.
51. Compression Ring.
52. Oil Scraper Ring.
53. Piston Pin.
54. Circlip for Piston Pin.
55. Distributor and Tachometer Driving Gear.
56. Mills Pin.
57. Oil Pump Drive Shaft.
58. Woodruff Key.
59. Distributor Pedestal.
60. Pedestal Joint Washer.
61. Tachometer Drive Gear.
62. Bearing for Tachometer Drive Gear.
63. Locating Screw for Bearing.
64. Lock Washer for Locating Screw.
65. Oil Seal.
66. Distributor Stud.

than .010″ in excess of the standard dimensions they should be renewed. It should be noted that maximum wear occurs at the top of the bore.

The camshaft and camshaft bore in early engines should also be dimensionally examined. Journal wear in excess of .003″ will necessitate a replacement shaft, while wear in the cylinder block bores of more than .0035″ will entail a replacement block.

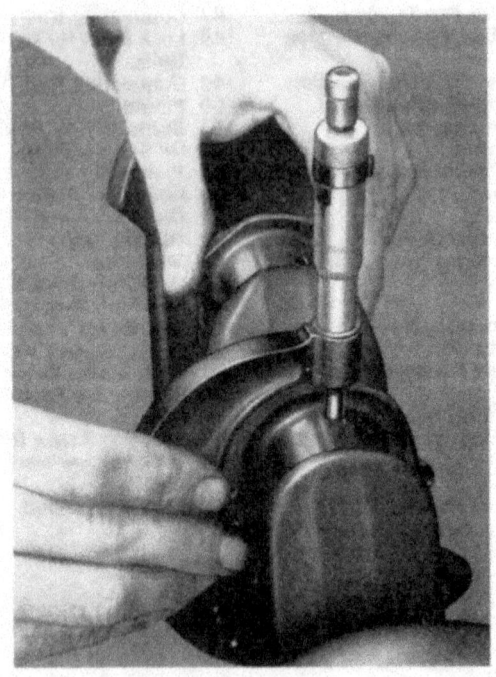

On later engines, remove the three shouldered setscrews on the left side of the block adjacent to the distributor drive and fuel pump drive bosses. **(Note:** the oil gallery sealing plugs are directly **below** the cam bearing setscrews. Do not confuse the two.) Drift out the rear bearing sealing disc. The bearings can be extracted using a suitable extractor. (Churchill No. S. 32)

To replace the bearings, align the oil feed hole and the location holes with those in the block; install the setscrews with new $\frac{1}{16}$″ plain steel washers under the heads and install a new rear bearing sealing disc.

The head should be examined and due attention paid to valve guides, valve seats, valve springs and the valves themselves. Valve guides should be replaced if they are more than .003″

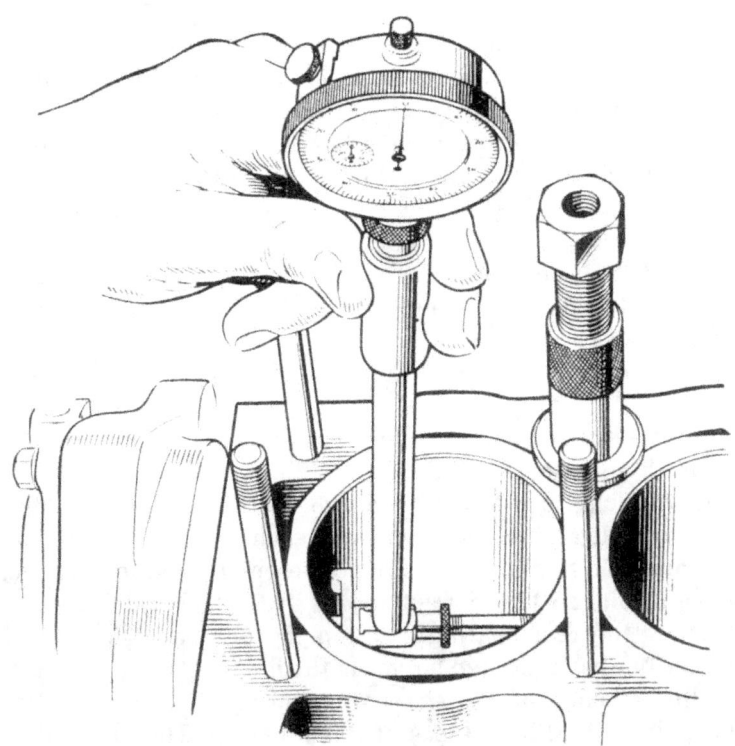

oversize.

Valve seats should be ground in, or if "pocketed," new seats should be shrunk in.

Valve springs should be thoroughly examined for cracks and dimensions.

Valves should be examined to ensure that their stems are perfectly straight and the faces recut.

The block and the head should be thoroughly cleaned or blown out by compressed air to ensure that all foreign matter has been removed. Bolts, setscrews and nuts are to be tightened to the torque loadings given in General Data Section.

All joint washers, gaskets, locking washers, lock plates and split pins must be renewed, then:

1. Check that the two halves of the rear oil seal bear the same number. These are machined as a mated pair and failure to observe this instruction may result in oil leakage. Shellac the top half of the oil seal and attach it loosely to the cylinder block by its four bolts and lock washers. Shellac and similarly fit the lower half of the oil seal to the rear bearing cap. Ensuring that the crankshaft mandrel is clean, lay it in the rear bearing housing (without the shell bearings). Fit the bearing cap and tighten

down sufficiently to nip the mandrel. Tighten the eight bolts to secure the oil seal to the cylinder block and bearing cap (torque loading of 8-10 lbs. ft.). Remove bearing cap from block.

2. Fit the upper half of the main bearings to the cylinder block; thoroughly clean and lubricate; place the crankshaft in position.

3. Fit the lower halves of the main bearings to the bearing caps, and lubricate.

4. Thread the two top halves of the thrust washers at the side of the center main bearing between the crankshaft and the cylinder block.

It is essential that the white metal side is toward the crankshaft.

Fit the thrust washers, one either side, to the center bearing cap and lightly secure with the two bolts and lock washers to cylinder block. Fit the two remaining caps to the cylinder block with two bolts and two lock washers each.

5. Commencing from the front of the engine tighten the bearings cap bolts to the correct torque (see "General Data"). On tightening the rear bearing cap, tap the oil seal lightly so that the joint between the two halves is flush.

In the absence of a crankshaft mandrel the oil seal attachment bolts will still be loose at this juncture. They should now be tightened to a torque loading of 8-10 lbs. ft. The bearing cap must be tightened down so that the oil seal division is flush.

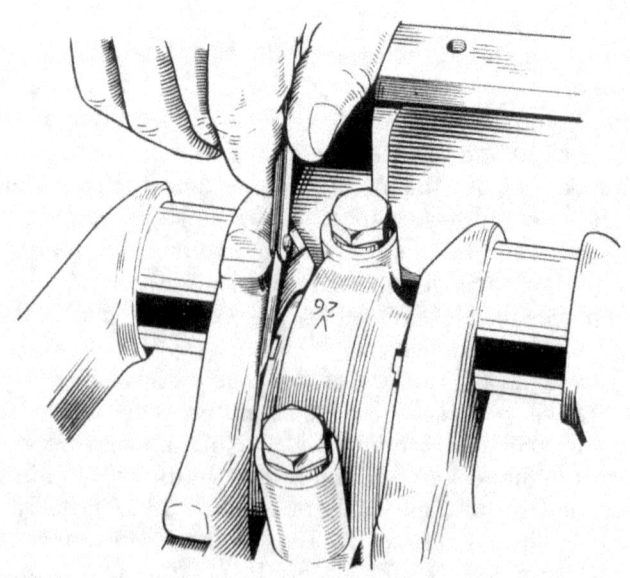

6. Check the crankshaft end float by the use of the feeler gauges or dial indicator gauge as shown. Should the end float determined be greater than .006", thicker thrust washers may be fitted; when the float is less than .004", thinner washers are needed or the existing ones should be rubbed down on emery paper.

7. Fit the front main bearing sealing block and tighten down the two cheese-headed bolts using a substantial screwdriver. Check that the face of the block is flush with the face of the cylinder block.

Plug the two cavities, one either end of the sealing block, with the sealing pad coated with shellac.

8. After dipping the felt packing strip into shellac force it into the recesses either side of the rear main bearing cap with the aid of a ³⁄₁₆" square brass drift. Two lengths about 9" long are necessary. Completely fill the groove and cut the felt off ¹⁄₆₄" proud of the cylinder block face. It is suggested that the felt strip is cut into approximately ³/₄" lengths for easy insertion.

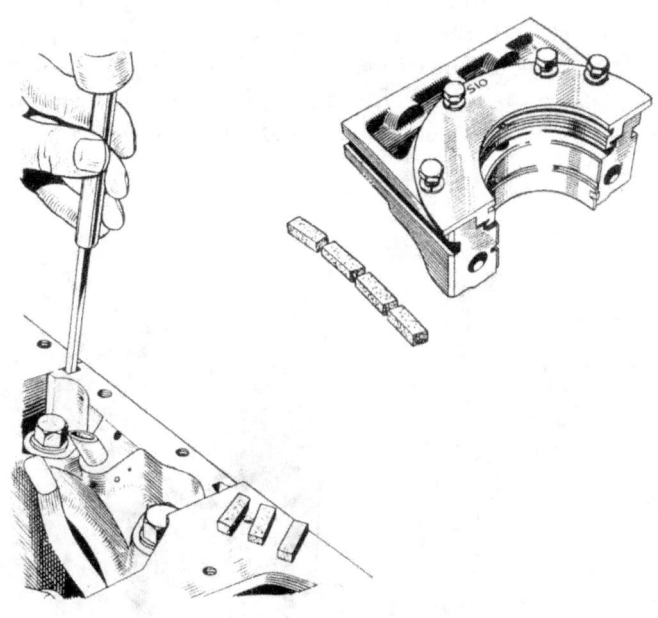

9. Check the connecting rods for alignment. Assemble the piston to the connecting rods so that the split of the skirt faces the cap side of the rod. It is suggested that the pistons be first submerged in hot water for a few moments and the piston pin

should then be a light push fit. Secure the pin with circlips, one either side. Dry the piston and rod assemblies thoroughly.

10. Fit the piston rings to the pistons, the two compression rings are uppermost with one oil scraper ring below. Lubricate freely.

On engines after No.TS9731-E a tapered compression ring is the second ring. This must be fitted with the taper towards the top and "T" or "Top" marking on upper face.

Move the rings so that their gaps are 180° removed from one another; failure to observe this point may lead to increased oil consumption. Wire brush the exterior of the cylinder liners to ensure that they are free from scale and all loose dirt on their machined surfaces. With the assistance of a piston ring compressor fit the piston assemblies to the cylinder sleeves bearing the same letter as the piston.

11. Arrange the piston and connecting rod assemblies now in their cylinder sleeves, so that the numbers stamped on the rods and caps run consecutively, i.e., 1, 2, 3, 4. Turn these assemblies upside down in pairs, 1 and 2, 3 and 4, with the flat of the liner adjacent to one another. The bearing caps are now all uppermost and must be turned to face one way. Remove the bearing caps and fit the shell bearings to rods and caps. Fit one figure of eight packing using a light coating of jointing compound on the flanged faces of each pair of cylinder sleeves and on the

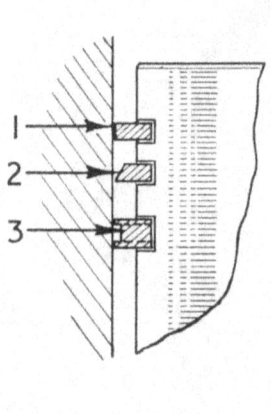
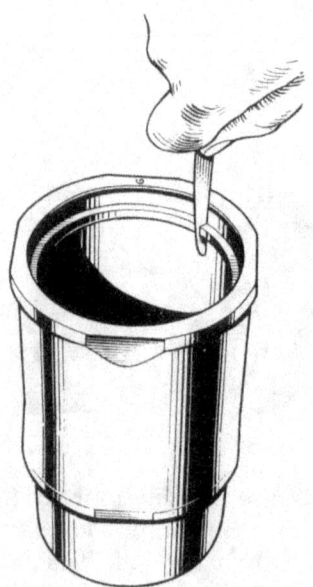

1 Plain compression ring
2 Taper faced compression ring
3 Oil control ring

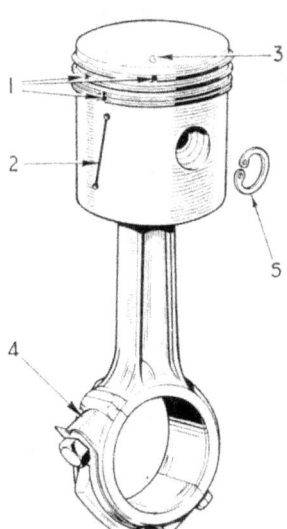

1 Piston rings
2 Slot in piston
3 Identification symbol
4 Cap
5 Circlip

mating faces in the cylinder block after ensuring that all components have been thoroughly cleaned of all loose deposits and the machined surfaces in which the cylinder sleeves spigot are clean and free from burrs, the sleeves with their respective piston assemblies can now be fitted to the block.

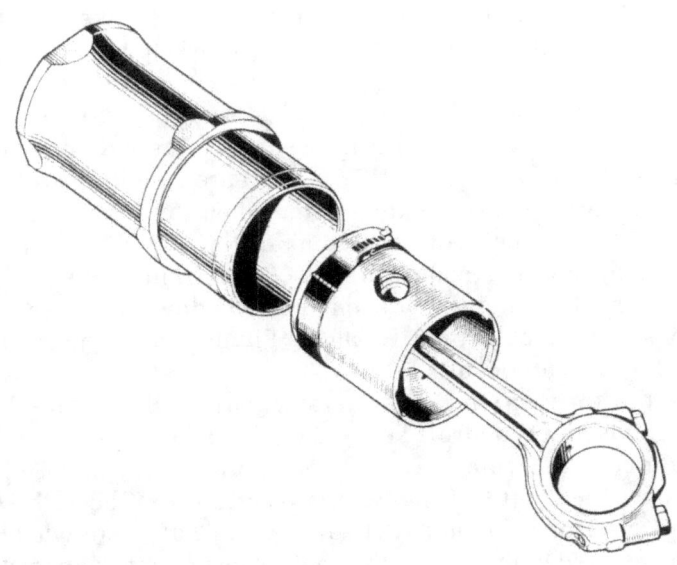

12. Locate the cylinder sleeves and piston assemblies in the cylinder block so that the cap of the connecting rod is adjacent to the camshaft side of the engine. The assembly which bears the number 1 on its connecting rod is fitted to the foremost position. The sleeves should stand .003° to .0055" proud of the cylinder block face.

13. It is essential that means are employed to prevent the cylinder sleeves from moving in the block. Messrs. V. L. Churchill & Co. Ltd. have manufactured special retainers for this purpose and it is suggested that these are employed. Until this is done the piston assemblies must not be moved, for any movement will be transferred to the sleeve and damage the figure of eight washers. If damage is undetected, water leakage will result. An alternate method is to insert the cylinder sleeve **alone** into the block, clamp them with the Churchill sleeve retainers to ensure no further movement and then fit the piston assemblies similarly as described above.

14. Having the sleeve retainers in position, the connecting rods may be fitted to the crankshaft, Nos. 1 and 4 cylinders, followed by 2 and 3 cylinders. The caps are fitted to their respective rods and in such a manner that the tubular dowel will sink into its recess and their identification numbers coincide. It should be noted that the bearing cap, because of this dowel, can only be fitted one way round. The cap is secured by two bolts and a locking plate. Tighten the bolts to the correct torque loading and turn over the tabs of the locking plates.

15. Push the oilite bush into the center of the crankshaft at its rear end and tap the flywheel locating dowel into position in the flange.

16. Fit flywheel located by the dowel so that the arrow marked on its periphery lines up with the center of the cylinder block with Nos. 1 and 4 pistons at T.D.C. Secure flywheel with the four setscrews and two locking plates when the setscrews have been tightened to their correct torque loading.

17. Utilizing jointing compound affix the front plate packing and locating the engine plate on the two dowels secure with the five bolts and locking washers. Fit the engine mountings secured by two nyloc nuts.

18. To the forward end of the crankshaft fit the sprocket locating shims, the Woodruff key and the sprocket.

19. Lubricate the camshaft and feed into the cylinder block and secure the front bearing with two setscrews. Check the end float as described previously. Rest the camshaft chainwheel on the camshaft spigot and turn the chainwheel about the camshaft

until the identification punch mark on the end of the camshaft can be seen through the punch marked hole in the chainwheel. Secure the chainwheel to the camshaft leaving the two setscrews finger tight. Check the alignment of the chainwheel with that of the sprocket on the crankshaft, taking into consideration the end float of the camshaft. The alignment can be adjusted by altering the thickness of the shim between the crankshaft sprocket and the abutement on the crankshaft.

20. Turn the camshaft chainwheel until the scribe line thereon lines up with the scribe line on the crankshaft sprocket. **Without moving** the camshaft remove the chainwheel and when removed fit the timing chain to this wheel and the one on the crankshaft. Reposition the camshaft chainwheel and check by simulating pressure of the chain tensioner that the timing marks have retained their positions and re-adjust if necessary. Tighten bolts to correct torque loading and turn over tabs of locking plates. Lubricate tappets and place in tappet chambers.

21. Fit the chain tensioner to its pin and secure with washer and split pin. Screw in timing cover support bolt to the engine plate and fit the oil deflector to the crankshaft so that the raised edge faces the timing cover.

22. Press the oil seal with its lip inwards into the timing cover and fit this cover with its packing to the engine plate utilizing one nut, eleven bolts with four nuts.

NOTE: See that the short ground bonding strap from engine to chassis frame is attached under the head of the bolt which aligns with L.H. rubber mounting attachment nut.

23. The machined faces on the cylinder head and the upper flanges of the cylinder sleeves, which contact the cylinder head gasket, should be lightly coated with sealing compound which retains its plasticity. This sealing is necessary to ensure a proper life for the gasket.

24. Assemble the valves and springs to the head and fit the assembly to the block, tightening the ten nuts and washers down in the order shown. Fit push rods in the chambers.

25. Assemble the rocker shaft as follows: To the rocker shaft fit No. 4 rocker pedestal in such a manner that the oil-feed holes coincide and secure with setscrews. To the shorter end of the shaft, fit No. 8 rocker, a double coil spring washer and a collar. Secure the collar to the shaft with a mills pin. On the longer end of the shaft feed the remaining rockers, springs and pedestals. After fitting No. 1 rocker, fit the double coil spring and collar securing the latter with a mills pin.

26. Loosen the ball pins and fit rocker shaft assembly to cylin-

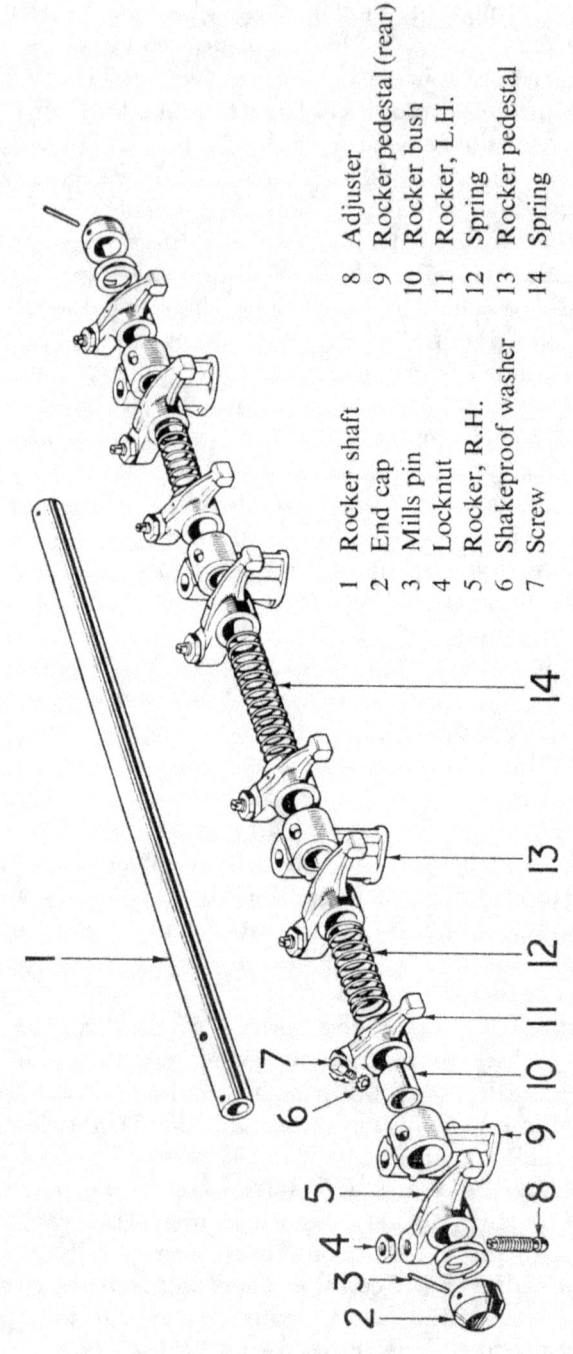

1 Rocker shaft
2 End cap
3 Mills pin
4 Locknut
5 Rocker, R.H.
6 Shakeproof washer
7 Screw
8 Adjuster
9 Rocker pedestal (rear)
10 Rocker bush
11 Rocker, L.H.
12 Spring
13 Rocker pedestal
14 Spring

der head securing the pedestals to the studs with four nuts and spring washers. Before exerting any pressure on the nuts it is recommended that the adjusting pins are slackened off to prevent them coming into too hard a contact with the push rods. Tighten down the nuts progressively to the correct torque loading.

27. Adjust valve clearances.

28. Fit the oil pump assembly and packing secured by three nuts and lockwashers to the inside of the cylinder block.

29. Fit the sump and packing to the cylinder block and secure with nineteen bolts and lock washers. The shorter bolt is fitted through the front flange of the sump into the sealing block. The rearmost bolt on the left-hand side accommodates the breather pipe clip and the bolt in front of this accommodates the clutch slave cylinder stay. When an aluminum sump is fitted, two packings are used, one either side of the tray.

30. Fit the breather pipe to the cylinder block and secure the clip.to the sump plate by the bolt, nut and lock washer with a distance piece between the two plates.

31. Fit ignition coil to side of cylinder block with two nuts and lock washers.

32. Fit distributor and adapter as described in "Distributor Timing."

33. To the pulley hub and hub extension assemble the fan pulley in such a manner that the T.D.C. indicating hole in the pulley is diametrically opposite the key way in the pulley hub center; secure with six nuts and bolts locked in pairs with locking plates. On later production cars with engine numbers after T.S. 4145E the locking plate and nut was replaced by a plain washer and nyloc nut.

34. Fit the Woodruff key to the crankshaft, offer up the pulley assembly and secure with the extension bolt. Shims are placed behind the head of this bolt, which incorporates the starting handle dogs, to provide the correct relation with the starting handle and the engine compressions. This position is obtained with Nos. 1 and 4 pistons at T.D.C. and the dog faces corresponding to "10 minutes to 4 o'clock."

35. To the fan assembly fit the split rubber bushes (four front and four to the rear) and slide into the bushes the four metal sleeves. Place on top of the rubber bushes four larger diameter plain washers, the lockwasher for the starting dog extension bolt followed by the balance piece placed in such a manner that the drilled holes coincide with the drill spot on the hub extension. To the securing bolts fit the locking plates and

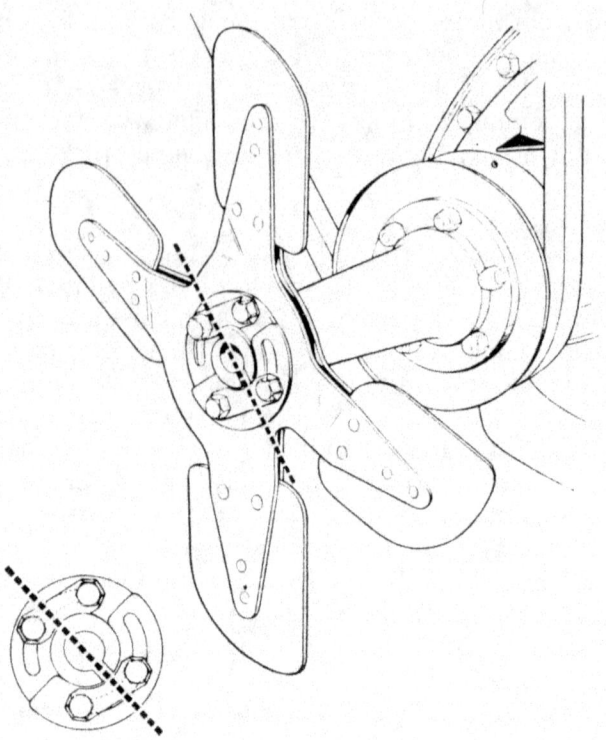

smaller diameter plain washers and feed through the holes in the fan blade assembly, and offer up the hub assembly to the crankshaft and secure, finally turning over the tab washers.

36. Using a new joint washer and sealing compound, offer up the water pump housing to the cylinder block and secure with two bolts and lock washers and tighten to the correct tightening torque. Affix a joint washer to the housing with sealing compound and offer up the water pump impeller. This is secured by two nuts with lock washers and a bolt with lock washer, the purpose of this bolt is twofold, it secures the impeller to the housing and the housing to the cylinder block. Attach the adjusting link with a bolt and tab washer to the right-hand side of the water pump housing but leave the bolt finger tight at this juncture.

37. Fit the generator bracket to cylinder block utilizing three setscrews and lock washers. Fit the pedestal to the front engine plate and secure with nyloc nut; offer up generator and secure finger-tight to the pedestal with a setscrew and lock washer and to the bracket at the rear by nut and bolt with lock washer. Secure the front of the generator by its second fixing point to

the adjusting link (already attached to the water pump) utilizing one setscrew with a plain washer either side.

38. Fit the fan belt and adjust to give $3/4''$ play either side of a center line. Tighten up all nuts and bolts securely including the bolt of the adjusting link and turn up tab of tab washer.

39. Fit thermostat housing and packing to cylinder head and secure with two bolts and lock washers, leaving finger tight at this juncture. Connect the water pump and thermostat housing with the by-pass hose and tighten hose clips.

40. Assemble the inlet manifold to the exhaust manifold leaving the two nuts finger tight. Position the manifold gaskets on the eight studs fitted in the cylinder head. Fit the manifold assembly to the cylinder head, positioning the four short clamps on the upper row of studs and the longer pair on the two inner studs of the bottom row. Fit the eight nuts and spring washers and tighten to 20-24 lbs. ft. Finally tighten the two nuts attaching the inlet to the exhaust manifold to 16-18 lbs. ft.

41. Fit the oil filter with packing to left-hand side of cylinder block. It is located by a tubular stud and secured by three bolts with lock washers. The tubular stud accommodates the oil pressure gauge pipe. This part is fitted to the stud with a copper washer either side of the banjo connection and secured by a cap nut. The pipe is also attached by a clip to the rear stud of the fuel pump.

42. Fit fuel pump and packing and secure with two nuts and lock washers. The rearmost stud of this mounting also accommodates the clip steadying the oil pressure pipe.

43. Connect fuel pipe from pump, clipping it to the thermostat housing, also the suction tube to the distribution union. The latter, a narrow section tube, is strapped to the fuel pipe.

44. Apply oil to the rocker arms and valve tops. Ensure that the rocker cover seal is in position and is in good order and secure cover to top of engine by the two nyloc nuts, each bearing on a fibre and plain washers. Ensure that the rocker cover does not foul the cylinder head nuts at the right-hand side of the engine.

45. Offer up the clutch driven plate and housing to flywheel, ensuring first that they are in good condition and the release levers of the housing are correctly adjusted. (See "Clutch" Section.) Settle the housing on the two dowels and secure the flywheel with six setscrews and lock washers, centralizing the clutch driving plate with a dummy constant pinion shaft or mandrel.

46. Ascertain that the gearbox, clutch release bearing and

clutch operating shaft are in working order before assembling to engine. Offer the gearbox up to the engine, locating it on two dowels and three studs, and secure with six bolts, nuts and lock washers, and three nuts and washers on the studs.

47. The engine and gearbox can be fitted to the chassis with the use of a hoist or moveable crane. Allow the rear extension of the gearbox to be lower than the sump and by slowly lowering the whole unit the mounting points can be found.

48. The attachment of the engine and gearbox to the chassis is the reveral of the detachment procedure.

49. The engine and the gearbox must be refilled with oil and the radiator with water before the car is used.

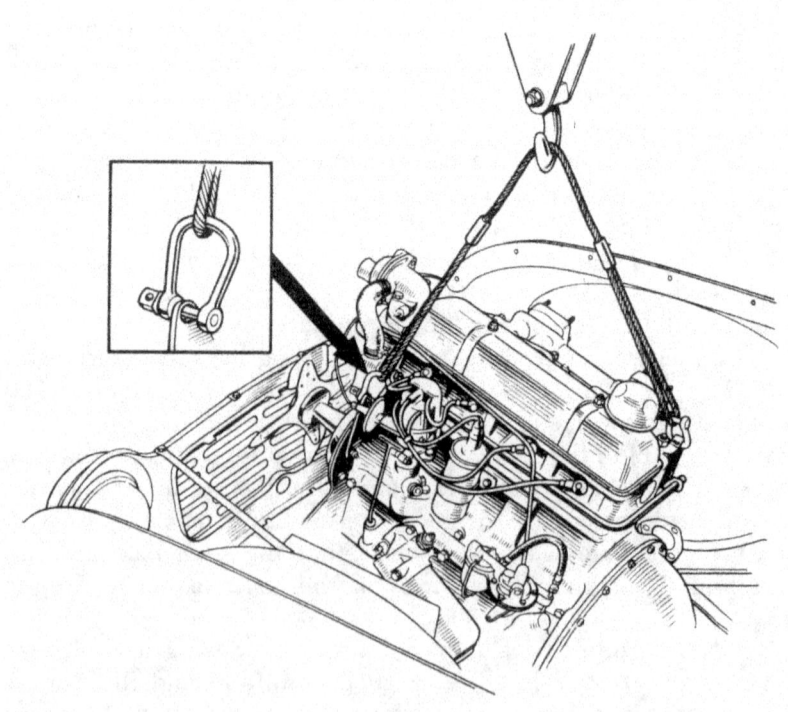

ENGINE FAULT DIAGNOSIS

Main Bearing Knock

This knock can usually be identified by its dully heavy metallic note which increases with frequency as the engine speed and load rises. A main bearing knock is particularly noticeable when the engine is running very slowly and consequently unevenly, it is more pronounced with advanced ignition.

When this bearing knock is experienced it can be explained by one of the following faults and should be treated accordingly.
1. Unsuitable grade of oil or badly diluted oil supply.
2. Low oil pressure.
3. Insufficient oil in sump.
4. Excessive bearing clearance caused by worn journal and/or bearings.

Crankshaft End Float Knock

When a knock is being caused by the development of end float, it will be found most noticeable when the engine is running at idling speeds. This knock can temporarily be eliminated by operating the clutch.

Big End Bearing Knock

A big end bearing knock is lighter in note than that experienced with a main bearing. It will be evident at idling speeds and will increase with engine speed.

The best test for this noise is to detach the lead from each spark plug in turn and reconnecting the lead while flicking the throttle open. On reconnection of the lead, a light thud will be audible where the bearing looseness or correcting misalignment exists, further investigation can be carried out to that particular rod or rods.

In addition to the knock being caused by excessive bearing clearance it is sometimes caused by:—
1. Unsuitable grade of oil or badly diluted supply.
2. Insufficient supply of oil.
3. Low oil pressure.

Small End Knocks

As the piston pin used in this model is able to float in the piston and the bearing in the connecting rod, a knock may arise owing to slackness in the small end bush or the piston bosses. The knock will make itself audible under idling conditions or at road speeds between 20-30 m.p.h. (32-48 km.p.h.).

To test for a piston pin knock, cut out each cylinder one at a time by disconnecting the plug leads. The offending pin will be identified by the fact that a double knock is caused when the disconnection of the plug lead is made.

With complaints of this nature, the following possible causes should be examined.
1. A too tight pin.
2. A pin slack in the connecting rod bush or piston boss.
3. Misalignment of connecting rod allowing connecting rod bush to foul the piston bosses.

Piston Knock (Piston Slap)

This will increase with the application of load up to 30 m.p.h. (48 km.p.h.) but only in very bad cases will it continue to be audible over that speed. In some cases piston knock will only be evident when the engine is started from cold and will disappear as the engine warms. In such cases it is suggested that the engine is left untouched.

A suggested method of locating the offending piston is to engage a gear and with the hand brake hard on, just let the clutch in sufficiently to apply a load with the engine at a moderate speed.

By detaching a spark plug lead and thus putting a cylinder out of action, it is possible to cut out the knock and so determine the offending piston.

Faults in the engine components listed below often contribute to piston slap and should therefore be examined:
1. Excessive clearance between piston and cylinder sleeve due to usage or to an unsuitable replacement part.
2. Pistons or rings striking ridge at the top of the sleeve after fitting a replacement. Such ridges should be removed before replacement parts are fitted.
3. Collapsed piston.
4. Broken piston ring grooves or excessive clearance in grooves.
5. Connecting rod misalignment.

Noisy Valve Rockers or Tappets

Noise due to valve rockers can be identified fairly easily owing to the fact that these are operated by the camshaft which revolves at half engine speed, the noise will seem to be slower than other engine noises. Valve rocker noise has a characteristic clicking sound which increases in volume as the engine speed rises.

Where rocker noise is caused by excessive tappet clearance, it can be eliminated by the insertion of a feeler gauge between the stem of the valve and the rocker toe while the engine is idling.

When this complaint is experienced and is found to be caused by incorrect tappet clearance the rockers should be adjusted.

Push rod noise may be caused by worn or rough rocker ball pins or push rod cups and can be cured by replacing the worn or damaged parts.

Ignition Knock (Pinking)

An ignition knock is recognized by its metallic ringing note, usually occuring when the engine is laboring or accelerating.

The knock can be caused by either detonation or pre-ignition. Detonation is the result of a rapid rise in pressure of the explosive mixture, thus causing the last portion of the charge in the cylinder to be spontaneously ignited, resulting in this striking the cylinder wall with a ringing sound; this noise being familiar to motorists as "pinking."

Pre-ignition may arise as a result of detonation owing to heat generated thereby but may also be caused by sharp edges or points in the combustion space, and where it arises should be treated accordingly.

When ignition knock is audible, the following possible causes should be investigated.
1. Excessive carbon deposits in head and on piston crowns.
2. Incorrect or faulty spark plugs causing incandescence.
3. Sharp edges or pockets in combustion space.
4. Engine overheating.
5. Too-weak fuel-air mixture, causing delayed combustion.
6. Unsatisfactory grade of fuel.
7. Too early ignition timing.
8. Faulty automatic advance and retard mechanism due to incorrect or weak centrifugal control springs.
9. Hot engine valves due to incorrect seating width, insufficient valve rocker clearances, valve edges thinned by excessive refacing. Valve of unsuitable material.

Back Firing into Carburetor

It is in order that with a cold engine back firing into the carburetors may occur, but this should cease when the engine attains normal working temperature.

If back firing still persists in spite of warming up, the following possible causes should be investigated.
1. Incorrect ignition timing.
2. Incorrect wiring of spark plugs.
3. Centrifugal or vacuum advance and retard mechanism not functioning correctly.
4. Incorrect valve timing.

5. Poor quality fuel.
6. Mixture is too weak or excessively rich.
7. Pre-ignition due to various causes.
8. Air leak into induction system giving rise to a weak mixture.
9. Valves, particularly inlet, not seating correctly.
10. Defective cylinder head gasket.

Excessive Oil Consumption

Excessive oil consumption is usually associated with a very worn engine, but can arise as a result of external leakages and due to other factors with comparatively new engines.

If excessive oil consumption is established, before commencing to dismantle the engine a check for external leakage should be carried out.

When an engine is burning oil it will be indicated by the emission of bluish grey smoke from the exhaust when the engine is raced after a period of idling.

A check for external leakage can be conveniently carried out by spreading paper on the ground under the forward part of the car, and running the engine at a moderate speed for a few minutes.

In this way it is possible to locate the position of leaks which, without the engine running, would not be evident. External leaks are caused by one or more of the following:—

1. Cracked sump or poor sump packing.
2. Flange faces of sump not true.
3. Drain plug loose or defective packing washer.
4. Defective filter packing, poor joint faces or loose attachment bolts.
5. Oil pressure pipe line leaking.
6. Defective fuel pump packing, poor joint faces or attachment nuts loosened.
7. Defective rocker cover packing, poor joint faces or attachment nuts loosened.
8. Defective front engine plate packing or poor joint faces.
9. Timing cover oil seal defective.
10. Timing cover cracked, defective packing or loose mounting bolts.
11. Leakage round camshaft welch plug.
12. Unsuitable grade of oil or excessively diluted, arduous driving conditions, excessively high pressure or crankcase temperatures.
13. Excessive clearance between piston and sleeve or incorrect replacements, damaged rings, rings stuck in grooves, in-

sufficient piston ring end gap, piston rings exercising insufficient radial pressure.

14. Excessive diameter and axial clearance due to wear associated with the possibility of oval and worn crankpins.

15. Excessive diameter clearance in main bearings and/or worn journals.

Low Oil Pressure

The correct oil pressure in the TR 2 is 40-60 lbs. per sq. in. for top gear for road speeds between 30-40 m.p.h. and 70 lbs. in the TR 3 & TR 4. With complaints of low oil pressure the following possible causes should be investigated:—

1. Insufficient oil in sump.
2. Unsuitable grade of oil or a very badly diluted supply.
3. Suction oil filter restricted by dirt in sump.
4. Oil pump loose on mountings.
5. Very badly worn or damaged oil pump.
6. Oil release valve in exterior oil filter head out of adjustment, is fitted. Careful consideration has been given to points where adequate cooling is necessary, such as spark plugs and valve dirt on valve seating, broken or weak release valve spring. Filter loose on bracket, damaged joint packing, poor joint faces.
7. Loose connections on pressure gauge pipe or defective pipe line and/or flexible connections.
8. Incorrect oil pressure gauge.
9. Worn engine bearings and/or crankshaft journals and pins.

High Oil Pressure

1. Using too heavy a grade of oil.
2. Faulty adjustment of oil relief valve, too heavy a relief valve spring.
3. Faulty oil pressure gauge.

COOLING SYSTEM

The cooling system is pressurized and thermostatically controlled, with an impeller pump to ensure efficient circulation of water at all times. The capacity is 13 points or 14 when a heater guides, etc.

To assist cooling when the car is stationary or travelling at low speeds a 12½" diameter four bladed fan attached to the crankshaft draws air through the radiator.

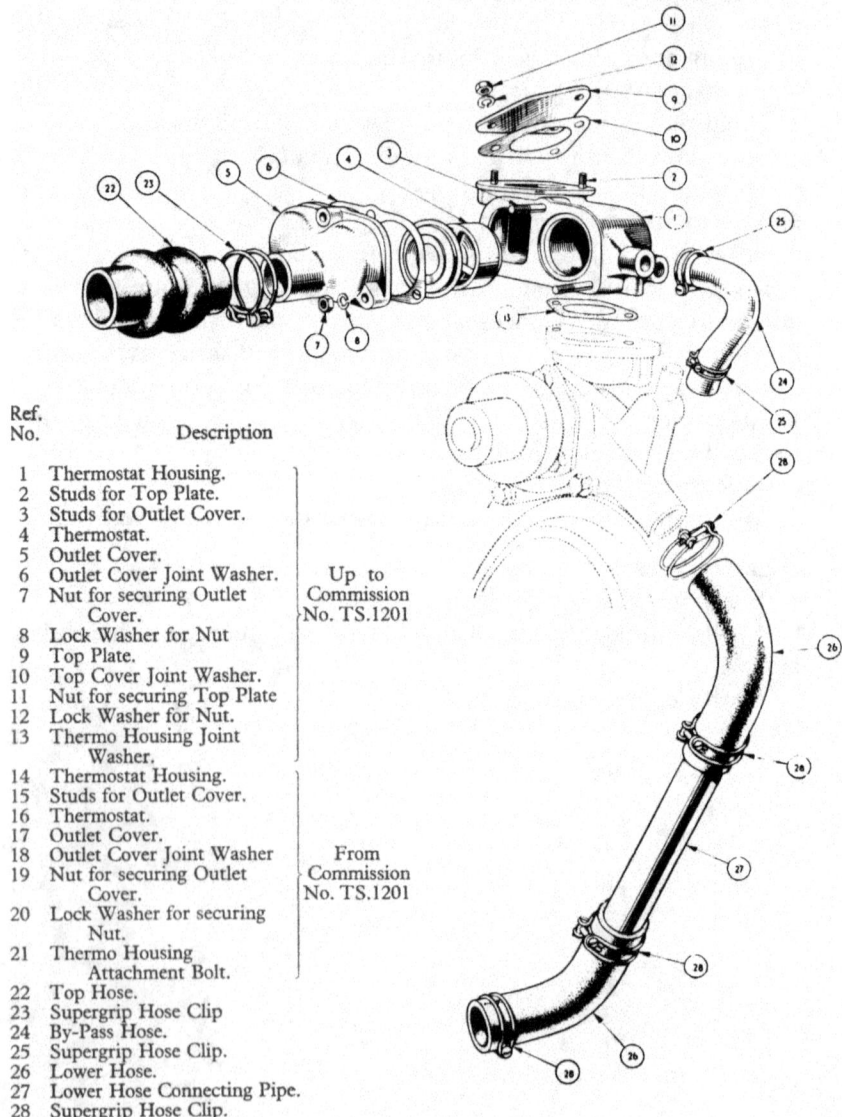

Ref. No.	Description	
1	Thermostat Housing.	
2	Studs for Top Plate.	
3	Studs for Outlet Cover.	
4	Thermostat.	
5	Outlet Cover.	
6	Outlet Cover Joint Washer.	Up to Commission No. TS.1201
7	Nut for securing Outlet Cover.	
8	Lock Washer for Nut	
9	Top Plate.	
10	Top Cover Joint Washer.	
11	Nut for securing Top Plate	
12	Lock Washer for Nut.	
13	Thermo Housing Joint Washer.	
14	Thermostat Housing.	
15	Studs for Outlet Cover.	
16	Thermostat.	
17	Outlet Cover.	
18	Outlet Cover Joint Washer	From Commission No. TS.1201
19	Nut for securing Outlet Cover.	
20	Lock Washer for securing Nut.	
21	Thermo Housing Attachment Bolt.	
22	Top Hose.	
23	Supergrip Hose Clip	
24	By-Pass Hose.	
25	Supergrip Hose Clip.	
26	Lower Hose.	
27	Lower Hose Connecting Pipe.	
28	Supergrip Hose Clip.	

To Drain Cooling System

1. Remove the radiator filler cap, this is necessary as the system is pressurized. If a heater is fitted ensure that the water shut-off valve is open.
2. Open both drain taps, one situated at the lower extremity of the radiator block and a second in the right hand side of the cylinder block below No. 4 inlet and exhaust manifold.

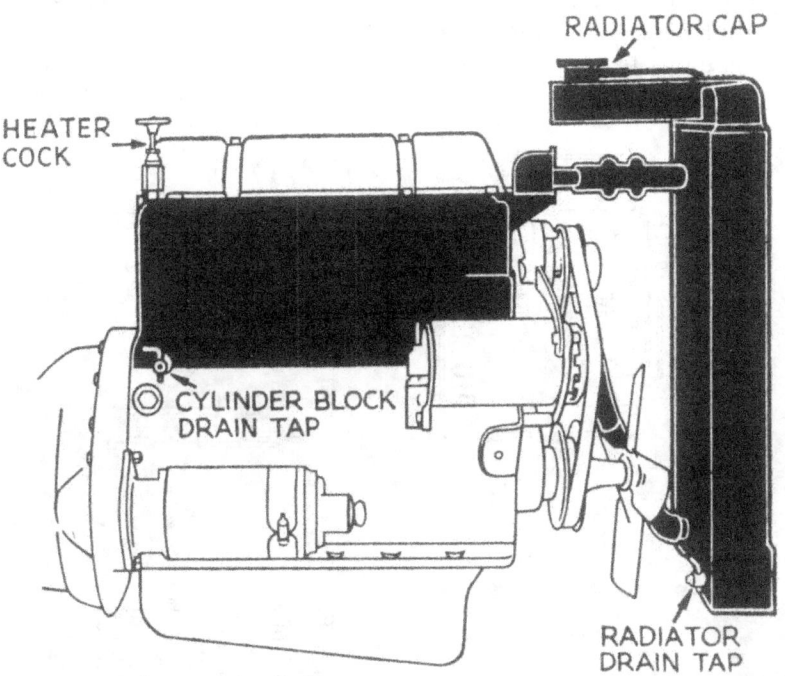

Fan Belt Adjustment

Fan belt adjustment is effected by repositioning the generator as follows:—
1. Loosen the three generator attachments:
a. The nyloc nut and bolt at the rear, attaching it to the bracket.
b. The bolt attaching the lower portion of the front flange to the fulcrum.
c. The bolt securing the upper portion of the flange to the adjusting link.
2. Move the generator to or away from the engine the fan belt is loosened or tightened respectively. When the belt has ³/₄" "play" in its longest run suitable adjustment is provided.
3. Tighten the adjusting link bolt, followed by the two lower attachments.

The Thermostat

This is fitted in the cooling system to control the flow of water before the engine has reached its normal working temperature.

When the engine is started from cold, water is circulated around the cylinder block by action of the water pump impeller through matched apertures in the impeller pump housing and the cylinder block. The water circulates round the block and cylinder head into the thermostat housing. If the water has not reached a temperature of 158°F. the thermostat will remain

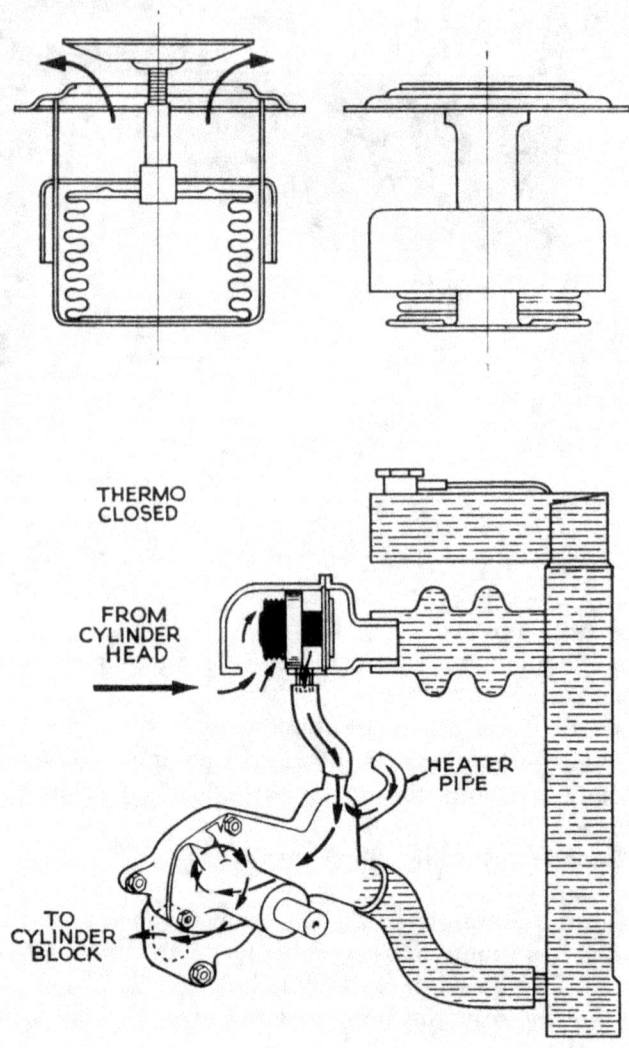

closed and the water will pass into the by-pass passage and down to the impeller pump housing to be recirculated through the block by the rotation of the impeller, being driven by a belt at twice crankshaft speed.

When the water temperature rises above 158°F. (70°C.) the thermostat will commence to open and allow the water to pass into the radiator. This new circulation of water allows the impeller pump to draw water from the lower part of the radiator. The thermostat is fully open at 197°F. (92°C.) and at this stage the by-pass is sealed off, this sealing off avoids loss of cooling efficiency when it is most required.

The radiator temperature for normal motoring should not exceed 185°F. (85°C.).

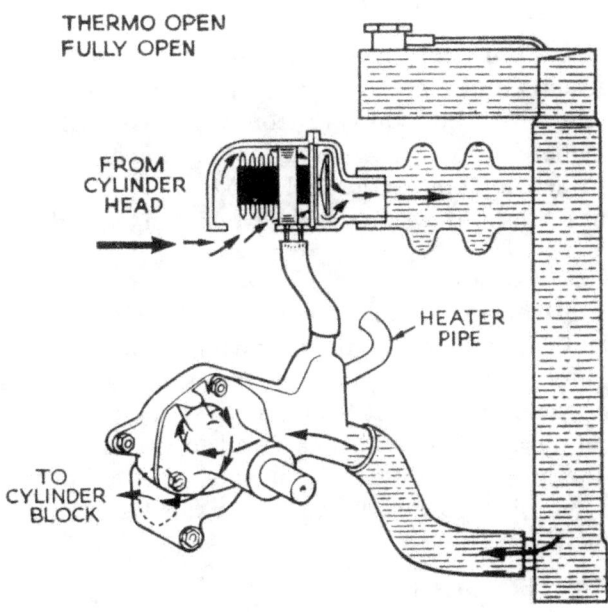

To Remove the Thermostat Housing (with thermostat)
1. Drain the cooling system.
2. Disconnect the top and by-pass hoses.
3. Loosen the nuts of the thermostat cover, and remove the lower nut to release the fuel pipe clip.
4. Remove the thermo gauge capillary tube by withdrawing the gland nut at the left hand side.
5. The thermostat housing can be removed by withdrawal of the two bolts attaching it to the combustion head.

6. The thermostat can be removed from housing by removing the remainder of the front cover nuts but **after** the removal of the joint washer.

To Replace Thermostat Housing

The replacement is the reversal of the removal but care should be taken concerning the following points.
1. That the contact surfaces of the housing and the cover are perfectly clean and do not bear traces of the old joint washer. Failure to observe this point may lead to water leakages.
2. The thermostat is fitted to the housing first and followed next by the joint washer. In no circumstances should the joint washer be fitted first.

To Remove the Thermostat Only

1. Drain the cooling system.
2. Disconnect the top hose.
3. Withdraw the thermostat housing front cover by removing the three nuts and lock-washers. Remove the pipe clip on the lower right hand stud. On cars from Commission No. TS. 1201 onwards there are only two front cover attachment studs. The lower one accommodates the fuel pipe clip.
4. Remove the joint washer **before** removing the thermostat.

To Replace Thermostat

The replacement is the reversal of the removal but care should be taken concerning the following points.
1. That the contact surfaces of the housing and the cover are perfectly clean and do not bear traces of the old joint washer. Failure to observe this point may lead to water leakage.
2. The thermostat is fitted to the housing first and followed next by the joint washer. In no circumstances should the joint washer be fitted first.

Testing the Thermostat

Remove the thermostat from its housing. It should be tested in water, at a suitable temperature employing a thermometer to ascertain that the valve does commence to open at the correct temperature 158°F. There is no need to check the temperature at which the valve is fully open as this follows automatically.

Water Temperature Gauge

The capillary of this instrument is secured in the thermostat housing by a gland nut and a dial on the instrument panel registers the temperature of the water on the engine side of the thermostat.

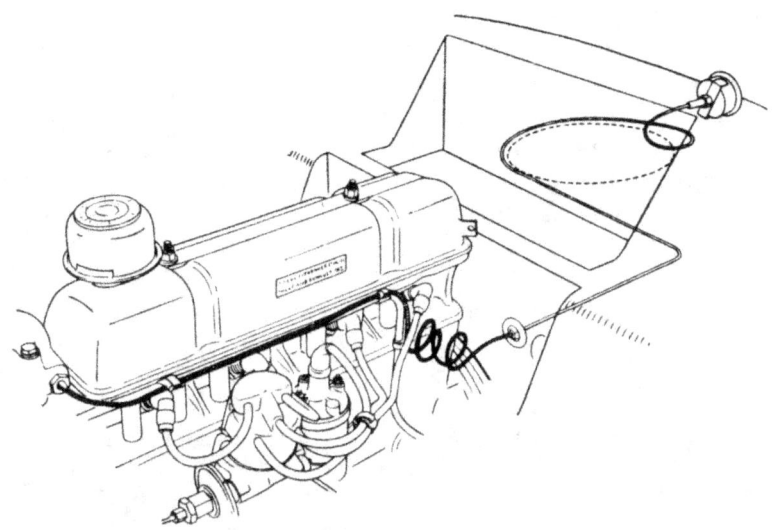

Care should be taken that the tubing is not kinked for this is liable to fracture the capillary tube thus rendering the instrument unserviceable.

To Remove Radiator
1. Remove the front cowling.
2. Drain the cooling system.
3. Remove top and bottom hoses and overflow pipe from radiator.
4. Remove the nuts and bolts from the two steady rods, one either side at the top of the radiator.
5. Remove the two bolts and lock washers from the brackets at the sides of the block. The packing between bracket and chassis frame can be removed **after** the radiator has been lifted.

The replacement of the radiator is the reversal of the removal.

Flexible Hose Connections

Four hoses are used in the system and all are moulded rubber with a fibre insert. They are secured to their mating parts by "Supergrip" hose clips.

The smaller diameter curved hose is the by-pass hose for the thermostat — water pump housing connection, the larger diameter straight corrugated hose connects the thermostat housing to the radiator.

The two large diameter curved hoses are assembled to a metal connecting pipe so that their ends are 90° removed from one another. This assembly connects the water pump housing to the radiator outlet.

The Water Pump Assembly

This assembly is attached to the cylinder block by three bolts of unequal length. The longer bolt is situated in the upper right hand position and its purpose is two-fold. In addition to attaching the pump assembly to the cylinder block it also secures the bearing housing to the pump body. The head of this bolt is

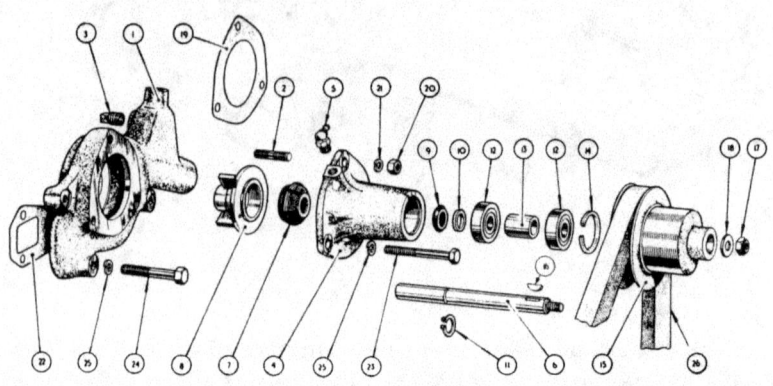

NOTATION FOR WATER PUMP HOUSING ASSEMBLY			
Ref. No.	Description	Ref. No.	Description
1.	Water Pump Body.	15.	Water Pump Pulley.
2.	Bearing Housing Attachment Stud.	16.	Woodruffe Key.
3.	Plug (removed when heater is fitted).	17.	Nyloc Nut.
4.	Bearing Housing.	18.	Plain Washer.
5.	Grease Nipple.	19.	Water Pump Joint Washer.
6.	Spindle.	20.	Nut.
7.	Water Pump Seal.	21.	Lock Washer.
8.	Impeller.	22.	Water Pump Housing Joint Washer.
9.	Synthetic Rubber Spinner.	23.	Bearing Housing to Cylinder Block Attachment Bolt.
10.	Abutment Washer.		
11.	Circlip.	24.	Pump Housing to Cylinder Block Attachment Bolt.
12.	Bearings.		
13.	Distance Collar.	25.	Lock Washer.
14.	Circlip.		

trapped by the belt pulley and the bolt cannot be removed until this pulley is first removed. The two remaining bolts are of equal length and are situated in the lower extremities of the impeller body.

To Remove the Water Pump Bearing Housing

1. Loosen the two lower generator attachments, remove the upper fixing bolt with the two plain washers and then remove the fan belt.

2. Loosen the two nuts and the bolt securing the bearing housing to the pump body progressively until the bearing housing can

be lifted away with its joint washer.

3. It will be noted that the bolt is trapped between the bearing housing and the pulley. Mark the position of the bolt on the bearing housing so that during assembly it can be returned to its original position.

To Replace the Water Pump Bearing Housing

1. The replacement of this assembly is the reversal of the removal, but the following points should be noted.

2. The attachment bolt must be fitted before the fan pulley is attached to the shaft. Looking at the pulley end of the assembly with the grease nipple positioned at 11 o'clock, the bolt will occupy the hole at approximately 7 o'clock.

3. Ensure that the contact surfaces of both components are perfectly clean and a replacement joint washer is used. Failure to observe this point may lead to water leaks.

To Remove Water Pump Body
(When bearing assembly has been removed)

1. Disconnect the by-pass hose, also the heater pipe if the car is so fitted.

2. Remove dynamo adjusting link which is secured to the pump body by a setscrew locked by a tabwasher.

3. Remove the remaining two bolts securing the pump body to the cylinder block.

4. Remove the body complete with its joint washer.

To Replace Water Pump Body

The replacement is the reversal of the removal, but care should be taken concerning the following point:

That the contact surfaces of the housing and the cover are perfectly clean and do not bear traces of the old joint washer. Failure to observe this point may lead to water leakages.

The Fan Assembly

The fan is built up on a hub and hub extension, then balanced as a unit. When this operation has been completed the balancing plate is drilled right through and the drill allowed to touch the hub extension.

If, for any reason, the fan is dismantled all that is necessary on re-assembly is to line up the component parts so that the drill holes are all in line with the dimple in the hub extension and the re-assembled unit is in balance. Only when replacement parts are fitted will it be necessary to re-balance the unit.

The hub extension is attached to the hub, the latter being keyed to the crankshaft by six nyloc nuts and bolts and the whole assembly is secured to the crankshaft by the extension bolt, the head of which acts as the starting handle dog and on re-assembly it will be necessary to place sufficient shims under the head of the extension bolt to bring it into such a position that when the starting handle is in use compression is felt just after the handle has left B.D.C.

To Remove the Fan Assembly from Engine Unit

1. Remove the front cowling.
2. Remove the radiator.
3. Scribe a mark on the balancing plate and fan assembly to ascertain the front of these components for re-assembly.
4. Turn back the tabs of the locking plates and withdraw the four bolts together with lock plates, plain washers, the balance plate (if one is fitted) and the extension bolt locking plate. The fan assembly, together with split rubber bushes, metal sleeves and larger diameter plain washer can now be removed.
5. Remove the extension bolt and shims from the hub extension.
6. By tapping the front flange of the hub extension remove the hub extension, hub and fan belt pulley from the crankshaft. Collect Woodruff key.
7. By releasing the tabs of the locking plates the nuts and bolts can be removed. On engines after Engine No. TS.4145E nyloc nuts and plain washers were fitted in place of lock plates and plain nuts. The hub extension can be removed and the hub withdrawn from the pulley pressings.

To Fit Fan Assembly to Engine Unit

1. Fit the Woodruff key to the crankshaft and slide on the hub and hub extension assembled as described in operations 1, 2 and 3 of "To assemble fan for balancing," hereafter.
2. Fit the two shims under the head of the extension bolt and insert through the center of hub extension and tighten until the abutment of the starting dog jaws, incorporated in the head of the extension bolt, assume a "10 to 4 o'clock" position to ensure correct relationship with compression when the starting handle is in use.
3. On to one pair of fan securing bolts feed one lock plate followed by one plain washer per bolt.
4. Offer up the fan assembly in such a manner that the hole in the web is over the dimple in the hub extension face. Fit the extension bolt locking plate with the larger diameter plain washer between it and the rubber bushes. Secure the extension bolt locking plate with the bolts, built up as described in operation 3 (above) utilizing the two tappings opposite those with

the $\frac{5}{32}$" drill hole.

5. The remaining pair of bolts are made up in a similar manner to those already mentioned, but with the balancer fitted. These bolts are assembled to the remaining tappings in the hub extension. Before tightening, the balancer is moved until the hole aligns with those in the fan assembly; after tightening the tabs of the locking plates are turned over.

6. Replace the radiator and hoses.

7. Replace the front cowling.

To Assemble Fan For Balancing

Check that the four fan blades riveted to the fan webs are free from movement. If for any reason replacement parts have been fitted the fan unit should be re-balanced. The dimple in hub extension face should be filled in with solder to avoid confusion during re-assembly.

1. Place the two pulleys pressings together, the flatter one with the drilled hole uppermost and the second pressing on top; feed the hub through the pressings with its keyway lowermost. It is necessary that this procedure is followed for it ensures a visual check of setting the engine at T.D.C. on Nos. 1 and 4 cylinders.

2. Position the six bolts and secure the hub extension with the nyloc nuts. On early production cars, nuts and locking plates were used.

3. Insert the rubber bushes in the fan assembly and locate the metal sleeves through the centers of these bushes.

4. Feed the four fan attachment bolts through the larger diameter plain washers and metal sleeves of the fan assembly and secure the latter to the hub extension.

5. Using a jig, ascertain the lighter side of the assembly and fit the balancer to that side. This can be moved to obtain perfect balance.

6. When the balanced condition is attained a $\frac{5}{32}$" drill hole should be put through the thinner edge of the balancer and fan assembly webs until it makes a small dimple in the face of the hub extension. Withdraw the four bolts and remove fan assembly from hub extension.

Anti-freeze Precautions

During frosty weather it is necessary to protect the engine from damage and this can be effected by draining the cooling system by opening the tap at the lowermost portion of the radiator, and the second tap at the right hand side of the cylinder block.

In severe frosty weather an anti-freeze additive to the cooling system is strongly recommended, for it is possible for the lower portion of the radiator to become frozen, even when the car is being driven, restricting the circulation of the water as well as causing possible damage to the radiator itself. Before adding the anti-freeze compound thoroughly flush out the radiator and cylinder block, and ascertain that all hoses and connections are in perfect condition. Check also that the cylinder head nuts are tight, for if due to leaks, any anti-freeze solution finds its way into the cylinder bores serious damage may result.

The anti-freeze solution itself does not usually evaporate, thus apart from leakage, it should only be necessary to top up with water as the level in the radiator head drops.

Many reputable anti-freeze compounds are available and the compound chosen should be used in accordance with the manufacturer's instructions.

SERVICE DIAGNOSIS.

OVERHEATING.

This difficulty may arise owing to one or more of the causes listed below :—

CAUSE	REMEDY
Ignition timing too late or auto advance and retard mechanism or suction not operating correctly.	Check ignition timing, automatic advance and retard mechanism and the suction pipe for the carburettor.
Fan belt slipping.	Adjust to give belt $\frac{3}{4}''$ play by moving dynamo outwards along adjusting link.
Insufficient water in cooling system.	Check all joints for leaks including combustion head gasket
Radiator and/or cylinder block restricted by the accumulation of sludge, dirt or other solid matter.	Flush out system with a detergent and refill, using clean, softened or soft water.
Thermostat not operating correctly.	Remove and test as described
Weak mixture caused by incorrect carburettor setting or air leaks in induction manifold.	Check carburettor manifold and carburettor joints, ensure tightness of manifold.
Initial tightness after an engine overhaul or insufficient clearance of replacement parts during an overhaul.	If due to the former, run-in engine most carefully and overheating should disappear. If overheating is caused by the latter it will not disappear, it can even get worse. The engine should be examined for badly fitting parts.
Overheating from bad lubrication, incorrect oil level or incorrect grade of oil. The use of certain brands of anti-freeze compound which have a lowering effect on the boiling point during warm weather.	Check oil level, grade and circulation, flushing system and refilling if necessary. Smiths " Bluecol " has a tendency to raise the boiling point.

FUEL SYSTEM

Fuel Master Valve

The valve, fitted at the end of the rigid fuel line, is secured to the chassis by a special welded fork bracket to the L.H. side chassis frame brace.

It is an Ewarts "pull and push" type which can be locked in the "on" position by turning the plunger head in an anti-clockwise direction approximately $1/8$ of a turn.

The purpose of this valve is to facilitate the disconnection of the fuel pipe at the pump without first draining the tank as the level of the fuel in the tank is above that of the pump.

AC Fuel Pump Type "UE"

The AC fuel pump, type "UE," is operated mechanically from an eccentric (H) on the engine camshaft (G). The illustration gives a sectional view of the pump, the method of operation is as follows:—

As the engine camshaft (G) revolves, the cam (H) lifts pump rocker arm (D) pivoted at (E) which pulls the pull rod (F) together with the diaphragm (A) downward against spring pressure (C) thus creating a vacuum in the pump chamber (M).

Fuel is drawn from the tank and enters at (J) into sediment chamber (K) through filter gauze (L), suction valve (N) into the pump chamber (M). On the return stroke the spring pressure (C) pushes the diaphragm (A) upwards, forcing fuel from the pump chamber (M) through the valve (O) and outlet (P) to the carburetor feed pipe.

When the carburetor float chambers are full the float will rise and shut the needle valve, thus preventing any flow of fuel from the pump chamber (M). This will hold diaphragm (A) downward against spring pressure (C), and it will remain in this position until the carburetors require further fuel and the needle valve opens. The rocker arm (D) operates the connecting link by making contact at (R) and this construction allows idling movement of the rocker arm when there is no movement of the fuel pump diaphragm.

Spring (S) keeps the rocker arm (D) in constant contact with cam (H) and eliminates noise.

Fuel Pump Oil Seal

During very fast cornering oil rises up the cylinder block walls and during right-hand turns passes into the lower body of the fuel pump below the diaphragm assembly and by action of the latter is pumped out by way of the breather hole.

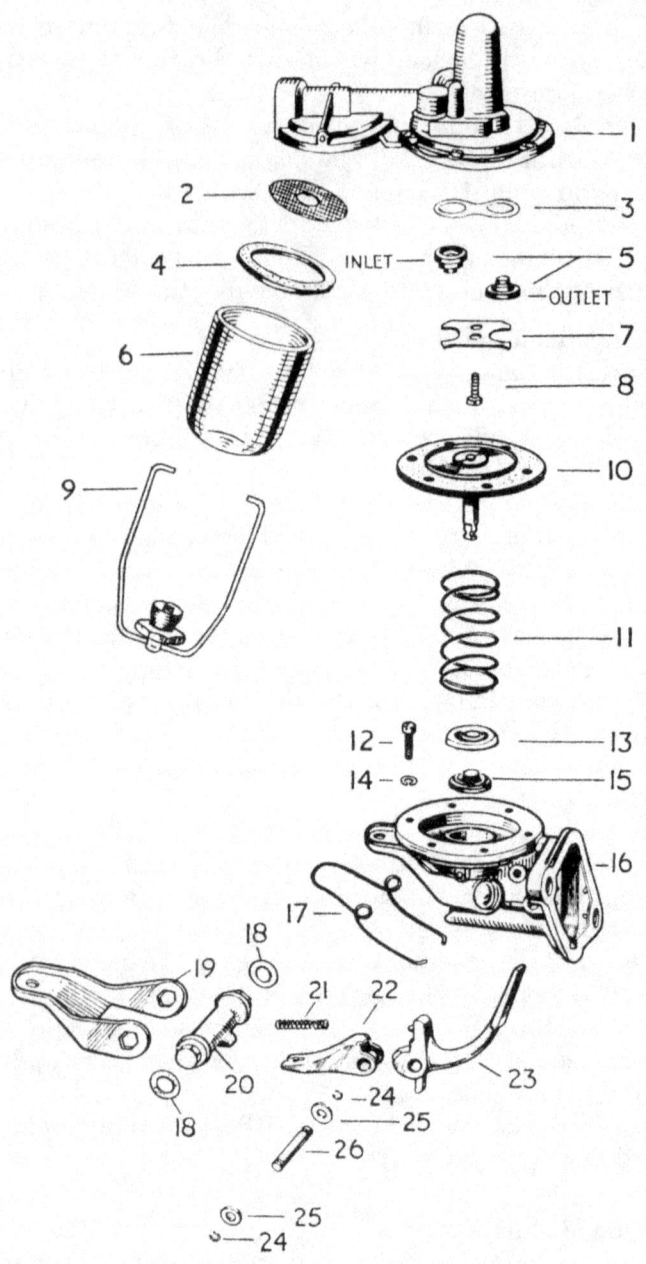

No.
1. Upper body.
2. Gauze filter.
3. Valve gasket.
4. Cork seal
5* Inlet and outlet valve assemblies.
6. Glass sediment bowl.
7. Valve retaining plate.
8. Screw for retaining plate.
9. Wire cage.
10. Diaphragm assembly.
11. Diaphragm spring.
12. Body securing screw.
13. Oil seal retainer.
14. Lock washer.
15. Oil seal.
16. Lower body.
17. Hand primer spring.
18. Cork washer.
19. Hand primer lever.
20. Hand primer lever shaft.
21. Rocker arm spring.
22. Link lever.
23. Rocker arm.
24. Retainer ring.
25. Washer.
26. Rocker arm pin.

---

*These valves are identical, but on fitting them to the upper body the spring of the inlet valve is pointing towards the diaphragm and the spring of the outlet valve away from the diaphragm, as shown in the illustration.

To obviate this condition an oil seal is fitted round the diaphragm assembly push rod and is prevented by rising with the action of the push rod by a metal retainer staked to the lower pump body.

Fuel pumps fitted with this oil seal were fitted to engines after No. TS.2074E.

During dismantling this oil seal should not be removed unless it is known to be defective.

To Clean the Pump Filter

The pump filter should be examined every 1,000 miles and cleaned if necessary.

Access to the filter is gained by loosening the thumb nut situated below the glass sediment chamber at the side of the pump body and swinging the wire frame to one side. The sediment chamber can be removed followed by the cork gasket and gauze filter.

The gauze filter should be cleaned by a blast of air or washing it in clean solvent. The cork gasket should be inspected for condition and replaced if broken or hard. The glass sediment chamber should be cleaned and its upper rim inspected for chips.

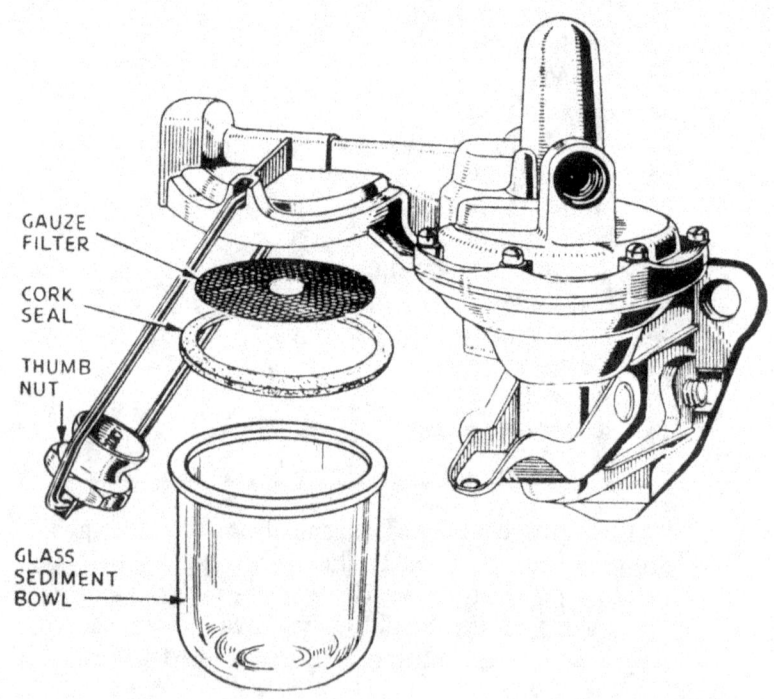

Testing While On Engine

With the engine stopped and switched off, the pipe to the carburetor should be disconnected at the pump and replaced by a shorter tube, leaving a free outlet from the pump. The engine is then turned over by hand. There should be a well defined spurt of fuel at every working stroke of the pump, namely, once every two revolutions of the engine.

To Remove Fuel Pump From Engine

1. Turn off master fuel valve and remove the flexible hose from the top first, then remove the hose from the pump.
2. Remove fuel feed from pump to carburetor at its pump connection.
3. Remove the two pump securing nuts and spring washers. Note the oil pressure pipe clip is attached to the rear stud.
4. The pump can be removed from the cylinder block, together with the packing.

To Fit Pump to Engine

1. Place a new packing of correct thickness on the pump attachment studs followed by the pump. Secure with foremost nut and lock-washer finger tight.
2. Position on the rear stud the oil pressure pipe clip, secure with nut and lockwasher. Tighten both nuts.
3. Attach the carburetor feed to pump and secure with union nut taking care to seat the pipe olive before attaching the union nut.
4. Attach the flexible hose to the forward end of the pump. Attach and secure the rigid end to the master valve.

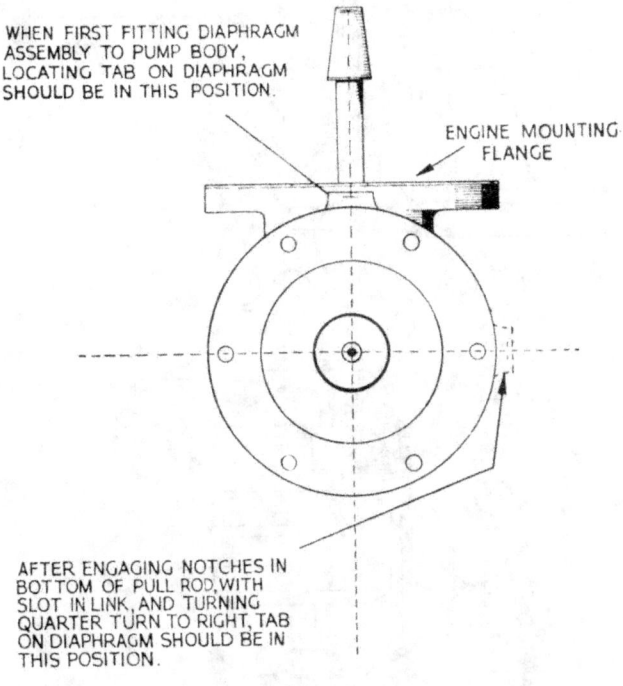

5. Turn on fuel and prime pump with hand lever, until the glass sediment chamber and carburetor float chambers are full.

6. Start and run the engine for a few moments and examine the connections for leaks.

The S.U. Carburetor

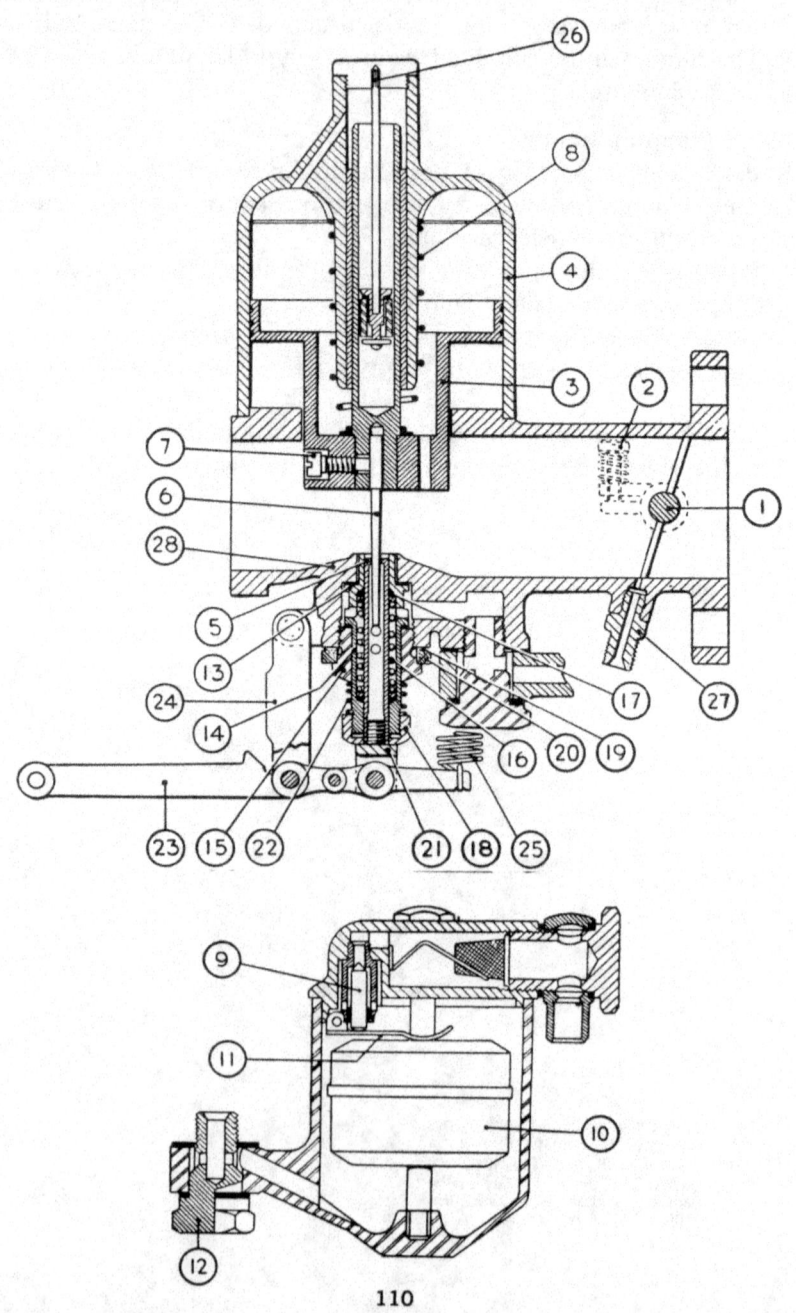

Description

The S.U. carburetor is of the automatically expanding choke type, in which the cross sectional area of the main air passage adjacent to the fuel jet, and the effective orifice of the jet, is variable. The variation takes place in accordance with the demand of the engine as determined by the degree of the throttle opening, the engine speed, and the load against which the engine is operating.

The distinguishing feature of the type of carburetor is that an approximately constant air velocity, and hence an approximately constant degree of depression, is at all times maintained in the region of the fuel jet. This velocity is such that the air flow demanded by the engine in order to develop its maximum power is not appreciably impeded, although good atomization of the fuel is assured under all conditions of speed and load.

The maintenance of a constant high air velocity across the jet, even under idling conditions, obviates the necessity for an idling jet. A single jet only is employed in the S.U. carburetor.

Construction

The main constructional features of the carburetor in its simplest form are shown in the accompanying drawings, which illustrate the horizontal-type carburetor. The diagrams illustrate the main body, butterfly throttle, automatically expanding choke and variable fuel-jet arrangement. They also indicate the means whereby the jet is lowered by a manual control to effect enrichment of the mixture for starting and warming up.

It will be seen that a butterfly throttle mounted on the spindle (1) is located close to the engine attachment flange, at one end of the main air passage, and that an adjustable idling stop screw (2) is arranged to prevent complete closure of the throttle, thus regulating the flow of mixture from the carburetor under idling conditions with the accelerator released. At the outer end of the main passage is mounted the piston (3), its lower part constituting a shutter, restricting the cross-sectional area of the main air passage in the vicinity of the fuel jet (5) as the piston falls. This component is enlarged at its upper end to form a piston of considerably greater diameter which moves axially within the bore of the suction chamber (4) and at the bottom of the piston is mounted the tapered needle (6) which is retained by means of the setscrew (7).

The piston component (3) is carried upon a central spindle which reciprocates and is mounted in a bush fitted in the central boss, forming the upper part of the suction chamber casting.

An extremely accurate fit is provided between the spindle and the bush in the suction chamber so that the enlarged portion of the piston is held out of contact with the bore of the suction chamber, within which, nevertheless, it operates with an extremely fine clearance. Similarly, the needle (6) is restrained from contacting the bore of the jet (5) which it is seen to penetrate, moving axially therein to correspond with the rise and fall of the piston.

It will be appreciated that, as the piston rises, the air passage in the neighborhood of the jet becomes enlarged, and passes an additional quantity of air. Provided that the needle (6) is of a suitably tapered form, its simultaneous withdrawal from the jet (5) ensures the delivery to the engine of the required quantity of fuel corresponding to any given position of the piston and hence to a given air flow.

The piston, under the influence of its own weight and assisted by the light compression spring (8) will tend to occupy its lowest position, two slight protuberences on its lower face contacting the bottom surface of the main air passage adjacent to the jet. The surface in this region is raised somewhat above the general level of the main bore of the carburetor, and is referred to as the "bridge" (28).

Levitation of the piston is achieved by means of the induction depression, which takes effect within the suction chamber, and thus upon the upper surface of the enlarged portion of the piston through drillings in the lower part of the piston which make communication between this region and that lying between the piston and the throttle. The annular space beneath the enlarged portion of the piston is completely vented to atmosphere by ducts not indicated in the diagram.

It will be appreciated that, since the weight of the piston assembly is constant, and the augmenting load of the spring (8) approximately so, a substantially constant degree of depression will prevail within the suction chamber, and consequently in the region between the piston and the throttle, for any given degree of lift of the piston between the extremities of its travel.

It will be clear that this floating condition of the piston will be stable for any given airflow demand as imposed by the degree of throttle opening, the engine speed and the load; thus, any tendency in the piston to fall momentarily will be accompanied by an increased restriction to air flow in the space bounded by the lower side of the piston and the bridge, and this will be accompanied by a corresponding increase in the depression between the piston and throttle, which is immediately communicated to the interior of the suction chamber, instantly counteracting the initial disturbance by raising the piston to an appropriate extent.

The float chamber is of orthodox construction, comprising a needle valve (9) located within a separate seating which, in turn, is screwed in the float chamber lid, and a float (10), the upward movement of which, in response to the rising fuel level, causes final closure of the needle upon its seating through the medium of the hinged fork (11).

The float-chamber is a unit separate from the main body of the carburetor to which it is attached by means of the bolt (12), suitable drillings being provided therein to lead the fuel from the lower part of the float chamber to the region surrounding the jet. It is steadied at its upper extremity by a suction chamber attachment screw.

The buoyancy of the float, in conjunction with the form of the lever (11) is such that a fuel level is maintained approximately $1/8''$ below the jet bridge. This can easily be observed after first detaching the suction chamber and suction piston, and then lowering the jet to its full rich position. The level can vary a further $1/4''$ downwards without any ill effects on the functioning of the carburetor. The only parts of importance not so far described are those associated with the jet.

Under idling conditions the piston is completely dropped, being then supported by the two small protuberances provided on its lower surface, which are in contact with the bridge (28); the small gap thus formed between piston and bridge permits the flow of sufficient air to meet the idling demand of the engine without, however, creating enough depression on the induction side to raise the piston.

The fuel discharge required from the jet is very small under these conditions, hence the diameter of the portion of the needle now obstructing the mouth of the jet is very nearly equal to the jet bore. Initial manufacture of the complete carburetor assembly to the required degree of accuracy to ensure perfect concentricity between the needle and the jet bore under these conditions is impracticable, and an individual adjustment for this essential centralization is provided.

It will be seen that the jet is not mounted directly in the main body, but is housed in the parts (13) and (14) referred to as the jet bushes, or jet bearings.

The upper jet bush is provided with a flange which forms a face seal against a recess in the body, while the lower one carries a similar flange contacting the upper surface of the hollow hexagon locking nut (15).

The arrangement is such that tightening of the hollow hexagon locking screw will positively lock the jet and jet bushes in position. Some degree of lateral clearance is provided between the jet bushes and the bores formed in the main body and the locking screw. In this manner the assembly can be moved laterally until perfect concentricity of the jet and needle is achieved, the screw (15) being slackened for this purpose. This operation is referred to as centering the jet," on completion the jet locking nut (15) is finally tightened.

In addition to this concentricity adjustment, an axial adjustment of the jet is provided for the purpose of regulating the idling mixture strength.

Since, the needle tapers throughout its length, it will be clear that raising or lowering the jet within its bearing will alter the effective aperture of the jet orifice, and hence the rate of fuel discharge. To permit this adjustment the jet is a variably mounted within its bearings and provided with adequate sealing glands.

A compression spring (16) which, at its upper end, serves to compress the small sealing gland (17) and thus prevents any fuel leakage between the jet and the upper jet bearing.

At its lower end this spring abuts against a similar sealing gland, thus preventing leakage of fuel between the jet and the lower jet bearing.

In both locations a brass washer is interposed between the end of the spring and the sealing gland to take the spring thrust. A further sealing gland (19), together with a conical brass washer (20) is provided, to prevent fuel leakage between the jet screw (15) and the main body.

It will be seen from the diagram that the upward movement of the jet is determined by the position of the jet adjusting nut (18) since the enlarged jet head (21) finally abuts against this nut as the jet is moved upwards towards the "weak" or running position.

The position of the nut (18) therefore determines the idling mixture ratio setting of the carburetor for normal running with the engine hot, and is prevented from unintentional rotation by means of the loading spring (22).

The cold running mixture control mechanism comprises the jet lever (23) supported from the main body by the link member (24) and attached by means of a clevis pin to the jet head (21). A tension spring (25) is provided, as shown, to assist in returning the jet-moving mechanism to its normal running position. Connection is made from the outer extremity of the jet lever (23) to a control situated within reach of the driver.

Drillings in the float-chamber attachment bolt (12), the main body of the carburetor, the jet (5) and slots in the upper jet bearing (13) serve to conduct the fuel from the float-chamber to the jet orifice.

It will be seen that the spindle upon which the piston (3) is mounted is hollow, and that it surrounds a small stationary damper piston suspended from the suction chamber cap by means of the rod (26). The hollow interior of the spindle contains a quantity of thin engine oil, and the marked retarding effect upon the movement of the main piston assembly, occasioned by the resistance of the small piston, provides the momentary enrichment desirable when the throttle is abruptly opened. The damper piston is constructed to provide a one-way valve action which gives little resistance to the passage of the oil during the downward movement of the main piston.

An ignition connecting is provided for use in conjunction with vacuum-operated ignition advance mechanism, and is fitted to the front carburetor only.

Throttle and Mixture Control Interconnection

A direct connection is provided between the jet movement and the throttle opening. Such an interconnection ensures that

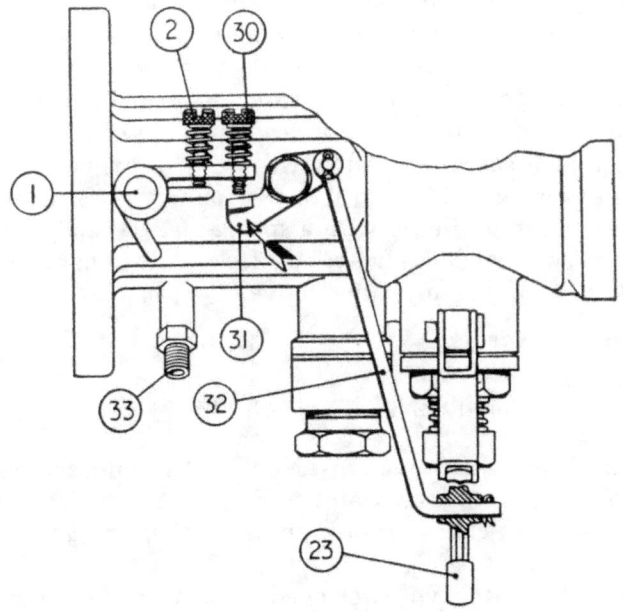

115

the engine will continue to run when the mixture is enriched by lowering the jet, without the additional necessity of maintaining a greater throttle opening than is normally provided by the setting of the slow-running screw (2).

The mechanism involved in this interconnection is shown above. It will be seen that a connecting rod (32) conveys movement from the jet lever (23) to a lever (31) pivoted on the side of the main body casting.

Movement of the jet lever in the direction of enrichment is thus accompanied by an upward movement of the extremity of the lever (31) which, in turn, abuts against the adjustable screw (30) and this opens the throttle to a greater degree than the normal slow-running setting controlled by the slow-running stop screw (2). The screw (30) should be so adjusted that it is just out of contact with the lever (31) when the jet has been raised to its normal running position, and the throttle is shut back to its normal idling condition, as determined by the screw (2).

Effect of Altitude and Climatic Extremes On Standard Tuning

The standard tuning employs a jet needle which is broadly suitable for temperate climates at sea level upwards to approximately 3,000 ft. Above this altitude it may be necessary, depending on the additional factors of extreme climatic heat and humidity, to use a weaker tuning than standard.

The factors of altitude, extreme climatic heat, each tend to demand a weaker tuning, and a combination of any of these factors would naturally emphasize this demand. This is a situation which cannot be met by a hard and fast factory recommendation owing to the wide variations in the condition existing and in such cases the owner will need to experiment with alternative weaker needles until one is found to be satisfactory.

If the carburetor is fitted with a spring-loaded suction piston, the necessary weakening may be affected by changing to a weaker type of spring or by its removal.

To Remove Jet Needle

1. Remove the air-cleaner.
2. Remove the damping piston from the top of the suction chamber.
3. Withdraw the three suction chamber securing screws and move the carburetor float chamber support arm to one side.
4. Lift the suction chamber and remove coil spring and washer from piston head.
5. Remove the piston with jet needle attached from the body

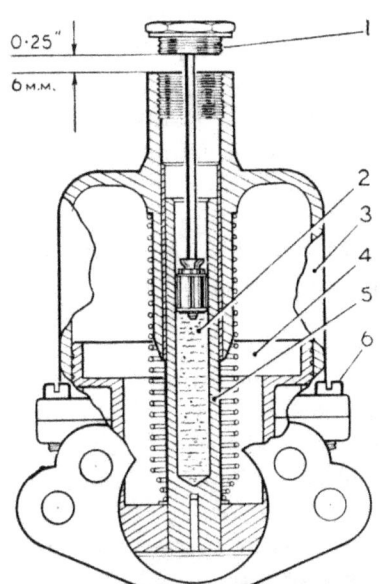

1 Damper
2 Oil well
3 Suction chamber
4 Piston
5 Piston rod
6 Screw

of the carburetor and empty away oil in the reservoir.
6. Loosen screw in base of piston and withdraw jet needle.

To Fit Needle
1. Ensure that the jet head is loose in the main body of the carburetor by loosening clamp ring.
2. Ascertain that the jet needle is perfectly straight and position it so that the shoulder is flush with the base of the piston, tighten screw to grip needle. Feed the needle into its recess in the jet head.
NOTE: On no account should the piston with the needle attached be laid down so that it rests on the needle. Failure to observe this point may cause carburetion defects due to a bent needle.
3. Position the washer and the spring on top of the piston and the suction chamber over the piston.
4. Secure with the three attachment screws with the foremost accommodating the float chamber support arm.
5. Fill the piston reservoir within thin oil and fit the damper to the suction chamber.
6. Centralize the jet as described below.

Centralization of Jet
1. Disconnect the throttle linkage to gain access to the jet head (21) and remove damper (26).

2. Withdraw the jet head (21) and remove adjusting nut (18) and spring (22). Replace nut (18) and screw up to its fullest extent.
3. Slide the jet head (21) into position until its head rests against the base of the adjusting nut.
4. The jet locking nut (15) should be slackened to allow the jet head (21) and bearings (13 and 14) assembly to move laterally.
5. The piston (3) should be raised, (access being gained through the air intake) and allowed to fall under its own weight. This should be repeated once or twice and the jet locking nut (15) tightened.
6. Check the piston by lifting to ascertain that there is complete freedom of movement. "If sticking is detected operation (4) and (5) will have to be repeated.
7. Withdraw jet head (21) and adjusting nut (18).
8. Replace nut (18) with spring (22) and insert the jet head (21).
9. Check oil reservoir and replace damper (26).
10. Tune the carburetors.

To Assemble the Carburetor

Having ensured the cleanliness and the serviceability of all component parts, it is suggested that the carburetor be assembled in the following sequence:

The front carburetor differs from that of the rear insomuch that there are certain additions. As and when the additions occur they will be specifically mentioned.)
1. Fit the ignition union to the front carburetor, this utilizes the tapped bore which breaks through into the mixture passage.
2. Position the throttle spindle in the body in such a manner that the spindle protrudes **less** on the left-hand side looking at the air cleaner ends.
3. Feed the throttle disc into the slot of the spindle and secure with two countersunk screws. These screws have split shanks which are now opened by the insertion of the screw driver blade.
4. Position the throttle stop with the two adjusting screws on the shorter end of the throttle spindle of the front carburetor body and secure with the taper pin; to the rear carburetor, fit the throttle stop with the single adjusting screw.
5. Feed the rocker lever bolt through the double coil washer and the rocker lever so that the platform of the lever is on the left viewing the bolt head. This assembly is fitted to the front carburetor with a plain washer between it and the carburetor. Ensure that the rocker lever moves freely.

6. Fit the throttle spindle return spring anchor plate on the longer end of the spindle and anchor it on the web provided. Follow it with the spring and the end clip then adjust the tension and lock the end clip with the pinch bolt.

7. To the bottom half of the jet bearing position the copper washer followed by the jet adjusting sealing nut (threaded portion uppermost) spring and secure with the jet adjusting nut. Position the alloy sealing ring, flatter side downwards, and the cork washer over the thread of the jet adjusting nut.

8. Insert the jet assembly through the jet adjusting nut and bottom half of the jet bearing from below. Position the cork gland washer, the copper gland washer, spring, a second gland washer and cork gland washer on the head of the jet assembly.

9. Position a copper washer on the shoulders of the upper half jet bearing and, with the shoulder uppermost, balance the top half bearing on the cork gland washer of the jet assembly.

10. Feed the assembly mentioned in (6) and (9) into the carburetor body and secure with the sealing nut.

11. Fit the float to the pillar of the float chamber, this is symmetrical and can be fitted either way up.

12. The needle valve body is secured in the float chamber cover, position valve needle and hinge lever and insert pin.

13. Assemble the splash overflow pipe to the cap of float chamber with a washer interposed between.

14. Fit the float chamber cover to the float chamber and attach cap nut. The nut is left loose at this juncture.

15. Fit the jet needle to the piston assembly and ensure that its lower shoulder is flush with that of the piston.

16. The piston and jet needle is now fitted to the body assembly so that the brass dowel in the carburetor body locates the longitudinal groove in the piston.

17. With the smaller diameter of the coil spring downwards, position the spring over the polished stem of the piston.

18. Fit the suction chamber over the spring and piston stem allowing the spring to position itself outside the suction chamber center.

19. The suction chamber is secured to the carburetor body by three screws, these are fitted but left loose at this juncture.

20. The float chamber is now attached to the carburetor body by the float chamber attachment bolt. Two large bore fiber washers with a brass washer between are positioned between the bolt head and the float chamber and a small bore washer between the float chamber and the body. With the washers so

placed the float chamber is attached to the body, the attachment bolt is left loose at this juncture.

21. Looking at the intake end of the carburetor body remove the right-hand suction chamber securing screw. With a shakeproof washer under its head feed the bolt through the float chamber steady bracket and replace to secure suction chamber. The three screws can now be fully tightened, the cap nut is, however, still left loose. The cap nut of the cover is tightened to secure the splash overflow pipe for tuning purposes when fitted to the car. Attach the jet lever return spring to the position provided between jet assembly and float chamber.

22. The jet and jet needle are now centralized.

23. The damper assembly is fitted to the suction chamber dry. The oil reservoir is not filled until the carburetors are fitted to the car.

24. Select the jet lever of the front carburetor, identified by having two holes at the extremity of the longer arm. This is attached to the jet assembly by a clevis pin and split pin, positioning the second end of the lever return spring to the jet lever.

25. Feed the upper end of the tension link through the rocker lever of the front carburetor from behind and the second end through the jet lever. Secure both ends with split pins.

26. Select the front carburetor jet lever link, this is distinguished by the pinch bolt at one end. This is attached to the lug at the rear of the jet assembly and again to the elbow of the jet lever in such a manner that the pinch bolt end of this link points to the rear. Both attachments are made by clevis pins and split pins.

The assembly of the jet lever and jet lever link to the rear carburetor is very similar. Both components are shorter than those fitted to the front carburetor.

To Adjust the Fuel Level in the Float Chamber

The level of the fuel in the float chamber is adjusted by setting the fork lever in the float chamber lid. It is suggested that the following procedure for its adjustment is adopted.

1. Remove the banjo bolt of the fuel connection and collect the two fiber washers and filter.
2. Loosen the screw securing the float chamber support arm to the carburetor body.
3. Withdraw the cap nut from the center of the float chamber lid and remove washers and splash overflow pipe.
4. Swing the support arm clear to lift the lid of the float chamber and joint washer.

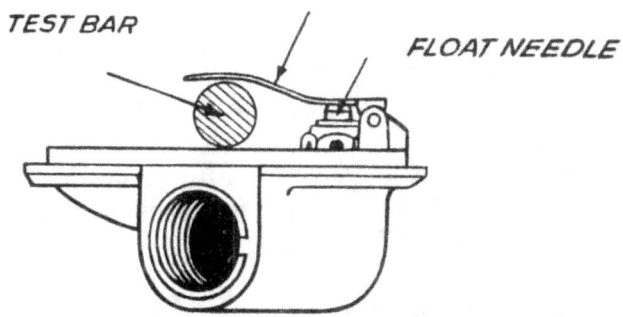

5. The set tof the forked lever is correct when, with the lid of the float chamber inverted and the shank of the fork lever resting on the needle of the delivery valve, it is possible to pass a 7/16" diameter rod between the inside radius of the forked lever and the flange of the lower face of the cover.

Carburetion Defects

In the case of unsatisfactory behavior of the engine, before proceeding to a detailed examination of the carburetor, it is advisable to carry out a general condition check of the engine, in respects other than those bearing upon the carburetion.

Attention should, in particular, be directed towards the following:—
1. The ignition system.
2. Incorrectly adjusted contact breaker gap.
3. Dirty or pitted contact breaker points, or other ignition defects.
4. Loss of compression of one or more cylinders.
5. Incorrect plug gaps.
6. Oily or dirty plugs.
7. Sticking valves.
8. Badly worn inlet valve guides.
9. Defective fuel pump, or chocked fuel filter.
10. Leakage at joint between carburetor and induction manifold, or between induction manifold flanges and cylinder head.

If these defects are not present to a degree which is thought accountable for unsatisfactory engine performance, the carburetor should be investigated for the following possible faults:

Pistons Sticking

The symptoms are stalling and a refusal to run slowly, or lack of power and heavy fuel consumption.

The piston (3) is designed to lift the jet needle (6) by the depression transferred to the top side from the passage facing the butterfly. This depression overcomes the weight of the piston and spring (8). The piston should move freely over its entire range and rest on the bridge pieces (28) when the engine is not running.

This should be checked by gently lifting the piston with a small screwdriver and any tendency for binding generally indicates one of the following faults:—

a. The damper rod may be bent causing binding and this can be checked by its removal. If the piston is now free the damper rod should be straightened and refitted.

b. The piston is meant to be a fine clearance fit at its outer diameter in the suction chamber and a sliding fit in the central bush. The suction chamber should be removed, complete with piston, and the freedom of movement checked after removal of the damper rod. The assembly should be washed clean and very lightly oiled where this slides in the bush and then checked for any tendency of binding. It is permissible to carefully remove, with a hand scaper, any high spots on the outer wall of the suction chamber, but no attempt should be made to increase the clearance by increasing the general bore of the suction chamber or decreasing the diameter of the piston. The fit of the piston in its central bush should be checked under both rotational and sliding movement.

Eccentricity of Jet and Needle.

The jet (14) is a loose fit in its recess and must always be centered by the needle before locking up the clamping ring (15).

The needle should be checked in the piston to see that it is not bent. It will be realized that it does not matter if it is eccentric as the adjustment of the jet allows for this, but a bent needle can never have the correct adjustment.

Flooding from Float Chamber or Mouth of Jet

This can be caused by a punctured float (10) or dirt on the needle valve (9) or its seat. These latter items can be readily cleaned after removal of the float chamber lid.

Leakage from Bottom of Jet adjacent to Adjustment Nut

Leakage in this vicinity is most likely due to defective sealing by the upper and lower gland assemblies. There is no remedy other than removing the whole jet assembly after disconnecting the operating lever and cleaning or replacing the faulty parts. It is very important that all parts are replaced in their correct sequence, as shown in the illustration, and it must be realized that centralization of the jet and needle and re-tuning will be necessary after this operation.

Dirt in the Carburetor

This should be checked in the normal way by examining and cleaning the float chamber, but it may be necessary if excessive water or dirt is present to strip down and clean all parts of the carburetor with solvent.

Failure of Fuel Supply to Float Chamber

If the engine is found to stop under idling or light running conditions, notwithstanding the fact that a good supply of fuel is present at the float chamber inlet union (observable by momentarily disconnecting this), it is possible that the needle has become stuck to its seating. This possibility arises in the rare cases where some gummy substance is present in the fuel system. The most probable instance of this nature is the polymerized gum which sometimes results from the protracted storage of fuel in the tank. After removal of the float chamber lid and float lever, the needle may be withdrawn, and its point thoroughly cleaned by immersion in alcohol.

Similar treatment should also be applied to the needle seating, which can conveniently be cleaned by means of a matchstick dipped in alcohol. Persistent trouble of this nature can only be cured properly by complete mechanical cleansing of the tank and fuel system. If the engine is found to suffer from a serious lack of power which becomes evident at higher speeds and loads, this is probably due to an inadequately sustained fuel supply, and the fuel pump should be investigated for

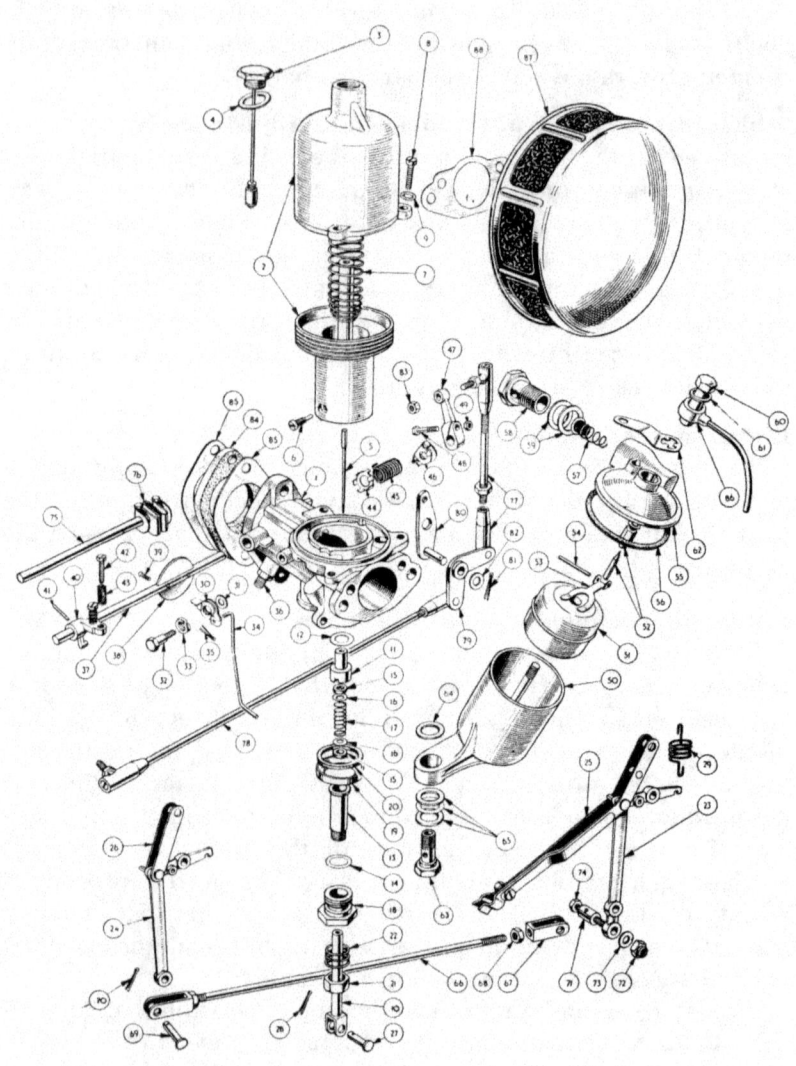

S.U. CARBURETTOR DETAILS

1	Body assembly.	45	Return spring.
2	Suction chamber and piston assembly	46	End clip.
3	Damper assembly.	47	Throttle lever.
4	Washer.	48	Pinch bolt.
5	Jet needle.	49	Nut for 48.
6	Needle locking screw.	50	Float chamber.
7	Piston spring.	51	Float.
8	Securing screw.	52	Needle and seat assembly.
9	Shake proof washer.	53	Hinged lever.
10	Jet head.	54	Pin for hinged lever.
11	Top half jet bearing.	55	Float chamber cover.
12	Washer.	56	Joint washer.
13	Bottom half jet bearing.	57	Petrol inlet filter.
14	Washer.	58	Banjo bolt
15	Cork gland washer.	59	Fibre washer.
16	Copper gland washer.	60	Cap nut.
17	Spring between gland washers.	61	Aluminium washer.
18	Jet locking nut.	62	Float chamber support arm.
19	Sealing ring.	63	Float chamber attachment bolt.
20	Cork washer.	64	Fibre washer.
21	Jet adjusting nut.	65	Washer.
22	Loading spring.	66	Jet control connecting rod. (Between front and rear jet levers.)
23	Jet lever. (Front carburettor.)		
24	Jet lever. (Rear carburettor.)	67	Fork end.
25	Jet lever link. (Front carburettor.)	68	Nut on fork end.
26	Jet lever link. (Rear carburettor.)	69	Clevis pin.
27	Clevis pin	70	Split pin.
28	Split pin.	71	Choke cable swivel pin.
29	Jet lever return spring.	72	Nyloc nut.
30	Rocker lever. (Front carburettor only.)	73	Plain washer.
31	Washer for 30. ,, ,,	74	Screw.
32	Rocker lever bolt. ,, ,,	75	Throttle spindle connecting rod.
33	Spring washer. ,, ,,	76	Folding coupling.
34	Connecting rod.	77	Short link rod assembly.
35	Split pin.	78	Long link rod assembly.
36	Ignition connection union. (Front carburettor only.)	79	Bell crank lever.
		80	Pivot lever.
37	Throttle spindle.	81	Split pin.
38	Throttle disc.	82	Plain washer.
39	Throttle disc attachment screws.	83	Nut.
40	Throttle stop. (Front carburettor only.)	84	Insulating packing.
41	Taper pin.	85	Joint washer.
42	Stop adjusting screw.	86	Carburettor splash and overflow pipe.
43	Locking screw spring.	87	Air cleaner.
44	Anchor plate.	88	Air cleaner gasket.

inadequate delivery, and any filters in the system inspected and cleansed.

Sticking Jet

Should the jet and its operating mechanism become unduly resistant to the action of lowering and raising by means of the enrichment mechanism, the jet should be lowered to its fullest extent, and the lower part thus exposed should be smeared with petroleum jelly, or similar lubricant. Oil should be applied to the various linkage pins in the mechanism and the jet raised and lowered several times in order to promote the passage of the lubricant upwards between the jet and its surrounding parts.

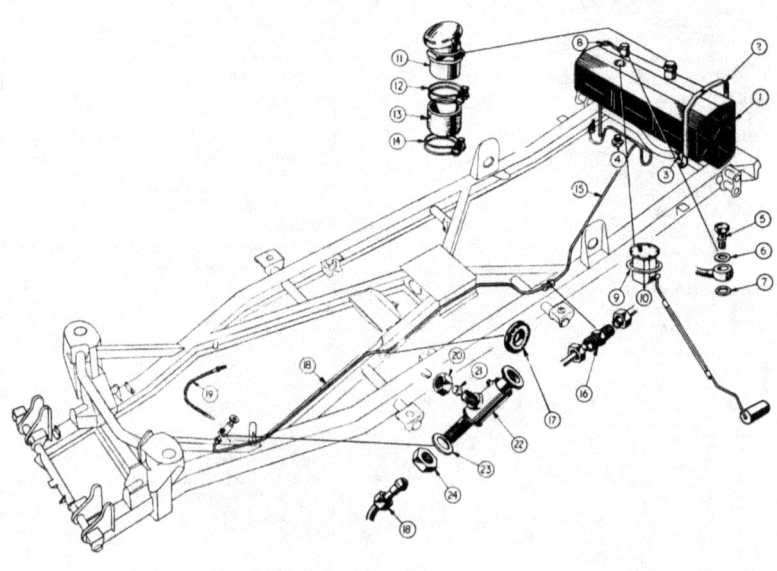

Ref. No.	Description	Ref. No.	Description
1	Petrol tank	13	Rubber hose connection
2	Petrol tank strap	14	Lower hose clip
3	Petrol tank strap fixing blot	15	Petrol pipe tank to connection
4	Drain plug	16	Pipe connection
5	Banjo bolt for vent pipe	17	Rubber grommet
6	Fibre washer above banjo connection	18	Petrol pipe (connection to stop tap)
7	Fibre washer below banjo connection	19	Flexible hose
8	Vent pipe	20	Stop tap outlet union nut
9	Cork washer	21	Brass olive
10	Petrol tank gauge unit	22	Petrol stop tap
11	Petrol filler cap and neck assembly	23	Plain washer
12	Upper hose clip	24	Jam nut for top attachment

ELECTRICAL EQUIPMENT

Batteries

Every 1,000 miles, or monthly (weekly in hot climates) examine the level of the electrolyte in the cells, and if necessary add distilled water to bring the level up to the top of the separators. A convenient method of adding the distilled water is by means of the Lucas Battery Filler, a device which automatically ensures that the correct level is attained. The action of resting the nozzle of the battery filler on the separators opens a valve and allows distilled water to flow into the cell, this being indicated by air bubbles rising in the filler. When the correct level has been reached air bubbles cease and the battery filler can then be withdrawn from the cell. A special non-spill nozzle prevents leakage from the filler.

Examine the terminals and, if necessary, clean them and coat them with petroleum jelly. Wipe away any foreign matter or moisture from the top of the battery, and ensure that the connections and the fixings are clean and tight.

Battery Cable Connectors

When fitting the diecast cable connectors, smear the inside of the tapered hole with petroleum jelly and push on the connector by hand. Insert the self-tapping screw and tighten with medium pressure only; fill in the recess around the screw with more petroleum jelly.

If the connectors are fitted dry and driven home on the tapered battery posts too tightly, difficulty may be experienced when it is required to remove them.

Generator

The generator is a shunt-wound two-pole two-brush machine, arranged to work in conjunction with a compensated voltage control regulator unit.

The output of the generator is controlled by the regulator and is dependent on the state and charge of the battery and the loading of the electrical equipment in use. When the battery is in a low state of charge, the generator gives a high output, whereas if the battery is fully charged, the generator gives only sufficient output to keep the battery in good condition without any possibility of overcharging. An increase in output is given to balance the current taken by lamps and other accessories when in use. Further, a high boosting charge is given for a few minutes immediately after starting.

Lubrication

Every 6,000 miles, inject a few drops of any high quality medium viscosity (S.A.E. 30) engine oil into the hole marked "oil" in the end of the bearing housing.

On earlier models, unscrew the cap of the lubricator on the side of the bearing housing, lift out the felt pad and spring and about half-fill the lubricator cap with high melting point grease. Replace the spring and felt pad and screw the lubricator cap back into position.

Performance Data

Model C-39 PV/2 fitted to TR 2-3 has a maximum output of 19 amperes at 1,900 - 2,150 rpm, at .3.5 generator volts on a resistance load of 0.7 ohm. Field resistance is 6.1 ohms.

Model C-40-1 fitted to TR 4 has a maximum output of 22 amperes at 2,050 - 2,250 rpm connected to a load of 0.61 ohms.

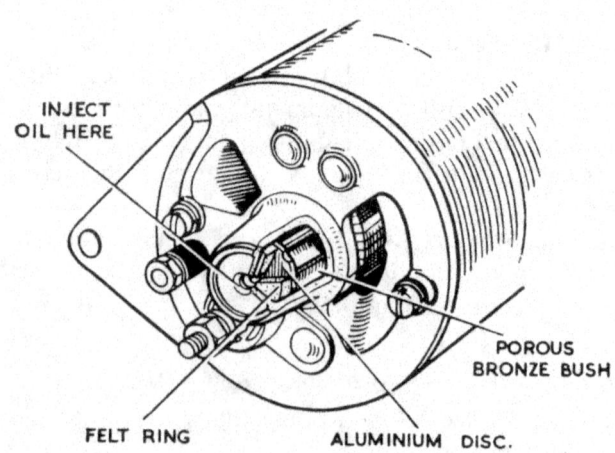

Generator
To test on vehicle

1. Make sure that belt slip is not the cause of the trouble. It should be possible to deflect the belt approximately ½ in. at the center of its longest run between two pulleys with moderate hand pressure. If the belt is too slack, loosen the two suspension bolts and then the belt of the slotted adjustment link. A gentle pull on the generator outwards will enable the correct tension to be applied to the belt and all three bolts should then be tightened firmly.

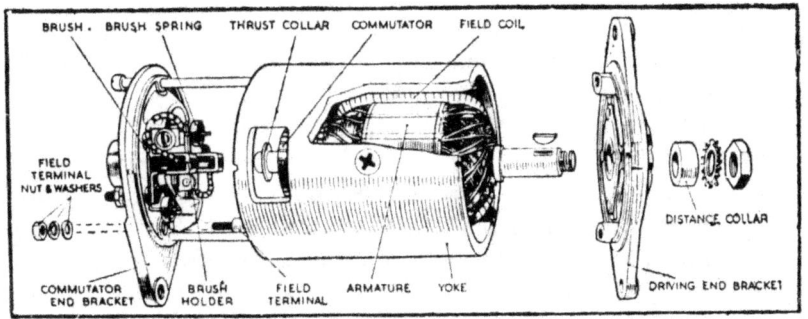

2. Check that the generator and control box are connected correctly. The generator terminal 'D' should be connected to the control box terminal 'D' and the generator terminal 'F' connected to the control box terminal 'F'.

3. After switching off all lights and accessories, disconnect the cables from the generator terminals marked 'D' and 'F' respectively.

4. Connect the two terminals with a length of wire.

5. Start the engine and set to run at idling speed.

6. Clip the negative lead of a moving-coil-type voltmeter, calibrated 0-20 volts, to one terminal and the other lead to a good ground point on the dynamo yoke.

7. Gradually increase the engine speed, when the voltmeter reading should rise rapidly and without fluctuation. Do not allow the voltmeter reading to reach 20 volts. Do not race the engine in an attempt to increase the voltage. It is sufficient to run the geenrator up to a speed of 1,000 r.p.m.

If there is no reading, check the brush gear.

If the reading is low (approximately 1 volt), the field winding may be faulty.

If the reading is approximately 5 volts, the armature winding may be faulty.

8. Remove the cover band and examine the brushes and commutator. Hold back each of the brush springs and move the brush by pulling gently on its flexible connector. If the movement is sluggish, remove the brush from its holder and ease the sides by lightly polishing on a smooth file. Always replace brushes in their original positions. If the brushes are worn so that they no longer bear on the commutator, or if the brush flexible lead has become exposed on the running face, new brushes must be fitted. If the commutator is blackened or dirty, clean it by holding a solvent-moistened cloth against it while the engine is turned slowly by hand-cranking. Re-test the gen-

erator; if there is still no reading on the voltmeter there is an internal fault and the complete unit should be renewed.

If the generator is in good order, leave the temporary link in position between the terminals and restore the original connections, taking care to connect the terminal 'D' to the control box terminal 'D' and the terminal 'F' to the control box terminal 'F'. Remove the lead from the 'D' terminal on the control box and connect the voltmeter between this cable and a good ground point on the vehicle. Run the engine as before. The reading should be the same as that measured directly at the generator. No reading on the voltmeter indicates a break in the cable to the generator. Carry out the same procedure for the 'F' terminal, connecting the voltmeter between cable and ground. Finally remove the link from the generator. If the reading is correct test the control box.

Removing and Replacing the Generator

To remove the generator, disconnect the leads from the terminals.

Slacken all four attachment bolts and pivot the generator towards the cylinder block to enable the fan belt to be removed from the pulley. The generator can then be removed by completely removing the two upper and one lower attachment bolts.

Replacement is an exact reversal of this procedure.

Dismantling the Generator
1. Take off the pulley.
2. Remove the cover band, hold back the brush springs and remove the brushes from their holders.
3. Unscrew the locknuts from the through-bolts at the commutator end. Withdraw the two through-bolts from the driving end.
4. Remove the nut, spring washer and flat washer from the smaller terminal (i.e. field terminal) on the commutator end bracket and remove the bracket from the yoke.
5. The driving end bracket, together with the armature, can now be lifted out of the yoke.
6. The driving end bracket which, on removal from the yoke, has withdrawn with it the armature and armature shaft ball bearing, need not be separated from the shaft unless the bearing is suspected and requires examination, in which event the armature should be removed from the end bracket by means of a hand press.

Servicing the Generator
Brushes

Test if the brushes are sticking. Clean them with gasoline and, if necessary, ease the sides by lightly polishing with a smooth file. Replace the brushes in their original positions.

Test the brush spring tension with a spring scale if available. The correct tension is 20-5 oz. Fit a new spring if the tension is low.

If the brushes are worn so that the flexible lead is exposed on the running face, new brushes **must** be fitted. Brushes are pre-formed so that bedding to the commutator is unnecessary.

Commutator

A commutator in good condition will be smooth and free from pits or burned spots. Clean the commutator with a solvent-moistened cloth. If this is ineffective, carefully polish with a strip of fine glass-paper while rotating the armature. To remedy a badly worn commutator, mount the armature (with or without the drive end bracket) in a lathe, rotate at high speed and take a light cut with a very sharp tool. Do not remove more metal than is necessary. Polish the commutator with very fine glass-paper. Undercut the mica insulation between the segments to a depth of $\frac{1}{32}$ in. with a hacksaw blade ground down to the thickness of the mica.

Field coils

Test the field coils, without removing them from the generator yoke, by means of an ohmmeter. The reading on the ohmmeter should be between 6.0 and 6.3 ohms. If this is not available, connect a 12-volt D.C. supply with an ammeter in series between the field terminal and the yoke. The ammeter reading should be approximately 2 amps. If no reading is indicated the field coils are open-circuited and most be renewed. To test for grounded field coils, unsolder the end of the field winding from the ground terminal on the yoke and, with a test lamp connected

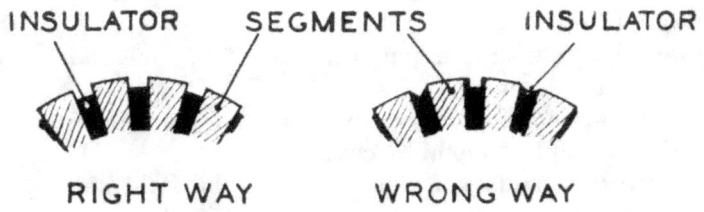

from supply mains, test across the field terminal and ground. If the lamp lights, the field coils are grounded and must be renewed.

When fitting field coils, carry out the procedure outlined below, using an expander and wheel-operated screwdriver:
1. Remove the insulation piece which is provided to prevent the junction of the field coils from contacting the yoke.
2. Mark the yoke and pole-shoes in order that they can be refitted in their original positions.
3. Unscrew the two pole-shoe retaining screws by means of the wheel-operated screwdriver.
4. Draw the pole-shoes and coil out of the generator yoke and lift off the coils.
5. Fit the new field coils over the pole-shoes and place them in position inside the yoke. Take care to ensure that the taping of the field coils is not trapped between the pole-shoes and the yoke.
6. Locate the pole-shoes and field coils by lightly tightening the fixing screw.
7. Insert the pole-shoe expander, open it to the fullest extent and tighten the screws.
8. Finally tighten the screws by means of the wheel-operated screwdriver and lock them by caulking.
9. Replace the insulation piece between the field coil connection and the yoke.

Armature

The testing of the armature winding requires the use of a voltage drop test and growler. If these are not available, the armature should be checked by substitution. No attempt should be made to machine the armature core or to true a distorted armature shaft.

Bearings

Bearings which are worn to such an extent that they will allow side movement of the armature shaft must be replaced by new ones.

To fit a new bearing at the commutator end of the generator proceed as follows:

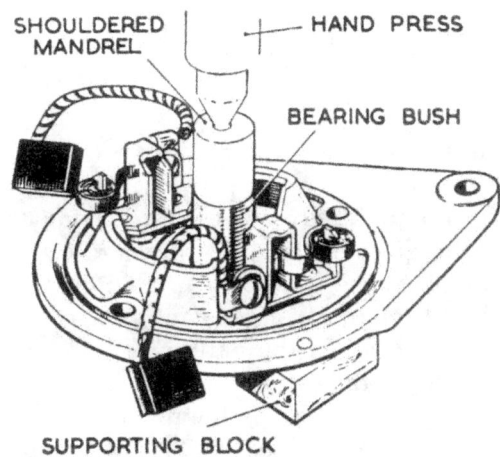

1. Press the bearing bush out of the commutator end bracket.
2. Press the new bearing bush into the end bracket, using a shouldered mandrel of the same diameter as the shaft which is to fit in the bearing.

Before fitting the new bearing bush allow it to stand completely immersed in thin engine oil for 24 hours, to fill the pores of the bush with lubricant.

The ball bearing at the driving end is renewed as follows:
1. Knock out the rivets which secure the bearing retaining plate to the end bracket and remove the plate.
2. Press the bearing out of the end bracket and remove the corrugated washer, felt washer and oil retaining washer.
3. Before fitting the replacement bearing see that it is clean and pack it with a high-melting-point grease.
4. Place the oil retaining washer, felt washer and corrugated

washer in the bearing housing in the end bracket.

5. Locate the bearing in the housing and press it home by means of a hand press.

6. Fit the bearing retaining plate. Insert the new rivets from the inside of the end bracket and open the rivets by means of a punch to secure the plate rigidly in position.

Reassembly

The reassembly of the generator is a reversal of the operations described above.

If the end bracket has been removed from the armature in dismantling, press the bearing end bracket into the armature shaft, taking care to avoid damaging the end plate and armature winding.

Add a few drops of oil through the hole in the armature end cover.

The Control Box
Regulator adjustment

The regulator is carefully set before leaving the factory to suit the normal requirements of the standard equipment, and in general it should not be necessary to alter it. If, however, the battery does not keep in a charged condition, or if the generator output does not fall when the battery is fully charged, it may be advisable to check the setting and, if necessary, to readjust it.

It is important, before altering the regulator setting, when the battery is in a low state of charge, to check that its condition is not due to a battery defect or to the generator belt slipping.

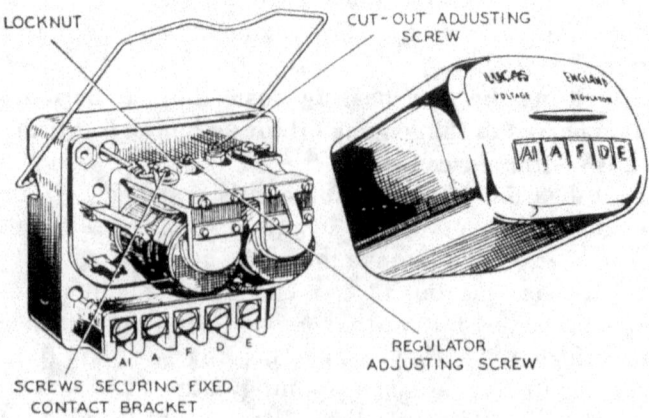

How to check and adjust electrical setting

The regulator setting can be checked without removing the cover of the control box.

Withdraw the cables from the terminals marked 'A' and 'A1' at the control box and join them together. Connect the negative lead of a moving-coil voltmeter (0-20 volts full-scale reading) to the 'D' terminal on the generator and connect the other lead from the meter to a convenient chassis ground.

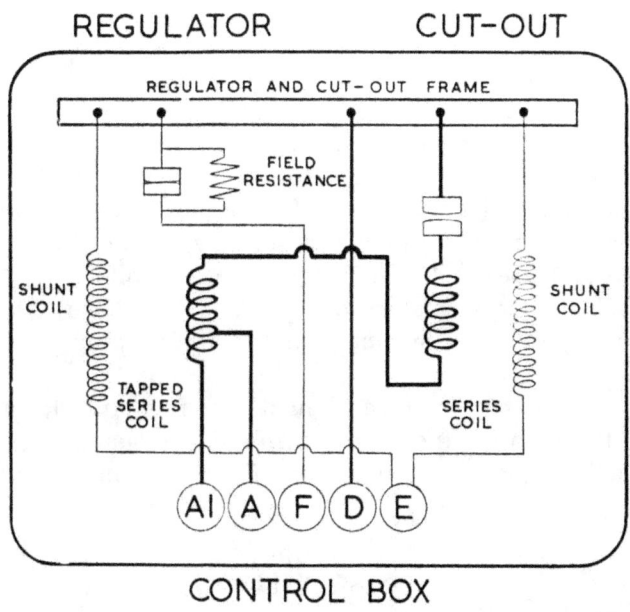

Slowly increase the speed of the engine until the voltmeter needle flicks and then steadies; this should occur at a voltmeter reading between the limits given below for the appropriate temperature of the regulator.

TR 2-3

Temperature	Voltage
10°C (50°F)	15.9 - 16.5
20°C (68°F)	15.6 - 16.2
30°C (86°F)	15.3 - 15.9

TR 4

Temperature	Voltage
10°C (50°F)	16.1 - 16.7
20°C (68°F)	16.0 - 16.6
30°C (86°F)	15.9 - 16.5

If the voltage at which the reading becomes steady occurs outside these limits, the regulator must be adjusted.

Shut off the engine, remove the control box cover, release the locknut (a) holding the adjusting screw (b) and turn the screw in a clockwise direction to raise the setting or in an anti-clockwise direction to lower the setting. Turn the adjusting screw a fraction of a turn and then tighten the locknut.

When the generator is run at high speed on open circuit, it builds us a high voltage. When adjusting the regulator, do not run the engine up to more than 3,000 r.p.m. or a false voltmeter reading will be obtained.

Mechanical setting

The mechanical setting of the regulator is accurately adjusted before leaving the factory, and provided that the armature carrying the moving contact is not removed, the regulator will not require mechanical adjustment. If, however, the armature has been removed from the regulator for any reason, the contacts will have to be reset. To do this, proceed as follows:

1. Slacken the two armature fixing screws (e). Insert a .020 in. feeler gauge between the back of the armature (a) and the regulator frame.
2. Press back the armature against the regulator frame and down onto the top of the bobbin core with the gauge in position and lock the armature by tightening the two fixing screws.

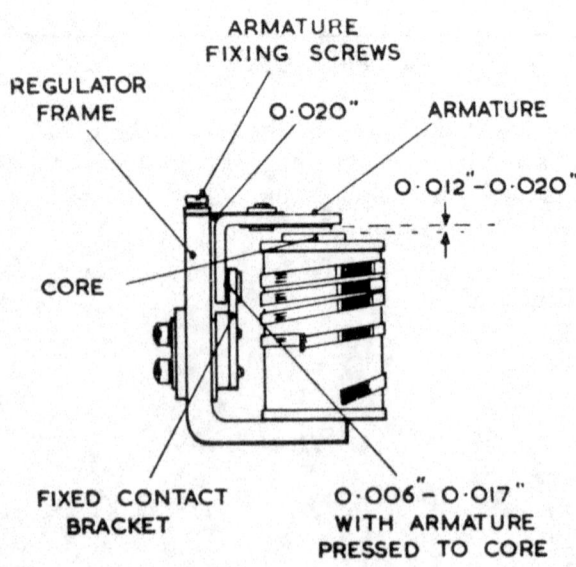

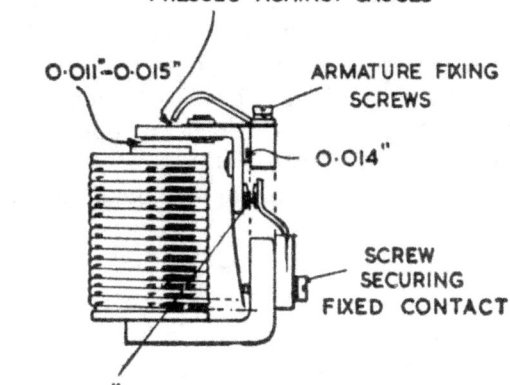

WITH 0·025" GAUGE BETWEEN ARMATURE SHIM
& CORE, CONTACT GAP TO BE 0·002"–0·006.

3. Check the gap between the under side of the arm and the top of the bobbin core. This must be .012 to .020 in. If the gap is outside these limits correct by adding or removing shims (f) at the back of the fixed contact (d) or, in later types, by carefully bending the fixed contact bracket.

4. Remove the gauge and press the armature down, when the gap between the contacts should be between .006 in. and .017 in.

Cleaning contacts

To render the regulator contacts accessible for cleaning, slacken the screws securing the plate carrying the fixed contact. It will be necessary to slacken the upper screw (c) a little more than the lower screw (d), so that the contact plate can be swung outwards. Clean the contacts by means of fine carborundum stone or fine emery-cloth. Carefully wipe away all traces of dirt or other foreign matter. Finally tighten the securing screws.

Cut-out
Adjustment

If it is suspected that the cutting-in speed of the generator is too high, connect a voltmeter between the terminals marked 'D' and 'E' at the control box and slowly raise the engine speed. When the voltmeter reading rises to between 12.7 and 13.3 volts the cut-out contacts should close.

If operation of the cut-out takes place outside these limits, it will be necessary to adjust. To do this, slacken locknut E and turn screw F in a clockwise direction to raise the voltage setting or in an anti-clockwise direction to reduce the setting. Turn the screw only a fraction of a turn at a time and then tighten the locknut. Test after each adjustment by increasing the engine speed and noting the voltmeter readings at the instant of contact closure. Electrical settings of the cut-out, like the regulator, must be made as quickly as possible because of the temperature-rise effects. Tighten the locknut after making the adjustment. If the cut-out does not operate, there may be an open circuit in the wiring of the cut-out and regulator unit, in which case the unit should be removed for examination or replacement.

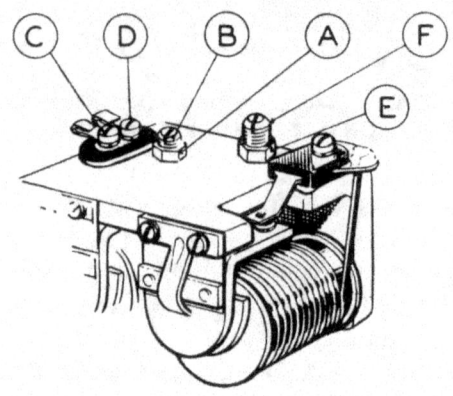

Mechanical Setting

If for any reason the cut-out armature has to be removed from the frame, care must be taken to obtain the correct air-gap settings on re-assembly. These can be obtained as follows: Slacken the two armature fixing screws, adjusting screw F and the screw securing the fixed contact.

Insert a 0.014" gauge between the back of the armature and the cut-out frame. (The air gap between the core face and the armature shim should now measure 0.011"-0.015". If it does not, fit a new armature assembly.) Press the armature back against the gauge and tighten the armature fixing screws. With the gauge still in position, set the gap between the armature and the stop plate arm to 0.030"-0.034" by carefully bending the gauge and tighten the screw securing the fixed contact.

Insert a 0.025" gauge between the core face and the armature. Press the armature down on to the gauge. The gap between the contacts should now measure 0.002" to 0.006" and the drop-off voltage should be between the limits given previously. If necessary, adjust the gap by carefully bending the fixed contact bracket.

Cleaning Contacts

If the cut-out contacts appear rough or burnt, place a strip of fine glass paper between the contacts — then, with the contacts closed by hand, draw the paper through. This should be done two or three times with the rough side towards each contact. Wipe away all dust or other foreign matter, using a clean fluffless cloth moistened with de-natured alcohol.

Do not use emery cloth or a carborundum stone for cleaning cut-out contacts.

Replacement Contacts

If the contacts are so badly worn that replacement is necessary, they must be renewed as a pair and not individually. The contact gap must be set to 0.014" to 0.016". This procedure allows for the initial "bedding-in" of the heel.

Starting Motor Drive

The drive embodies a combination of rubber torsion member and friction clutch in order to control the torque transmitted from the starter to the engine flywheel and to dissipate the energy in the rotating armature of the starter at the moment when the pinion engages with the flywheel.

It also embodies an overload release mechanism which functions in the event of extreme stress, such as may occur in the event of a very heavy backfire, or if the starter is inadvertently meshed into a flywheel, rotating in the reverse direction.

When the starter is energized, the torque is transmitted by two paths, one via the outer sleeve of the rubber coupling and through the friction washer to the screwed sleeve, while the other path is from the outer to the inner sleeve through the rubber coupling and then directly to the screwed sleeve.

The torque through the rubber limits the total torque which the drive transmits and since the rubber is bonded to the inner sleeve, under overload conditions slipping will occur between the rubber bush and the outer sleeve of the coupling. Slipping does not take place under normal engagement conditions, when the rubber acts merely as a spring with a limiting relative twist on the two members of approximately 30°.

Under conditions of unduly severe overload which might cause damage to the drive or its mounting, the rubber slips in its housing so that a definite upper limit is set to the torque transmitted and to the stresses which may occur.

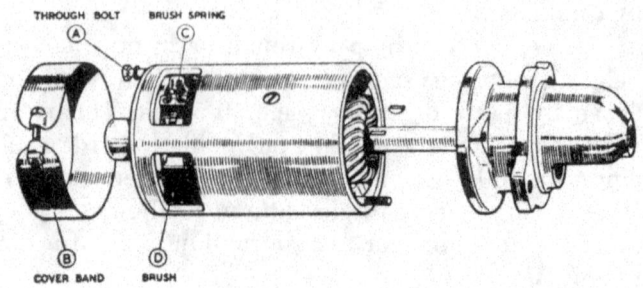

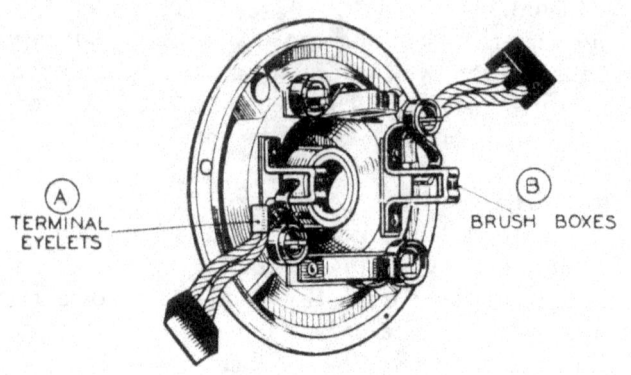

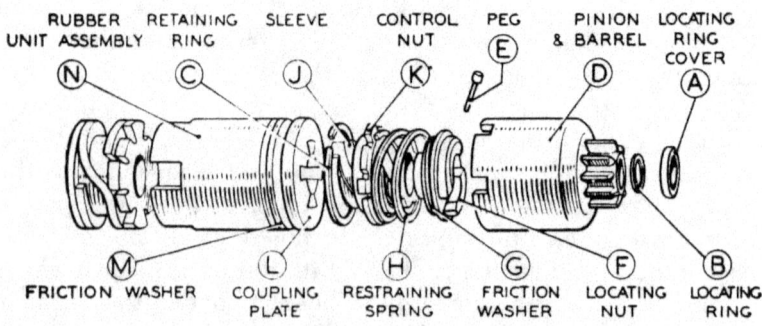

Routine Maintenance

If any difficulty is experienced with the starting motor not meshing correctly with the flywheel, it may be that the drive requires cleaning. The pinion should move freely on the screwed sleeve; if there is any dirt or other foreign matter on the sleeve it must be washed off with kerosene.

In the event of the pinion becoming jammed in mesh with the flywheel, it can usually be freed by turning the starter motor armature by means of a wrench applied to the shaft extension at the commutator end. This is accessible by removing the cap which is a push fit.

Construction

The construction of the drive will be clear from the illustration. The pinion is carried on a barrel type assembly which is mounted on a screwed sleeve.

The screwed sleeve is secured to the armature shaft by means of a location nut and is also keyed to the inner sleeve of the rubber coupling by a center coupling plate. A friction washer is fitted between the coupling plate and rubber assembly and the outer sleeve of the rubber coupling is keyed at the armature end of the starter by means of a transmission plate.

A pinion restraining spring is fitted in the barrel assembly to prevent the pinion vibrating into mesh when the engine is running.

The Starter
To test on vehicle

Switch on the lamps and operate the starter control. If the lights do dim, but the starter is not heard to operate, an indication is given that current is flowing through the starter windings but that the starter pinion is meshed permanently with the geared ring on the flywheel. This was probably caused by the starter being operated while the engine was still running. In this case the starter must be removed from the engine for examination.

Should the lamps retain their full brilliance when the starter switch is operated, check that the switch is functioning. If the switch is in order, examine the connections at the battery, starter switch and starter, and also check the wiring between these units. Continued failure of the starter to operate indicates an internal fault and the starter must be removed from the engine for examination.

Sluggish or slow action of the starter is usually caused by a poor connection in the wiring which produces a high resistance in the starter circuit. Check as described above.

Damage to the starter drive is indicated if the starter is heard to operate but does not crank the engine.

Removing and Replacing the Starter

Release the starter cable from the terminal and unscrew the two starter securing bolts. Maneuver the starter forwards below the oil filter, then rearwards and upwards.

Servicing the Starter
Examination of commutator and brush gear

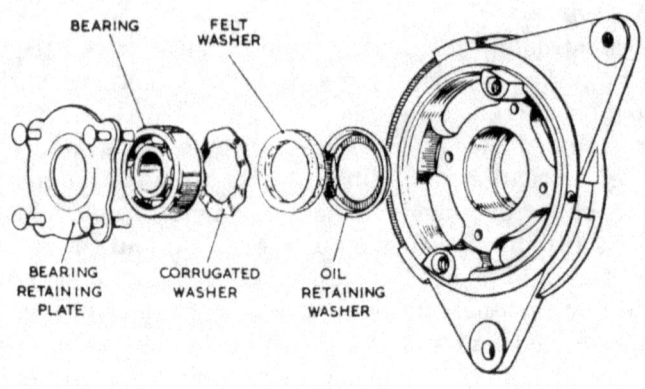

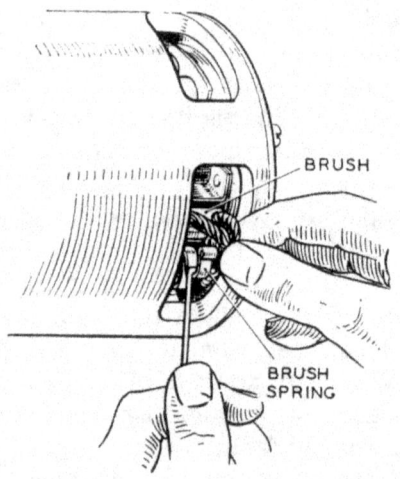

Remove the starter cover band (a) and examine the brushes (c) and the commutator. Hold back each of the brush springs (b) and move the brush by pulling gently on its flexible connector. If the movement is sluggish remove the brush from its holder and ease the sides by lightly polishing with a smooth file. Always replace brushes in their original positions. If the brushes are worn so that they no longer bear on the commutator, or if the brush flexible lead has become exposed on the running face, they must be renewed.

If the commutator is blackened or dirty, clean it by holding a solvent-moistened cloth against it while the armature is rotated.

Secure the body of the starter in a vice and test by connecting it with heavy-gauge cables to a battery of the correct voltage.

One cable must be connected to the starter terminal and the other held against the starter body or end bracket. Under these light load conditions the starter should run at a very high speed.

If the operation of the starter is still unsatisfactory, the starter should be dismantled for detailed inspection and testing.

Dismantling

Take off the cover band "A" at the commutator end, hold back the brush springs "B" and take out the brushes "C" from their holders.

Withdraw the jump ring and shims from the armature shaft at the commutator end and remove the armature complete with drive from the commutator end bracket and starter frame.

Remove the terminal nuts "E" and washers "F" from the terminal post "G" at the commutator end bracket and also withdraw the two through bolts. Remove the commutator end bracket and the attachment bracket from the starter frame.

Brushes

1. Test the brush springs with a spring scale. The correct tension is 30-40 oz. Fit a new spring if the tension is low.
2. If the brushes are worn so that they no longer bear on the commutator, or if the flexible connector has become exposed on the running face, they must be renewed. Two of the brushes are connected to terminals eyelets attached to the brush boxes on the commutator end bracket. The other two brushes are connected to tappings on the field coils.

The flexible connectors must be removed by unsoldering and the connectors of the new brushes secured in place by soldering. The brushes are pre-formed, so that bedding of the working face to the commutator is unnecessary.

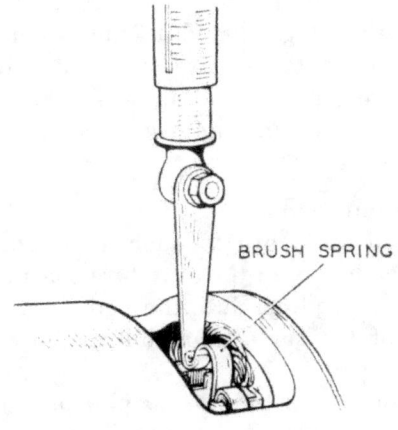

Commutator

A commutator in good condition will be smooth and free from pits and burned spots. Clean the commutator with a cloth moistened with solvent. If this is ineffective, carefully polish with a strip of fine glass-paper, while rotating the armature. To remedy a badly worn commutator, dismantle the starter drive as described above and remove the armature from the end bracket. Now mount the armature in a lathe, rotate it at a high speed and take a light cut with a very sharp tool. Do not remove any more metal than is absolutely necessary, and finally polish with very fine glass-paper.

The mica on the **starter** commutator **must not be undercut.**

Field coils

The field coils can be tested for an open circuit by connecting a 12-volt battery, having a 12-volt bulb in one of the leads, to the tapping point of the field coils to which the brushes are connected, and the field terminal post. If the lamp does not light, there is an open circuit in the wiring of the field coils.

Lighting of the lamp does not necessarily mean that the field coils are in order, as it is possible that one of them may be grounded to a pole shoe or to the yoke. This may be checked by removing the lead from the brush connector and holding it on a clean part of the starter yoke. Should the bulb now light it indicates that the field coils are grounded.

Should the above tests indicate that the fault lies in the field coils, they must be renewed. When renewing field coils carry out the procedure detailed in the generator section.

Armature

Examination of the armature will in many cases reveal the cause of failure, e.g. conductors lifted from the commutator due to the starter being engaged while the engine is running and causing the armature to be rotated at an excessive speed. A damaged armature must in all cases be renewed — no attempt should be made to machine the armature core or to true a distorted armature shaft.

Bearings (commutator end)

Bearings which are worn to such an extent that they will allow excessive sideplay of the armature shaft must be renewed. Press the new bearing bush into the end bracket, using a shouldered mandrel of the same diameter as the shaft which is to fit in the bearing.

The bearing bush is of the porous phosphor-bronze type, and

before fitting, **new bushes should be allowed to stand completely immersed for twenty-four hours in thin engine oil in order to fill the pores of the bush with lubricant.**

Reassembly

The reassembly of the starter is a reversal of the operations described in this section.

KEY TO CABLE COLOURS

1	BLUE
2	BLUE WITH RED
3	BLUE WITH YELLOW
4	BLUE WITH WHITE
5	BLUE WITH GREEN
6	BLUE WITH PURPLE
7	BLUE WITH BROWN
8	BLUE WITH BLACK
9	WHITE
10	WHITE WITH RED
11	WHITE WITH YELLOW
12	WHITE WITH BLUE
13	WHITE WITH GREEN
14	WHITE WITH PURPLE
15	WHITE WITH BROWN
16	WHITE WITH BLACK
17	GREEN
18	GREEN WITH RED
19	GREEN WITH YELLOW
20	GREEN WITH BLUE
21	GREEN WITH WHITE
22	GREEN WITH PURPLE
23	GREEN WITH BROWN
24	GREEN WITH BLACK
25	YELLOW
26	YELLOW WITH RED
27	YELLOW WITH BLUE
28	YELLOW WITH WHITE
29	YELLOW WITH GREEN
30	YELLOW WITH PURPLE
31	YELLOW WITH BROWN
32	YELLOW WITH BLACK
33	BROWN
34	BROWN WITH RED
35	BROWN WITH YELLOW
36	BROWN WITH BLUE
37	BROWN WITH WHITE
38	BROWN WITH GREEN
39	BROWN WITH PURPLE
40	BROWN WITH BLACK
41	RED
42	RED WITH YELLOW
43	RED WITH BLUE
44	RED WITH WHITE
45	RED WITH GREEN
46	RED WITH PURPLE
47	RED WITH BROWN
48	RED WITH BLACK
49	PURPLE
50	PURPLE WITH RED
51	PURPLE WITH YELLOW
52	PURPLE WITH BLUE
53	PURPLE WITH WHITE
54	PURPLE WITH GREEN
55	PURPLE WITH BROWN
56	PURPLE WITH BLACK
57	BLACK
58	BLACK WITH RED
59	BLACK WITH YELLOW
60	BLACK WITH BLUE
61	BLACK WITH WHITE
62	BLACK WITH GREEN
63	BLACK WITH PURPLE
64	BLACK WITH BROWN
65	DARK GREEN
66	LIGHT GREEN

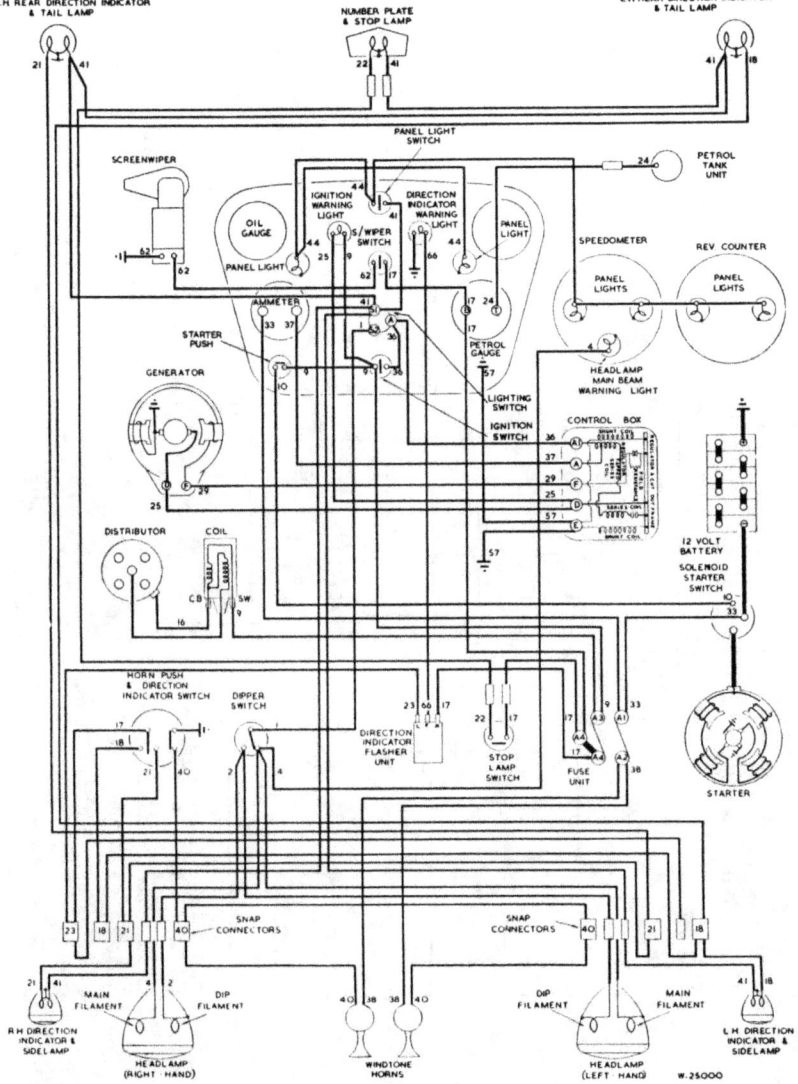

TR3 Wiring Diagram.

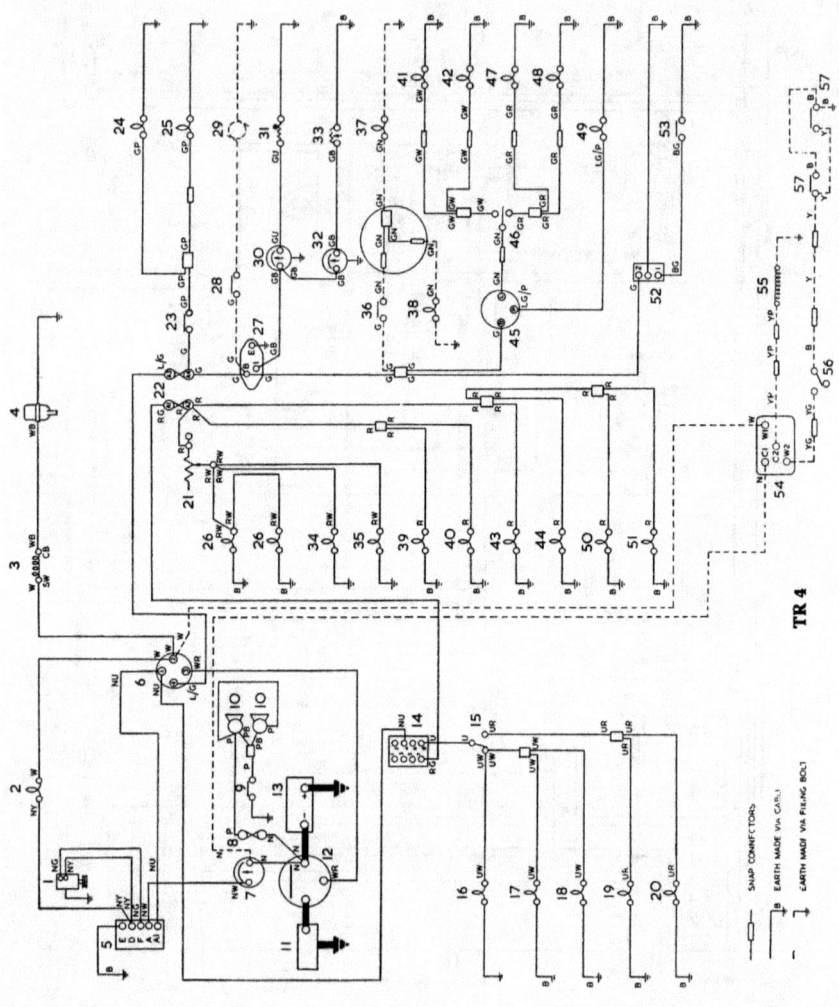

1 Generator
2 Ignition warning lamp
3 Ignition coil
4 Distributor
5 Control box
6 Ignition switch
7 Ammeter
8 Horns fuse
9 Horn push
10 Horns
11 Starter motor
12 Starter solenoid
13 Battery
14 Lighting switch
15 Dipper switch
16 High beam indicator lamp
17 Headlamp high beam, R.H.
18 Headlamp high beam, L.H.
19 Headlamp dip beam, R.H.
20 Headlamp dip beam, L.H.
21 Instrument illumination rheostat
22 Fuse unit
23 Stop lamp switch
24 Stop lamp, R.H.
25 Stop lamp, L.H.
26 Ammeter and gauges illumination
27 Voltage stabilizer
28 Heater blower motor switch } Optional Extra
29 Heater blower motor
30 Temperature indicator gauge
31 Temperature transmitter
32 Fuel gauge
33 Tank unit
34 Speedometer illumination
35 Tachometer illumination
36 Reversing lamp switch } Optional Extra
37 Reversing lamp
38 Reversing lamp
39 Parking lamp, R.H.
40 Parking lamp, L.H.
41 Direction indicator, R.H. Front
42 Direction indicator, L.H. Front
43 Tail lamp, R.H.
44 Plate illumination lamp, R.H.
45 Flasher unit
46 Direction indicator switch
47 Direction indicator, R.H. Rear
48 Direction indicator, L.H. Rear
49 Direction indicator monitor lamp
50 Tail lamp, L.H.
51 Plate illumination lamp, L.H.
52 Windscreen wiper motor
53 Windscreen wiper motor switch
54 Relay } Overdrive Optional Extras
55 Solenoid
56 Column control
57 Transmission switches

CABLE COLOUR CODE

B Black	S Slate		
U Blue	W White		
N Brown	Y Yellow		
G Green	D Dark		
K Pink	L Light		
P Purple	M Medium		
R Red			

TR 4

Distributor—Model DM2 (TR 2-3)

Mounted on the distributor driving shaft, immediately beneath the contact breaker, is a centrifugally operated timing control mechanism. It consists of a pair of spring-loaded governor weights, linked by lever action to the contact breaker cam. Under the centrifugal force imparted by increasing engine speed, the governor weights swing out against the spring pressure to advance the contact breaker cam and thereby the spark, to suit engine conditions at the greater speed.

A built-in vacuum-operated timing control is also included, designed to give additional advance under part-throttle conditions. The inlet manifold of the engine is in direct communication with one side of a spring-loaded diaphragm. This diaphragm acts through a lever mechanism to rotate the heel of the contact breaker about the cam, thus advancing the spark for part-throttle operating conditions. There is also a micrometer adjustment by means of which fine alterations in timing can be made to allow for changes in running conditions, e.g., state of carbonization, change of fuel, etc.

A completely sealed metallized paper capacitor is utilized. This has the property of being self-healing; should the capacitor break down, the metallic film around the point of rupture is vaporized away by the heat of the spark, so preventing a permanent short circuit. Capacitor failure will be found to be most infrequent.

The H.T. pick-up brush is of a composite construction, the top portion consisting of a resistive compound and the lower of softer carbon to prevent wear taking place on the rotor electrode. The resistive portion of this carbon brush which is in circuit between the coil and the distributor gives a measure of radio interference suppression. Under no circumstance must a short non-resistive brush be used as a replacement for one of these longer resistive brushes.

The Pre-tilted Contact Breaker Unit

An improved contact breaker unit was introduced on the DM2P4 distributor. Important features of this pre-tilted contact breaker unit are: improved sensitivity of vacuum control and elimination of any tendency for the moving contact breaker plate to rock at high cam speeds. Contact adjustment has also been simplified.

Routine Maintenance

In general, lubrication and cleaning constitute normal main-

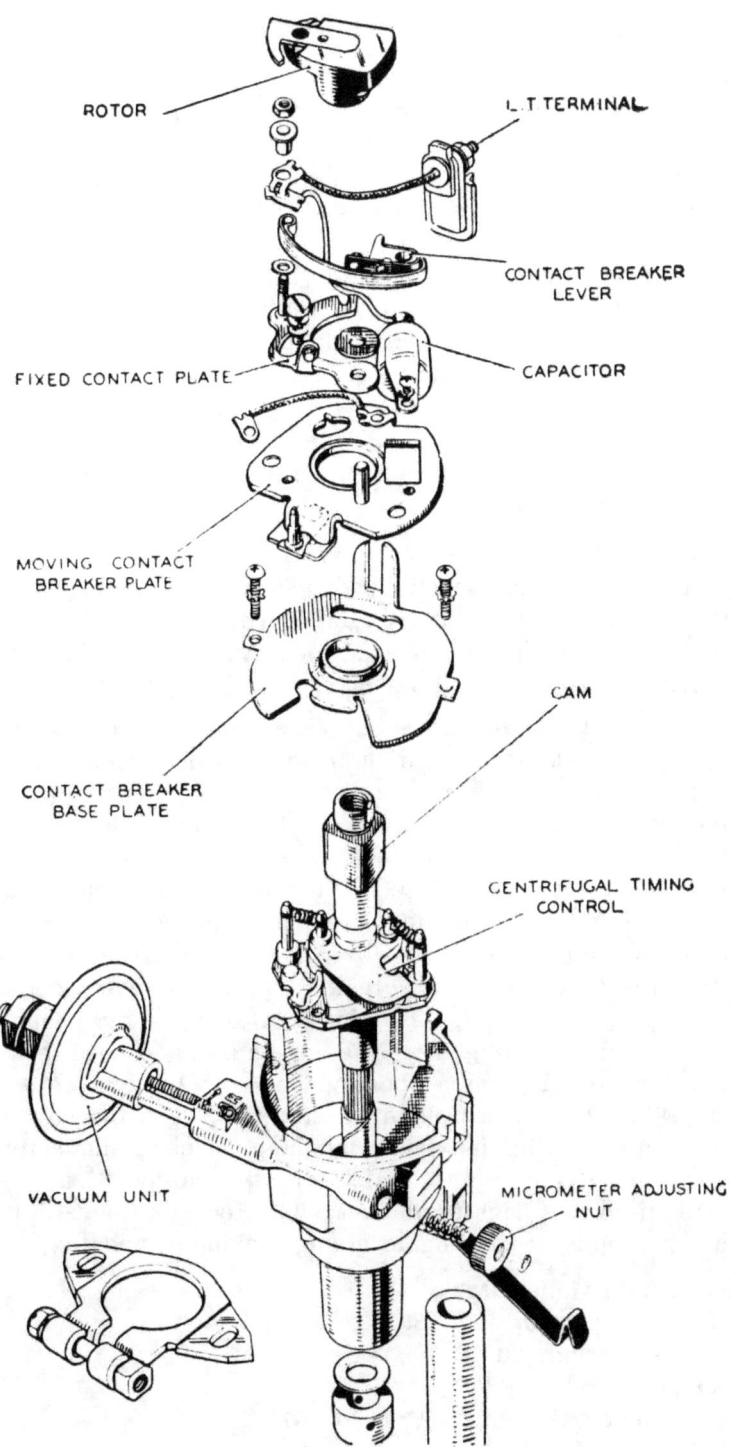

tenance procedure.

Lubrication—every 3,000 miles

Take great care to prevent oil or grease from getting on or near the contacts.

Add a few drops of thin machine oil through the aperture at the end of the contact breaker to lubricate the centrifugal timing control.

Smear the cam with Mobilgrease No. 2.

Lift off the rotor arm and apply to the spindle a few drops of Ragosine Molybdenized non-creep oil or thin machine oil to lubricate the cam bearing. It is not necessary to remove the exposed screw, since it affords a clearance to permit the passage of oil. Replace the rotor arm carefully, locating its moulded projection in the keyway in the spindle and pushing it on as far as it will go.

Cleaning—every 6,000 miles

Thoroughly clean the moulded distributor cover, inside and out, with a soft dry cloth, paying particular attention to the spaces between the metal electrodes. Ensure that the carbon brush moves freely in its holder.

Examine the contact breaker. The contacts must be quite free from grease or oil. If they are burned or blackened, clean them with very fine carborundum stone or emery cloth, then wipe with a gasoline-moistened cloth. Cleaning is facilitated by removing the contact breaker lever. To do this, remove the nut, washer, insulating piece and connections from the post to which the end of the contact breaker spring is anchored. The contact breaker lever may now be removed from its pivot. Before refitting the contact breaker, smear the pivot post with non-creep oil or Mobilgrease No. 2. After cleaning, check the contact breaker setting. Turn the engine by hand until the contacts show the maximum opening. This should measure 0.014" to 0.016". If the measurement is incorrect, keep the engine in the position giving maximum opening, slacken the screw(s) securing the fixed contact plate and adjust its position to give the required gap. Tighten the screw(s). Recheck the setting for other positions of the engine giving maximum opening.

Design Data Model DM2
a. Firing angles: $0°, 90°, 180°, 270°, \pm 1°$.
   Closed period: $60° \pm 3°$.
   Open period: $30° \pm 3°$.
b. Contact breaker gap: 0.014" to 0.016".

c. Contact breaker spring tension, measured at contacts: 20-24 ozs.
d. Capacitor: 0.2 microfarad.
e. Rotation: Anti-clockwise.
f. Checking Automatic timing control:
1. Advance due to centrifugal control:
Set to spark at zero degrees at minimum r.p.m.
Run distributor at 2,700 r.p.m. Advance should lie between 13° and 15°.
Check advance at following decelerating speeds:—

Speed r.p.m.	Advance (degree)
2,000	$12^{1}/_{2}$ - $14^{1}/_{2}$
750	$8^{1}/_{2}$ - $10^{1}/_{2}$
600	$6^{1}/_{2}$ - 9
200	0 - 2

Part No(s). of auto advance springs: 421218, 421219.
2. Advance due to vacuum control:
Apply a vacuum of 18" of mercury. Advance to lie between 6° and 8°. Check advance at the following points, as the vacuum is reduced:

Vacuum (in hg.)	Advance (degrees)
$9^{1}/_{2}$	5 - 7
$4^{3}/_{4}$	$^{1}/_{2}$ - $2^{1}/_{2}$

No advance below 2" of mercury.

NOTE: for design data of Model 25 D4 distributor fitted to TR 4, see accompanying specification table. Service and repairs are carried out in substantially the same manner as detailed here for the earlier type.

Servicing

Before starting to test, make sure that the battery is not fully discharged, as this will often produce the same symptoms as a fault in the ignition circuit.

Testing in Position to Locate Cause of Uneven Firing

Run the engine at a fairly fast idling speed.

If possible, short circuit each plug in turn with the blade of an insulated screwdriver or a hammer head placed across the terminal to contact the cylinder head. Short circuiting the plug in the defective cylinder will cause no noticeable change in the running note. On the others, however, there will be a pronounced increase in roughness. If this is not possible, due to the spark plugs being fitted with a shrouded cable connector, remove each plug connector in turn. Again, removal of the connection to the defective cylinder will cause no noticeable

SPECIFICATIONS

Distributor
    Model .. .. 25.D4.
Part Numbers

Compression Ratio	Lucas Service No.	Standard-Triumph Part No.
9	40795	208972
7	40842	209092

Design Data
    Firing angles .. .. 0°, 90°, 180°, 270°, ±1°.
    Closed period .. .. 60° ± 3°.
    Open period .. .. 30° ± 3°.
    Contact breaker gap .. .. 0·015″.
    Rotation (viewed on rotor arm) .. .. .. Anti-clockwise.

Centrifugal Timing Advance Tests

9 : 1 Compression Ratio
1. Set at 0° at a speed of less than 100 r.p.m.
2. Run distributor up to 1,200 r.p.m.—advance to be 9°—11°.
3. Check at following decelerating speeds:—

Speed R.P.M.	Advance Degrees
800	9—11
600	5—7
350	0—2

No advance below 225 r.p.m.

7 : 1 Compression Ratio
1. Set at 0°.
2. Run distributor up to 2,500 r.p.m.—advance to be 9° maximum.
3. Check at following decelerating speeds:—

Speed R.P.M.	Advance Degrees
1900	7—9
1350	4—6
700	$\frac{1}{2}$—2$\frac{1}{2}$
400	0—1

No advance below 250 r.p.m.

VACUUM ADVANCE TESTS CHECK ON RISING

Inches H.G.	Advance Degrees	Inches H.G.	Advance Degrees
2	0	2	0
3	1	3	1$\frac{1}{2}$
4	1$\frac{3}{4}$	5	4$\frac{1}{2}$
5	2$\frac{1}{2}$	7	7$\frac{1}{4}$
Maximum 6	2$\frac{3}{4}$	Maximum 8	10

Windscreen Wiper Motor
    Lucas Model DR.3A .. .. Shunt wound single speed.
    Light running speed .. .. 44 to 48 cycles per minute of wiper blades.
    Stall current .. .. 13—15 amps.
    Light running currents .. .. 2·7—3·4 amps. (Measured less cable and rack).
    Resistance of field winding at 20°C. (68°F.) .. 8·0—9·5 ohms.
    Resistance of armature winding at 20°C. (68°F.) .. 0·29—0·352 ohms. (Measured between adjacent commutator segments).
    Brush tension .. .. 125—140 grammes.
    Maximum permissible force to move rack in protective tubing with wiper motor disconnected and wiper arms removed .. .. 6 lbs. (2·7 kgs.).

change in the running note, but there will be a definite increase in roughness when the other plugs are disconnected. Having thus located the defective cylinder, stop the engine and remove the cable from the plug terminal.

Restart the engine and hold the cable end about $\frac{3}{16}''$ from the cylinder head. If spark is strong and regular, the fault lies with the spark plug, and it should be removed, cleaned and adjusted, or a replacement fitted. If, however, there is no spark, or only weak irregular sparking, examine the cable from the plug to the distributor cover for deterioration of the insulation, renewing the cable if the rubber is cracked or perished. Clean and examine the distributor moulded cover for free movement of the carbon brush. If a replacement brush is necessary, it is important that the correct type is used. If tracking has occurred, indicated by a thin black line between two or more electrodes or between one of the electrodes and the body, a replacement distributor cover must be fitted.

Testing in Position to Locate Cause of Ignition Failure

Spring back the clips on the distributor head and remove the moulded cover. Lift off the rotor, carefully levering with a screwdriver if necessary.

Switch on the ignition and while the engine is slowly cranked, observe the reading on the car ammeter, or on an ammeter connected in series with the battery supply cable.

The reading should rise and fall with the closing and opening of the contacts if the low tension wiring is in order. When a reading is given which does not fluctuate, a short circuit, or contacts remaining closed, is indicated. No reading indicates an open circuit, or badly adjusted or dirty contacts.

Check the contacts for cleanliness and correct gap setting. Ensure that the moving arm moves freely on the pivot. If sluggish, remove the arm and polish the pivot post with a strip of fine emery cloth. Smear the post with non-creep oil or Mobilgrease No. 2, replace the arm. If the fault persists, proceed as follows:

Low Tension Circuit — Fault Location
1. **No reading in ammeter test**

Refer to wiring diagram and check circuit for broken or loose connections, including ignition switch. Check the ignition coil by substitution.

2. **Steady reading in ammeter test**

Refer to wiring diagram and check wiring for indications of a short circuit.

Check capacitor (either by substitution or on a suitable tester). Check ignition coil by substitution. Examine insulation of contact breaker.

3. **High Tension Circuit**

If the low tension circuit is in order, remove the high tension lead from the center terminal of the distributor cover. Switch on the ignition and turn the engine until the contacts close. Flick open the contact breaker lever while the high tension lead from the coil is held about $\frac{3}{16}''$ from the cylinder block. If the ignition equipment is in good order, a strong spark will be obtained. If no spark occurs, a fault in the circuit of the secondary winding of the coil is indicated and the coil must be replaced.

The high tension cables must be carefully examined and replaced if the rubber insulation is cracked or perished, using 7 mm. rubber covered ignition cable.

The cables from the distributor to the spark plugs must be connected in the correct firing order, i.e. 1.3.4.2.

4. **Dismantling**

When dismantling, carefully note the positions in which the various components are fitted, in order to ensure their correct replacement on reassembly. If the driving dog or gear is offset, or marked in some way for convenience in timing, note the relation between it and the rotor electrode and maintain this relation when re-assembling the distributor. The amount of

dismantling necessary will obviously depend on the repair required.

Spring back the securing clips and remove the moulded cover. Lift the rotor arm off the spindle, carefully levering with a screwdriver if it is tight.

Disconnect the vacuum unit link to the moving contact breaker plate and remove the two screws at the edge of the contact breaker base. The contact breaker assembly, complete with external terminal, can now be lifted off. Remove the circlip on the end of the micrometer timing screw and turn the micrometer nut until the screw and the vacuum unit assembly are freed. Take care not to lose the ratchet and coil type springs located under the micrometer nut.

The complete shaft assembly, with automatic timing control and cam foot can now be removed from the distributor body.

Contact Breaker

To dismantle the assembly further, remove the nut, insulating piece and connections from the pillar on which the contact breaker spring is anchored. Slide out the terminal moulding. Lift off the contact breaker lever and the insulating washers beneath it. Remove the screw(s) securing the fixed contact plate, together with the spring and plain steel washers and take off the plate. Withdraw the single screw securing the capacitor and, on earlier models, the contact breaker ground lead.

Dismantle the contact breaker base assembly by turning the base plate clockwise and pulling to release it from the moving contact breaker plate. On earlier models remove the circlip and star washer located under the base plate.

Shaft and Action Plate

To dismantle the assembly further, take out the screw inside the cam and remove the cam and cam foot. The weights, springs and toggles (when fitted) of the automatic timing control can now be lifted off the action plate. Note that a distance collar is fitted on the shaft underneath the action plate.

Bearing Replacement

The single long bearing bush used in this distributor can be pressed out of the shank by means of a shouldered mandrel.

If the bearing has been removed the distributor must be assembled with a new bush fitted. The bush should be prepared for fitting by allowing it to stand completely immersed in medium viscosity (S.A.E. 30-40) engine oil for at least 24 hours. In cases of extreme urgency, this period of soaking may be shortened by heating the oil to 100°C. for two hours, then

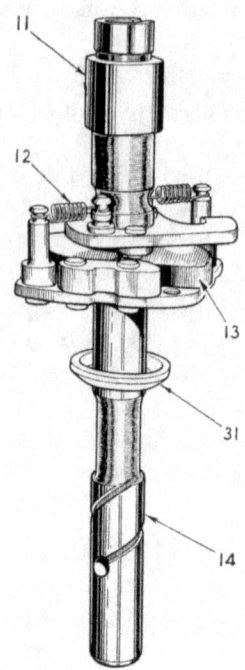

allowing to cool before removing the bush.

Press the bearing into the shank, using a shouldered, polished mandrel of the same diameter as the shaft.

Under no circumstances should the bush be overbored by reaming or any other means, since this will impair the porosity and thereby the effective lubricating quality of the bush.

Re-assembly

The following instructions assume that **complete** dismantling has been undertaken.

1. Place the distance collar over the shaft, smear the shaft with non-creep oil or clean engine oil, and fit it into its bearing.
2. Refit the vacuum unit into its housing and replace the springs, milled adjusting nut and securing circlip.
3. Re-assemble the centrifugal timing control. See the the springs are not stretched or damaged. Place the cam and cam foot assembly over the shaft, engaging the projections on the cam foot with the toggles, and fit the securing screw.
4. Before re-assembling the contact breaker base assembly, lightly smear the base plate with non-creep oil or Mobilgrease No. 2. On earlier distributors, the felt pad under the rotating contact breaker plate should be moistened with a few drops of thin machine oil.

Fit the rotating plate to the contact breaker base plate and secure with the star washer and circlip. Refit the contact breaker base into the distributor body. Engage the link from the vacuum unit with the bearing bush in the rotating plate and secure with the split pin. Insert the two base plates securing screws, one of which also secures one end of the ground lead.
5. Fit the capacitor into position, on earlier models the eyelet on the other end of the contact breaker ground lead is held under the capacitor fixing screw. Place the fixed contact plate in position and secure lightly with securing screw(s). One plain and one spring washer must be fitted under each of these screws.
6. Place the insulating washers on the contact breaker pivot post and on the pillar on which the end of the contact breaker spring locates. Refit the contact breaker lever and spring.
7. Slide the rubber terminal block into its slot.
8. Thread the low tension connector and capacitor eyelets on to the insulating piece, and place these on to the pillar which secures the end of the contact breaker spring. Refit the washer and securing nut.
9. Set the contact gap to 0.014" to 0.016" and tighten the securing screw(s) of the fixed contact plate.
10. Refit the rotor arm, locating the moulded projection in the rotor arm with the keyway in the shaft and pushing fully home.

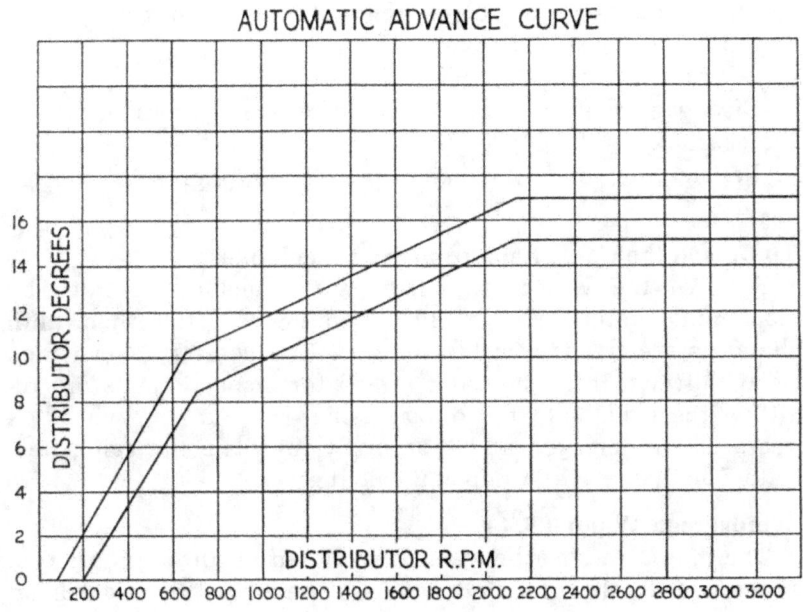

AUTOMATIC ADVANCE CURVE

Windscreen Wiper TR 2-3

Normally the windscreen wiper will not require any servicing apart from the occasional renewal of the rubber blades. In the event of irregular working, first check for loose connections, chafed insulation, discharged battery, etc., before removing the gearbox or commutator covers.

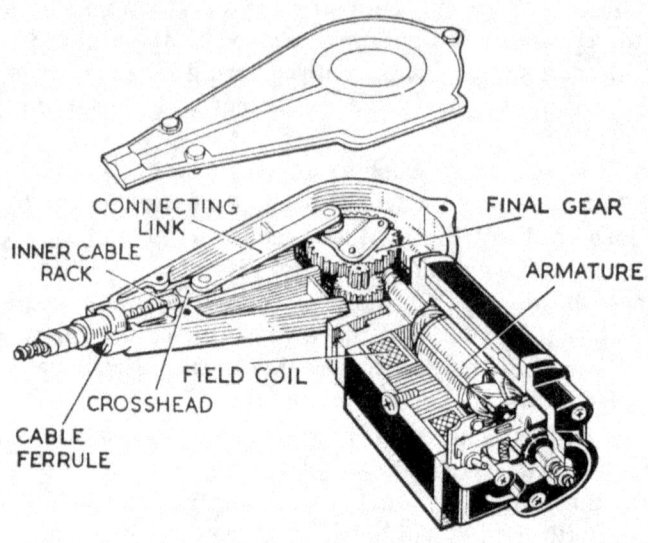

To Detach the Cable Rack from the Motor and Gearbox
1. Remove the gearbox cover.
2. Lift off the connecting link.
3. Disengage the outer casing, cable rack and crosshead from the gearbox.
4. Replace the gearbox cover to prevent the ingress of foreign matter.

To Detach the Cable Rack from the Wheelboxes
Remove the wiper arms from the wheelbox spindles by slackening the collet nuts and continuing to rotate them until the arms are freed from the spindles. The cable rack can then be withdrawn from the outer casing for inspection. Before refitting the cable into the outer casing, see that the wheelbox gears are undamaged and thoroughly lubricate the cable rack with Duckham's HBB or an equivalent grease.

Windscreen Wiper TR 4
The motor and gearbox unit is mounted on three pillars cast integral with the unit body and is located on the right-hand

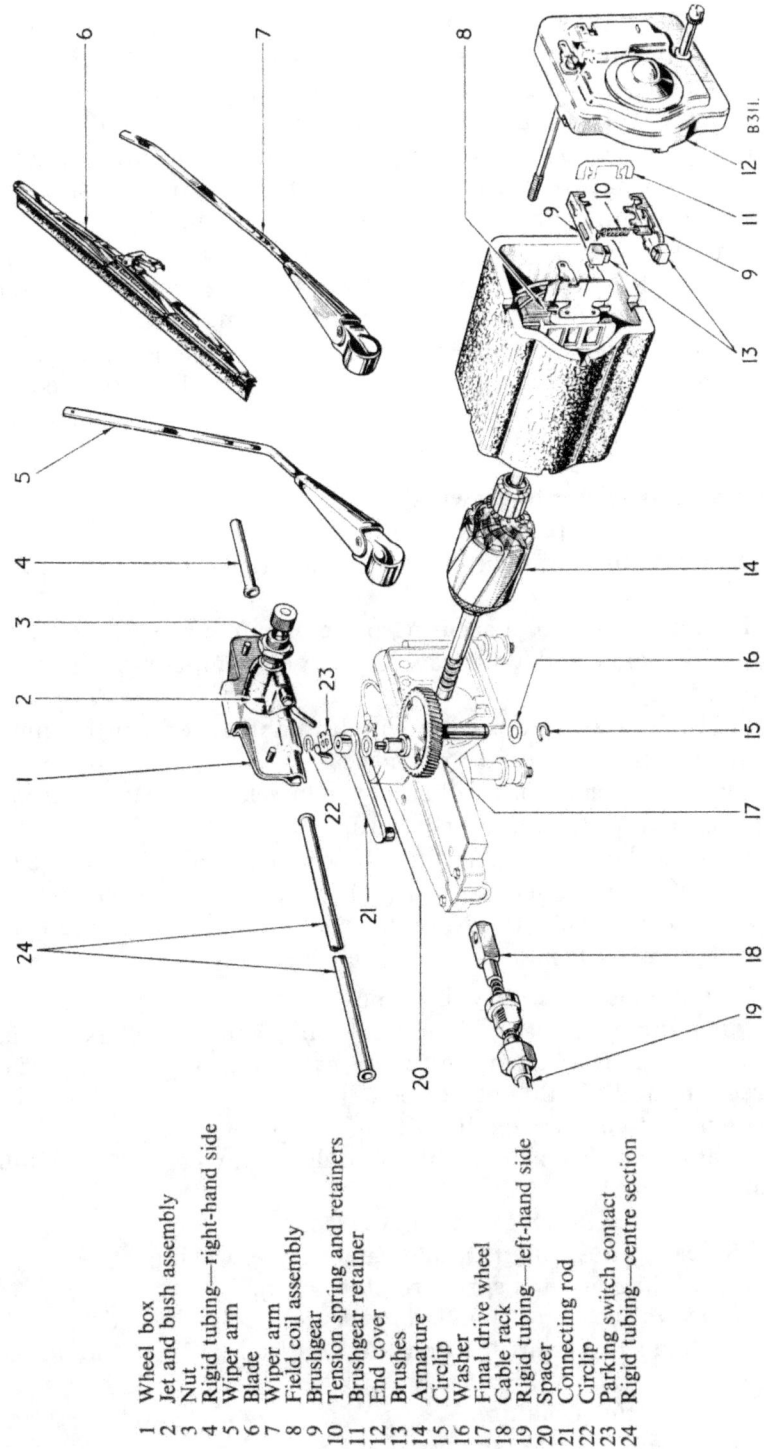

1. Wheel box
2. Jet and bush assembly
3. Nut
4. Rigid tubing—right-hand side
5. Wiper arm
6. Blade
7. Wiper arm
8. Field coil assembly
9. Brushgear
10. Tension spring and retainers
11. Brushgear retainer
12. End cover
13. Brushes
14. Armature
15. Circlip
16. Washer
17. Final drive wheel
18. Cable rack
19. Rigid tubing—left-hand side
20. Spacer
21. Connecting rod
22. Circlip
23. Parking switch contact
24. Rigid tubing—centre section

side of the dash panel in the engine compartment. Rotary motion of the motor armature is converted to a reciprocating movement by a single stage worm and nylon gear to which a connecting rod is attached. This actuates the cable rack which consists of a flexible core of steel wire wound with a wire helix to engage with a gear in each wheelbox for transmitting the reciprocating motion to the wiper arm spindles.

A parking switch is incorporated in the domed cover of the gearbox. On switching off at the wiper control switch, the motor continues to run until the moving contact of the parking switch reaches the insulated sector portion and so interrupts the ground return circuit and stops the motor. The domed cover is adjustable to give the correct park position of the wiper blades.

Dismantling (Refer to drawing)
1. Remove the wiper arms and blades.
2. Unscrew the large nut securing the outer tubing (19) to the gearbox.
3. Remove three bolts securing the motor mounting bracket to the dash panel and withdraw the motor complete with inner cable rack.
NOTE: The force required to withdraw the rack from the inner tubing should not exceed 6 pounds.
4. Mark the dome limit switch cover in relation to the gearbox lid, and remove the lid (four screws).
5. Release the circlip (22) and lift off limit switch wiper (23).
6. Lift off the connecting rod (21) from the final drive wheel (17) and cable rack (18). Note the spacer (20) between the connecting rod (21) from the final drive wheel (17).
7. The cable is now free to be removed.
8. Push the rack back into the tubing and wheelboxes and withdraw the rack from the tubing using a spring balance. The force required should not exceed 6 lbs.
9. Remove two bolts and lift off the end cover (12).
10. Check brush tension. This should be between 125 and 140 grams.
11. Lift out the brush gear retainers (11).
12. Release the spring (10) and remove the brush gear (9) complete with brushes and spring retainers (12).
13. Remove the body complete with field coil; the red cable is long enough to permit the body to be lifted clear of the armature.
14. Remove the armature.

If further dismantling is required:
1. Remove the circlip (15) with washers (16). Use a fine file and remove any burrs from around the circlip groove.
2. Remove the final drive wheel (17).
3. Clean the wheel and associated parts and examine for wear or damage.
4. Mark the yoke and field coil in relation to each other.
5. Remove two screws and withdraw the field coil pole piece and field coil.

Re-assembly

Re-assembly is a reversal of the dismantling procedure.

The adjusting screw in the side of the gearbox should be set and firmly locked to permit 0.008" to 0.012" end play of the armature.

Lubrication

The commutator and brush gear must be free of oil or grease. Apply engine oil to the bearings and bushes of the shafts of the final drive wheel and armature.

If the gearbox has been washed clean, use 25 to 35 cubic centimeters of Ragosine Listate grease to refill.

Wiper Wheel Boxes

To Remove

Remove wiper motor and working under the facia, remove:
1. Demister nozzles.
2. Cover plate, located beneath each wheel box (two screws in each).
3. Remove the nut (3) from each wheel box.
4. Withdraw the jet and bush assembly (2) for approximately 2" and disconnect the water pipes.
5. Pass a piece of thin wire around the right-hand rigid tubing (4) to retain it in position.
6. Remove the back plate of the wheel box (two screws) and move the rigid tubing outward.
7. Grip the back of the wheel box with long nose pliers and withdraw it through the aperture.

To Refit
1. Clean all trace of old sealing compound from the body jet and bush assembly using solvent or alcohol.
2. Push the wheel box back into position and re-connect the assembly with Seelastick.
3. Re-connect the water pipes and the securing nut (3).

4. Clean the contacting surfaces of the cover plate and the underside of the facia. Apply fresh sealing compound to the surfaces and refit the cover plates.
5. Refit the wiper motor.

Flasher Unit Direction-Indicator Model FL.5

Housed in a small cylindrical container, the FL.5 Flasher

Unit incorporates an actuating wire which heats and cools alternately to operate the main armature and associated pair of contacts in the flasher lamp supply circuit. Simultaneously a secondary armature operates the pilot contacts which cause a warning light to flash when the system is functioning correctly.

Defective Flasher Units cannot be dismantled for subsequent reassembly and must therefore be renewed. Handle the Flasher Unit with care, otherwise the delicate setting may be disturbed and the unit rendered unserviceable.

Trace the cause of faulty operation as follows:
1. Check the bulbs for broken filaments.
2. Check all flasher circuit connections.
3. Switch on the ignition and check the voltage at terminal "B" (12 volts).
4. Connect terminals "B" and "L" together and operate the direction-indicator switch. If the flasher lamps light, the Flasher Unit is defective. If the flasher lamps do not light, check the direction-indicator switch.

CLUTCH

General Data — Model A 6 G 9"

Hydraulically operated from twin bore master cylinder which incorporates the brake master cylinder.

Ball bearing release bearing.

Clearance between ball bearing release bearing and release levers — .0625".

Nine, 120-130 lb. cream thrust springs.

Single dry plate with six springs. All six springs cushion the driving torque, while three cushion the overrun.

Free travel on clutch pedal = .820".

Clearance between piston rod and master cylinder piston = .030".

End float in Slave Cylinder fork assembly = .079".

Height of release lever tip from face of flywheel = 1.895".

Long portion of hub towards Gearbox.

An improved clutch driven plate incorporating a Belleville washer friction center was fitted after Engine No. TS.7830E.

The new driven plate can be recognized by four small tongues (or tabs) protruding through the spring retaining plates adjacent to the longer side of the splined hub and by the color of the six cushioning springs, white and light green.

The clutch is hydraulically operated and has a twin bore master cylinder (see Brake Section for full explanation) attached to the bulkhead and a slave cylinder secured to the gearbox bell housing by a support plate, these are connected together by a length of Bundy-tubing and a flexible hose.

When pressure is applied to the foot pedal of the master cylinder it is transmitted through the pipe line to the slave cylinder. The piston of this cylinder operates a rod attached to the lever of the clutch operating shaft, a fork mounted on the latter engages in an annular grove of the release bearing mounting sleeve and moves the release bearing into engagement with the release levers.

Twin Bore Master Cylinder

The unit consists of an integrally cast body with a common fluid reservoir for the two identical bores, one connected to the brakes and the second to the clutch. Each bore accommodates a piston having a main cup loaded on to its head by a return spring. In order that the cup shall not tend to be drawn into the holes in the piston head, a piston washer is interposed between the main cup and the piston head.

Unlike the brake cylinder bore, with that for the clutch,

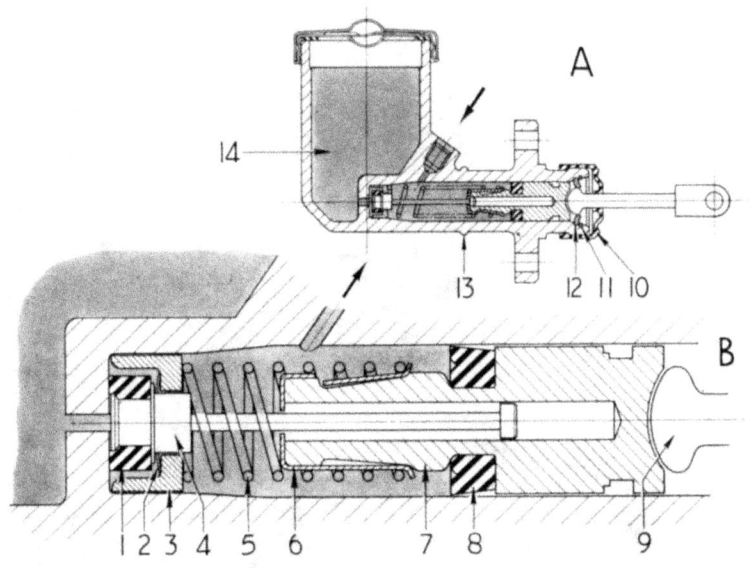

1	Valve seal	6	Spring retainer	11	Circlip
2	Spring (valve seal)	7	Plunger	12	Push rod stop
3	Distance piece	8	Plunger seal	13	Identification ring
4	Valve shank	9	Push rod	14	Fluid reservoir
5	Plunger return spring	10	Dust cover		

there is no check valve fitted at the delivery end of the return spring and this spring uses the body as an abutment.

The absence of this check valve precludes the risk of residual line pressure which would tend to keep the release bearing in contact with the release levers, causing excessive wear on the bearing and possible clutch slip.

Clutch Slave Cylinder

The slave cylinder is mounted on a support plate which is attached by the two lower bell housing bolts to the left-hand side of the engine unit. A steady bracket, attached at its forward end to the engine unit by one of the sump bolts, forms the slave cylinder and plate upper attachment by means of a jam nut and a nyloc nut. The lower attachment being effected by nut and bolt wih washer. A return spring is fitted to a plate on the clevis pin of the fork assembly to the lower portion of the support plate.

The inner assembly of the slave cylinder is made up of a coil spring, cup filler, rubber cup and a piston. The piston moves in the highly polished bore when hydraulic pressure is applied through the pipe line.

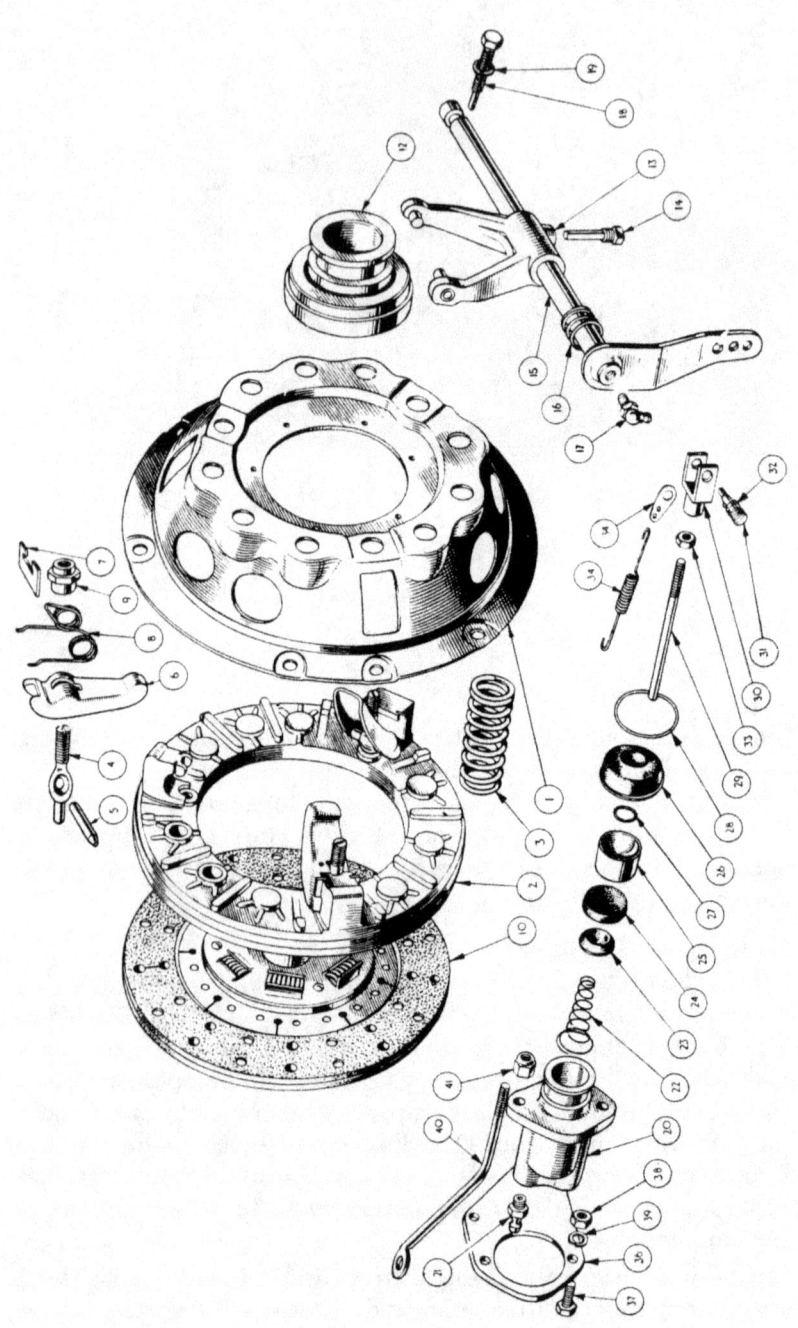

NOTATION FOR CLUTCH ASSEMBLY

1. Clutch Cover.
2. Pressure Plate.
3. Thrust Springs.
4. Release Lever Eye Bolt.
5. Release Lever Pin.
6. Release Lever.
7. Release Lever Strut.
8. Anti-Rattle Spring.
9. Adjusting Nut.
10. Driven Plate Assembly.
11. Driven Plate Facings.
12. Ball Bearing, Release Bearing and Pressed-in Sleeve.
13. Clutch Operating Fork.
14. Taper Pin.
15. Clutch Operating Shaft.
16. Spring on Operating Shaft.
17. Grease Nipple (one each end of shaft).
18. Shaft Locating Bolt.
19. Locking Washer for Locating Bolt.
20. Slave Cylinder Body.
21. Bleed Screw.
22. Cup Filler Spring.
23. Cup Filler.
24. Rubber Cup.
25. Piston.
26. Rubber Boot.
27. Small Circlip for Rubber Boot.
28. Large Circlip for Rubber Boot.
29. Fork Assembly Rod.
30. Fork End.
31. Clevis Pin.
32. Clevis Pin Spring.
33. Fork End Locking Nut.
34. Clutch Shaft Return Spring.
35. Anchor Plate for Return Spring.
36. Slave Cylinder Support Bracket.
37. Lower Attachment Bolt.
38. Nut.
39. Lock Washer.
40. Slave Cylinder Stay.
41. Nyloc Nut.

The Clutch Operating Shaft

This shaft is carried in the bell housing in two "Oilite" bushes, it is positioned by a fixing screw, the shank of which locates the reduced diameter portion of the shaft. A short coil spring is placed between the shaft lever and the bell housing which steadies the shaft and prevents rattle.

Mounted on the shaft is the release bearing operating fork, being secured thereto by a tapered pin, the shank of which passes into the shaft, while its head is locked to the fork by a short length of wire.

The shaft is lubricated by grease nipples and over-lubrication must be avoided.

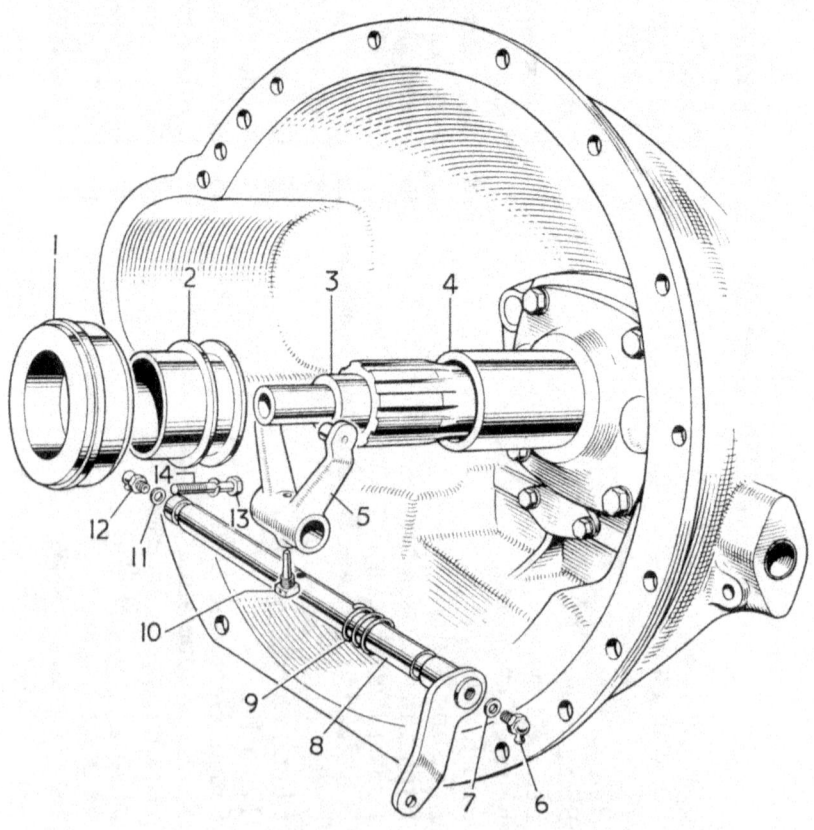

1	Release bearing	8	Cross-shaft
2	Bearing sleeve	9	Anti-rattle spring
3	Input shaft	10	Tapered locking bolt
4	Front cover	11	Fibre washer
5	Fork	12	Grease nipple
6	Grease nipple	13	Locating bolt
7	Fibre washer	14	Lockwasher

The Release Bearing

This is a ball bearing housed in a cover. A sleeve pressed into the inner race of this bearing, is grooved externally to accomodate the pins of the clutch operating fork mounted on its shaft in the bell housing of the gearbox. The sleeve, pressed into the bearing, moves on an extension of the front gearbox cover which ensures its correct angular engagement with the three release levers.

The ball bearing is grease packed during its manufacture and does not require re-greasing.

Cover Assembly

This assembly consists of a steel pressing to which the component parts are assembled, being attached with the Driven Plate Assembly to the flywheel.

The cover assembly contains a cast iron pressure plate loaded by nine cream thrust springs (120-130 lbs.). Mounted on the pressure plate are three release levers which pivot on floating pins retained by eye bolts. Adjusting nuts are screwed on the eye bolts, which pass through the cover pressing these nuts being secured by staking.

Driven Plate Assembly

This is the Borglite spring type, having a splined hub and a disc adapter fitted with nine cushioned segments which carry two facings attached by rivets.

The hub flange and disc adapter are slotted to carry six springs positioned by a retaining plate which is secured to the disc adapter by stop pins. This flange is drilled to carry three steel balls positioned by the two friction plates located by tabs in holes in the hub flange.

A spacer is fitted between the disc adapter and one friction plate and another spacer is fitted between the retaining plate and the second friction plate.

Maintenance

It is essential that the master cylinder is at least half full of Lockheed Brake Fluid at all times, and should be checked every 5,000 miles.

Only Lockheed Brake Fluid should be used in this system. This fluid has been selected as it has no injurious effects on the rubber seals and flexible hoses used.

Before removing the filler cap, wipe the top of the master cylinder and the cap clean with a non-fluffy material. Cleanliness is particularly important and every precaution should be taken to ensure no dirt or foreign matter is allowed to enter the system. Failure to observe this point may lead to blockages or damage to the highly polished bores and pistons, resulting in expensive replacements.

Ensure also that the breather hole in the filler cap is not restricted and that the sealing washer and pipe lines are in good order.

Bleeding the Hydraulic System

Bleeding is only necessary when a portion of the system has been disconnected or if the level of the fluid has been allowed to fall so low that air has been allowed to enter the system. If bleeding is carried out for the latter reason the brake system will need to be bled also, as they share the same reservoir.

1. Fill the reservoir with Lockheed Brake Fluid and keep at least half full throughout the operation. Failure to observe this point may lead to air being drawn into the system and the operation of bleeding will have to be repeated.
2. Attach a length of rubber piping to the bleed screw and allow the free end to be submerged in a little Lockheed Brake Fluid contained in a clean glass jar, open the bleed port by giving the screw one complete turn.
3. Depress the clutch pedal with a slow full stroke and before the pedal reaches the end of its travel the bleed screw is tightened sufficiently to seat it.
4. Repeat this operation until air bubbles cease to appear from the end of the tube.
5. Ensure that there is sufficient fluid in the reservoir, at least half full, and replace cap first, ensuring that its seal is in good order and its vent is unobstructed.

Greasing of the Clutch Operating Shaft

Hand grease gun lubrication should be used when greasing this shaft. Two strokes of the gun to each nipple after 5,000 miles of running will provide adequate lubrication.

Over-lubrication, from generous use of pressure lubricating may lead to grease finding its way on to the clutch facing.

Adjusting the Clutch

The adjustment connection between pedal and master cylinder is set on initial assembly and should not need re-adjustment.

During complete overhauls or the repair of accidental damage the master cylinder may have to be disturbed. Its replacement is dealt with in the Brake Section and the adjustment is described in this section below.

The clutch pedal will provide no sensitive indication of loss of release bearing clearance (1/16″) consequent upon wear of the facings. Adjustment at the slave cylinder fork assembly must therefore be checked periodically, at whatever intervals the operating conditions may dictate. The adjusting sequence is described below.

The adjustment is said to be correct when there is .079″ end float in the slave cylinder fork assembly.

Adjusting the Master Cylinder

It is important to provide .030″ free travel of the push rod before it reaches the piston. This clearance is necessary to ensure that the piston will return to its stop in its cylinder and thus prevent the possibility of the lip of the main cup covering the by-pass port. If such a condition were to exist the excess fluid drawn into the cylinder during the return stroke of the piston will find no outlet and pressure will build up in the system causing the clutch to slip.

1. Loosen the jam nut of the clutch pedal stop at the forward end of the master cylinder support bracket.
2. Turn the adjuster screw inwards and testing the push rod eliminate all end float. Tighten jam nut finger tight, holding adjuster screw.
3. Unscrew the adjuster together with the jam nut until a .030″ feeler can be placed in between the jam nut and the master cylinder bracket.
4. Holding adjuster screw, lock jam nut to the bracket.

Adjusting the Slave Cylinder

1. Unlock the jam nut on the slave cylinder fork assembly.
2. Turn the rod until ALL end float is just eliminated.

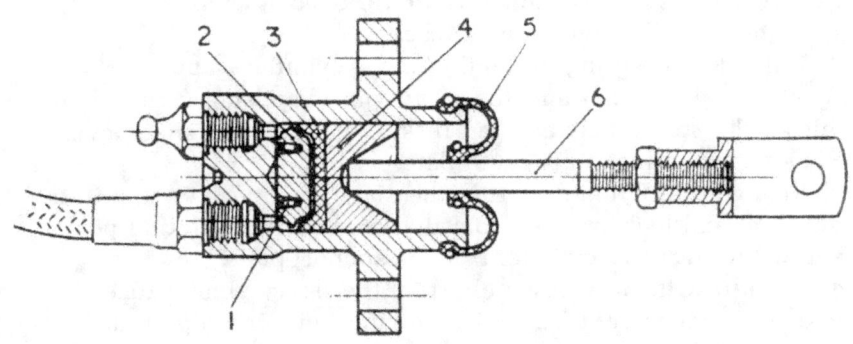

3. Hold the push rod and turn the jam nut until a .079" feeler gauge will pass in between the nut and the fork end.

4. Screw the rod together with the jam nut to the fork and lock. Check by moving the fork assembly and readjust if necessary.

To Remove the Flexible Hose
1. Drain the hydraulic system.
2. Holding the hexagon of the flexible hose, withdraw the Bundy tubing by first removing the union nut.
3. Still holding the hexagon of the flexible hose, remove the locking nut and shake proof washer.
4. Withdraw the flexible hose from its bracket and disconnect it from the slave cylinder.

Ensure that its whole length is turned while unscrewing as any twist will impair the life of the hose.

To Fit the Flexible Hose
Ensure that all connections are perfectly clean. Dirt being allowed to enter the system may cause blockages, or damage to the highly polished bores and pistons resulting in expensive replacements.
1. Utilizing a new copper gasket, attach and secure the flexible hose to the lower port of the slave cylinder.
2. Feed the hose into the bracket welded on the left hand chassis member. Gripping the hexagon of the hose with a spanner set the hose in such a manner that it will have a free run, away from all obstructions and rubbing contacts.
3. Still holding the hexagon of the hose secure it to the chassis bracket with the shakeproof washer and lock-nut.
4. Insert the Bundy tubing into its housing and check that it is correctly seated before securing with the union nut.
5. Bleed the clutch system as described.

Removal of the Slave Cylinder (with fork-rod assembly)
1. Remove the flexible hose as described.
2. Unhook the spring from the slave cylinder support plate. Remove the split pin and the clevis pin exercising care not to mislay the spring between the fork and the clutch shaft lever. Remove the spring attachment plate.
3. Remove the nyloc nut from the slave cylinder stay and the nut, bolt and lock washer from the lower cylinder fixing point and withdraw slave cylinder from its support plate.
4. Withdraw the fork assembly from the slave cylinder together with the rubber boot by first removing the wire clip from the exterior of the boot and slave cylinder.

To Replace Slave Cylinder
1. Seat the slave cylinder in the support bracket with the bleed screw uppermost.
2. Secure at the uppermost point by a nyloc nut on the threaded end of the stay and at the lowermost point with nut, bolt and lock washer.
3. Fit the small coil spring and spring anchor plate either side of the clutch operating lever, followed by the fork assembly. Secure with the clevis pin and lock with split pin.
4. Attach the return spring to the spring anchor plate of the fork end assembly and anchor the other end to the slave cylinder support bracket.
5. Fit the flexible hose as described.
6. Adjust the clutch at the fork end assembly as described.

Dismantling the Slave Cylinder
1. Remove the slave cylinder assembly from its mounting. Remove bleeder screw.
2. Remove the wire circlip from the rubber boot and ease the rubber boot from the alloy body.
3. The rubber boot can be removed from the fork end assembly by first removing the wire circlip. The assembly can now be drawn through the rubber.
4. By applying low air pressure through one of the tapped holes the piston can be removed from the cylinder bore followed by the rubber cup, the cup filler and spring.
5. The components should be washed in Lockheed Brake Fluid and any component that shows excess wear should be replaced. Particular attention must be paid to the cylinder bore and piston.

Assembly of the Slave Cylinder
1. Give the component parts a liberal coating of Lockheed Brake Fluid and also the bore of the cylinder.
2. Assemble the spring to the cup filler and insert both, spring first, into the bore of the cylinder.
3. Fit the rubber cup, lip first, into the bore, exercising great care that the edges do not curl up inside the bore. After assembly it will be noticed that the flat surface of the rubber cup is uppermost and will accommodate the piston.
4. Slide the piston into the cylinder, flat side first, the piston may be assisted in the travel by the rod of the fork end assembly.
5. Insert the push rod of the fork assembly into the rubber in such a manner that the push rod end is nearer to the lips of

the boot. Secure the rubber boot to the rod with a small circlip.
6. Fit the fork end assembly and rubber boot to the slave cylinder body and secure with the large wire circlip.
7. Fit the bleed screw to one of the ports in the slave cylinder body.

To Remove Release Bearing and Clutch Operating Shaft

1. Remove the gearbox from the car as described in the Gearbox Section.
2. Break and remove the wire locking the taper pin to the clutch bearing operating fork, remove taper pin.
3. Withdraw the release bearing and sleeve from the front end cover of the gearbox.
4. Remove grease nipple and fibre washer from right hand end of clutch operating shaft.
5. Withdraw the shaft locating bolt and lock washer from right hand side of bell housing.
6. Holding the clutch operating fork withdraw the shaft from the left.
7. Remove spring and grease nipple with fibre washer from lever end of shaft.

NOTE: To effect the removal of the shaft from cars prior to Commission No. TS. 411, there is no necessity to remove the grease nipple and the shaft locating bolt is situated on the left hand side of the bell housing.

To Replace Clutch Operating Shaft and Release Bearing

The replacement of the clutch operating shaft and release bearing is the reversal of the removal. It will be found, however, that light pressure will be necessary to compress the spring on the operating shaft to insert and tighten the shaft locating bolt.

When fitting the ball bearing release bearing, locate the pegs of the operating fork in the groove of the bearing. Secure the operating fork to the shaft with the taper pin and lock the head with wire.

Removal of the Clutch from Flywheel with Gearbox Removed

1. Slacken the six holding bolts, in the outer rim of the cover pressing, a turn at a time by diagonal selection until the thrust spring pressure is relieved.
2. Remove the six bolts and lift away the cover assembly and driven plate assembly from the two locating dowels.
3. Inspect the two dowels in the flywheel for looseness and burrs and replace if necessary.

Replacement of Clutch to Flywheel

1. Place the driven plate assembly on the flywheel with the larger portion of the splined hub towards the gearbox. Centralize this plate with Churchill Tool No. 20S. 72 or the splined portion of a constant pinion shaft.
2. Fit the cover assembly over the driven plate and locate it on the two dowels in the face of the flywheel.
3. Secure the cover assembly to the flywheel with six bolts and lock washers, tighten them a turn at a time by diagonal selection to the correct tightening torque, 20 lbs. ft.
4. Remove the driven plate centralizer only when the cover assembly is attached to the flywheel.

It is essential that the driven plate assembly is central at all times during the assembly of the cover to flywheel. Failure to observe this point may lead to difficulty in attaching the gearbox, for the constant pinion shaft may not have a free passage to the pilot bearing bush **in the rear end** of the crankshaft.

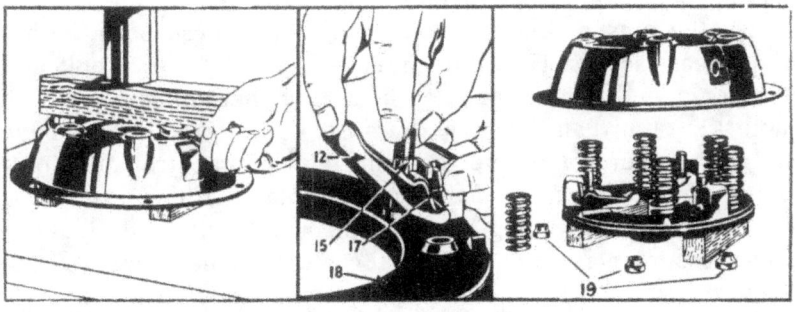

Dismantling the Cover Assembly Without a Churchill Clutch Fixture

In the event of a Churchill Fixture not being available the following method is suggested.

This method utilizes a hydraulic press and suitable size wooden blocks; two blocks on which to stand the pressure plate and allow the cover pressing downward movement. Before dismantling the cover assembly suitably mark the following parts so that they can be re-assembled in the same relative positions to each other and so preserve the balance of the cover assembly:—

a. Cover pressing.
b. Lugs on the pressure plate.
c. Release levers.

1. Lay the assembly on the bed of the press with the pressure plate resting on the two wooden blocks so arranged that the cover pressing is free to move downwards when pressure is applied.
2. Lay another wooden block on top of the cover pressing in such a manner that it will contact the ram of the press and will also move downward between the release levers.
3. Lower the ram of the press sufficiently to bring the cover pressing in contact with the bed of the press. Secure the ram and remove the three adjusting nuts, considerable torque will be necessary as the staking of these nuts has to be overcome.
4. Release the pressure of the press slowly to prevent the thrust springs from flying out.
5. Remove the cover pressing and collect the component parts.

To Assemble Cover Assembly Without Churchill Fixture

Before assembly note the markings on the various components and return them to their original positions. Grease the components slightly at their contact faces with Lockheed Expander Lubricant or equivalent.
1. Fit the pins to the eye bolts and locate these parts within the release levers. Hold the threaded end of the eye bolt and the inner end of the lever as close together as possible and, with the other hand, engage the strut within the slots in a lug on the pressure plate and the other end of the strut push outwards to the periphery of the pressure plate. Offer up the lever assembly, first engaging the eye bolt shank within the hole in the pressure plate, then locate the strut in the groove of the release lever. Fit the remaining levers in a similar manner.
2. Place the pressure plate on the wooden blocks on the base of the press and position the thrust springs on the bosses on the pressure plate.
3. Place the cover pressing, with the anti-rattle springs fitted, over the pressure plate ensuring that the lugs protrude through the cover slots.
4. Arrange a wooden block across the cover and apply pressure to compress the whole assembly. Screw the adjusting nuts on to the eye bolts sufficiently so that pressure can be released.

Inspection of Cover Assembly

Before re-assembling the clutch unit the parts should be cleaned and inspected. Any components which show considerable wear on its working surface should be replaced. The thrust springs and anti-rattle springs should be checked against new ones of the correct strength, and any found to be obviously weak should be replaced. The anti-rattle springs should be assembled to the cover pressing. The working face of the cast iron pressure plate should also be inspected and if the ground face is deeply scored or grooved it should be either reground or replaced by a new plate.

If any parts are changed or a new pressure plate fitted, it is essential it should be statically balanced.

Adjusting the Release Levers

In service, the original adjustments made by the clutch manu-

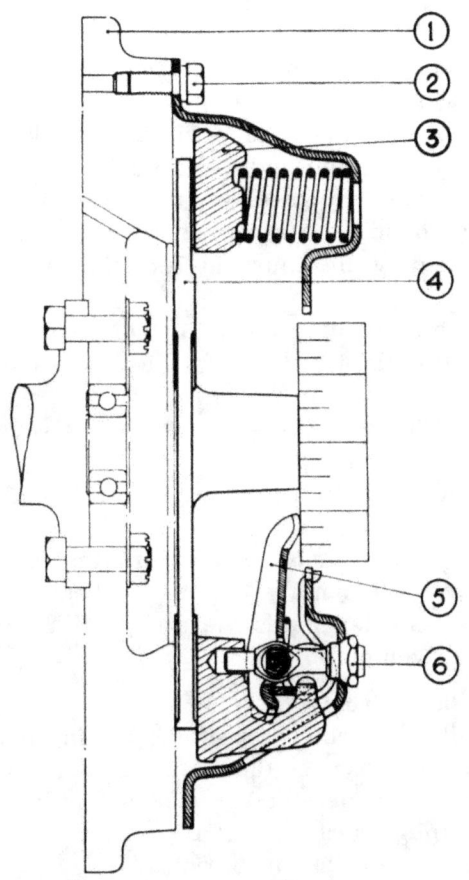

1 Flywheel.
2 Cover assembly attachment bolts.
3 Pressure plate.
4 Borg and Beck gauge plate No. **CG 192.**
5 Release lever.
6 Adjusting nut.

facturer, will require no attention and re-adjustment is only necessary if the cover assembly has been dismantled.

There are three methods by which the release levers may be adjusted.
1. Churchill No. 99A Clutch Fixture.
2. Borg and Beck No. CG 192 gauge plate.
3. In the absence of the above the Driven Plate Assembly may be used.

Utilizing the Driven Plate Assembly

This method of setting the levers is not highly accurate and should only be used when the Churchill Fixture or the Borg and Beck Gauge Plate are not available.

The drawback to this method is that although the driven plate is produced to close limits, it is difficult to ensure absolute parallelism. Although the error in the plate is small it becomes magnified at the lever tip due to lever ratio.
1. Utilizing the actual flywheel, lay the driven plate in position and clamp the cover plate assembly over it. The driven plate can be centralized by the Churchill Tool No. 20S. 72 (or similar tool).
2. By turning the adjusting nut adjust the height of the lever tips to 1.895" from the flywheeel face utilizing a suitable depth gauge.
3. Operate the Clutch by using a small press several times in order to settle the mechanism.
4. Check the height of the release lever tips and re-adjust if necessary.
5. Slacken the cover assembly and turn the drive plate 90°. Reclamp the cover assembly to the flywheel and check the height of the release lever tips as a safeguard against any lack of truth in the driven plate.

Condition of Clutch Facings

The possibility of further use of the driving plate assembly is sometimes raised, because the clutch facings have a polished appearance after considerable service. It is perhaps natural to assume that a rough surface will give a higher friction value against slipping, but this is not correct.

Since the introduction of non-metallic faces of the moulded asbestos type, in service, a polished surface is a common experience, but it must not be confused with a glazed surface which is sometimes encountered due to conditions discussed hereafter.

The ideal smooth polished condition will provide a normal

contact, but a glazed surface may be due to a film or a condition introduced, which entirely alters the frictional value of the facings. These two conditions might be simply illustrated by the comparison between a polished wood and a varnished surface. In the former the contact is still made with the original material, whereas in the latter instance, a film of dried varnish is interposed between the contact surfaces.

The following notes give useful information on this subject:

After the clutch has been in use for some little time, under perfect conditions, with the clutch facings working on a true and polished material, without the presence of oil, and with only that amount of slip which the clutch provides for under normal condition, then the surface of the facings assumes a high polish, through which the grain of the material can be clearly seen. This polished facing is of a mid-brown color and is then in perfect condition, the co-efficiency of friction and the capacity for transmitting power is up to a very high standard.

NOTE: The appearance of Wound or Woven type facings is slightly different but similar in character.

Should oil in small quantities gain access to the clutch in such a manner as to come in contact with the clutch facings it will burn off, due to the heat generated by slip which occurs during normal starting conditions. The burning off of the small amount of lubricant, has the effect of gradually darkening the clutch facings, but providing the polish on the facing remains such that the grain of the material can be clearly distinguished, it has very little effect on clutch performance.

Should increased quantities of oil or grease attain access to the facings, one or two conditions or a combination of the two, may arise, depending on the nature of the oil, etc.

a. The oil may burn off and leave on the surface facings a carbon deposit which assumes a high glaze and causes slip. This is a very definite, though very thin deposit, and in general it hides the grain of the material.

b. The oil may partially burn and leave a resinous deposit on the facings, which frequently produce a fierce clutch and may also cause a spinning clutch due to a tendency of the facings to adhere to the flywheel or pressure plate face.

There may be a combination of 1 and 2 conditions, which is likely to produce a judder during clutch re-engagement.

Still greater quantities of oil produce a black soaked appearance of the facings, and the effect may be slip, fierceness or **judder** in engagement etc., according to the conditions. If these conditions are experienced, the clutch driven plate assembly should be replaced by one fitted with new facings, the cause of the presence of oil removed and the clutch cover housing assembly and flywheel thoroughly cleaned.

Reconditioning of Driven Plate Assembly

While a much more satisfactory result is obtained by the complete replacement of this assembly, circumstances may force the renewal of the clutch facings. These notes will prove useful:

a. Ensure that the metal components of the assembly are in good condition and pay particular attention to the following:—
1. Uneven spline wear.
2. Cracked segments.
3. Springs are not broken.
4. Test the drive and over run.

b. Drill out the rivets securing the facings to the plates.

c. Rivet the new facings onto the plate assembly. It is suggested than an old flywheel is used as an anvil and the rivets supported by short pieces of $\frac{3}{16}$" dia. mild steel rod.

d. Mount the driven plate assembly on a mandrel between the centers of a lathe and check for run out with a dial test indicator set as near to the edge of the assembly as possible.

Where the run-out exceeds .015" locate the high spot and true the assembly by prying over in the requisite direction. Care must be taken not to damage the facings.

NOTE: When offering up the driven plate assembly to the flywheel, the LONGER side of the splined hub must be nearer to the gearbox.

CLUTCH

SERVICE DIAGNOSIS.

SYMPTOM	CAUSE	REMEDY
1. Drag or Spin.	(a) Oil or grease on the driven plate facings.	Fit new facings.
	(b) Misalignment between the engine and gearbox shaft.	Check over and correct the alignment.
	(c) Improper pedal adjustment not allowing full movement to release bearing.	Correct pedal adjustment.
	(d) Warped or damaged pressure plate or clutch cover.	Renew defective part.
	(e) Driven plate hub binding on splined shaft.	Clean up splines and lubricate with small quantity of high melting point grease such as Duckham's Keenol.
	(f) Pilot or operating shaft bearings binding.	Renew or lubricate bearings.
	(g) Distorted driven plate due to the weight of the gearbox being allowed to hang in clutch plate during erection.	Fit new driven plate assy. using a jack to take the overhanging weight of the gearbox.
	(h) Broken facings of driven plate.	Fit new facings.
	(j) Dirt or foreign matter in the clutch.	Dismantle clutch from flywheel and clean the unit, see that all working parts are free. **Caution.** Never use petrol or paraffin for cleaning out clutch.
	(k) Air in hydraulic line or insufficient fluid.	Bleed or replenish.
2. Fierceness or Snatch.	(a) Oil or grease on driven plate facings.	Fit new facings and ensure isolation of clutch from possible ingress of oil or grease.
	(b) Misalignment.	Check over and correct the alignment.
	(c) Binding of clutch pedal mechanisms.	Free and lubricate journals.
	(d) Worn out driven plate facings.	New facings required.
3. Slip.	(a) Oil or grease on the driven plate facings.	Fit new facings and eliminate cause of foreign presence.
	(b) Improper pedal adjustment indicated by lack of the requisite .820″ free or unloaded foot pedal movement—.030″ at master cylinder, .079″ at slave cylinder.	Correct pedal adjustment and/or clearances.
4. Judder.	(a) Oil, grease or foreign matter on the driven plate facings.	Fit new facings and eliminate cause of foreign presence.
	(b) Misalignment.	Check over and correct alignment.

CLUTCH

SYMPTOM	CAUSE	REMEDY
	(c) Pressure plate out of parallel with flywheel face in excess of of permissible tolerance.	Re-adjust levers in plane and, if necessary, fit new eyebolts.
	(d) Contact area of friction facings not evenly distributed. Note that friction facing surface will not show 100% contact until the clutch has been in use for some time, but the contact area actually showing should be evenly distributed round the friction facings.	This may be due to distortion, if so fit new driven plate assembly.
	(e) Bent splined shaft or buckled driven plate.	Fit new shaft or driven plate assembly.
	(f) Unstable or ineffective rubber engine mountings.	Replace and ensure elimination of endwise movement of power unit.
5. Rattle.	(a) Damaged driven plate, *i.e.*, broken springs, etc. (b) Worn parts in release mechanism. (c) Excessive back lash in transmission. (d) Wear in transmission bearings. (e) Bent or worn splined shaft. (f) Ball release bearing loose on operating sleeve.	Fit new parts as necessary.
6. Tick or Knock.	(a) Hub splines badly worn due to misalignment.	Check and correct alignment, then fit new driven plate.
	(b) Worn pilot bearing.	Pilot bearing should be renewed.
7. Fracture of Driven Plate.	(a) Misalignment distorts the plate and causes it to break or tear round the hub or at segment necks in the case of Borglite type.	Check and correct alignment and introduce new driven plate.
	(b) If the gearbox during assembly be allowed to hang with the shaft in the hub, the driven plate may be distorted, leading to drag, metal fatigue and breakage.	Fit new driven plate assembly and ensure satisfactory re-assembly.
8. Abnormal Facing Wear.	Usually produced by overloading and by the excessive slip starting associated with overloading.	In the hands of the operator.

THE GEARBOX

The gearbox is a four-speed and reverse type with remote gear lever. Top, third and second gears are synchronized. Reverse is a compound gear which is disengaged when in neutral or any forward gear. The remote control shift lever is carried in a tower formed in the rear end of the top cover and extends approximately half the length of the rear extension. Gear selection is made in the conventional H pattern. An overdrive unit is fitted in production on order. Lubricant capacity is: 1.5 pints or 3 pints with overdrive.

To Remove Gearbox Leaving Engine In Position
1. Disconnect battery lead.
2. Remove both seats by withdrawing sixteen nuts, eight from beneath each seat cushion.
3. Remove gear lever and grommet, after slackening the locknut and unscrew gear lever from its ball end.
4. Withdraw floor center section and carpet after the withdrawal of sixteen setscrews located round the edges of the pressing. Similarly remove the "U" plate (R.H. side) secured with two P.K. screws.
5. Disconnect the propeller shaft at the front end by withdrawing the four bolts and nyloc nuts.
6. Disconnect speedometer cable from gearbox by unscrewing the knurled collar from its adaptor.
7. Remove clutch slave cylinder with its mounting bracket after withdrawing two nuts and bolts from the bell housing and one sump bolt securing the steady rod. The slave cylinder push rod can be removed from the clutch operating shaft after the withdrawal of the split pinned clevis pin from the operating fork to which is attached the clutch return spring.
8. Disconnect the two wires from their terminals on the solenoid if an Overdrive is fitted.
9. Remove gearbox mounting after the withdrawal of two nuts by jacking up the unit, using a block of wood between jack and sump to avoid damage.
10. Remove starter motor bolts and slide starter motor forwards clear of the bell housing.
11. Remove nuts and bolts from bell housing and withdraw gearbox.

To Replace Gearbox
Carry out the above procedure in reverse, but it is advisable before doing so to check the **alignment** of the clutch unit with

GEARBOX

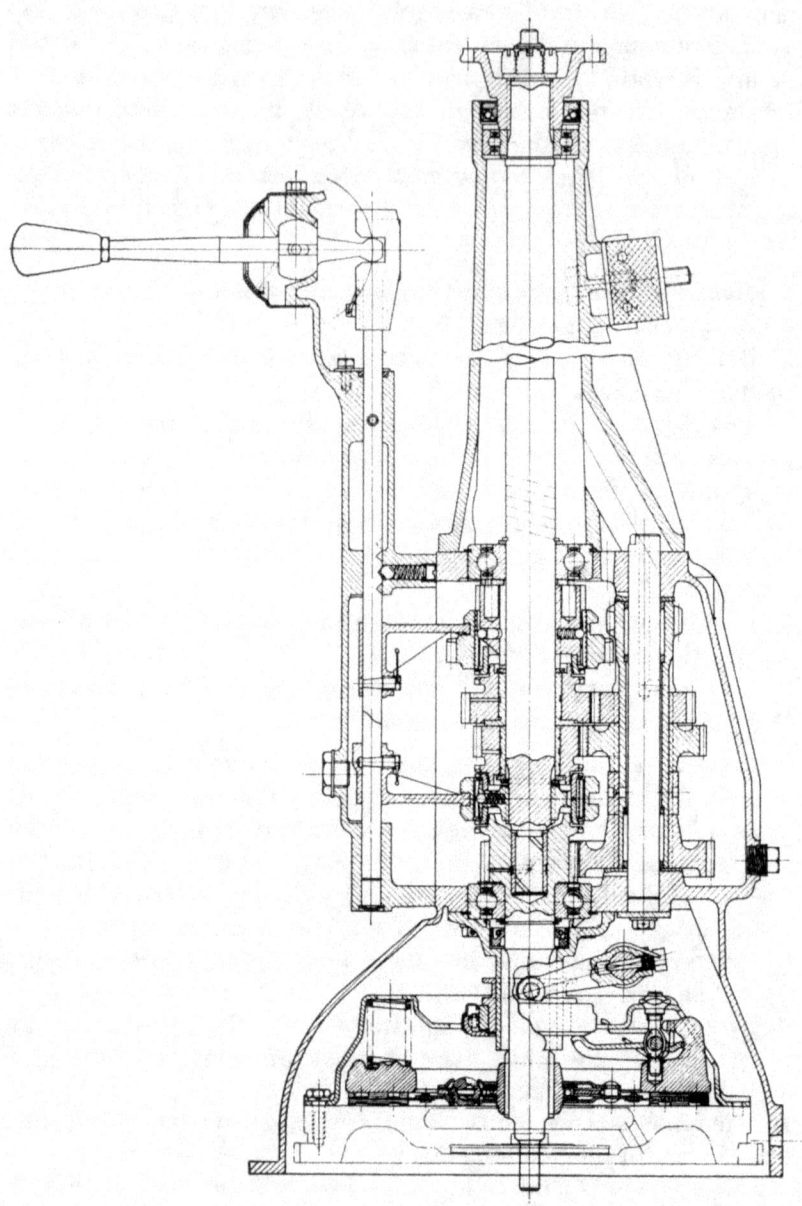

a suitable mandrel. If this is found to be incorrect slacken the clutch cover assembly bolts until the mandrel slides in freely, then re-tighten the bolts.

To Dismantle
1. Remove eight setscrews from the top cover assembly and withdraw complete with selector mechanism.
2. Remove top cover paper joint.
3. Break locking wire on clutch operating fork positioning setscrew and withdraw.
4. Remove clutch operating shaft positioning bolt and grease nipple with fibre washer from R.H. of clutch shaft. Then withdraw operating shaft, coil spring, operating fork, clutch throwout bearing and sleeve.
5. Detach the speedometer drive after removal of the special securing setscrew.
6. Withdraw propeller shaft coupling, having first removed split pin, nut and plain washer.
7. Remove gearbox extension and paper joint after the withdrawal of six securing setscrews and spring washers. The oil seal and ball race will remain in position in the housing but can easily be tapped out with a suitable drift.
8. Withdraw the countershaft locating setscrew.
9. After removal of the countershaft front end cover plate which is secured by two wired setscrews, plain washers and lead linger drive out the countershaft using a suitable tube to retain the 48 needle rollers in position maintaining contact throughout between the tube and countershaft.
10. Remove the gearbox front end cover and paper joint after cutting the wire in the setscrew heads and withdrawing them complete with their plain washers and lead linger.
11. Extract the constant pinion shaft assembly and remove the mainshaft spigot bush located in the pinion itself. The further dismantling of this assembly necessitates the removal of the small circlip and thrustwasher which fit against the inner ring of the ball race and calls for an extractor tool or press. After extraction of ball race the oil thrower may be withdrawn, but owing to probable damage to this thrower during the dismantling operation a new one may be required when re-assembling the unit.
12. Tap the mainshaft towards the rear with a soft metal drift sufficiently to clear the bearing from the casing. Next tilt the shaft sufficiently to enable the third and top synchro unit to be withdrawn. Note the position of the short boss on the synchro

GEARBOX

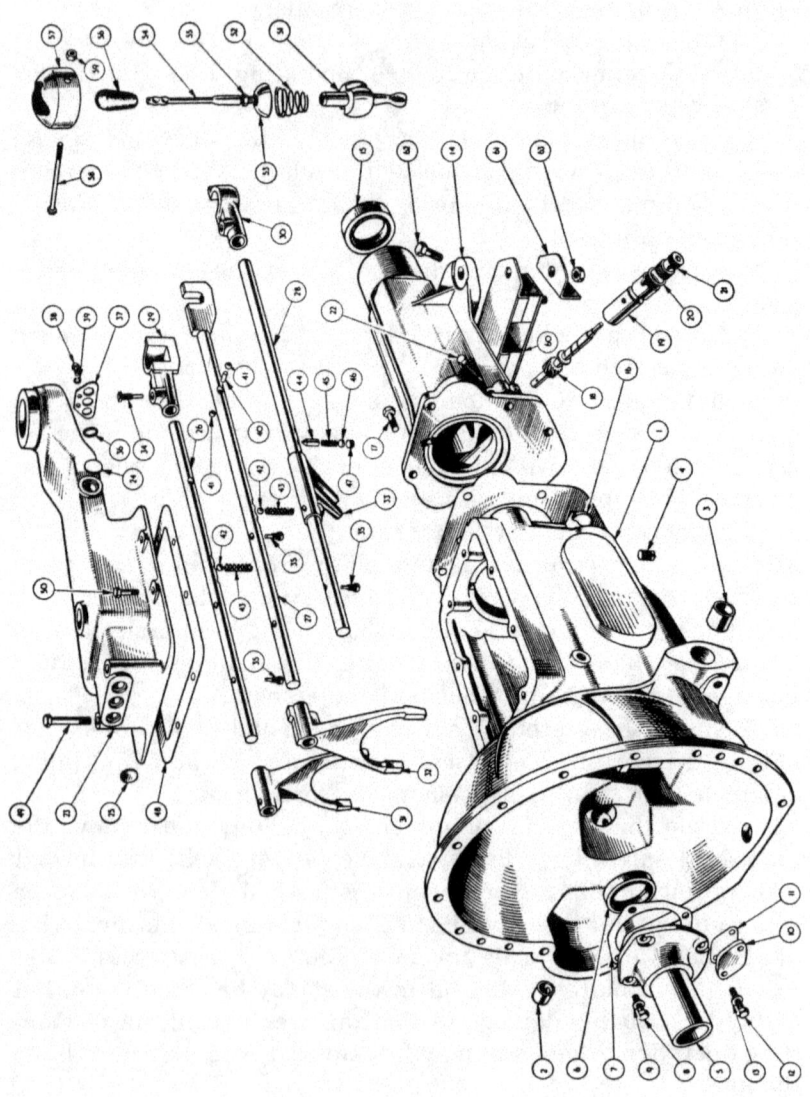

Ref. No.	Description	Ref. No.	Description
1	Clutch and Gearbox Casing.	33	Reverse Selector.
2	Bush for Clutch Shaft.	34	Taper Screw.
3	Bush for Clutch Shaft.	35	Stop Screw.
4	Drain Plug.	36	Sealing Ring.
5	Front End Cover.	37	Cover Plate.
6	Oil Seal.	38	Setscrew for Cover Plate.
7	Joint Washer.	39	Lock Washer.
8	Setscrew for Cover.	40	Interlock Roller 3rd/Top.
9	Plain Washer for 8.	41	Interlock Balls.
10	Countershaft Cover.	42	Selector Shaft Ball.
11	Joint Washer.	43	Spring for Ball.
12	Setscrew.	44	Reverse Shaft Plunger.
13	Plain Washer.	45	Spring for Plunger.
14	Gearbox Extension.	46	Distance Piece.
15	Oil Seal.	47	Plug.
16	Joint Washer.	48	Joint Washer.
17	Extension Attachment Bolt.	49	Attachment Bolt (long). ⎫ Top cover.
18	Speedometer Drive.	50	Attachment Bolt (short). ⎭
19	Speedometer Bearing.	51	Ball End.
20	Washer.	52	Spring.
21	Screwed Adaptor.	53	Spring Retainer.
22	Locating Screw.	54	Lever Assembly.
23	Top Cover.	55	Lever Locknut.
24	Core Plug.	56	Knob.
25	Selector Shaft Welch Washer.	57	Cap.
26	Selector Shaft (1st and 2nd Gear).	58	Bolt.
27	Selector Shaft (Top and 3rd Gear).	59	Nyloc Nut.
28	Reverse Selector Shaft.	60	Rear Mounting.
29	1st/2nd Gear Selector.	61	Steady Bracket.
30	Reverse Gear Selector.	62	Bolt.
31	1st/2nd Selector Fork.	63	**Nut.**
32	3rd/Top Selector Fork.		

hub is towards the mainshaft circlip.

13. Remove mainshaft circlip with the special Churchill No. 20SM69 extractor. The extraction of this circlip is made somewhat difficult by the adjacent thrust washer which has three lugs, equally spaced, and engaging alternate splines on the mainshaft. Quite apart from the necessity to engage the three available splines with the full length prongs, in some cases it may be necessary to tap the circlip round on these prongs, to free it from its recess before it can be withdrawn. A new circlip should always be used when re-assembling.

14. Withdraw thrust washer, third mainshaft constant gear and bush, second mainshaft constant gear and bush, thrust washer with three lugs to fit splines and the second speed synchro unit which also incorporates the first mainshaft gear. The mainshaft can now be withdrawn.

15. Remove the small seeger circlip and thrust washer which locates the ball race on the mainshaft and extract the race. The triangular washer can then be removed from behind the race.

16. After removal of the lock nut and locating screw the reverse selector shaft and bronze selector fork can be withdrawn. A steel selector shaft insert located at the rear of the casing and a welch plug at the front can easily be removed.

Ref. No.	Description	Ref. No.	Description
1	Mainshaft.	30	Synchro Spring.
2	Triangular Washer.	31	Synchro Ball.
3	Centre Bearing (Interchangeable with 36).	32	3rd and TOP Gear Sychronising Sleeve.
4	Outer Circlip for Centre Bearing (Interchangeable with 37).	33	Constant Pinion Shaft.
		34	Constant Pinion Bush.
5	Circlip for Centre Bearing.	35	Oil Thrower.
6	Washer for Centre Bearing.	36	Ball Bearing.
7	Washer for Rear Bearing.	37	Outer Circlip for Constant Pinion Bearing.
8	Rear Bearing.	38	Circlip.
9	Driving Flange.	39	Washer between Bearing and Circlip.
10	Slotted Nut.	40	Countershaft.
11	Plain Washer.	41	1st Speed Countershaft Gear.
12	Split Pin.	42	2nd Speed Countershaft Gear.
13	1st Gear Synchro Hub.	43	3rd Speed Countershaft Gear.
14	Interlock Plunger.	44	Distance Piece Countershaft Gear.
15	Interlock Ball.	45	Constant Gear.
16	Synchro Spring.	46	Needle Rollers.
17	Synchro Ball.	47	Retaining Ring for 46.
18	1st Gear Synchronising Sleeve.	48	Front Thrust Washer.
19	2nd Speed Synchronising Cup.	49	Rear Thrust Washer.
20	Washer.	50	Reverse Spindle.
21	2nd Gear.	51	Reverse Wheel.
22	2nd Speed Bush.	52	Lock Washer.
23	3rd Speed Gear.	53	Countershaft Retaining Screw.
24	3rd Speed Bush.	54	Reverse Operating Fork.
25	Circlip.	55	Operating Rod.
26	Washer.	56	Bush on rear end of Rod.
27	3rd and TOP Gear Synchronising Cup.	57	Rod Retaining Screw.
28	3rd and TOP Gear Synchronising Hub.	58	Locknut.
29	Synchro Spring Shim.		

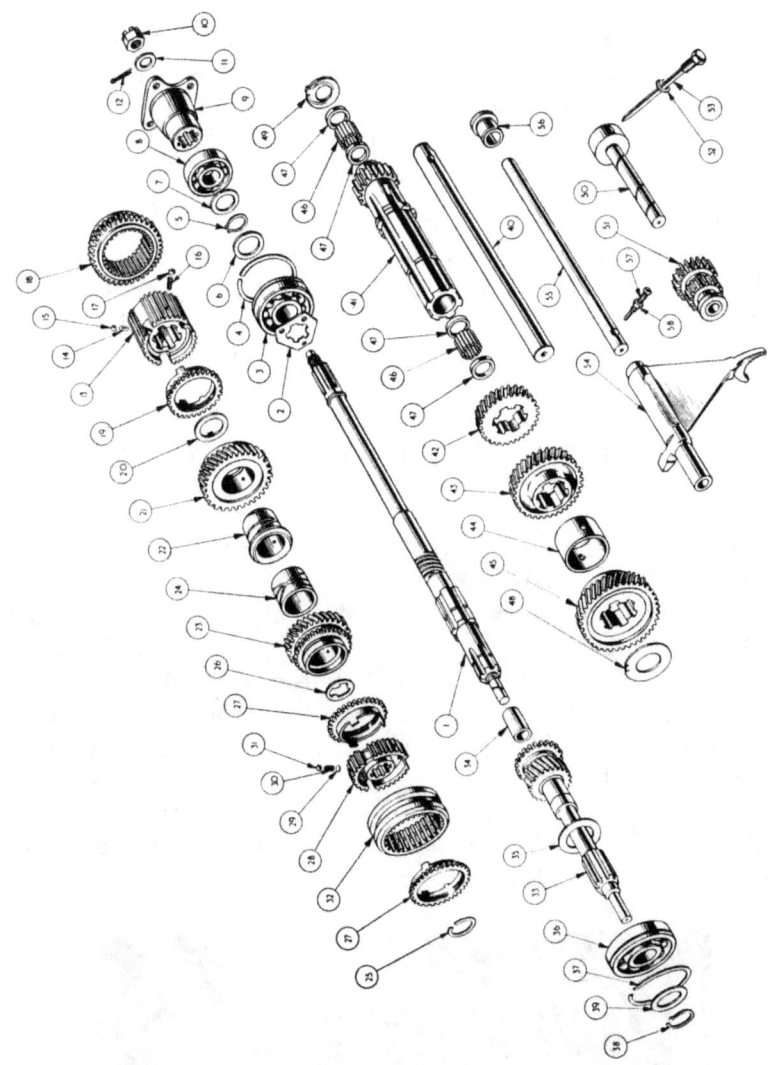

17. Lift out the reverse pinion (compound gear) after tapping out its spindle through the rear of the casing, the retaining setscrew having been removed in a previous operation.

18. The countershaft assembly can now be lifted out of the casing with the needle roller retaining tube still locating the 24 rollers at each end of the countershaft in their respective recesses. Lay aside the two phosphor bronze thrust washers for re-assembly.

19. The countershaft gears and distance sleeve can now be removed from the splined portion of the countershaft, noting

their position for re-assembly.

20. If it is desired to examine the needle rollers they can be removed by withdrawing the retaining tube. Note the correct number of 48 for re-assembly (24 at each end) and the needle roller retaining rings can be tapped out with a suitable drift.

To Assemble

1. Thoroughly clean out the casing and examine for cracks, ball race housings for wear or other damage.

2. Fit needle roller retaining rings if necessary. Fit 24 needle rollers at each end of the countershaft ensuring that the locating rings are in position. The chamfer on each retainer ring should be placed towards the bottom of the bore in the case of the inner ones, outwards for the outer ones. The rollers should be retained in grease and counted after installation to ensure that they have not become displaced before fitting the retainer tube.

3. Assemble countershaft, noting correct position for the gears, observed when dismantling.

4. Install the countershaft assembly, positioning the thrust washers on the casing with grease. The correct end float for the countershaft gears should be between .006"-.010". If there is insufficient end float the distance piece should be reduced as necessary by rubbing it down on a sheet of emery cloth placed on a surface plate. Where too much end float exists new thrust washers and/or distance piece should be fitted.

5. Fit reverse pinion (compound gear) with smaller gear towards front of box, having first ensured that there is no tooth

damage or wear in bushes; leave the fitting of the locating setscrew until the countershaft has been assembled in its normal fitted position.

6. Install the reverse selector shaft and bronze selector fork position with setscrew and tighten lock nut. The selector shaft steel insert and welch plug can now be fitted.

7. Install the triangular washer on its splines on the mainshaft. Press ball race on to mainshaft with Churchill fixture. Then fit the thrust washer and small seeger circlip. A large circlip should be fitted into the annular groove in the outer ring of the bearing.

8. Before the mainshaft is assembled into the gearbox the following points should be checked:
a. The 2nd speed constant gear float on its bush (.004"-.006").
b. The 3rd speed constant gear float on its bush (.004"-.006").
c. Overall bush float on mainshaft (.007"-.012").

To check gear bush end float, fit 2nd speed mainshaft gear thrust washer, ensuring that its three lugs engage in the mainshaft splines, 2nd and 3rd mainshaft gear bushes and 3rd mainshaft gear thrust washer fitted with oil scroll towards the bush. Install the original circlip and measure float with a feeler gauge.
d. Axial release loading of 2nd speed synchro unit 25-27 lbs.
e. Axial release loading of 3rd and top speed synchro unit 19-21 lbs.

If (d) & (e) are found to be incorrect, steel shims can be added or removed from below the axial release loading springs to increase or decrease respectively the axial release load as required.

9. After completion of checks the mainshaft circlip, thrust washers and constant gear bushes can be removed. The mainshaft can then be installed into the gearbox casing, and assembled as follows:

a. Second speed synchro unit incorporating the first mainshaft gear.
b. Thrust washer with three lugs to fit splines.
c. Second mainshaft constant gear and bush.
d. Third mainshaft constant gear, bush and thrust washer fitted with oil scroll towards gear.
e. New mainshaft circlip.
f. Third and top speed synchro unit with the short boss of the synchro hub towards the mainshaft circlip or rear of gearbox. The mainshaft and ball race can then be driven into the gearbox casing, positioning the gap of the circlip on the outer ring of the bearing in line with the atmosphere hole in the casing.

10. Assemble oil thrower on to constant pinion shaft and press ball race on the shaft, ensuring that this goes right home and that in this position with the correct thrust washer fitted, the small seeger circlip fits properly into its recess. When passing this circlip along the ground portion of the constant pinion shaft, take care not to score the shaft as such damage may cause subsequent leakage of oil. Fit larger circlip into the annular groove in the outer ring of the ball race.

11. Fit Oilite spigot bush into constant pinion, placing the internally bevelled portion of it towards the mainshaft.

12. Drive the constant pinion shaft and bearing into the gearbox casing, positioning the gap in the circlip on the outer ring of the bearing in line with the oil hole in the casing.

Utilizing a feeler gauge, measure the distance between the dog teeth of all the mainshaft synchro gears, and the dog teeth of their respective baulk rings.

Move the outer synchro sleeve towards the gear being measured thus forcing the baulking ring on to its cone. In this position the dimension should be between .035" and .040" for new components and .005" to .010" less for components which have been run-in.

13. Utilize a pilot to align thrust washers and countershaft gear assembly driving out needle roller retaining tube, subsequently ejecting the pilot tool with the actual countershaft. It is important when carrying out this operation that the pilot tool should maintain contact with the retaining tube or counter-

shaft, as appropriate, throughout the operation, alternatively there is danger that the needle rollers may leave their recess.
14. Install locating setscrew through countershaft, and reverse spindle, first checking the alignment of the holes in the reverse gear spindle and countershaft.
15. Fit countershaft front end cover plate and paper joint securing with two setscrews and washers using lead linger and wiring as necessary.
16. Assemble gearbox extension and paper joints, securing with six setscrews and washers, using lead linger and wiring as necessary.
17. Install thrust washer and ball race into gearbox extension with suitable tool.
18. Locate gearbox extension oil seal.
19. Fit plain washer, slotted nut, tightening to 95-100 lbs.i/ft., and install split pin.
20. Install speedometer driving gear and accommodating bush, securing with special setscrew.
21. Fit front cover, having installed oil seal, utilizing fitting tool to protect oil seal.

Fit four setscrews and plain washers with lead linger after positioning the slot in the face of the front cover horizontally at 9 o'clock and wire setscrew heads.
22. Assemble clutch throw-out bearing and sleeve and install with clutch operating shaft coil spring and clutch operating fork, positioning both with special securing setscrews, wire locking the latter. Install grease nipple with fibre washer into R.H. end of clutch operating shaft.
23. Fit top cover assembly with selector mechanism, paper joint, securing with eight setscrews.

To Dismantle Top Cover Assembly
1. Remove oil level dipstick.
2. Ensure that the selector mechanism is in the neutral position.
3. Remove change speed lever positioning bolt, nyloc nut and setscrew. This enables the change speed lever complete with knob, cap, spring retainer, spring and ball end to be removed as an assembly. Further dismantling requires the removal of the knob and/or the removal of the screwed change speed lever ball end.
4. Remove 1st and 2nd speed selector shaft wire locked stop screw and ³/₈" dia. positioning ball, spring and retaining screw, then 1st and 2nd speed bronze selector fork wire locked positioning setscrew, and slide selector shaft rearwards clear of the casting to enable the selector fork to be removed.

5. Remove reverse selector fork and shaft, carrying out procedure as in (4) except that the shaft is positioned by a plunger spring, distance piece and retaining screw instead of the ball, spring and retaining screw.

6. Remove 3rd and top speed selector shaft and fork, carrying out the procedure as in (4).

NOTE: It is important that no attempt is made to move more than one selector shaft at a time otherwise damage will be caused to the selector shaft bores by the interlock mechanism consisting of two $3/8''$ dia. ball bearings located in the top cover casting either side of the 3rd and top speed selector shaft, and the .185'' dia. interlock roller made of key steel which makes contact with these balls being installed, in a hole drilled transversely through the 3rd and top speed selector shaft.

The interlock roller and steel balls can easily be shaken or pushed out of position if it is desired to examine them.

7. Further dismantling of the selector shafts only requires the removal of the selector shaft end pieces on the 1st and 2nd and reverse rods, they are located by a wired setscrew; on the 3rd and top they are silver soldered together.

8. Remove the two setscrews and spring washers from the oil sealing ring cover plate, enabling the plate and three rubber sealing rings at the end of the selector shaft bores to be removed.

9. The three 16G pressing selector shafts welch plugs located at the front of top cover and the two 14G pressing welch plugs either side of top cover can easily be removed with a suitable drift.

10. The threaded plug located on the top cover can also be removed.

To Assemble

Carry out the reverse procedure to that of dismantling, but for ease of assembly install the $3/8''$ dia. interlock mechanism balls after the 3rd and top speed selector shaft has been fitted but before the reverse and 1st and 2nd selector shafts.

Important: While fitting the selector shafts make sure that the selector shaft or shafts already fitted are in the neutral position.

PROPELLER SHAFT

When the rear axle rises and falls, with the flexing of the springs, the arc of the axle's travel necessitates variations in the length of the propeller shaft which is provided for by the fitting of a sliding spline at the front end of the assembly.

A universal joint is supplied at each end, consisting of a central spider having four trunnions, four needle roller bearings and two yokes.

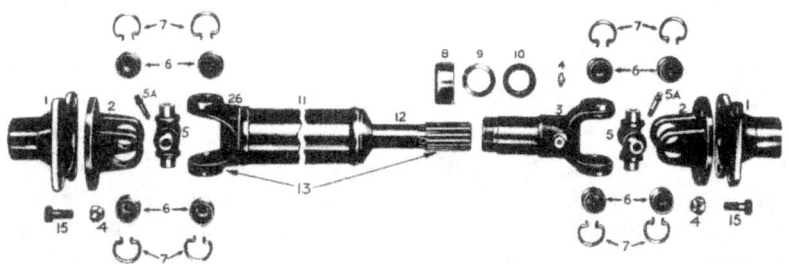

Ref. No.	Description	Ref. No.	Description
1	Companion Flange.	8	Dust Cap.
2	Flange Yoke.	9	Steel Washer.
3	Sleeve Yoke Assembly.	10	Cork Washer.
4	Nipple for Splines.	11	Tube.
5	Spider Journal Assembly (less Nipple).	12	Splined Stub Shaft.
5A	Nipple for Journal Assembly.	13	Propeller Shaft Assembly.
6	Bearing Race Assembly.	14	Simmonds Nut.
7	Snap Ring.	15	Flange Attachment Bolts.

Each spider is provided **with an oil nipple** and there is one fitted on the sleeve yoke assembly to lubricate the sliding spline. After dismantling and before reassembly, the inside splines of the sleeve yoke should be liberally smeared with oil. Each of the two journal assemblies are provided with an oil nipple which should be lubricated each 5,000 miles.

If a large amount of oil exudes from the oil seals, the joint should be dismantled and new oil seals fitted.

Wear on the thrust faces is located by testing the lift in the joint by hand.

Any circumferential movement of the shaft relative to the flange yokes indicates wear in the needle roller bearings and/or the sliding splines.

Removal of Propeller Shaft

1. Jack up one rear wheel clear of the ground to enable the propeller shaft to be rotated.

2. Remove nuts from bolts at both flange yokes engaging first gear, as necessary to hold the shaft from turning when slackening nuts.

3. Tap out bolts and remove propeller shaft assembly.

To Dismantle Propeller Shaft

Before commencing to dismantle propeller shaft see if "arrow" location marks are visible when the parts are clean. If no markings are visible, re-mark to ensure correct re-assembly.

Having unscrewed the dust cap pull sleeve yoke assembly off shaft. Clean enamel from snap rings and top of bearings races. Remove all snap rings by pinching ears together with a suitable pair of circlip pliers and subsequently prying out these with a screwdriver. If ring does not snap out of groove readily, tap end of bearing race lightly inwards to relieve the pressure against ring. Holding joint in left hand with splined sleeve yoke lug on top, tap yoke arms lightly with a soft hammer. Top bearing should begin to emerge, turn joint over and finally remove with fingers.

If necessary tap bearing race from inside with small diameter bar taking care not to damage the bearing race. This operation will destroy the oil seal and necessitate fitting replacement parts when re-assembling, keep joint in this position while removing bearing race, so as to avoid dropping the needle

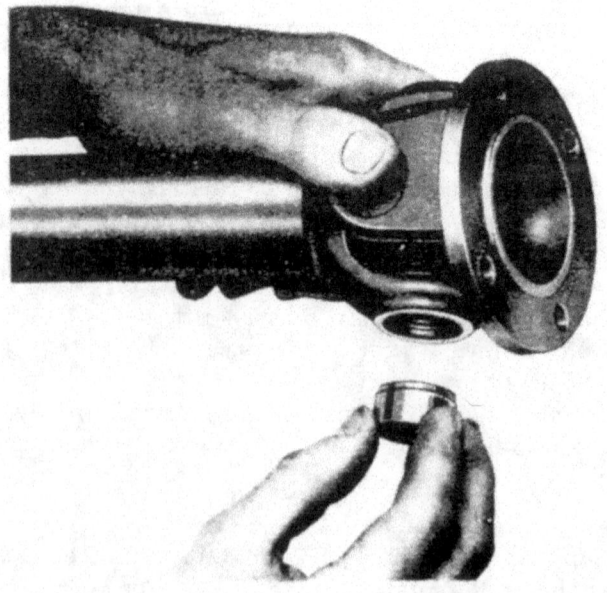

rollers.

Repeat the operation described in previous paragraph for opposite bearing. The splined sleeve yoke can now be removed.

Rest the two exposed trunnions on wood or lead blocks, then tap flange yoke with soft hammer to remove the two remaining bearing races.

The parts most likely to show signs of wear after long usage are the bearing races and spider trunnions. Should looseness in the fit of these parts, load markings, or distortion be observed, they must be renewed complete, as no oversize journal bearing races are provided. It is essential that bearing races are a light drive fit in the yoke. In the rare event of wear having taken place in the yoke cross holes, the holes will most certainly be oval, and such yokes must be replaced.

In the case of wear of the cross holes in a fixed yoke, which is part of the tubular shaft assembly, only in cases of absolute emergency should this be replaced by welding in a new yoke. The normal procedure is to replace by a complete shaft assembly. The other parts likely to show signs of wears are the splines of the sleeve yoke, or splined stub shaft. A total of .004" circumferential movement, measured on the outside diameter of the spline, should not be exceeded.

In the event of the splined stub shaft requiring renewal this must be dealt with in the same way as the fixed yoke, i.e., a replacement tubular shaft assembly fitted.

To Assemble

See that the trunnion assemblies are well lubricated with one of the oils recommended. Assemble needle rollers in bearing recess, smearing the walls of the races with vaseline, or lubricant, to retain the rollers in place.

It is advisable to replace cork gaskets and gasket retainers (oil seals) on the trunnions using a tubular drift. The spider journal shoulders should be shellacked prior to fitting retainers to ensure a good oil seal. Ensure that the trunnions are clean and free from shellac before fitting needle rollers.

Insert spider in flange yoke. Then using a soft-nosed drift about ½₂" smaller in diameter than the hole in the yoke, tap the bearing into position. It is essential that bearing races are a light drive fit in the yoke holes. Repeat this operation for the other three bearings.

Refit snap rings with a suitable pair of circlip pliers, ensuring that rings engage properly with their respective grooves. If joint appears to bind after assembly, tap lightly with a soft hammer, thus relieving any pressure of the bearings on the ends of the trunnions.

When replacing sliding joint on shaft be sure that sliding and fixed yokes are in the same plane and arrow markings coincide. A single universal joint does not transmit uniform motion when the driving and driven shafts are out of line, but when two joints are used as in the case of a propeller shaft, and are set in correct relation the one to the other, the errors of one are corrected by the discrepancies of the other, and uniform motion is then transmitted. Hence the importance of re-engaging the splines correctly when they have been taken apart.

To Fit Propeller Shaft

Wipe companion flange and flange yoke faces clean, to ensure the pilot flange registering properly and joint faces bedding evenly all round. Insert bolts, and see that all nuts are evenly tightened all round and are securely locked. Dust cap to be screwed up by hand as far as possible. Sliding joint is always placed towards front of vehicle.

REAR AXLE

The rear axle is of the hypoid semi-floating type with shim adjustment for the differential bearings and for the endwise location of the pinion in relation to the crown wheel. The axle sleeves are pressed into the center casing and each sleeve is located by four pegs.

The center casing is a casting which accommodates the differential cage and the attached crown wheel, together with the hypoid pinion. A detachable pressed steel cover, at the rear of the casing, allows access to the differential unit and crown wheel, the removal of this cover clears the way for the dismantling of the axle. The hypoid pinion is mounted on two taper roller bearings which are separated from one another by a tubular spacer. The pinion's endwise relation with the crown wheel is adjusted by means of shims inserted between the "head" bearing outer ring and the casing. Preloading of bearings is adjusted by means of shims between the spacer and tail bearing.

The differential casing contains two sun and two planet wheels and also carries the crown wheel, which is bolted in position by ten bolts passing through the casing and into tapped holes in the back of the wheel itself.

NOTE: The crown wheel is attached to the differential casing by bolts locked by tab washers. The crown wheel showed a tendency to work loose after exacting rally acceleration and reversing gear tests and to obviate this possibility the 5/15" UNF attachment bolts were replaced by 3/8" UNF in axles numbered TS.4731 onwards.

The two planet wheels are mounted on a cross spindle, this spindle being provided with a hole at one end and located by a pin passing through the hole and the differential casing.

NOTE: The locating pin used in early cars was a "stepped" shape but this changed to the "parallel" type pin and incorporated in axle No. TS.6260 onwards.

The axle shafts are splined at both ends. The inner end fitting into the sun wheels and the outer extremity accommodating the shell bearing and hub. The hub is secured to the splined end of the axle shaft by means of a splined taper collar, a shaped washer and a castellated nut.

The wheel bearing is accommodated in the axle sleeve and a housing which is bolted to the flanged end of each axle tube. The inner portion of the wheel bearing is gripped between the hub and a flange on the axle **shaft.**

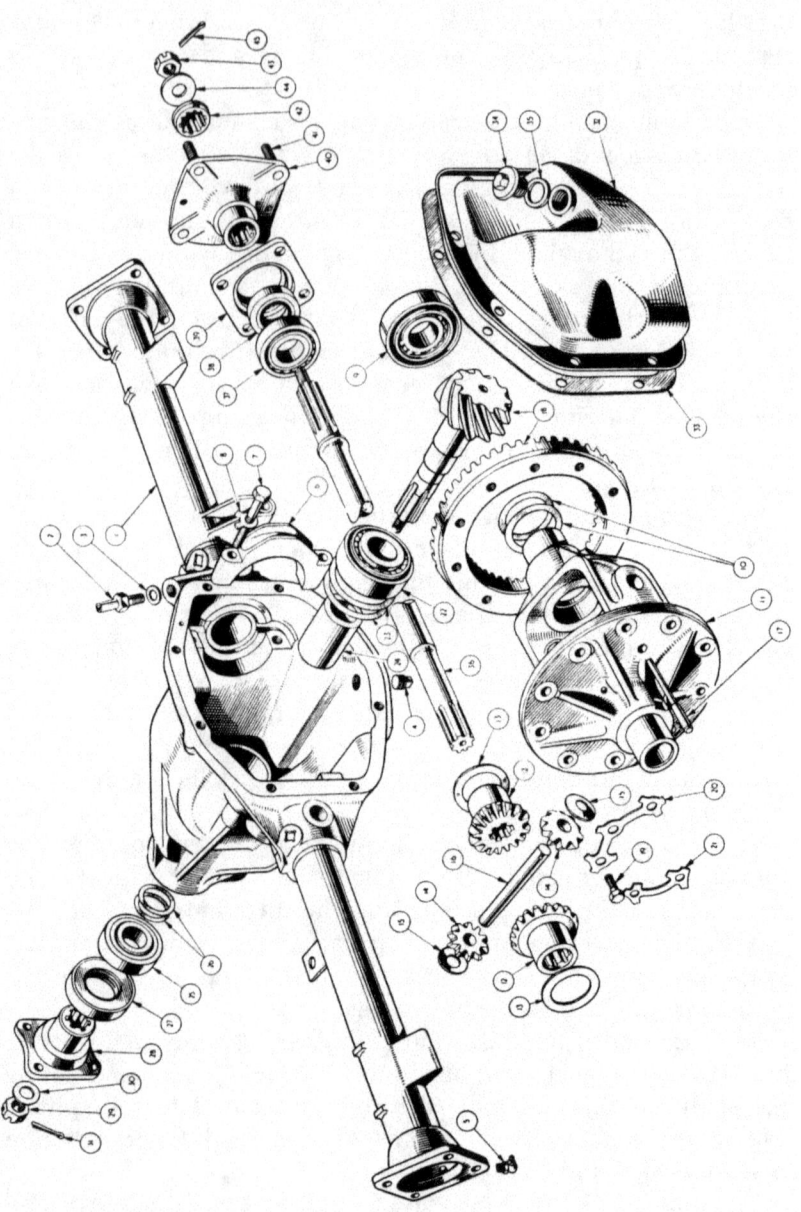

Ref. No.	Description	Ref. No.	Description
1.	Axle casing assembly	23.	Pinion head bearing ring shim.
2.	Breather.	24.	Pinion bearing spacer.
3.	Fibre washer.	25.	Pinion tail bearing.
4.	Drain plug.	26.	Pinion shaft shims.
5.	Grease nipple.	27.	Pinion shaft oil seal.
6.	Bearing cap.	28.	Pinion driving flange.
7.	Bearing cap setscrew.	29.	Castellated nut.
8.	Tab washer.	30.	Washer.
9.	Differential bearing.	31.	Cotter pin.
10.	Shims.	32.	Rear cover.
11.	Differential casing.	33.	Joint washer.
12.	Sun gear.	34.	Oil filter plug.
13.	Thrust washer.	35.	Washer.
14.	Planet gear.	36.	Rear axle shaft.
15.	Thrust washer.	37.	Hub bearing.
16.	Cross pin.	38.	Hub oil seal.
17.	Locating pin. (See note 1 page, 4).	39.	Bearing housing.
18.	Crown wheel and pinion.	40.	Hub assembly.
19.	Crown wheel bolt. (See note 2, page 4).	41.	Wheel stud.
20.	Tab washer.	42.	Splined collar.
21.	Tab washer.	43.	Castellated nut.
22.	Pinion head bearing.	44.	Washer.
		45.	Cotter pin.

DATA

Crown wheel run out	Not more than .003"
Backlash between crown wheel and pinion	.004" — .006"
Distance from ground thrust face on pinion to centre of crown wheel	3.4375"
Pinion bearing pre-load, measured without oil seal	15 — 18 in. lbs.
Pre-load for differential bearings	Allowance for .002" to .004" shims, spread over both bearings
Diameter of differential bearings	2.8446" — 2.8440"
Later production cars	2.8460" — 2.8450"
Pinion nut tightening torque	85 — 100 lbs. ft.
Hub securing nut tightening torque	110 — 125 lbs. ft.
	125—145 lbs. ft. with special nut fitted to axle No. TS.8039 onwards.

The differential casing is mounted on two taper roller bearings, the position of these being adjusted by means of shims interposed between them and the casing itself. The disposition of these shims decides the crown wheel and pinion depth of engagement and the thickness of these the amount of preloading.

To Remove Hubs (Disc Wheels)

1. Withdraw the split pin from end of axle shaft. Partly release the torque on the castellated hub securing nut.
2. Jack up the car, remove the castellated nut, the road wheel and by the withdrawal of the two countersunk setscrews remove the brake drum.
3. Remove the washer and the splined taper collar from the axle shaft.
4. Fit the Churchill hub removing tool No. M86 or S132/2 or suitable hub puller and withdraw the hub from the shaft.

An alternate method is to withdraw the half shaft with the hub in position, this method necessitates the removal of the brake backing plate and the severing of the hydraulic and hand brake connections.

To Replace Hubs

The replacement of the hubs is the reversal of removal but the following notes should be considered:

The axle shafts of later production cars provide an interference fit with the hub splines. To facilitate the replacement of the hubs, the Churchill hub replacing Tool No. S125 was introduced. Should the axle shafts be out of the axle casing it will still be necessary to use the hub replacing tool or a fly press.

To Remove Center Lock Hubs

1. Jack up the car and remove the hub cap by tapping the lugs with a copper faced mallet. Remove the road wheel.
2. Remove the split pin through the aperture in the barrel of the hub.
3. Remove the hub securing nut from the axle shaft. It may be necessary to replace the wheel and lower the car when torque is applied to the nut. After removing the nut withdraw the washer and splined collar.
4. By inserting a screwdriver blade into the cut of a split tapered collar, the collar willl expand and allow it to be withdrawn from the hub.
5. Remove the two countersunk brake drum securing screws and withdraw the brake drum.
6. Fit the Churchill hub removing Tool No. S132 or a suitable puller and remove the hub. It should be remembered that the hubs have right or left-hand threads and care must be exercised when selecting the removal rings.

An alternate method of hub removal is to remove the axle shaft complete as described below. This necessitates the severing of the hand brake and hydraulic connections and removing the brake backing plate.

To Replace Center Lock Hubs

The replacement of the hubs is the reversal of their removal. However the following points should be noted.

1. The axle shafts of later production cars provide an interference fit with the hubs. To facilitate the replacement of the hubs the Churchill hub replacing Tool No. S125 was introduced.
2. When the axle shafts are out of the casing it is still necessary to use the hub replacing tool or a fly press.

To Remove Axle Shaft

1. Jack up car and remove road wheel.
2. If the car is equipped with wire wheels remove the split tapered collar by inserting a screwdriver blade into the cut of the ring. It can now be drawn off the barrel of the hub.
3. Withdraw the two countersunk brake drum securing screws and remove the brake drum.
4. Drain the hydraulic system, disconnect the pipe line and the hand brake cable at the wheel cylinder.
5. Remove the four bolts and nyloc nuts which secure the brake backing plate and the bearing housing to the axle flange.
6. Withdraw the axle shaft assembly from the axle casing together with the brake backing plate assembly.
7. Grip the axle in the protected jaws of a vice and utilizing the aperture in the barrels of the center lock hub, remove the split pin. Remove the castellated nut, washer and splined taper collar. Remove the hub with the Churchill hub remover, Tool No. S132 or equivalent.
8. To remove the disc wheel hub, first remove the split pin at the axle end followed by the castellated nut, washer and splined taper collar. Remove the hub with the Churchill hub remover, Tool No. M86 or S132/2.

The extraction of each hub will release the oil seal and bearing housing but leave the hub bearing on the axle shaft.

9. Remove the hub bearing from the shafts, utilizing the Churchill Tool No. S4615 Codes 8 and 10.
10. The oil seal can now be drifted out of the bearing housing if it is seen to be unserviceable.

To Replace Axle Shaft

The replacement of the axle shaft is the reversal of their removal. On later production cars the axle shaft provided an interference fit with the hub and it is necessary to replace the hub, utilizing the Churchill hub replacing Tool No. S125. On completion of the replacement operations it will be necessary to bleed the brakes.

To Remove Axle Unit

NOTE: As the axle has to be tilted it may be desirable to drain off the oil.

1. Jack up car and remove road wheels.
2. Detach propeller shaft from pinion flange by the removal of four bolts and nyloc nuts.
3. Disconnect hand brake cable from the compensator lever.
4. Drain the hydraulic system and disconnect the line at the

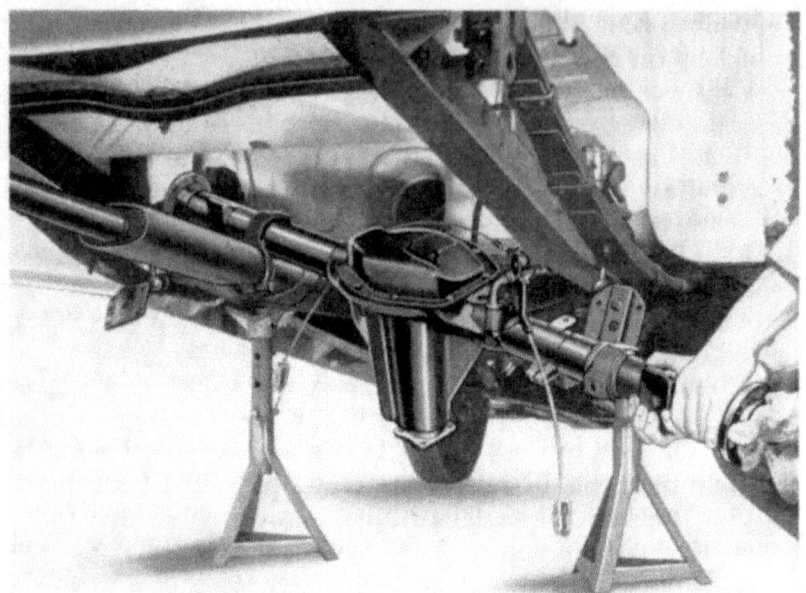

front end of the flexible hose. (See Brake Section.)
5. Remove the brake drums after withdrawing the two countersunk setscrews. If wire wheels are fitted the split taper ring will have to be removed first, this can be effected by inserting the blade of a screwdriver into the split to expand the ring which can then be drawn off the hub.
6. First disconnect the Bundy Tubing and the hand brake cables at the wheel cylinders and then remove the bolts and nyloc nuts securing the brake back plate to the axle casing.

The hubs, together with the half shafts, oil seals, bearings and brake backing plate, can now be removed from the axle. These can be dismantled as described previously.
7. Remove the axle check straps by first removing the four nuts and lock washers.
8. Remove the nyloc nuts from the "U" bolts securing the axle to the road spring and swing the shock absorber arm (attached to the spring plate) clear. The "U" bolts may now be removed from the axle.
9. Lift the axle clear of the spring and move it to the left, allow the right-hand side to be lowered when the axle end is clear of the right-hand spring. By moving the axle to the right it can be withdrawn from the chassis.

To Replace the Axle

If a replacement axle is being fitted it will be necessary to remove the complete brake assemblies at the axle ends.

It is not necessary to remove the hubs, for these can be removed with the half shafts and brake backing plates.

The axle must be tilted during the fitting operations and filling the axle with oil should be delayed until the axle has been fitted to the car.

The fitting is the reversal of the removal. For the bleeding of the hydraulic system see Brake Section.

To Dismantle

1. Drain oil.
2. Remove wheel securing cones (wire wheel hubs only). This enables the brake drug securing screws to be removed and the drums withdrawn.
3. Remove split pins and hub securing nuts. Preventing the hubs from rotating by means of a road wheel, the conical washers can then be removed and the hubs, complete with their splined tightening cones, withdrawn with a suitable tool or press. Churchill Tool No. M86 or S132/2.

NOTE: Some difficulty may be experienced in the slackening of the nuts due to rotation of the hubs, but since the axle is going to be completely dismantled the hubs can be removed at a later stage, which means that the half shaft, hubs, brake backing plates, etc., must be removed as an assembly.

4. Remove brake shoes and return springs.
5. Withdraw the brake backing plates after removal of the eight bolts, spring washers and nyloc nuts, four from either back plate. Further dismantling of the brake backing plates only require the removal of the hydraulic wheel cylinders and anchor blocks, the latter being secured by spring washers and two nuts, the former can be withdrawn provided the hydraulic connections, rubber dust sealing boots, etc., have been removed.
6. The half shafts can now be withdrawn from the axle casing, the bearing housings tapped off the bearings and the bearings withdrawn with a suitable puller. The grease seal can then be tapped out of the bearing housings.

NOTE: If the hubs have not been previously withdrawn due to difficulties in slackening the hub nuts mentioned in (5) they can now be slackened by gripping the axle shaft in the vice, and the hubs then pressed off the axle shafts with a suitable tool or press.

7. Remove axle center casing cover and joint after withdrawal of eight setscrews.
8. Remove the differential bearing caps, noting the markings stamped on the top of these and the corresponding abutting

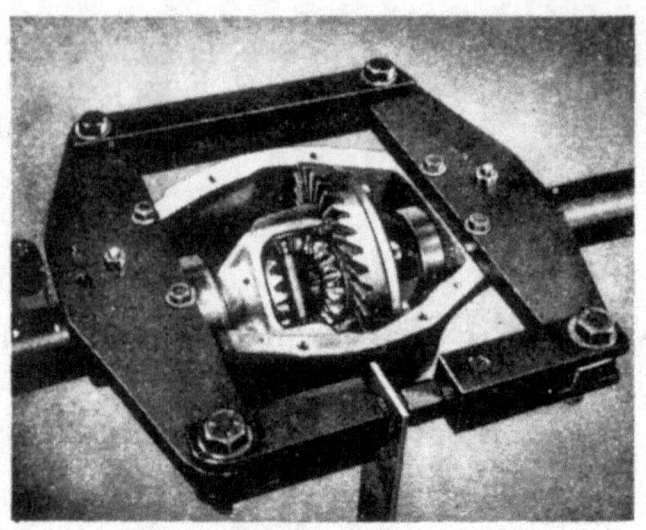

portions of the casing. The existing relation between the caps and casing must be retained when re-assembling.

9. Apply axle casing spreader and lift differential assembly out of the axle center casing. Spreading should be limited to that required to just free the assembly in the casing.

10. Suitably identify the respective outer portion of the differential bearings with their inner races. The inter-relation of the component parts of these races must be retained when re-assembling the rear axle.

11. Remove the crown wheel from its mounting flange after the withdrawal of the ten fixing bolts, leaving further dismantling of the differential unit until a later stage.

12. After removal of split pinned flange nut and having removed the flange, drive the pinion out through the casing with a hide faced hammer. Lay aside the shims which are fitted between the spacer and tail race for possible use when re-assembling. Remove pinion head bearing inner cone.

13. Drive out the pinion outer rings. The removal of the outer ring of the tail bearing will also eject the oil seal and tail bearing inner cone. The ejection of the head bearing outer ring will uncover the shims fitted between this and the casing. These shilms should be laid aside with the component parts of this bearing as a guide when re-assembling.

14. Replace the differential assembly in the axle casing and release the tension from the axle casing spreader.

15. Check the "run out" of the crown wheel mounting flange; this should not exceed .003". The crown wheel itself can be

checked on a surface table with the aid of a set of feeler gauges. Having satisfactorily completed these checks, the differential assembly can be removed from the axle casing and dismantled as follows:

a. Drive out the cross pin locating pin and withdraw the cross pin.

b. Rotate the sun wheels which will in turn rotate the planet wheels until the planet wheels with their respective thrust washers are opposite the cut away portions of the crown wheel carrier from which they can easily be withdrawn.

c. Remove the sun wheels and their thrust washers, so completing the dismantling of the rear axle.

To Re-assemble

All parts must be examined carefully and a decision should be made as to which items require renewal. Where it is found necessary to replace the crown wheel or pinion for any reason the gears must be replaced as a pair, as they are "lapped" together in manufacture.

The first consideration, after replacing damaged or worn parts, must be the correct interrelations between the crown wheel and pinion. The assembled relation of these two gears must very closely approximate that used when the gears were "lapped" together after heat treatment during manufacture.

The datum position of the pinion with relation to the crown wheel is specified as 3.4375" from the ground thrust face on the back of the pinion to the center line of the differential bearings. It is also important that not only should this datum position be achieved, but that sufficient bearing preload should be arranged to ensure the maintenance of the specified relations in service.

Having cleaned the abutment faces and bearing housings thoroughly, and removed an excrescences from these surfaces, the following procedure for re-assembly is recommended.

1. Fit the outer rings of the pinions two bearings, pulling them into place with a special tool.

2. Fit the dummy pinion (M.84), the pinion bearing inner cones and install into the axle center casing; tightening the flange nut progressively until the correct pinion pre-load of 15-18 in. lbs. is obtained.

3. Install the pinion setting gauge in the axle center casing (after zeroing the dial with a ground button held firmly on the gauge plunger) and tighten bearing caps. This gauge is used to assess the shim thickness which is required under the pinion

datum position mentioned earlier. Due to the fact that the bearing inner cones are a slide fit on the dummy pinion and a press fit on the actual pinion to be used, bearing expansion will undoubtedly take place in the latter case. A pack of shims .002"-.003" below the gauge reading will be required to allow for this expansion and thus ensure the pinion is in its correct datum position.

4. Although the packing shims are supplied to nominal thicknesses, the dimensions should be measured with a micrometer gauge. It is important that no damaged shims are used and that they are thoroughly cleaned before measurement.

5. Remove the pinion setting gauge, dummy pinion and pinion bearing outer rings.

6. Insert the measured pack of shims on the pinion head bearing outer ring abutment face and replace the pinion bearing outer rings, pulling them into place with the special tool.

7. Press the pinion head bearing inner cone on to the pinion shaft.

8. The bearing spacer is fed on to the pinion shaft with the chamfer outwards. The shims previously removed when dismantling the axle are placed in position on the pinion and the assembly fitted into the axle center casing. The thickness of shims fitted will probably have to be adjusted to provide the correct pre-load figure.

9. The inner cone of the pinion tail bearing is tapped into position on the pinion and up against the shims on the distance collar.

10. The driving flange is fitted on the end of the pinion shaft and firmly secured with the castellated nut and plain washer to a tightening torque of 85-100 lbs. ft. **The oil seal is not fitted until the bearing preload has been checked as described in the next operation.**

11. The fixture shown is now applied and the pre-load of the bearings checked. The correct pre-load should fall between 15-18 in. lbs. If the preload is inadequate shims must be with-

drawn, whereas if an excessive figure is obtained additional shims must be fitted.

12. When the correct pinion pre-load is obtained remove driving flange and fit the oil seal, after which the flange should be replaced, the castellated nut tightened to the correct torque and split pinned.

13. The differential assembly bearings are now fitted without, as yet, installing any packing shims. A suitable driver should be used for driving the bearings on to the crown wheel carrier.

14. The axle bearing seats are carefully cleaned and any excresences removed. The differential casing is positioned and the bearing caps, fitted with regard to the identification markings, are tightened down and then slackened off a ¼ turn. This will prevent the bearings tilting but allow sideways movement. A dial indicator gauge is mounted on the axle center casing with the plunger resting on the crown wheel mounting flange. The assembly is forced away from the dial gauge and then the indicator set to zero. The assembly should then be levered in the opposite direction until the taper roller bearings go hard home. The reading on the dial gauge (.062″ for exam-

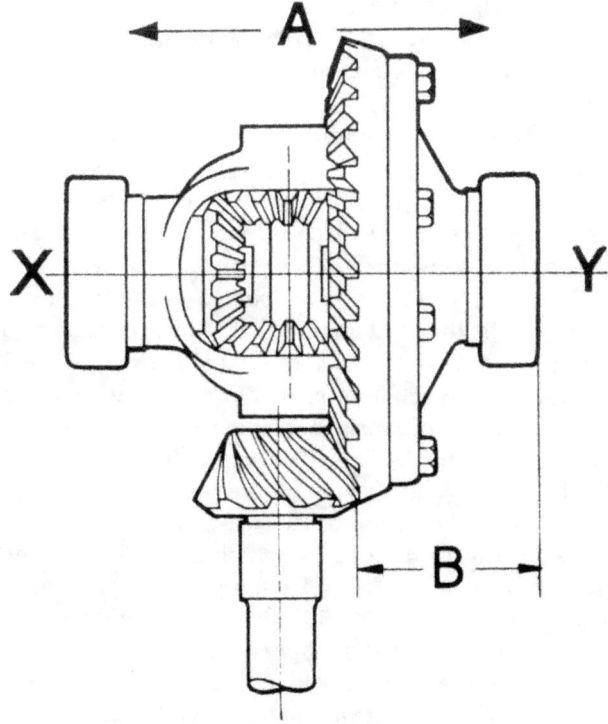

ple) will indicate the total side float of the crown wheel carrier and should be noted for later reference.

15. The crown wheel carrier is now removed from the axle center casing so that the sun gears, planet gears and thrust washers can be assembled, the cross pin being used to locate the two planet gears with their respective thrust washers temporarily in position. Subsequently, the planet gears are rotated round the sun wheel through 90 degrees, the cross pin being withdrawn to allow the gears to assume their normal fitted position, and the cross pin finally fitted and secured by its locking pin, this pin being located by "center popping."

16. The crown wheel is fitted to the crown wheel carrier, the fixing bolts thoroughly tighten to 22-24 lbs. ft. and secured with their respective locking plates.

NOTE: The crown wheel attachment bolts were increased in diameter from $\frac{5}{16}''$ to $\frac{3}{8}''$ at rear axle No. TS.4731.

The crown wheel is checked for flush fitting against the flanged face of the carrier with a feeler gauge, thus ensuring that the crown wheel goes right home and also that there can be no question of casting distortion. The maximum permissible run out of the crown wheel and crown wheel mounting flange is .003". The flange can be checked before the fitting of the crown wheel by rotating it on its bearings, using a dial indicator, the crown wheel itself on a surface table with the aid of feeler gauges.

17. The differential assembly is installed in the casing in a similar manner to operation (14), but in this instance the D.T.I. plunger bears against the back of a crown wheel fixing bolt.

18. The assembly is now forced away from the dial gauge until the teeth on the crown wheel go fully home with those on the pinion. The dial gauge is now set to zero and the assembly levered towards the dial gauge. Let this dimension be .045".

19. The side float of the assembly measured in the last operation, less the crown wheel and pinion backlash specified, will indicate the shim thickness required on the crown wheel side. The backlash is specified as between .004" and .006" and an average figure of .005" should be used for this calculation giving .040" to be fitted on the crown wheel side.

20. To obtain the thickness of the shims required between the other differential bearing and casing, the figure arrived at in previous operation, i.e., .040", should be subtracted from the total side float measured in operation (14), plus an allowance of .005" to provide the necessary degree of bearing pre-load. This gives a total shim thickness of .067" and thus shims on

two bearings will be .040" already estimated and .067" — .040" equals .027" on the other side.

21. Having decided the thickness of shims required behind each differential bearing, these bearings are extracted with a puller. The respective shim packs are measured with a micrometer gauge after ensuring that the shims are clean and undamaged and allocated to their respective sides of the crown wheel carrier.

22. As each bearing is extracted, the two portions of each must be laid aside for refitting in the same relation and position as that used during initial assembly. Failure to fit these bearings in their original positions will upset the measurements made in previous operations.

23. Having fitted the two packs of shims in their respective positions the bearing inner cones are driven on to the carrier with a suitable sleeve tool and the outer rings applied.

24. The differential assembly is now fitted into the axle center casing and, owing to the pre-loading of the bearings, a certain amount of casing spreading is desirable to complete this operation. **The casing spreader shown should be used and the spreading of the case limited to that just required to enable the differential assembly to enter the casing.**

25. The bearing caps are then fitted in their respective positions so that the number stamped on the caps, coincide with those stamped on the axle casing, tightening them to their correct torque of 34-36 lbs. ft.

26. The pinions and crown wheel backlash is checked with a dial gauge and should be .004"-.006": an average should be taken of several teeth. Should the backlash be incorrect, the transfer of shims from one side of the differential carrier to the other will be necessary. If the backlash is too great, then a shim or shims will have to be taken from the side opposite the crown wheel and the same shims added to the crown wheel side, always maintaining the same overall total. Should the backlash be insufficient, then the reverse procedure must be adopted.

27. A tooth marking test should now be carried out, and to enable this to be done a few teeth should be painted with a suitable marking compound. The pinion should be rotated backwards and forwards by the driving flange, over the marked teeth one the crown wheel, and the markings compared with the diagram, and the instructions on this diagram regarded.

28. A new axle cover packing is fitted, together with the cover itself, and the latter secured with the eight setscrews.

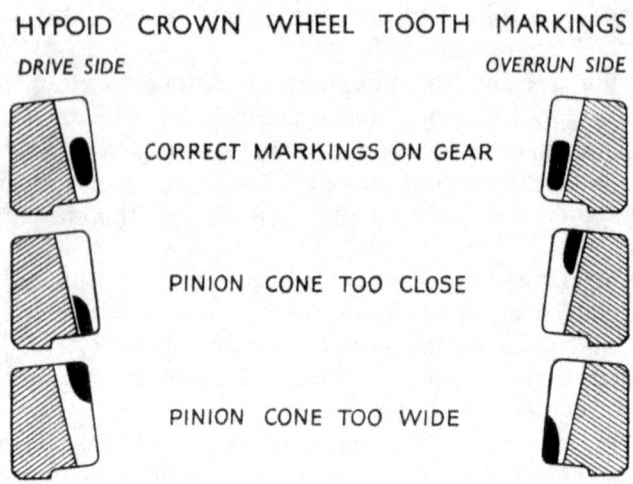

HYPOID CROWN WHEEL TOOTH MARKINGS
DRIVE SIDE   OVERRUN SIDE

CORRECT MARKINGS ON GEAR

PINION CONE TOO CLOSE

PINION CONE TOO WIDE

29. Drive the wheel bearings on to their respective axle shaft and assemble to the axle unit.

30. The grease seals should now be tapped into the bearing housings and the assemblies fitted to each axle sleeve, followed by the brake backing plate and shoe assembly.

31. The four bolts are fitted through each bearing housing and brake backing plate, ensuring that both these items assume their appropriate relation with the axle sleeve, the nuts are screwed into position and firmly tightened.

32. The hubs are next fitted by means of a special tool or press and secured by the splined hub tightening cones, conical washers and hub securing nuts. A substantial spanner will be required to tighten the castellated securing nut. (A tightening torque of 110-125 lbs. ft. is specified. After axle No. TS.8039 the torque was increased to 125-145 lbs. ft. when a nut of a different material was introduced.) Having thoroughly tightened up this nut, the hole in the axle shaft is lined up with one of the slots in the castellated nut and the split pin is fitted.

33. The brake drum is next fitted to each hub and secured thereto by means of the two countersunk grub screws.

34. Fit wheel securing cones (wire wheel hubs only).

Service Diagnosis

Rear axle noise is usually apparent as a hum in moderate cases or as a growl in very severe cases.

Noises from the rear wheel bearings, propeller shaft bearing or tires is often diagnosed as rear axle troubles.

Always ascertain that the noise attributed to the rear axle does actually emanate from that unit before dismantling parts.

CAUSE	REMEDY
Axle Noise	
a. Inadequate or improper lubrication.	a. Drain, flush casing out with flushing oil and replenish with correct grade of oil.
b. Teeth broken off gears.	b. Replace damaged parts.
c. Contact of crown wheel and pinion not correctly adjusted.	c. Noise during coasting; move the pinion away from crown wheel. Noise during driving; move the pinion toward the crown wheel. Do not move the pinion more than .004" when making these adjustments.
Lubricant Leakage	
a. Leakage in general.	a. Reduce level of oil if overfull. Clean out breather.
b. Leakage at hub.	b. Clean out breather. Renew oil seal if leakage persists.
c. Leakage at pinion head.	c. Clean out breather. Renew oil seal if leakage persists.
Axle Knock	
a. Splines on axle shafts or in differential gears badly worn.	a. Replace worn parts.
b. Splines on hub shell or center of wire wheel badly worn.	b. Replace worn parts.
c. Incorrect shimming of planet gears in differential unit.	c. Replace present ones in use with thicker ones.

FRONT SUSPENSION AND STEERING

Front Suspension Data

Track at Ground (Static Laden)	45″
Castor Angle	Nil
King Pin Inclination (Static Laden)	7°
Wheel Camber (Static Laden)	2°
Wheel Camber (Full Bump 3″)	$1/2$°
Wheel Camber (Full Rebound 2.25″)	1°
Turning Circle	32′
Back Lock	31°
Front Lock	28.5°

A 20° Back Lock gives an 18.75° Front Lock.

Front Wheel Alignment	Parallel to $1/8$″ toe in
Length of Center Tie Rod	19.44″
Length of Outer Tie Rod	7.68″
End Float of Lower Outer Shackle Pin Assembly	.004″ to .012″

NOTE: At TR 4 Commission No. CT6344 (wire wheels) and CT6390 (disc wheels) and thereafter, 3° positive camber (instead of 0°) has been incorporated by modification of the upper wishbone arms, ball joints and vertical links.

Description

The two front suspension units are of wishbone construction. Road shocks are absorbed by low periodicity coil springs, each of these springs is controlled by a double acting telescopic shock absorber fitted inside the coil spring.

The upper wishbones are rubber bushed at their inner ends to a fulcrum pin which is attached to the spring housing, they are shaped to form a "U" and the outer ends are interlaced to accommodate a distance piece and are secured together by the screwed shank of a ball joint. This joint is fitted to, and provides the axial movement for, the upper end of the vertical link. The inner ends of the lower wishbone arms are bushed on each side and are attached to the fulcrum pin mounted on the upper side of the chassis frame. The fulcrum is steadied at its extremities by two support brackets.

The outer ends of the wishbone arms, are mounted on either end of a shackle pin. The shackle pin is splined centrally to fit transversely into the manganese bronze trunnion which is threaded to accommodate the lower end of the vertical link.

Each bushed end of the wishbone arms is located sideways on the shackle pin by means of a white metal covered steel thrust washer, bearing on the screwed trunnion on the inside and on the outer side against a steel washer which is secured by a split-pinned castellated nut. During production, the outer lower ends of the wishbone arms are assembled to the shackle pin to give an end float of .004" to .012". The need for adjustment should only occur when the front suspension units have been disturbed. Road dirt and weather are excluded from the grease lubricated bearings by special oil resisting rubber seals.

The screwed trunnion at the lower end and the ball joint at the upper end of the vertical link provide the bearings for the pivoting of the road wheels. Road dirt and weather are excluded from these bearings by a rubber gaited interposed between the vertical link and the ball joint assembly at its upper end, at the lower end a circular rubber seal is fitted between the trunnion and the link. The thread of the trunnion is sealed off by a disc let into the lower end of the threaded bore. The steering lock stock consists of an eccentric roller bolted to the upper side of the trunnion and abuts against a machined face on the vertical link. The vertical link, which couples the upper and lower wishbone arms as previously described, is a carbon steel stamping and carries the stub axle shaft, the brake backing plate and the steering lever.

The stub axle is of manganese molybdenum steel, mounted as a press taper fit in the vertical link and secured by a split pin locked castellated nut.

The brake backing plate, with the brake shoes and hydraulic wheel cylinders attached, is secured to a machined flange on the vertical link by two setscrews with a lock plate at the lower two points and two bolts of unequal length at the upper two points. The longer of these bolts passes through the front bore of the brake plate, the vertical link, a distance piece and the steering lever and is secured by a nyloc nut; the shorter bolt is similarly secured and utilizes the lower bore.

The front hub is mounted on a pair of opposed taper roller bearings carried on the stub axle shaft. The inner bearing abuts against a projecting shoulder on the vertical link and its outer ring against a flange machined in the hub. The outer ring of the outer bearings bears against the flange machined in the hub and in the hub and the inner cone of the race against a "D" washer, all are secured to the stub axle by a castellated nut and split pin. These bearings are adjusted by the castellated securing nut but are not pre-loaded.

Provision is made against the loss of grease by fitting a felt washer between the vertical link and inner bearing.

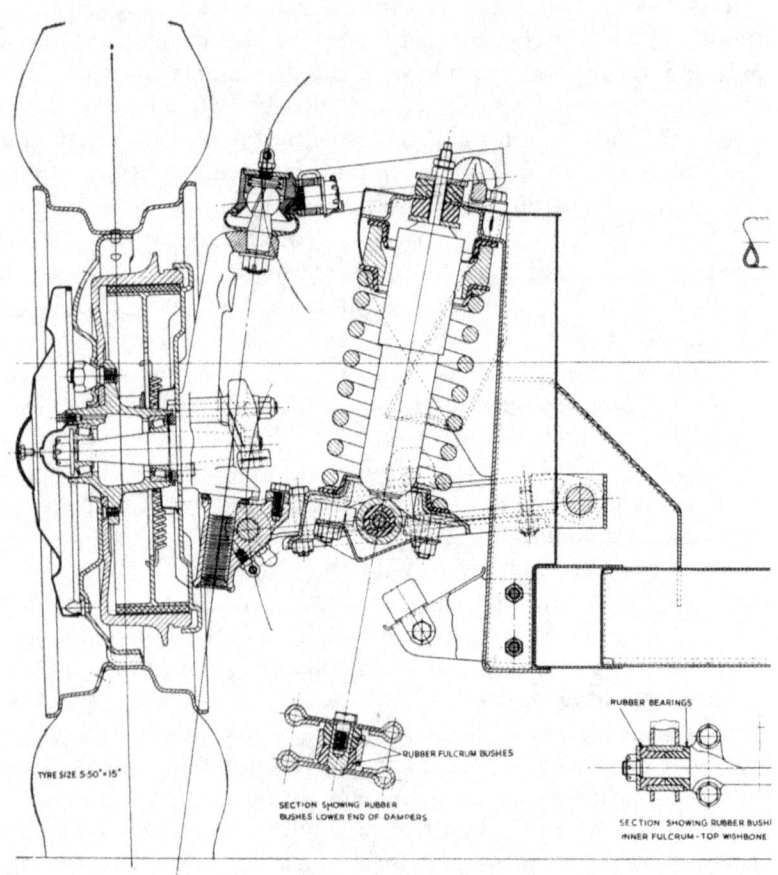

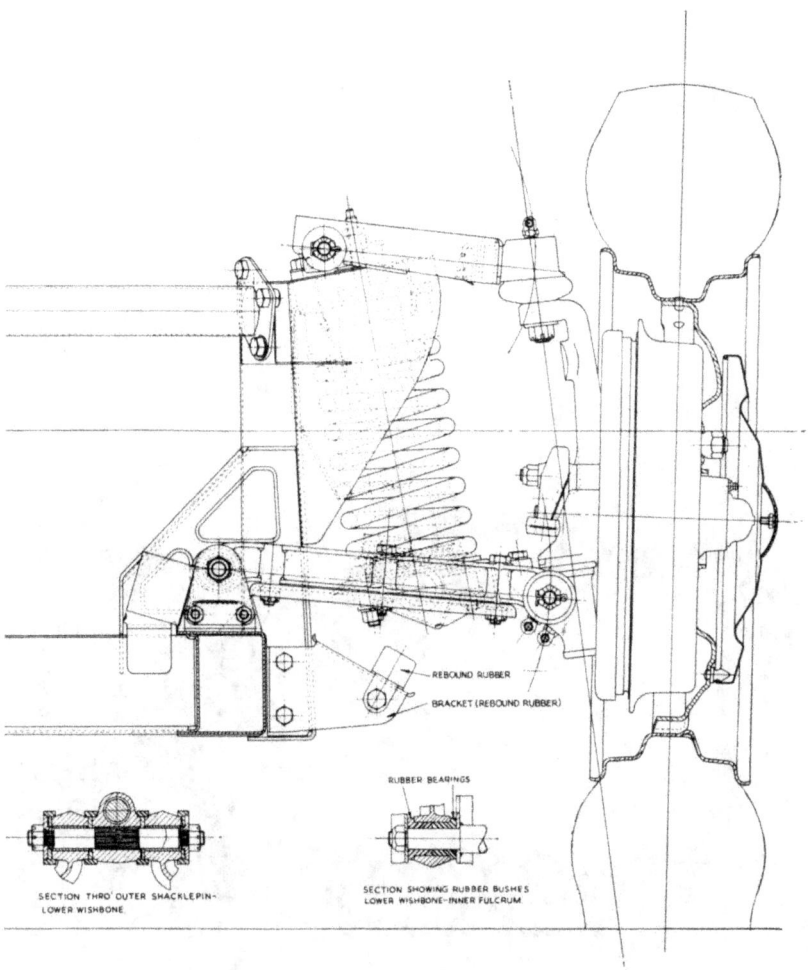

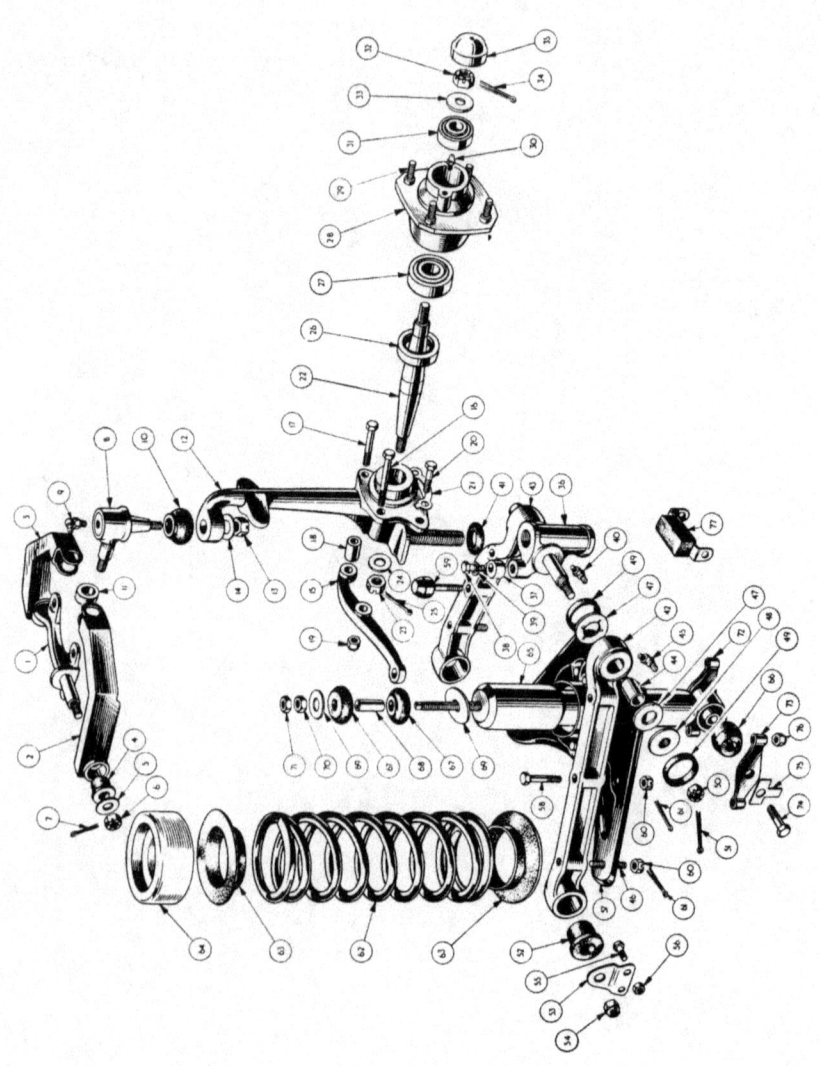

Ref. No.	Description	Ref. No.	Description
1.	Inner Upper Fulcrum Pin.	41.	Oil Seal.
2.	L.H. Front Upper Wishbone Arm.	42.	L.H. Front Lower Wishbone Arm Assembly.
3.	R.H. Front Upper Wishbone Arm.	43.	R.H. Front Lower Wishbone Arm Assembly.
4.	Rubber Bush.		
5.	Plain Washer.	44.	Bush for Wishbone Arm.
6.	Castellated Nut.	45.	Grease Nipple.
7.	Split Pin.	46.	Spring Pan Studs
8.	Upper Wishbone Ball Joint Assembly.	47.	Thrust Washer.
9.	Grease Nipple.	48.	Lock Washer.
10.	Rubber Gaiter.	49.	Grease Seal.
11.	Upper Wishbone Distance Piece.	50.	Castellated Nut.
12.	Vertical Link.	51.	Split Pin.
13.	Castellated Nut.	52.	Rubber Bush.
14.	Plain Washer.	53.	Support Bracket.
15.	Steering Lever.	54.	Nyloc Nut.
16.	Bolt.	55.	Bolt.
17.	Bolt.	56.	Nut.
18.	Steering Lever Distance Piece.	57.	Lower Spring Pan Assembly.
19.	Nyloc Nut.	58.	Bolt.
20.	Setscrew.	59.	Bump Rubber.
21.	Locking Plate.	60.	Castellated Nut.
22.	Stub Axle.	61.	Cotter Pin.
23.	Castellated Nut.	62.	Front Road Spring.
24.	Plain Washer.	63.	Rubber Washer.
25.	Split Pin.	64.	Packing Piece.
26.	Oil Seal.	65.	Shock Absorber.
27.	Front Hub Inner Bearing.	66.	Lower Rubber Mounting.
28.	Front Hub.	67.	Upper Rubber Mounting.
29.	Wheel Stud.	68.	Metal Sleeve.
30.	Grease Nipple, fitted up to Commission No. TS.5348.	69.	Washer.
		70.	Nut.
31.	Front Hub Outer Bearing.	71.	Lock Nut.
32.	Castellated Nut.	72.	Shock Absorber Bracket and Fulcrum Pin.
33.	"D" Washer under nut.		
34.	Split Pin.	73.	Shock Absorber Bracket.
35.	Grease Retaining Cap.	74.	Setscrew.
36.	Bottom Trunnion.	75.	Tab Washer.
37.	Steering Lock Stop.	76.	Nut.
38.	Bolt for Steering Lock Stop.	77.	Rebound Rubber.
39.	Spring Washer.		
40.	Grease Nipple.		

Maintenance

The maintenance necessary is largely confined to periodical greasing (see Lubrication Chart in General Data Section).

The hub bearings are not pre-loaded and it will be necessary to ensure this condition is attained when carrying out adjustments.

As a precautionary measure it is most desirable to check that an end float of .004" to .012" in the lower outer wishbone arm attachment to the shackle lin is maintained. Each arm is adjusted independently. Apart from damage at this point, tightness at this point can appreciably affect the ride of the car.

Front Wheel Alignment

The track should be between parallel and $1/8''$ toe in with normal tires. $1/16''$ toe in with Michelin tires.

The outer tie rods are adjustable for length and usually to give correct track the distance between the centers of the ball joint assemblies will be 7.68", TR 2 & 3; 8.55" for TR 4.

If the wheel alignment is in doubt and a check is to be made it will be necessary to satisfy the following initial requirements:
a. Tire pressures are correct for all tires.
b. The amount of wear on both front tires must be the same.
c. The front wheels are true and in balance.
d. The checking floor must be level.
e. The car is in the static laden condition.

To Adjust Front Wheel Alignment

1. With the car satisfying the initial requirements, set the front road wheels in the straight ahead position and push the car forward a short distance.
2. Check the alignment of the wheels with an optical gauge, similar instrument, or by measuring with alignment rod.
3. If only a fractional correction is necessary it can be made on the outer tie rod on the opposite side to the steering box.
4. To carry out this adjustment it is first necessary to loosen the two lock nuts and turn the tube to shorten or lenghten the tie-rod assembly. Lock the tube by the two nuts and move the car forward half a revolution of a wheel and check, and make a further adjustment if necessary.
5. If an appreciable amount of maladjustment has to be corrected, check first the length of the outer tie-rods. Should these lengths be equal make the necessary correction to both. When they are found to be of unequal length first correct the rod nearest the steering box and then make any adjustment to the further one. After making such adjustments it is a wise pre-

caution to measure the length and if found to differ greatly from 7.68" or 8.55" the front suspension should be checked for accidental damage.

Steering Lock Stops

The steering lock stop consists of an eccentric roller mounted on each bottom trunnion by means of a setscrew and lock washer.

It is most important that the steering lock stops come into action before the conical peg of the rocker shaft follower reaches the end of its cam path. This movement is not more than 33° either side of the mid point of the cam and will allow the steering wheel to travel approximately $2^{1}/_{4}$ turns from lock to lock.

The correct adjustment of the lock stops should allow a "Back lock" of 31° and a "Front lock" of $28^{1}/_{2}°$.

When checking this adjustment it is necessary to satisfy the following requirements.
a. The tire pressures must be correct for all four tires.
b. The testing ground must be flat.
c. Car must be in the static laden condition.

To Set Steering Lock Stops
1. Select a space of level ground and run the car gently forward so that the front wheels run on to the Churchill Turning measure or similar radius gauge and the back wheels on to blocks as high as the gauge. This will ensure that the car maintains its level.
2. Measure the wheel movement from the straight ahead position.
3. Adjust the eccentric roller by first loosening the setscrew and then turn the roller itself.
4. When the correct degree of adjustment is attained, tighten down the setscrew so that the roller will remain in contact with the vertical link.

NOTE: If it is impossible to obtain the correct lock positions by adjustment of the steering lock stop, this condition will indicate either a damaged steering drop arm, steering lever, or in rare cases, a fault in the steering unit. Where such difficulties do arise steps must be taken to diagnose the cause and necessary replacements fitted.

To Remove Front Hub and Stub Axle
1. Jack up the front of the car, remove road wheel.
2. Remove grease retaining cap and grease nipple from end of hub. Grease nipples were discontinued after Commission No.

TS.5348.

3. Withdraw split pin and remove castellated nut and washer from end of stub axle.
4. Remove hub.
5. The outer hub bearing can be removed when the hub is released from the hub remover.
6. Remove the four nuts, spring washers and bolts securing the hub grease catcher to the brake backing plate.
7. Remove the inner wheel bearing from the stub axle, followed by the grease seal.
8. The stub axle can be removed from the vertical link if so desired by the removal of the split pin, castellated nut and plain washer from the inner side of the vertical link.

To Replace Front Hub and Stub Axle
1. Fit the stub axle to the vertical link and secure with the plain washer, castellated nut locked by a split pin on the inner side of the vertical link.
2. Seat the grease seal on its spigot of the vertical link with the felt pad towards the center of the car, followed by the inner wheel bearing.
3. Place the hub grease catcher in position in such a manner that the shaped end of the pressing is below the vent hole in the brake backing plate. Secure grease catcher to backing plate with four screws, spring washers and nuts.
4. Fit the hub and outer bearing followed by the "D" aperture washer and attach castellated nut.

These front wheel bearings should **not** be pre-loaded.

5. The castellated nut should be tightened to a torque loading of 10 lbs. ft. and then slackened off $1^{1}/_{2}$ to 2 flats according to the position of the split pin hole. The hub bearings are now considered to be correctly adjusted and the castellated nut can be locked with the split pin.
6. Fit the grease retaining cap and grease nipple to hub, and grease hub.
7. Replace road wheel. Remove lifting jack from under front of car.

To Remove Front Shock Absorber TR 2-3
1. Jack up the car, place supporting stands under the chassis frame and remove lifting jack. Remove road wheel.
2. Partially compress the front road spring by placing a small lifting jack under the spring pan.
3. Remove the lock nut and nut from upper end of shock absorber, followed by a plain washer and upper rubber mount-

ing.
4. Detach the rebound rubber and its bracket from the side of the chassis frame after removing the nuts, lock washers and two long bolts.
5. Remove the lifting jack from below the spring pan.
6. Remove the four nuts and lock washers from the underneath and center of the spring pan. After withdrawing the rebound rubber abutment plate the shock absorber can be withdrawn through the spring plate.
7. After removing the shock absorber from the car, its lower attachment brackets can be removed. Lift the tabs of the locking plate and remove the setscrew followed by one bracket and a rubber bush.
8. The second bracket is removed from the shock absorber together with the rubber bush, the latter can be withdrawn from the fulcrum pin of the bracket assembly.

To Fit Shock Absorber
1. Examine all rubber bushes to ascertain that they are in good order. Also ensure that the fulcrum pin is securely welded to the shock absorber attachment bracket.
2. Press a rubber bush on to the fulcrum pin attachment bracket and feed this assembly, bush first, into the eye of the shock absorber. Press a second rubber bush on to the protruding fulcrum pin.
3. Position second attachment bracket with the tab washer and secure with the setscrews. Turn over tab of washer.
4. Place a large plain washer in position on the upper end of the shock absorber followed by a rubber mounting (spigot uppermost) with the metal sleeve in its center.
5. Feed the shock absorber assembly through the spring pan in such a manner that the two attachment brackets locate on the studs of the spring pan assembly and at the same time the upper attachment will pass through the spring abutment on the chassis frame. It may be necessary to compress the road spring by placing a jack under the lower wishbone assembly.
6. Attach the second rubber mounting (spigot downwards) to the upper end of the damper which is protruding through the chassis frame, threading it on to the metal sleeve and followed by the plain washer and securing nut.
7. Tighten this nut sufficiently to nip the plain washers and metal sleeve and lock with a second nut.
8. Place the rebound rubber abutment plate in position on the lower attachment studs (welded to the spring pan) with the

apex of the wedge pointing towards the center of the car. Secure with nuts and lock washers.

9. Utilizing two long bolts, nuts and lock washers secure the rebound rubber and its bracket to the chassis frame.

10. Remove the lifting jack from under the lower wishbones and replace the road wheel.

11. Jack up front of car to remove support stands, finally remove jack.

To Remove Front Road Spring

1. Remove front shock absorber.
2. Withdraw the split pins from the castellated nuts on the underside of the lower wishbones. Remove the center nut and bolt from the front wishbone arm and the bump rubber assembly from the rear wishbone arm. Feed two guide pins into the vacant holes.
3. Place a small lifting jack under the spring pan, with a suitable packing between jack and pan to prevent damage to the shock absorber attachment studs on the latter.
4. Remove the four remaining nuts securing the spring pan to the wishbone arms and lower jack, easing the guide pins through the wishbone arms.
5. The spring can be withdrawn from its upper abutment together with rubber washers and distance piece.

An alternative method is to utilize the Churchill Tool, No. M50, or a spring compressor in the following manner:—

a. Carry out operation 1 and 2 as previously described.
b. Remove the flynut, bearing and plate from the threaded rod of the Churchill Tool followed by the "C" washer.
c. Feed the rod, notched end first, through the spring pan and upper shock absorber abutment, to the protruding end fit the "C" washer.
d. Feed the plate on to the threaded portion of the rod protruding from the spring pan in such a manner that the bearing seat is downwards, ensure too that the holes in the block locate on the studs of the spring pan.
e. Feed bearing on to threaded rod followed by the fly nut, tighten to compress spring a small amount.
f. Remove the four remaining nuts securing the spring pan to the wishbone arms.
g. By slowly unscrewing the fly nut the spring pan can be lowered down the guide pins.
h. When all tension is released from the road spring the guide pins and the "C" washer can be removed from the upper end of the shaft.

i. Withdraw the Churchill Tool from the suspension unit together with the spring pan, spring, rubber washers and distance piece.

To Fit Road Spring

1. Attach the rod of the Churchill Tool No. M50 to the spring abutment bracket of the front suspension unit and fit the guide pins through the center holes of the lower wishbone arms.
2. Assemble the alloy distance piece (spigot downward) on the road spring with a rubber washer interposed between, and position a second rubber washer on the spring's lower extremity.
3. The spring and distance piece assembly is offered up to the front suspension unit followed by the spring pan, the latter located on the guide pins.
4. Fit the plate to the threaded rod of the Churchill Tool in such a manner that the bearing will seat in its recess and the studs of the spring pan in their recesses. Follow with the bearing and fly nut.
5. The fly nut of the tool is turned to compress the spring. Ensure that, when the spring pan closes to the wishbone arms that it is located on the attachment studs at the inner ends of the wishbone. Secure and lock washers and castellated nuts and fit two bolts with castellated nuts and lock washers at the trunnion end of the wishbone arm.
6. When the spring pan is secured to the wishbone arms the Churchill Tool can be removed and the guide pins withdrawn from the wishbone arm.
7. The spring pan is finally secured to the wishbone arms by a nut, bolt and lock washer at the front arm and a bump rubber assembly at the rear arm.
   Lock all six nuts with split pins.
8. The shock absorber can now be fitted.

To Remove and Dismantle Front Suspension Unit

Before dismantling the units, suitably mark the components so that they can be returned to their relative positions.

Carry out instructions as detailed for "To Remove Front Hub and Stub Axle" and "To Remove Front Road Spring" then proceed as follows:—
1. Drain the hydraulic system and disconnect the flexible hose as described in Brake Section. Remove the grease catcher by removing four nuts and bolts. Release the tabs of the locking plates and withdraw the lower two of the four bolts securing the brake backing plate to the vertical link, followed by the

upper two bolts. These bolts pass through the vertical link and distance pieces and thence through the steering lever, on the withdrawal of these bolts it will be necessary to hold the steering lever and collect the bushes. Alternately the brake plate can be removed from the vertical link without draining the system.

2. Remove the nyloc nuts from the ends of the lower wishbone fulcrum pin, followed by the nuts, bolts and lock washers securing the fulcrum pin support brackets to the chassis frame. The support brackets can now be removed.

3. Remove the split pins from the outer ends of the lower shackle pins. Remove the castellated nuts, grease seals and washers from both ends of the shackle pin.

4. The wishbone arms can now be removed and the thrust washer and grease seal withdrawn from the shackle pin.

5. Remove the two bolts, nuts, plain and locking washers, followed by the two setscrews and spring washers, from the upper fulcrum pin.

6. The front suspension unit can now be lifted away from the car.

7. Withdraw the split pin from the castellated nut securing the ball joint assembly to the upper wishbone arm. Remove the castellated nut and withdraw the ball joint assembly from the wishbone arms, collecting the distance piece as the ball joint is moved.

8. Withdraw the split pin and remove the nut and plain washer securing the ball joint assembly to the vertical link and withdraw ball joint.

9. Withdraw the split pin from the castellated nuts at the outer ends of the upper inner fulcrum pin. Remove the large diameter plain washers and the outer rubber bushes.

10. The wishbone arms can now be removed and the second rubber bush withdrawn from the fulcrum pin.

11. Remove the steering stop screw from the lower end of the vertical link and detach the bottom trunnion assembly from the vertical link and collect the oil seal situated between the vertical link and the trunnion assembly.

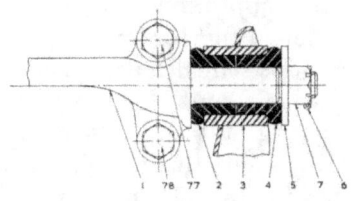

Section through upper inner fulcrum

To Assemble and Replace Front Suspension Unit

Assembly is made with strict regard to the markings on certain parts to ensure that they are returned to the same relative position.

1. Fit a bush to each end of the upper fulcrum pin.
2. Feed the fulcrum pin into the upper wishbone arm, press the second rubber bush into the wishbone and fit the large plain washer followed by the castellated nut. This nut should be left loose at this juncture.
3. While similarly fitting the second wishbone arm ascertain that the other ends of the arm are positioned correctly to receive the ball pin assembly and distance piece. With the ball pin assembly toward the operator the wishbone flange on the right overlaps the one on the left. This applies to both left and right suspension units.
4. Feed through the upper attachment of the ball joint assembly with the distance piece between the wishbone arms and secure with the plain washer and castellated nut locked by the split pin. Tighten castellated nuts of inner upper fulcrum pins and lock with split pins.
5. Fit the ball pin taper into the vertical link with the rubber gaiter in position and secure with the plain washer and castellated nut. Fit split pin in nut.
6. Offer up the inner upper fulcrum pin to the chassis frame and secure by bolts with a plain washer under its head and a lock washer with the nut at the points near the center line of the car. Setscrews and lock washers are used for the attachment points nearer the ball joint assembly.
7. Ascertain that the shackle pin of the bottom trunnion assembly is mounted centrally. This pin is a press fit in the body of the casting and is prevented from turning by the imbedding of the splines, it can be centralized by the use of a press or gentle tapping with a copper faced mallet.
8. Fit the rubber sealing ring to the lower end of the vertical link followed by the bottom trunnion assembly, which is a screw fit on the vertical link. The trunnion is screwed home and then turned back approximately one turn so that the shackle pin lies parallel to the fore and aft line of the car but between the base of the vertical link and the chassis frame.
9. Feed the locking washer and steering lock stop bush on to the steering stop securing bolt and attach to the bottom trunion assembly. The bolt is left finger tight at this juncture.
10. Fit two rubber bushes to the inner lower fulcrum pin situated on the upper face of the chassis frame, one to each side.

11. Fit two thrust washers to the shackle pin, one to each side, followed by the grease seal.

12. The lower wishbone arms are now fitted over the rubber bushes on the inner fulcrum pin and on to the shackle pin simultaneously. Fit a second pair of rubber bushes on to the inner fulcrum pin (and into the lower wishbone arm) followed by the support bracket, the two holes of which are lowermost. Secure with the nyloc nut but do not fully tighten at this juncture.

13. Secure the support brackets to the brackets welded to the chassis frame utilizing bolts, nuts with lock washer. Tighten the nyloc nuts of the inner lower fulcrum pins until they are solid.

14. Fit to both ends of the shackle pin at the outer end of each wishbone arm, a thrust washer followed by a special lock washer (collar inwards) followed by the rubber grease seals. These lock washers are prevented from rotating by self cutting splines. Feed on the castellated nuts to the ends of the shackle pin and obtain the necessary end float before locking with the split pin.

15. It is essential to have .004" to .012" end float for the outer boss of each lower wishbone arm. As it is not possible to ascertain the end float by the usual method owing to the presence of the rubber grease seals, the following procedure is suggested.

a. Equal tightening should be applied to the two castellated nuts and continued until the assembly is solid.

b. The nuts should then be turned back $1^{1}/_{2}$ - 2 flats according to the position of the split pin hole and then split pinned.

c. The wishbone arms should then be lightly tapped outwards to displace the lock washers (now a splined fit to the shackle pin) and this should be carried out alternately on each arm to avoid altering the relationship of the shackle pin and trunnion.

d. This method will give the recommended end float but as a final precaution the assembly should be checked for freedom of movement over its full range of operation before fitting the road spring.

Apart from damage at this point, tightness will affect the ride of the car.

16. Attach the rod of the Churchill Tool No. M.50 to the spring abutment bracket and the guide rods through the center of the lower wishbone arms.

17. Assemble the alloy distance piece (spigot downward) on the road spring with a rubber washer interposed, fit a second

rubber washer to the lower extremity of the road spring.

18. The spring and distance piece assembly is offered up to the front suspension unit followed by the spring pan, the latter being located on the guide pins. It will be found that the rod of the Churchill Tool No. M.50 protrudes downward from the unit. Fit the plate to this rod in such a manner that the clamp bearing will seat in the recess and the studs of the spring pan fit into their recesses.

19. The fly nut of the tool can be turned to compress the spring. Ensure that, as the spring pan closes to the wishbone, it is located on the attachment studs. Attach the lock washers and castellated nuts adjacent to the bottom trunnion assembly.

20. When the spring pan is secured to the wishbone arms the Churchill Tool can be removed.

21. Remove the guide pins from the center holes and fit the bump rubber assembly to the rear wishbone arm and secure with a lock washer and castellated nut. Fit bolt, lock washer and castellated nut to vacant hole in front wishbone arm. Lock all six nuts with split pins.

22. Fit the shock absorber.

23. Ensuring that the taper bore of the vertical link and the taper of the stub axle are perfectly clean, feed axle into link and secure with plain washer, castellated nut and lock with a split pin.

24. Place the brake backing plate in position on the vertical link and secure by the lower bolt holes first, utilizing two short setscrews and a locking plate. Through the upper holes of the brake backing plate feed the longer of the two remaining bolts, on to the shank of these bolts protruding inwards through the plate and vertical link feed a distance piece (one to each bolt). Selecting the correct steering lever, it must point forward and downward when fitted, fit this also on the protruding bolts and secure with two nyloc nuts. Finally tighten the lower pair of setscrews and turn up tabs of locking plate.

25. Check that the length of outer tie-rod is correct and then connect the outer tie-rod to the steering arm and secure with the nyloc nut with plain washer.

26. Connect the flexible hose to the hydraulic line as described in Brake Section.

27. Fit the hub bearings and hub.

28. Bleed the hydraulic system if the system has been drained and adjust brakes.

29. Fit road wheel, and remove jacks.

30. Check front wheel alignment.

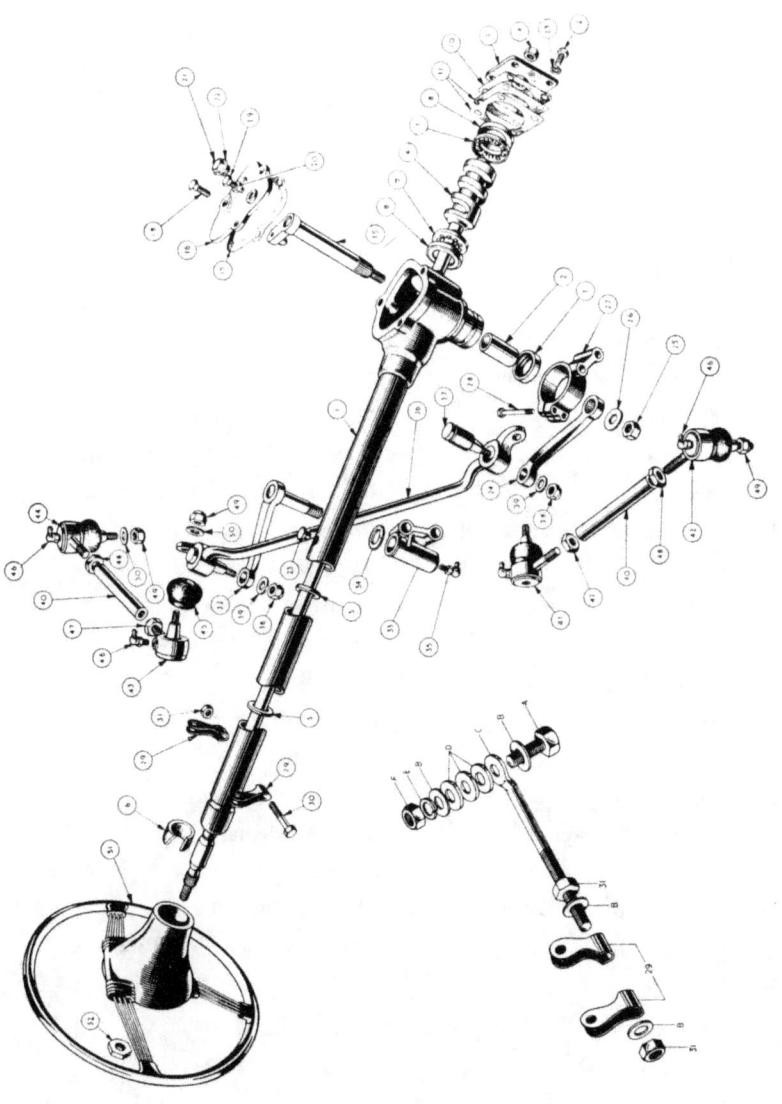

1. Outer Tube and Box Assembly.
2. Rocker Arm Bush.
3. Rocker Arm Oil Seal.
4. Inner Column and Cam.
5. Rubber Ring.
6. Felt Bush.
7. Inner Column Ball Cage.
8. Ball Cage Race.
9. End Cover.
10. Joint Washer.
11. Adjusting Shims.
12. Bolt.
13. Lock Washer.
14. End Plate Gland Nut.
15. Rocker Shaft Assembly.
16. Top Cover.
17. Joint Washer.
18. Bolt.
19. Rocker Shaft Adjusting Bolt.
20. Lock Nut.
21. Oil Filler.
22. Washer.
23. Rubber Plug.
24. Drop Arm.
25. Nut.
26. Lock Washer.
27. Trunnion Bracket.
28. Bolt.
29. Steering Column Clamp.
30. Bolt.
31. Nut.
32. Idler Bracket.
33. Idler Bracket.
34. Oil Seal.
35. Grease Nipple.
36. Center Tie-rod.
37. Silentbloc Bush and Fulcrum Pin.
38. Nyloc Nut.
39. Plain Washer.
40. Tie-rod.
41. R.H. Inner End Assembly.
42. R.H. Outer End Assembly.
43. L.H. Inner End Assembly.
44. L.H. Outer End Assembly.
45. Rubber Gaiter.
46. Grease Nipple.
47. R.H. Threaded Lock Nut.
48. L.H. Threaded Lock Nut.
49. Nylock Nut.
50. Plain Washer.
51. Steering Wheel.
52. Steering Wheel Nut.
A. Bolt
B. Plain Washer
C. Tie Rod
D. Thick Washers
E. Lock Washer
F. Nut
Fitted in place of
30 after Comm. No. TS.1390.

31. Set the steering lock stop.

Steering — TR 2-3

The steering gear is of the cam and lever type with a ratio of 12 to 1. The rocker shaft travel should be limited to 33° either side of the mid point of the cam by the steering lock stops and this will allow the steering wheel to travel approximately $2^{1}/_{4}$ turns from lock to lock. The cam takes the form of a spiral, while the lever carries a conical shaped peg which engages in this cam.

As the conical peg does not reach the bottom of the spiral cam the depth of engagement can be adjusted. This is effected by a hardened steel setscrew mounted on the top cover, the screw when turned clockwise contacts the lever's upper face and holds the conical peg in engagement with the cam.

The steering gear is a self contained and oil tight unit. The cam is attached permanently to the inner column which in turn is mounted on caged ball bearings immediately above and below the cam, with a graphite impregnated bearing at its other end.

The lever, to which the conical shaped peg is attached, is an integral part of the rocker shaft assembly and the latter is mounted in a plain bearing, the bore has an oil seal fitted at its lower extremity. The shaft which protrudes through the case is splined to receive the drop arm.

The stator tube which carries the control wires of the electric horn and flashing indicators is held in position by the bottom cover plate, a gland nut and an olive, the latter also provides an oil tight seal.

The unit is attached to the chassis frame by a trunnion bracket at its lower end and braced in the body of the car to the facia panel.

Maintenance

An oil filler is provided in the form of a rubber plug, which is located on the steering column at approximately 12" from the steering box.

A high pressure oil should be used for replenishment. (See Lubrication Chart for recommended lubricants.)

The felt bush in the top of the column outer tube is graphite impregnated and should, therefore, require no additional lubrication. If owing to extreme climatic conditions a "squeak" should develop in the bush, extra lubrication should be by colloidial graphite. Oil should not be used since it tends to make the bearing "sticky."

An occasional check for tightness should be made to the steering drop arm, the ball joints and also the steering box securing bolts.

Adjustment of the steering box can be affected in two ways, firstly by shims interposed between the steering box and its end cover, and secondly by a setscrew mounted in the top cover.

Adjustment of Steering Box

Means of adjustment to take up wear is provided at two points, both of which are accessible with the steering column in position.

The first means of adjustment is made by adding to, or taking from, the shim pack located between the end cover and the steering box.

The thickness of the shim pack controls the amount of "float," or pre-load, of the inner column.

While a slight amount of pre-load is permissible, in no circumstances must there be any end float.

The second means of adjustment is by a hardened setscrew and locknut, situated on the top cover plate.

This screw controls the amount of lift in the rocker shaft and is adjusted with the rocker shaft in the center of the box, that is, the straight ahead position.

The cam gear, which is integral with the inner column, is similar in shape to a spiral cam, having a greater diameter at its center than at its extremities.

When adjusting the rocker shaft it will be noticed that at the extremities of the arc through which the rocker shaft moves, a certain amount of lift can be felt, and as the shaft moves to the center, the amount of lift is progressively reduced.

The correct adjustment of the rocker shaft is when on turning the steering wheel from lock to lock, a very slight resistance is felt at the center of the travel.

The point of resistance should correspond with the straight ahead position of the steering.

NOTE: The adjustment of the rocker shaft should only be made after ensuring that **NO** end float exists in the inner column.

To Remove Control Head From Steering Wheel

1. Disconnect the horn and flasher control wires at the "snap connectors" situated on the fender valance. Suitably identify these wires for subsequent reconnection if the coloring is not distinguishable.

2. Slacken off the gland nut which secures the stator tube to the end cover of the steering box.

3. Slacken the three grub screws which are situated radially in the steering wheel hub.

4. Withdraw the control head and stator tube from the steering column.

5. The stator tube can now be withdrawn from the control head. These components are a slide fit just below the control

To Fit Control Head and Stator Tube to the Steering Wheel

1. Place the steering wheel in the straight ahead position. This position can be checked by inspecting the alignment of all four wheels.

2. Feed the stator tube, with the anti-rattle springs in position, into the innter column of the steering unit with the tube slot uppermost and at the 12 o'clock position. Allow approximately 1 inch of tube to protrude from the end cover of the steering box.

3. Fit the brass olive to the protruding stator tube and secure with the gland nut. Loosen nut back one turn, this is retightened in a later operation.

4. Feed the wires from the short tube of the control head into and through the stator tube now in the steering unit. With the flasher control lever of the head at 12 o'clock ensure that the vertical lever of the stator tube plate it at the 6 o'clock position. Failure to observe this point will mean that the flashing indicators will not cancel correctly.

5. Secure the control head in the boss of the steering wheel by tightening the three grub screws situated radially in the steering wheel hub. Do not move the steering wheel during this operation.

6. Tighten the gland nut to secure the stator tube to the steering box end cover and reconnect wires according to the colors or identification marks.

To Remove Steering Wheel

1. First remove the stator tube and control head as described above.

2. Remove the steering wheel securing nut. If it is so desired the wheel and the top of the inner column can be "center punched" for identification and simplified replacement.

3. Utilizing the Churchill steering wheel remover Tool No. 20SM.3600 or suitable puller remove the wheel.

To Fit Steering Wheel
1. Place the car on level ground and set the wheels in the straight ahead position.
2. Feed the steering wheel on to the inner column of the steering unit in such a manner that the two horizontal spokes lie across the fore and aft axis of the car. If on dismantling the column and wheel previously the components have been marked it is merely necessary to align the marks.
3. Fit the securing nut and tighten down.
4. Fit stator tube and control head.

To Remove Steering Unit
1. Disconnect battery lead and jack up front of car. Place stands securely under frame and remove jacks.
2. Remove the road wheel nearest to the steering column.
4. Using a suitable lever remove the center tie-rod from the drop arm of the steering unit.
5. Remove the control head from the center of the steering wheel.
6. Remove the steering wheel.
7. Loosen the clamp securing the column to the facia panel by slackening off the two nuts on the lower support stay (this is a nut and bolt on early production cars) and the two nuts secur-

ing the clamps to the anchor bracket.
8. Remove the clip from the rubber draught excluder.
9. Withdraw the two bolts securing the steering unit trunion bracket to the chassis frame.
10. The steering unit may be drawn forward and downward.
11. After the removal of the steering unit the drop arm can be detached from the rocker shaft, utilizing a suitable puller when the securing nut and lock plate have been first removed.
12. Slacken off the two pinch bolts securing the trunnion bracket and withdraw it from the steering unit.

To Fit Steering Unit
1. Adjust the end float of the inner column and the rocker shaft for depth of engagement.
2. Fit the trunnion bracket so that the chassis mounting points are forward. Do not fully tighten these two bolts at this juncture.
3. Attach the drop arm to the splined end of the rocker shaft in such a manner that the scribe lines on these components align and appear to be continuous. Position lock plate and tighten securing nut, lock this nut with the plate by turning its edge over the "flat" machined on the drop arm and another part of the lock plate over the nut.
4. Place screw clip on draught excluder and feed the column of the steering unit upwards from the front of the car and under the facia panel. Position the trunnion bracket in the chassis bracket and attach with two bolts and lock washers, the longer bolt also accommodates the stiffening bracket for the bumper and is fitted to the lowermost hole, the shorter of the two bolts utilizes the upper hole. Leave both bolts loose at this juncture.
5. Secure the column to the mounting bracket under the facia panel by tightening the two nuts on the lower support stay (this was a nut and bolt on early production cars) and the nuts securing the clamps to the anchor bracket.
6. Tighten the two bolts securing the trunnion bracket to the chassis frame and finally the two bolts of the trunnion bracket to the steering unit.
7. Fit the center tie-rod to the drop arm and secure with the nyloc nut and plain washer.
8. Tighten the draft-excluded clip.
9. Fit the steering wheel.
10. Fit the control head and stator tube.
11. Fill steering box with high pressure oil.
12. Fit front apron and front bumper.

13. Replace road wheel, jack up car to remove stands and lower car to ground. Reconnect battery.

To Dismantle Steering Unit
1. Remove nut and lock plate and utilizing a suitable puller remove the drop arm. On no account must the drop arm be removed by hammer blows as this may seriously damage the conical pin on the rocker shaft and also the cam of the center column.
2. Slacken off the two pinch bolts attaching the trunnion bracket to the body of the rocker shaft housing, and remove bracket.
3. Remove cover and joint washer after withdrawing the set-screws of the steering box cover. Allow the oil to drain away.
4. Withdraw the rocker shaft while protecting the rocker shaft oil seal with a thin clinder of shim steel.
5. Remove the setscrews and lock washers securing the end cover to the steering box, followed by the shims and joint washer.
6. The lower bearing race and ball cage can now be removed allowing the cam to be withdrawn, together with the upper ball cage and rubber rings attached to the inner column.
7. The split felt bush situated in the top of the outer case can now be withdrawn.
8. The upper bearing race can be drifted out from the steering box.
9. Drift out the bearing bush and oil seal of the rocker shaft.

To Assemble Steering Unit
1. Feed the rocker shaft bearing bush into the outer column and box assembly and press into position.
2. Slide the trunnion bracket into position on the rocker shaft housing. The chassis mounting points should point forward and downward. The two bolts should be tightened just sufficiently to keep the bracket in position at this juncture.
3. Fit the upper ball race to the steering box. Feed the inner column with the rubber rings and ball cage in position into the box.
4. Place the second ball cage in position on the lower bearing face of the cam followed by the race.
5. Locate a fresh washer together with the old shim pack on the end cover and fit to the steering box, utilizing four bolts and lock washers.
6. Check for end float. All float **must** be eliminated but a small amount of pre-loading is permitted. End float is adjusted by

the removal or addition of shims interposed between the steering box and the end cover. Their removal decreases the end float while the addition of these shims increases the end float.

7. Press the oil seal into the lower extremities of the rocker shaft body.

8. Feed the rocker shaft into its bore through the top of the steering box and allow the conical pin to settle in the groove of the cam.

While this shaft is being fitted it is essential that the oil seal lip is protected from damage, otherwise oil leaks will result.

9. Withdraw the adjusting screw in the top cover to ensure that its shank does not bear down on the rocker shaft lever when the cover is secured to the unit. Secure cover with three setscrews and lock washers, utilizing a new joint washer.

10. Ensure that the mounting bracket is in position as described, for this cannot be fitted when the drop arm is attached to the rocker shaft. Position the drop arm on the splined rocker shaft so that the scribe lines align; secure with nut and lock plate, the edge of the latter is turned up to secure nut and drop arm.

11. Having removed **all** end float adjust the depth of engagement of the rocker shaft and the cam by means of the screw mounted in the top cover. The screw is turned clockwise to increase the depth of engagement or anti-clockwise to reduce the depth. The engagement is said to be correct when slight resistance is felt when the rocker shaft is in the straight ahead position.

12. Fit the graphite impregnated bush to the upper end of the outer column. The steering wheel securing nut is loosely attached to the inner column for safe keeping.

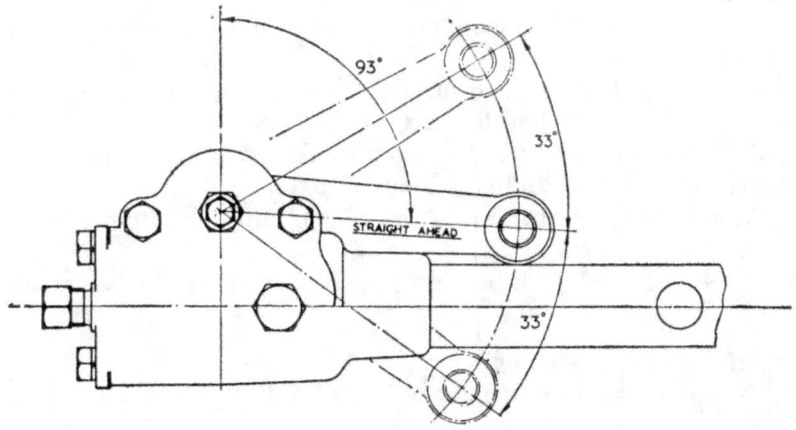

Removal and Replacement of Drop Arm

It should be noted **that it is not possible to remove the drop arm of the steering unit without first removing the unit for the car.** The drop arm must only be removed by a special puller, Tool No. M.91 is recommended, a hammer must not be used since any blow would be transferred to the hardened conical pin in the rocker shaft lever which would in turn indent the cam gear and damage the unit.

The drop arm should only be replaced when the trunnion bracket is in position on the rocker shaft housing. The arm is set in such a manner that it will point rearwards and downwards and the scribe line on the end of the rocker shaft will align with that on the drop arm and appear to be continuous.

Should there be an absence of scribe lines on these components the rocker shaft must be set in the straight ahead position and the drop arm fitted so that it is offset 3° to the left of a line passing through the center of the rocker shaft parallel to the center line of the column.

To Remove Idler Unit
1. Jack up the car and place stands securely under the chassis frame, remove the jacks and remove the road wheel nearest to the idler unit.
2. Remove nyloc nut and plain washer and utilizing a suitable lever disconnect the center rod from the idler lever.
3. Remove the two bolts from the chassis frame brackets, lift out idler unit.
4. The idler unit can be further dismantled by unscrewing the lever and fulcrum assembly from its bracket body. The oil seal can now be removed from the base of the fulcrum pin.

To Fit Idler Unit
1. Ensure that the lever and fulcrum pin have full movement, this is allowed by screwing the pin into its housing and unscrewing one full turn; ensure also that the grease seal is in good condition and that the unit is fully greased.
2. Offer up the unit to its bracket welded to the chassis frame and secure with two bolts and lock washers.
3. Attach center tie-rod to the idler lever and secure with nyloc nut and plain washer.
4. Fit road wheel, jack up car, remove stands and lower car to ground.

Steering Column Bracing

To provide greater steering column stability, the nut and bolt fixing for the column attachment clamps at the facia panel were replaced by a tie-rod. This tie-rod is attached at its inner end to the facia-battery box stay and grips the column clamps at its outer end by two nuts and plain washers. Cars with Commission No. TS.1390 onwards are fitted with this tie-rod.

The rod is attached to the facia stay by a $1^{1}/_{8}''$ long bolt. The bolt with a thin plain washer under its head is fed through the eye of the tie-rod with the off set uppermost, three thick plain washers are now fitted to the bolt. This assembly is offered up to the underside of the facia stay and held in position by a nut with a plain and lock washer.

An additional support bracket, clamped to the steering column by two nuts and bolts and to the front suspension unit by a third nut and bolt, was introduced at Commission No. TS. 5777. This bracket is situated between the front suspension unit and the steering box. To remove the column it will be necessary to loosen the two clamping bolts and re-tightening them on replacement of the column.

Telescopic (Adjustable) Steering Unit

This unit is very similar to the normal equipment apart from three main features:—

a. The inner column is of similar length, but its steering wheel attachment splines are of a much greater length.

b. The outer column is shorter than the normal equipment to allow the increased length of the inner column splines to be utilized.

c. The distance of the steering wheel from the driver can be increased by $2^{1}/_{2}$ inches.

Steering Wheel

The steering wheel is the three equidistance spoke type and is a slide fit on the splines of the inner column, it is held at its maximum point of extension by a circlip fitted in an annular recess machined at the top of the splines.

The lower length of splines, between the underside of the steering wheel and the top of the outer column is covered by a telescopic metal shroud.

This metal shroud is supported at its smaller (bottom) end by a spigotted bakelite washer and positioned at its upper end under the steering wheel locking sleeve by a plated steel cup washer.

The steering wheel hub consists of a steel internally splined sleeve as its center, with a cast aluminum surround. The lower end extruding portion of the steel insert is split, threaded and is provided with an externally tapered flange to accommodate aluminum steel lined locking sleeve.

An internal taper, corresponding to that on the lower extension of the steering wheel hub, is machined at the bottom of the locking sleeve bore. When the locking sleeve is screwed to the hub insert, a chuck action is developed, thus locking the steering wheel to the external splines on the inner column.

The length of these splines permit the range of adjustment, and the circlip mounted in its annular groove limits the upwards movement. The telescopic metal shroud covers and protects the splines at all points of adjustment.

The Control Head

The control head mounted in the steering wheel center is similar to the normal equipment with the exception of the stator tube. This consists of a short tube with indents at its lower end to form a key, and a longer tube with a slot at its upper end. The two tubes telescope together, the indents engaging with the slot provided.

The purpose of this key and slot is two fold, firstly to prevent rotation with the steering wheel and secondly to provide telescopic action as the steering wheel is adjusted on its splines.

To Remove Telescopic Steering Wheel and Steering Unit
1. Proceed as described under "To remove Steering Unit."

2. Remove the control head and stator tube as described under "To remove Control Head" below.
3. Loosen the clamping nut of the steering wheel hub and lower the wheel to its fullest extent. The hub and inner column may be marked for simplified replacement.
4. Remove the circlip from its annular groove situated at the top of the inner column.
5. Loosen the hub clamp to allow the steering wheel to be drawn from its column and at the same time hold the metal shroud assembly.
6. Remove the cupped washer from the top of the metal shroud, followed by the shroud and bakelite washer from the top of the outer column.
7. Proceed with operation as detailed in "To remove Steering Unit."

Steering Stiffness

If after greasing all points of the steering, stiffness persists, the following procedure is recommended.
1. Jack up the front of the car and turn the steering wheel from lock to lock. A very slight resistance should be felt when the steering is almost in the straight ahead position. If this stiffness is appreciable and extends to a distance either side of the straight ahead position, the rocker shaft adjusting screw situated in the steering box top cover is bearing too heavily on the lever head of the shaft. The screw should be unlocked and slackened off by a fraction of a turn and then relocked. Should this fail to improve the condition further investigation must be carried out.
2. Loosen off completely the nuts of the steering column tie situated under the facia panel, followed by the two nuts securing the clamps to the anchor bracket. If the column moves more than $1/4''$ from its clamped position, reposition by slackening the bolts securing the steering box to its mounting bracket and the mounting bracket to the chassis frame.
3. Move the steering unit to its correct position. Secure the mounting bracket to the chassis and the steering unit to the mounting bracket.
4. The clamp attachments to the anchor bracket should be made finger tight and the two clamps brought together round the steering column in such a manner that the column is not displaced. Tighten the jam nuts up to the clamps and finally tighten the nuts of the clamp to anchor bracket attachment.
5. If stiffness still persists remove the center tie-rod from the

drop arm by removing the nyloc nut and plain washer and so isolate the steering unit from the suspension unit. Check the inner column for pre-load by loosening the four bolts attaching the end cover from the steering box. Should the movement of the steering wheel become easier shims must be placed between box and end cover.

Remove the control head and steering followed by the felt bearing situated at the top of the column. Check the inner column relative to the outer column, if column appears to be displaced, it can be assumed that the inner column is bent and must be replaced.

6. If the stiffness is traced to the ball joint assemblies, isolate the joint by removing the outer tie-rods from the steering levers. The offending ball joint can now be located and corrected.

7. Should no stiffness be traced, the car must be jacked up and the upper and lower bearings of the vertical link examined.

TR 4 Rack and Pinion Steering

The rack and pinion steering unit introduced on the TR 4 model is essentially a trouble-free mechanism which needs only lubrication every 6,000 miles as noted in the lubrication chart. In case of damage by accident it is best to replace the rack and pinion as a unit rather than separately.

To Remove the Unit from the Car

1. Jack up the front of the vehicle, support it on stands and remove the road wheels.
2. Drain the cooling system and remove the bottom radiator hose.
3. Remove the bolt from the steering coupling.
4. Remove the nyloc attachment nuts and separate the outer tie-rod ball joints from the rod levers.
5. Remove the nyloc nuts, U bolts and aluminum packing pieces.
6. Release the steering unit by moving it forward to disengage the splined shaft from the coupling.
7. Remove unit by withdrawing it through the wheel arch.

To Replace the Steering Unit

Having checked the steering unit dimensions as given in the accompanying illustration, count the number of turns required to move the rack from lock to lock. Turn the shaft back to centralize rack and move the wheels to a straight ahead position.
1. Fit the unit by entering the splined pinion shaft into the coupling.
2. Assemble the aluminum packing pieces behind the rack and the two front aluminum blocks, entering their dowels into the holes in the rack tube.
3. Fit the U bolts and nyloc nuts.
4. Enter the taper pins of the outer tie-rod ball joints into the steering levers.
5. Fit washers and bolts.
6. Refit bolt and nyloc nut to the steering coupling.
7. Refit the road wheels and check front wheel alignment.

STEERING

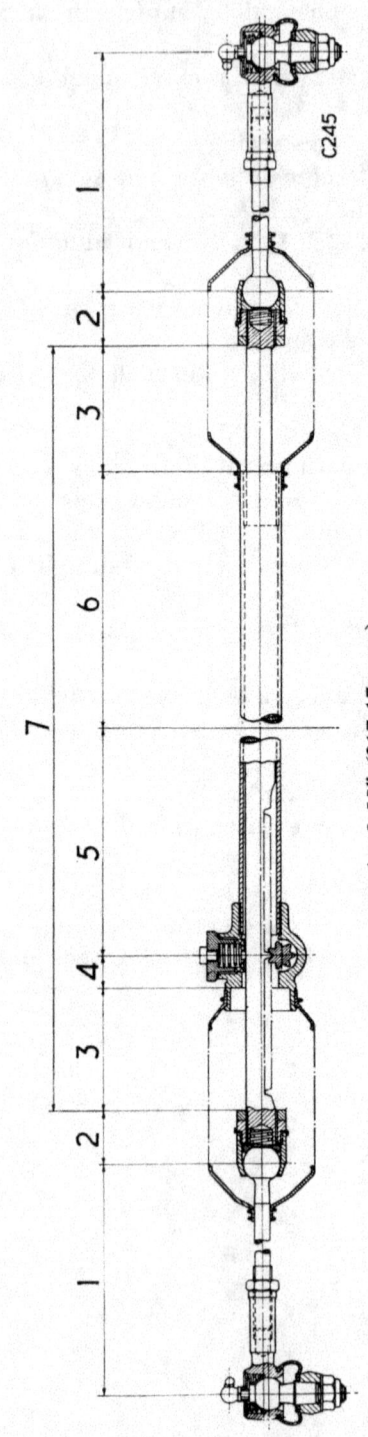

1 8·55" (217·17 mm.).
2 1·42" (36·06 mm.).
3 3·09" (78·5 mm.).
4 0·88" (22·35 mm.).
5 8·00" (203·2 mm.).
6 8·88" (225·55 mm.).
7 23·94" (60·8 cm.).

STEERING UNIT DIMENSIONS

ROAD SPRINGS AND SHOCK ABSORBERS

Rear Road Springs

Semi-elliptical laminated springs are used which have their location point with the axle below and forward of the center, so that the longer end of each spring is fitted toward the rear of the car.

The forward fulcrum of the spring has a silentblock bush and is mounted on a bolt protruding from the outer side of the chassis frame. The attachment is completed by a "D" washer and split pinned castellated nut. The rear fulcrum is a shackle assembly utilizing split rubber bushes interposed between the pins, the spring or the chassis frame. The attachment is completed by nuts and lock washers situated between the spring and the chassis frame.

Maintenance

The only lubrication required is that for the spring leaves, on no account must the rubber or silentblock bushes be lubricated. Over-lubrication of the spring leaves should be avoided. After the springs have been cleaned, brush the blades at their edges with engine oil, this will allow sufficient oil to penetrate between the leaves and provide inter-leaf lubrication.

Lubrication of spring blades is chiefly required at the ends of the leaves where one presses upon the next and where the

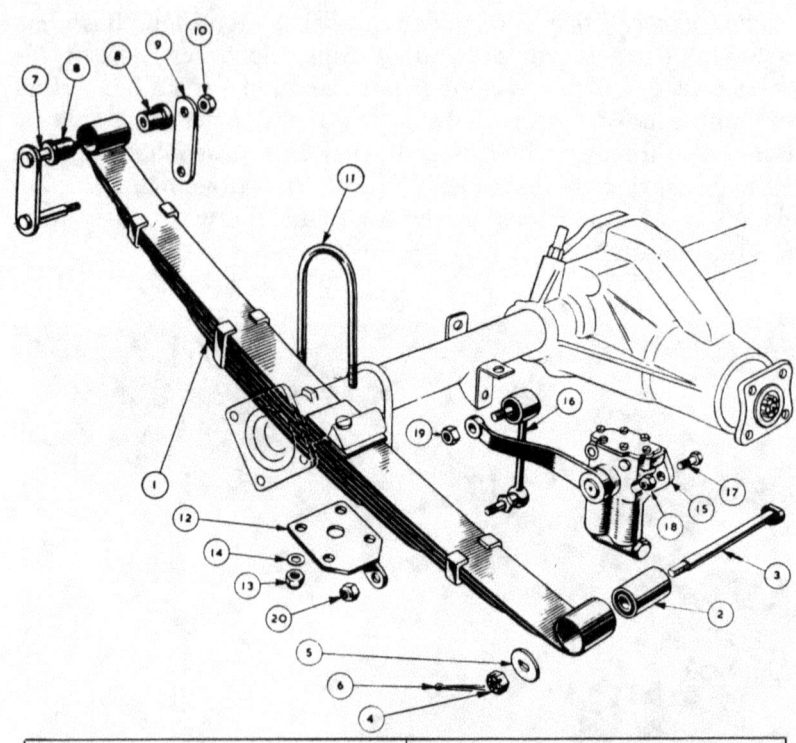

Ref. No.	Description	Ref. No.	Description
1.	Rear Road Spring	12.	Right Hand Shock Absorber Plate Assembly.
2.	Silentbloc Bush.	13.	Nyloc Nut.
3.	Front Attachment Bolt.	14.	Plain Washer.
4.	Castellated Nut.	15.	Shock Absorber.
5.	"D" Washer.	16.	Shock Absorber Link.
6.	Split Pin.	17.	Attachment Bolt.
7.	Shackle Pin and Plate Assembly.	18.	Attachment Nut.
8.	Rubber Bush.	19.	Nut for Link Upper Attachment.
9.	Shackle Plate.	20.	Nut for Link Lower Attachment.
10.	Nut.		
11.	"U" Bolt.		

maximum relative motion occurs.

The clips should be inspected and any looseness corrected by pinching the ears closer to the spring. Failure to keep these clips tight often causes "knocks" at the rear of the car.

To Remove Rear Road Spring
1. Jack up the body at the rear of the car sufficiently to take the weight off the road spring.
2. Remove the rear fender stay situated behind the rear wheel between the chassis and fender itself.
3. Holding the hexagon of the shock absorber-link remove the nyloc attachment nut.
4. Remove the two nuts and lock washers, followed by the plate of the shackle assembly at the rear end of the spring. Withdraw the plate and pin assembly and collect the rubber bushes from the spring eye and the chassis bracket.
5. Screw a $5/16''$ - 24 UNF bolt into the head of the forward fulcrum bolt to a depth of $1/2''$. Withdraw the split pin to remove nut and "D" washer. Utilizing a lever under the head of the $5/16''$ UNF bolt, the fulcrum bolt can now be withdrawn from the spring and chassis frame.
6. Supporting the spring by a small jack remove the four nyloc nuts of the two "U" bolts attaching the spring to the axle, remove the "U" bolts and the spring plate from the shock absorber link.
7. The road spring and the supporting jack is now removed from under the car to a bench.
8. The silentbloc bush can now be removed from the forward eye of the spring.

To Fit Rear Road Spring
1. Press the silentbloc bush into the forward eye of the road spring and ensure that the eight split rubber bushes are in good condition.
2. Offer up the spring, short end forward, to a position above the rear shackle bracket of the chassis frame and below the axle. Support the spring on a small jack and attach spring plate loosely to the shock absorber link.
3. Fit the "U" bolts over the axle either side of the spring and through the spring plate, secure with four nyloc nuts.
4. Secure shock absorber link to spring plate.
5. Feed the front attachment bolt from inner side of the chassis frame through its support tube into the silentbloc bush of the road spring and allow the machined flat on its head to bed against its abutment on the inner side of the chassis frame.

Secure the fulcrum bolt on its outer side by a "D" washer and castellated nut locked by a split pin.

6. Fit the two rubber half bushes to the road spring rear eye — one from each side. Press a second pair of half bushes into the shackle eye on the chassis frame.

7. Press the shackle pins of the shackle assembly through the rubber bushes and after positioning the inner shackle plate on the pin extremities, between the shackle assembly and chassis side member, fit and secure the two nuts and lock washers.

8. Replace the rear fender stay, positioning it behind the rear wheel in the fender valance and chassis bracket provided and securing with bolts, nuts, plain and lock washers.

9. Remove the packs from under the body of the car.

Rear Road Spring Overhaul

The best procedure to adopt when dealing with a road spring which has settled badly or where blades have broken is to fit a replacement.

Front Shock Absorber

A telescopic type shock absorber is fitted, utilizing a stem fixing at the top with rubber bushes, large diameter steel washers and lock nuts. At the lower end it is first attached to a fulcrum pin bracket with rubber bushes interposed between shock absorber eye and fulcrum pin, the bracket assembly is secured to the lower side of the spring pan. The body of the shock absorber is in the center of the coil spring.

Maintenance

The shock absorber is a sealed unit and requires no topping up. If it is found to be unserviceable it must be replaced.

The only maintenance that can be required is the renewal of the rubber mountings.

Rear Shock Absorber

The shock absorber body is attached to brackets welded to the upper sides of the chassis frame and linked to the rear axle by an arm splined to the shock absorber spindle and a connecting link to a plate assembly mounted on the underside of the road spring.

The body has two equal sized cylinders accommodating steel pistons which are reciprocated through short connecting rods and are coupled to the crank plate which is attached to the spindle.

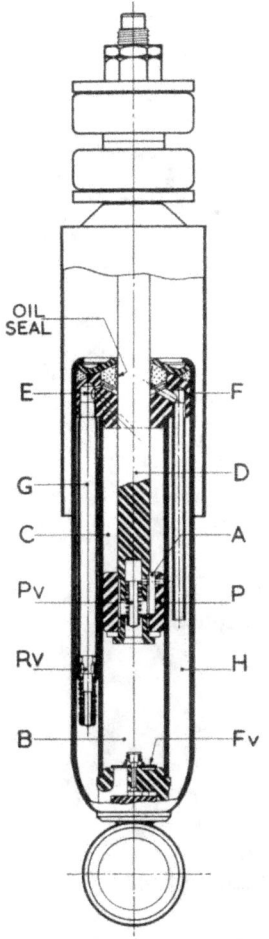

A. Port in Piston.
B. Portion of Cylinder below Piston.
C. Portion of Cylinder above Piston.
D. Piston Rod.
E. Port in Piston Rod Guide.
F. Piston Rod Guide.
Fv. Foot Valve.
G. Foam Tube.
H. Oil Reservoir.
P. Piston
Pv. Piston Valve.
Rv. Rebound Valve.

When the axle moves relative to the car (this movement is allowed by the road spring) the arm is moved up or down, and as it is splined to a spindle, the latter rotates. The spindle is a splined fit in the crank plate, this plate being coupled by means of connecting rods to the pistons, in which are situated lightly loaded recuperating valves. The pressure is built up in one cylinder or the other and since the cylinders are connected by ports in the body to the valve chamber, this pressure is dependent on the valve setting.

The unit is filled to the base of the filler plug boss which prevents over filling and maintains the necessary air space essential to saitsfactory operation. The working mechanism is completely submerged in oil which is prevented from leaking along the spindle by means of oil seals.

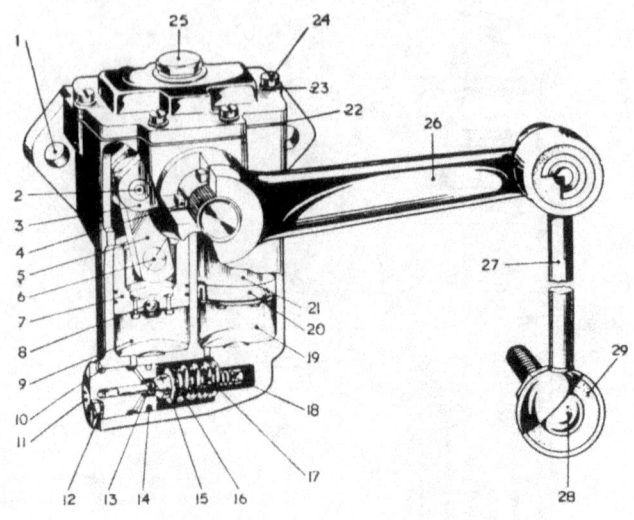

Ref.
No.   Description
1. Mounting Holes.
2. Crank Pin.
3. Crank Plate.
4. Oil Seal.
5. Connecting Rod.
6. Piston Pin.
7. Compression or Bump Piston.
8. Recuperating Valve.
9. Compression or Bump Cylinder.
10. Ring Seal.
11. Valve Screw.
12. Valve Screw Washer.
13. Rebound Valve.
14. Ring Seal.
15. Compression Valve.
16. Compression Washer.
17. Compression Spring.
18. Rebound Spring.
19. Rebound Cylinder.
20. Rebound Piston Seal.
21. Rebound Piston.
22. Gasket.
23. Shake Proof Washer.
24. Lid Screw.
25. Filler Plug.
26. Arm.
27. Connecting Link.
28. Ball End Bolt.
29. Rubber Cushion.

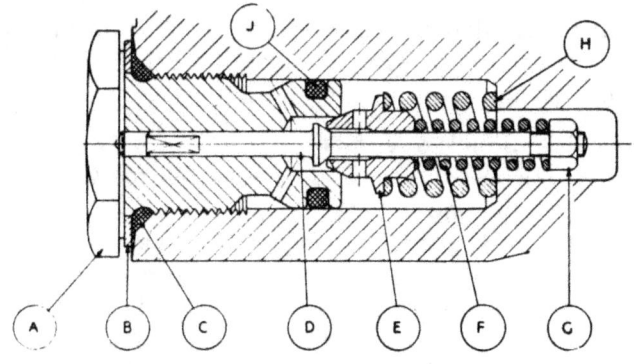

A Valve Screw
B Valve Screw Washer
C Ring Seal
D Rebound Valve
E Compression Valve
F Rebound Valve Spring
G Rebound Valve Spring Nut
H Compression Spring
J Ring Seal

Maintenance

The damper requires very little attention but the fluid level should be checked every 15,000 miles. It should be topped up to the lower reaches of the filler boss and only Armstrong Shock Absorber Oil No. 624 should be used, **the guarantee of this particular component becomes void if any other oil is used.**

Every precaution must be taken to ensure that no lubrication is given to the rubber mountings of the connecting link.

Valve Operation

To accomplish general damping of the car springs, a small bleed is built into the valve. This operates both on compression (axle moving up) and on rebound (axle moving down). As bumps become more severe on compression, pressure builds up in the compression cylinder and blows the compression valve off its seat at a pre-determined pressure controlled by the outer spring.

As the speed of the rebound increases, pressure is built up

in the rebound cylinder and blows the rebound valve off its seat at a pre-determined pressure controlled by the inner spring.

It will be clear that by suitable selection of springs in the valve, any range from zero to a maximum rating of the shock absorber can be obtained in either direction.

To Remove Rear Shock Absorber
1. Jack up the rear of the car and remove the road wheel nearest to the shock absorber.
2. Remove the nyloc nut and plain washer from the connecting rod attachment to the spring plate. It may be necessary to hold the hexagon on the inner side of the spring plate.
3. Remove the nut and lock washer from the upper joint of the connecting link. Utilizing a suitable extractor, remove the link from the shock absorber arm, this is a taper fit. Remove the connecting link from between chassis frame and spring.
4. Remove the bolts and nyloc nuts securing the body of the shock absorber to its bracket on the chassis frame and withdraw the shock absorber and connecting link.

To Fit Rear Shock Absorber
1. Remove the connecting link from the shock absorber arm.
2. Offer up the shock absorber to its bracket on the chassis frame in such a manner that the body faces outwards and the arm points rearwards. Secure with two bolts and nyloc nuts.
3. With the spherical knuckle of the connecting link lowermost, offer up the link to the shock absorber arm and spring plate, the link should be positioned between the road spring and chassis frame, with the nuts away from the center line. Holding the hexagon of the lower attachment bolt secure the link to the spring plate with a nyloc nut and plain washer.
4. Utilizing a nut and lock washer secure the connecting link to the shock absorber arm.
5. Fit road wheel and remove jacks.

WHEELS AND TIRES

Construction of Tire

One of the principal functions of the tires fitted to a car is to eliminate high frequency vibrations. They do this by virtue of the fact that the unsprung mass of each tire — the part of the tire in contact with the ground — is very small.

Tires must be flexible and responsive. They must also be strong and tough to contain the air pressure, resist damage, give long mileage, transmit driving and braking forces, and at the same time provide road grip, stability, and good steering properties.

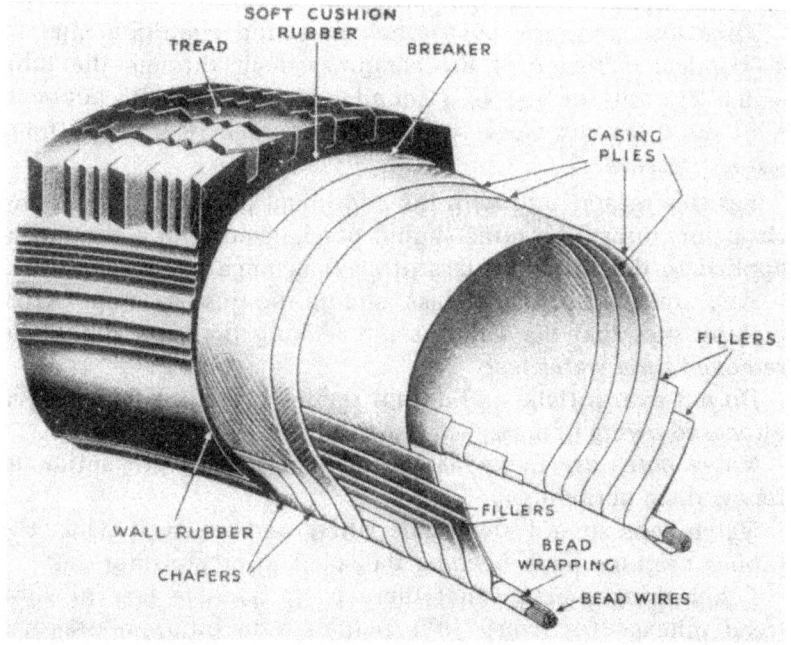

Strength and resistance to wear are achieved by building the casing from several plies of cord fabric, secured at the rim position by wire bead cores, and adding a tough rubber tread.

Part of the work done in deflecting the tires on a moving car is converted into heat within the tires. Rubber and fabric are poor conductors and internal heat is not easily dissipated. Excessive temperature weakens the structure and reduces the resistance of the tread to abrasion by the road surface.

Heat generation, comfort, stability, power consumption, rate of tread wear, steering properties and other factors affecting the performance of the tires and car are associated with the degree of tire deflection. All tires are designed to run at predetermined deflections, depending upon their size and purpose.

Load and pressure schedules are published by all tire makers and are based on the correct relationship between deflection, size, load carried and inflation pressure. By following the recommendations, the owner will obtain the best results both from the tires and the car.

Tire Pressures

For correct tire pressures see the accompanying chart.
NOTE: Pressures should be checked when the tires are cold, such as after standing overnight, and not when they have attained normal running temperatures.

Tires lose pressure, even when in sound condition, due to a chemical diffusion of the compressed air through the tube walls. The rate of loss in a sound car tire is usually between 1 lb. and 3 lbs. per week, which may average 10% of the total initial pressure.

For this reason, and with the additional purpose of detecting slow punctures, pressures should be checked with a tire guage applied to the valve not less often than once per week.

Any unusual pressure loss should be investigated. After making sure that the valve is not leaking the tube should be removed for a water test.

Do not over-inflate, and do not reduce pressures which have increased owing to increased temperature.

Valve cores are inexpensive and it is a wise precaution to renew them periodically.

Valve caps should always be fitted, and renewed when the rubber seatings have become damaged after constant use.

Other things being equal there is an average loss of 13% tread mileage for every 10% reduction in inflation pressure below the recommended figure. The tire is designed so that there is minimum pattern shuffle on the road surface and a suitable distribution of load over the tire's contact area when deflection is correct.

Moderate under-inflation causes an increased rate of tread wear although the tire's appearance may remain normal. Severe and persistent under-inflation produces unmistakable evidence on the tread. It also causes structural failure due to excessive friction and temperature within the casing.

Pressures which are higher than those recommended for the car reduce comfort. They may also reduce tread life due to a

concentration of the load and wear on a smaller area of tread, aggravated by increased wheel bounce or uneven road surfaces. Excessive pressures overstrain the casing cords, in addition to causing rapid wear, and the tires are more susceptible to impact fractures and cuts.

Effect of Temperature

Air expands with heating and pressures increase as the tires warm up. Pressures increase more in hot weather than in cold weather and as the result of high speed. These factors are taken into account when designing the tire and in preparing Load and Pressure Schedules.

Pressures in warm tires should not be reduced to standard pressures for cold tires. "Bleeding" the tires increases their deflections and causes their temperatures to climb still higher. The tires will also be under-inflated when they have cooled.

Speed

High speed is expensive and the rate of tread wear may be

twice as fast at 50 m.p.h. as at 30 m.p.h.

High speed involves:—

a. Increased temperatures due to more deflections per minute and a faster rate of deflection and recovery. The resistance of the tread to abrasion decreases with increase in temperature.
b. Fierce acceleration and braking.
c. More tire distortion and slip when negotiating bends and corners.
d. More "thrash" and "scuffing" from road surface irregularities.

Braking

"Driving on the brakes" increases rate of tire wear, apart from being generally undesirable. It is not necessary for the wheels to be locked for an abnormal amount of tread rubber to be worn away.

Other braking factors not directly connected with the method of driving can affect tire wear. Correct balance and lining clearances, and freedom from binding, are very important. Braking may vary between one wheel position and another due to oil or foreign matter on the shoes even when the brake mechanism is free and correctly balanced.

Brakes should be relined and drums reconditioned in complete sets. Tire wear may be affected if shoes are relined with non-standard material having unsuitable characteristics or dimensions, especially if the linings differ between one wheel position and another in such a way as to upset the brake balance. Front tires, and particularly near front tires, are very sensitive to any condition which adds to the severity of front braking in relation to the rear.

"Picking up" of shoe lining leading edges can cause grab and reduce tire life. Local "pulling up" or flats on the tread pattern can often be traced to brake drum eccentricity. The braking varies during each wheel revolution as the minor and major axes of the eccentric drum pass alternately over the shoes. Drums should be free from excessive scoring and be true when mounted on their hubs with the road wheels attached.

Climatic Conditions

The rate of tread wear during a reasonably dry and warm summer can be twice as great as during an average winter.

Water is a rubber lubricant and tread abrasion is much less on wet roads than on dry roads. Also the resistance of the tread to abrasion decreases with increase in temperature. Increased abrasion on dry roads, plus increased temperatures of tires and roads cause faster tire wear during summer periods. For the same reasons tire wear is faster during dry years with comparatively little rainfall than during wet years.

When a tire is new its thickness and pattern depth are at their greatest. It follows that heat generation and pattern distortion due to flexing, cornering, driving and braking are greater than when the tire is part worn. Higher tread mileage will usually be obtained if new tires are fitted in the autumn or winter rather than in the spring or summer. This practice also tends to reduce the risk of road delays because tires are more easily cut and penetrated when they are wet than when they are dry. It is therefore advantageous to have maximum tread thickness during wet seasons of the year.

Tire and Wheel Balance

In the interests of smooth riding, precise steering, and the avoidance of high speed "tramp" or "wheel hop," all Dunlop tires are balance checked to predetermined limits.

To ensure the best degree of tire balance the covers are marked with white spots on one bead, and these indicate the lightest part of the cover. Tubes are marked on the base with black spots at the heaviest point. By fitting the tire so that the marks on the cover bead exactly coincide with the marks on the tube, a high degree of balance is achieved. When using tubes which do not have the colored spots it is usually advantageous to fit the covers so that the white spots are at the valve position.

Some tires are slightly outside standard balance limits and are corrected before issue by attaching special loaded patches to the inside of the covers at the crown. These patches contain no fabric, they do not affect the local stiffness of the tire and should not be mistaken for repair patches. They are embossed "Balance Adjustment Rubber."

The original degree of balance is not necessarily maintained and it may be affected by uneven tread wear, by cover and tube repairs, by tire removal and refitting or by wheel damage and eccentricity. The car may also become more sensitive to unbalance due to normal wear of moving parts.

If roughness or high speed steering troubles develop, and mechanical investigation fails to disclose a possible cause, wheel and tire balance should be suspected.

Dynamic Balance

Static unbalance can be measured when the tire and wheel assembly is stationary. There is another form known as dy-

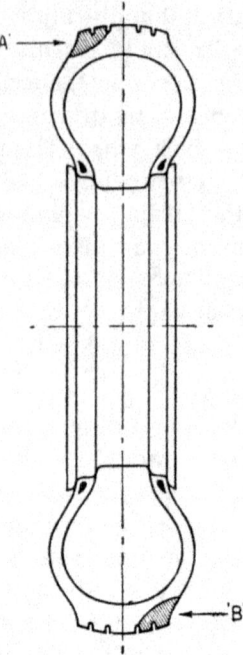

DYNAMIC OR
COUPLE UNBALANCE

EQUAL EXCESS MASSES
AT 'A' AND 'B'

namic unbalance which can be detected only when the assembly is revolving.

There may be no heavy spot — that is, there may be no natural tendency for the assembly to rotate about its center due to gravity — but the weight may be unevenly distributed each side of the tire center line. Laterally eccentric wheels give the same effect. During rotation the offset weight distribution sets up a rotating couple which tends to steer the wheel to right and left alternately.

Dynamic unbalance of tire and wheel assemblies can be measured on a suitable balancing machine and corrections made when cars show sensitivity to this form of unbalance. Where it is clear that a damaged wheel is the primary cause of severe unbalance it is advisable for the wheel to be replaced.

Rotation of Tires

There have been references to irregular tread wear and there may be different rates of wear between one tire and another. It has also been stated that irregular wear is confined almost entirely to front tires and that the left-hand front tire is likely to be more affected than the right-hand front tire.

The causes may lie in road conditions, traffic conditions, driving methods and certain features of design which are essential to the control, steering and driving of a car. Close attention to inflation pressures and the mechanical condition of the car will not always prevent irregular wear.

It is therefore recommended that front tires be interchanged with rear tires at least every 3,000 miles. Diagonal interchanging between left-hand front and right-hand rear and between right-hand front and left-hand rear provides the most satisfactory first change because it reverses the directions of rotation.

Subsequent interchanging of front and rear tires should be as indicated by the appearance of the tires, with the object of keeping the wear of all tires even and uniform.

Pressed Steel Wheels

Wobble

The lateral variation measured on the vertical inside face of a flange shall not exceed $\frac{3}{32}''$.

Lift

On a truly mounted and revolving wheel the difference between the high and low points, measured at any location on either tire bead seat, shall not exceed $\frac{3}{32}''$.

Radial and lateral eccentricity outside these limits contribute to static and dynamic unbalance respectively. Severe radial eccentricity also imposes intermittent loading on the tire. Static balancing does not correct this condition which can be an aggravating factor in the development of irregular wear.

A wheel which is eccentric laterally will cause the tire to "snake" on the road but this in itself has no effect on the rate of tread wear.

At the same time undue lateral eccentricity is undesirable and it affects dynamic balance.

There is no effective method of truing eccentric pressed steel wheels economically and they should be replaced.

Wheel nuts should be free on their studs. When fitting a wheel all the nuts should be screwed up very lightly, making sure that their seatings register with the seatings in the wheel.

Final tightening should be done progressively and alternately by short turns of opposite nuts to ensure correct seating and avoid distortion.

Wheels with damaged or elongated stud holes, resulting from slack nuts, should be replaced.

Rim seatings and flanges in contact with the tire beads should be free from rust and dirt.

Wire Wheels

To Remove Wheels
1. Jack up the car.
2. With the copper headed mallet tap the lugs of the hub cap in the direction stated thereon:—

UNDO—	UNDO	Caps fitted on right-hand
RIGHT SIDE		side of car.
UNDO	—UNDO	Caps fitted on left-hand
LEFT SIDE		side of car.

3. By gripping the tire with both hands the wheel can be pulled off the hub.

To Replace Wheels
1. Lightly grease the splines of the hub, and the thread of the hub cap.
2. Slide wheel on to hub and secure the hub caps.
3. Tap the lugs of the cap with the copper headed mallet to secure the wheel.

Right-hand side caps are turned anti-clockwise to tighten.

Left-hand side caps are turned clockwise to tighten.
4. Remove jacks.

Examination

This should be done periodically every 5,000 miles or at more frequent intervals if the car is used for competition driving or racing.

After cleaning the wheels they should be examined for faults paying particular attention to the following:—

a. **Spokes** — Looseness can be corrected and damaged spokes replaced but care must be taken to ensure that the position of the rim relative to the hub shell is not disturbed.

No undue load must be placed on any one spoke and all spokes must be under the same relative tension. The correct tension is that that will give a flexible but strong wheel. If the tension is too high the wheel will become rigid and lose its advantage over the disc wheel. Or, if too loose, undue strain will be placed on the spokes resulting in breakages.

This tension can be ascertained by drawing a light spanner or similar metal object across the spokes.

When the spokes are correctly tensioned they will emit a ringing note, however, if the spokes are slack the ring will be flat.

Spoke tensioning is best carried out with the tire and the tube removed and any protruding spoke heads filed off flush to the nipple.

NOTE: The building of wire wheels is a specialized trade and the wheel manufacturers advise that a wheel specialist is consulted if the condition of the wheel is in doubt.

b. **Hub Shells** — The splines should be examined for wear, this is often caused by looseness of the wheel on the axle hub. Excessive wear on these splines will mean the replacement of the hub shell. Rust caused by water entering from outside should be cleaned off and a smear of grease used to protect the interior of the shell and ease the fitting and removing of the wheel from the axle hub.

c. **Rims** — All rust should be cleaned off the exterior of the rim and the affected portion protected with enamel or similar finish. When the tires are changed the interior of the rims can be inspected for corrosion. Particular attention must be paid to the corrosion, if it is not cleaned away the tire will become affected.

BRAKES

TR 2

Lockheed Hydraulic Brakes are fitted to all four wheels. Two leading shoe type are used on the front wheels and leading and trailing shoe type on the rear wheels.

A foot pedal operates the brakes hydraulically on all four wheels simultaneously, while the handbrake operates the rear brakes only by means of a cable.

The foot pedal is coupled by a push rod to the master cylinder bore in which the hydraulic pressure of the operating fluid is originated. The second bore of the master cylinder is connected to the clutch operating mechanism.

A supply tank, integral with the master cylinder, provides a fluid reservoir for both cylinders, a pipe line consisting of tube, flexible hose and unions connect the master cylinder bore to the wheel cylinders.

The pressure created in the master cylinder, by application of the foot pedal, is transmitted with equal force to all wheel cylinders simultaneously. This moves the piston which in turn forces the brake shoes outward and in contact with the brake drum. An independent mechanical linkage, actuated by a hand lever, operates the rear brakes by mechanical expanders attached to the rear wheel cylinder and acts as a parking brake.

The handbrake is situated in the center of the car on the right-hand side of the gearbox tunnel. It is operated by pulling the grip rearwards and operating the push button on top by the thumb; when the button is depressed the lever will remain in that rearward position. To release the handbrake it is only necessary to pull the lever rearward sharply and then let it travel forward.

Brake Operation
1. Master cylinder to front connection pipe
2. Two-way connection
3. Banjo bolt
4. Large copper gasket
5. Small copper gasket
6. Right to left-hand front connection pipe
7. Front banjo connection
8. Banjo bolt
9. Large copper gasket
10. Small copper gasket
11. Stop light switch
12. Flexible hose
13. Hose locknut
14. Large shake proof washer
15. Front to rear connection pipe
16. Flexible hose
17. Hose locknut
18. Large shake proof washer
19. Copper gasket
20. Three-way connection
21. Connection attachment bolt
22. Right-hand brake pipe
23. Left-hand brake pipe
24. Rear axle clips

Clutch Operation
25. Master cylinder to frame bracket pipe
26. Flexible hose

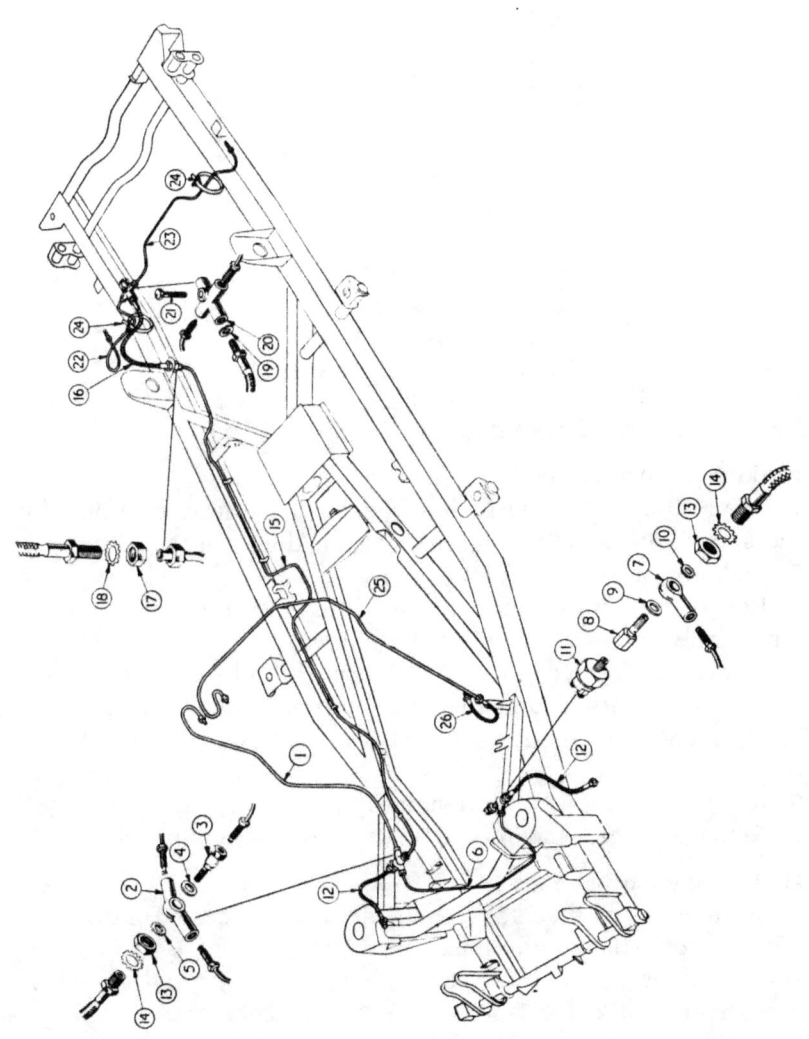

Ref.
No.
1 Front brake plate
2 Wheel cylinder
3 Wheel cylinder body
4 Spring in body
5 Cup filler
6 Cup
7 Piston assembly
8 Rubber seal
9 Wheel cylinder attachment bolt
10 Lock washer
11 Bleed screw
12 Bridge pipe
13 Brake shoe assembly
14 Micram adjuster
15 Micram adjuster mask
16 Brake shoe pull off spring
17 Hub grease catcher
18 Brake drum

Brake Shoe Adjustment
1. Apply the brakes hard while the car is stationary to position the shoes centrally in the brake drum, then release brake.
2. Jack up car, remove road wheels.
3. Rotate hub until hole provided in brake drum coincides with screwdriver slot in micram adjuster.
4. Insert screwdriver in slot and turn the adjuster until brake shoes contact the drum, then turn adjuster back one notch.
5. On front wheels repeat operations with second micram adjuster.
6. Repeat operations with remaining wheels.
7. Replace wheels. Lower car to ground and remove jacks.

Handbrake Adjustment
Adjustment of the brake shoes already described automatically readjusts the handbrake mechanism.

The cables are correctly set during assembly and only maladjustment will result from altering the mechanism.

From the compensating linkage to the brake levers mounted on the wheel cylinders are transverse cables which are of a set length when leaving the works. They are however adjustable at their inner ends and should these have been tampered with it is necessary to check the following:

The cable assembled to the right-hand cylinder lever is 12.97" ± .06" between centers.

BRAKES

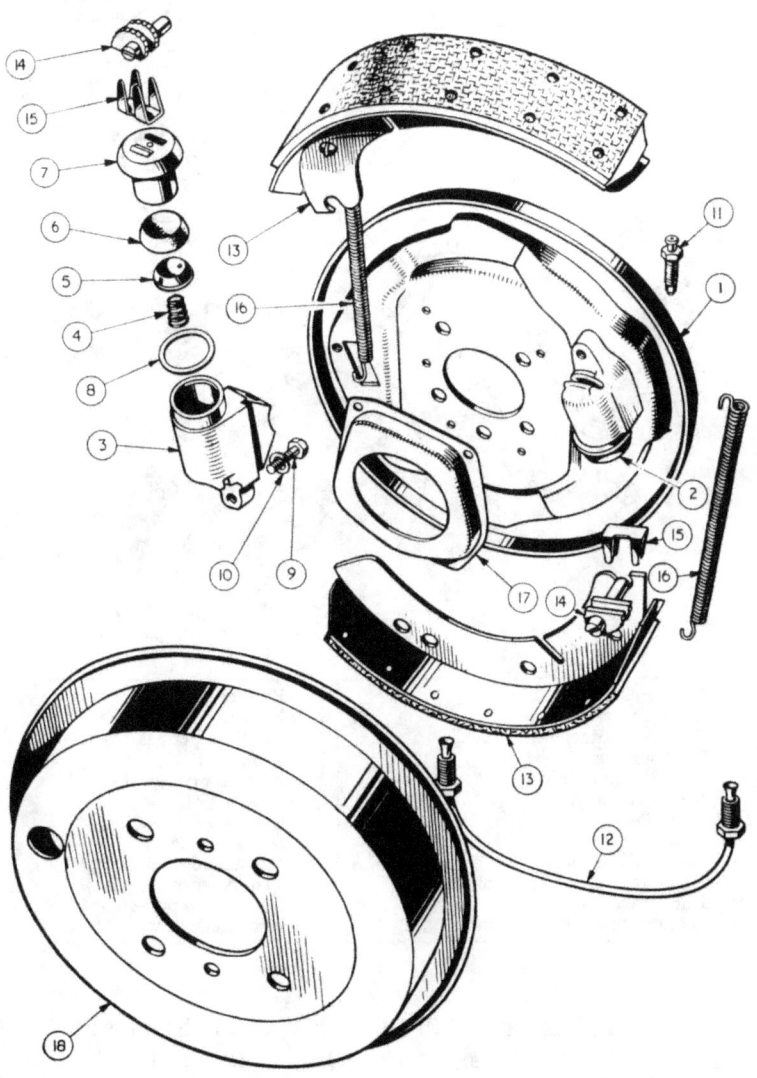

BRAKES

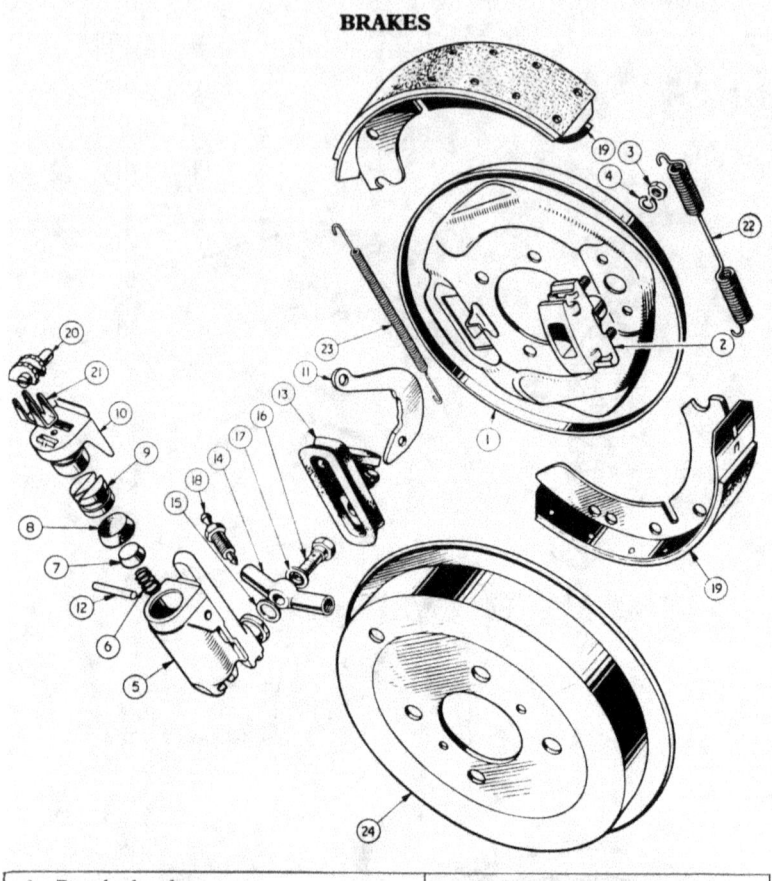

1	Rear brake plate.	13	Rubber boot.
2	Abutment assembly.	14	Banjo connection.
3	Abutment attachment nut.	15	Small copper gasket.
4	Lock washer.	16	Banjo bolt.
5	Wheel cylinder body.	17	Large copper gasket.
6	Spring in body.	18	Bleed nipple.
7	Cup filler.	19	Brake shoe assembly.
8	Cup.	20	Micram adjuster.
9	Hydraulic piston.	21	Micram adjuster mask.
10	Handbrake piston assembly.	22	Tension spring.
11	Handbrake lever.	23	Brake shoes pull-off spring.
12	Handbrake lever pivot pin.	24	Rear brake drum.

The left-hand is 26.85" ± .06", this gives the correct angle of the compensator lever as 17°. Only when a complete overhaul is necessary should the handbrake cables require resetting.

To carry out this operation, the brake shoes should be locked up in the brake drums with the handbrake in the "off" position. Any slackness that is in the cable from compensator to handbrake lever should be removed at the handbrake lever end.

Routine Maintenance

Examine the fluid level in the master cylinder periodically and replenish if necessary to keep the level $1/2''$ below the underside of the cover plate.

Do not fill completely. The addition of fluid should only be necessary at infrequent intervals and a considerable fall in fluid level indicates a leak at some point in the system, which should be traced and rectified immediately.

Ensure that the air vent in the filler cap is not choked, blockage at this point will cause the brakes to drag.

Adjust the brakes when the pedal travels to within $1''$ of the toe board before solid resistance is felt. If it is desired, adjustment may be carried out before the linings have become worn to this extent.

Brake Lining Identifications

To afford maximum braking efficiency brake linings of an improved material have been progressively introduced. To enable identification linings are color marked at their edges.

The following tabulation will give these identification marks and also the Commission number of the car on which they were first used.

Data

Front Brakes $10'' \times 2^{1}/_{4}''$.

Rear Brakes $9'' \times 1^{3}/_{4}''$ up to Commission No. TS.5481. Rear Brakes $10'' \times 2^{1}/_{4}''$ after TS.5481.

Transverse rear brake cable lengths:

Right-hand 12.97″ ± .06″ 12.47″ 10″
Left-hand 26.85″ ± .06″ 26.35″ brakes.

These lengths are measured from pin center of each fork-end.

Front brake shoes are interchangeable with one another providing they have the same lining.

Rear brake shoes are interchangeable with one another providing they have the same lining and also interchangeable with front brake shoes of the same diameter and lining type.

LINING	IDENTIFICATION	INCORPORATION	REMARKS
DM.7 Front and Rear	3 narrow blue striped markings on lining edges.	**FT.** TS.1 to TS.3247 **R.** TS.1 to TS.3219	
DM.8	2 narrow blue and 1 wide blue marking, with aluminium coloured metal impregnation of lining.	**FT.** TS.3248 to TS.5216 **R.** TS.3220 to TS.5480	
M.20 Front only. (DM.8 fitted on rear brakes).	5 green stripe markings with bronze coloured metal impregnation	TS.5217 to TS.5480	For 10′ brake only.
M.20 Front and Rear	As above.	TS.5480 and future.	Introduction of 10′ brakes for rear wheels

To Bleed Hydraulic System

Except for periodic inspection of the reservoir in the master cylinder, no attention should be required. If, however, a joint is uncoupled at any time, or air has entered the system the system must be bled in order to expel the air which has been admitted. Air is compressible and its presence in the system will affect the working of the brakes.

The method detailed hereafter is suitable only for the braking system; the procedure to be adopted when bleeding the clutch is detailed in the "Clutch Section."

1. Ensure an adequate supply of Lockheed Brake Fluid is in the reservoir of the Master Cylinder Unit and keep the level at least half full throughout the operation. Failure to observe this point may lead to air being drawn into the system and the operation of bleeding will have to be repeated.
2. Clean the bleed nipple on one of the wheel cylinders and fit a piece of rubber tubing over it, allowing the free end of the tube to be submerged in a glass jar partly filled with clean Lockheed Brake Fluid.
3. Unscrew the bleed nipple one full turn. There is only one bleed nipple to each brake.
4. Depress the brake pedal completely and let it return without assistance. Repeat this operation with a slight pause between each depression of the pedal. Observe the fluid being discharged into the glass jar and when all air bubbles cease to appear hold the brake pedal down and securely tighten the bleed nipple. Remove rubber tubing only when nipple is tightened.

NOTE: Check the level of the fluid in the master cylinder frequently and do not allow the level to fall below half full. Seven or eight strokes of the brake pedal will reduce the fluid level from full to half full.

5. Repeat the operation for the remaining three wheels.
6. Top up master cylinder with Lockheed Brake Fluid and road test car.

Leakage of Fluid from Master Cylinder

Leakage of fluid from the reservoir of the master cylinder can be explained as follows:

1. Overfilling which allows fluid to be trapped in the filler cap and leak through the breather hole. The fluid level should never be higher than 1″ measured from the top of the filler orifice or $1/2''$ measured from the underside of the cover plate.
2. The breaking up of the filler seal due to foreign matter be-

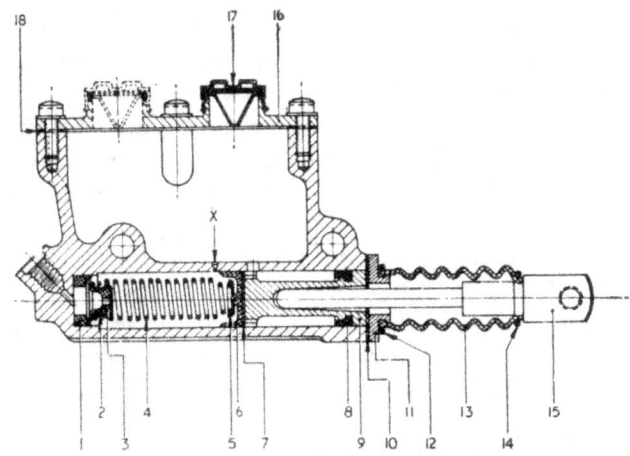

Sectional view of Brake Master Cylinder. To prevent fluid leakage the cover plate is turned 180° (the dotted outline of the filler cap shows this condition) on later production cars.

tween it and the rim of the orifice.

3. Leakage has been traced to jets of fluid from one of the cylinder recuperating holes finding its way past a defective filler cap sealing ring or via the breather hole.

The latter condition can be corrected by removing the cover plate and turning it 180° so that the filler cap is no longer directly above the jets.

Brake and Clutch Pedal Adjustment

The pedal adjustment is set when the car is assembled and should not require attention unless the assembly or adjustment has been disturbed.

A minimum clearance of .030″ is necessary between each push rod and the piston which it operates, this free movement can be felt at the pedal pad when it is depressed gently by hand.

The movement at the pedal pad will be magnified owing to the length of the lever and this movement will become between $1/2''$ to $5/8''$. Should this free movement not be apparent, first check that the pedals are free on their shaft and not prevented to return by some other fault than insufficient clearance between push rod and piston.

Adjusting the Brake Pedal

1. Loosen the jam nut on the shank of the pedal limit stop screw and screw it anti-clockwise approximately $1/8''$ away from the master cylinder support bracket.

2. Push the operating push rod end into the master cylinder

until it just contacts the piston. Screw up limit stop screw to meet the push rod fork end, but do not allow the rod to be pushed further into the piston. Screw the jam nut so that it makes contact with the master cylinder support bracket.

3. Unscrew the pedal limit stop screw together with the jam nut so that a .030" feeler gauge will pass between nut and support bracket.

4. Holding the pedal limit stop screw turn the jam nut to the support bracket and tighten.

NOTE: The clutch pedal is set in a similar way but it must be remembered that adjustment at the slave cylinder may also be necessary to obtain the correct free pedal movement.

Twin Bore Master Cylinder

Description

This unit consists of a body which has two identical bores, one connected to the brakes and the second to the clutch. Each of the bores accommodates a piston having a rubber cup loaded into its head by a return spring; in order that the cup shall not tend to be drawn into the holes of the piston head, a piston washer is interposed between these parts. At the inner end of the bore connected to the brakes, the return spring also loads a valve body, containing a rubber cup, against a valve seat; the purpose of this check valve is to prevent the return to the master cylinder of fluid pumped back into the line while bleeding the brake system, thereby ensuring a charge of fresh fluid being delivered at each stroke of the brake pedal and a complete purge of air from the system.

During normal operation, fluid returning under pressure and assisted by the brake shoe pull-off springs, lifts the valve off its seat, thereby permitting fluid to return to the master cylinder

Ref. No.		Ref. No.	
1	Body	17	Gasket between plate and body
2	Cover plate	18	Plate attachment screw
3	Joint washer	19	Shake proof washer
4	Filler cap and baffle	20	Push rod assembly
5	Cover plate attachment screw	21	Push rod boot
6	Shake proof washer	22	Large clip (Boot to fixing plate)
7	Valve seat ⎫	23	Small clip (Boot to push rod)
8	Valve cup ⎬ Brakes only	24	Slave cylinder pipe adapter (clutch)
9	Valve body ⎭	25	Gasket
10	Valve return spring	26	Bracket assembly
11	Spring retainer	27	Jam nut
12	Main cup	28	Master cylinder attachment bolt.
13	Washer between main cup and piston	29	Plain washer. (On front bolt only)
14	Piston	30	Nut
15	Piston secondary cup	31	Lock washers under nuts
16	Boot fixing plate		

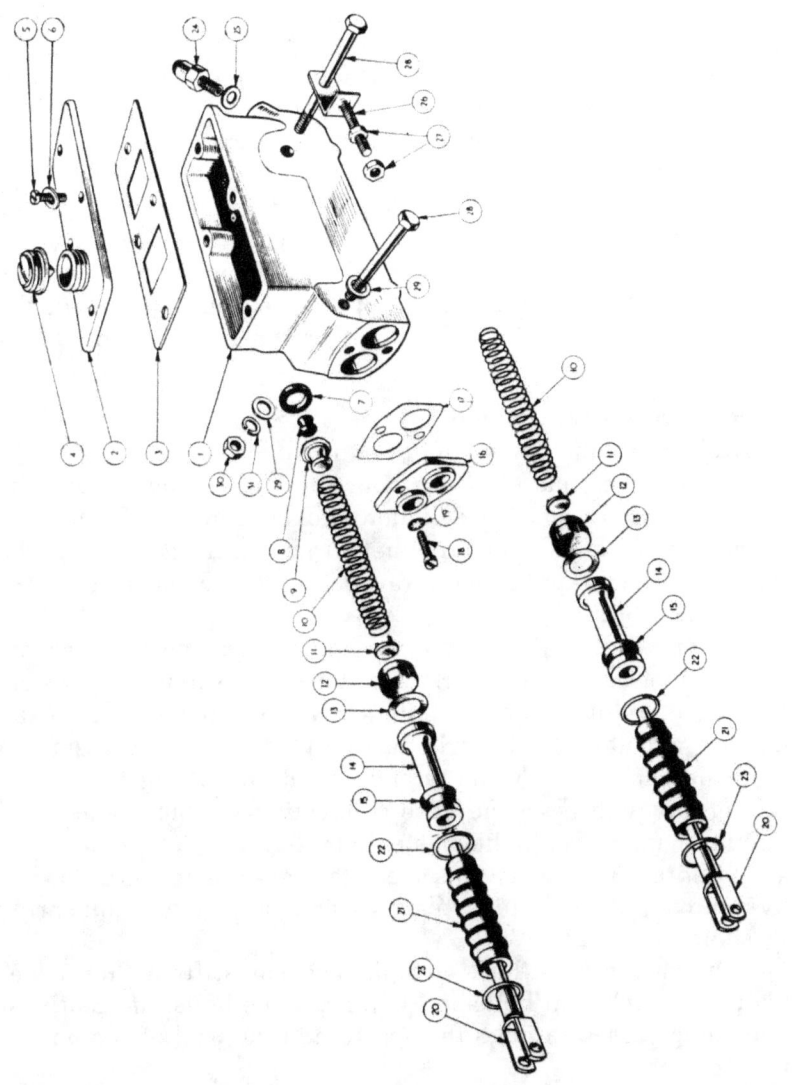

275

and the brake shoes to the "off" position.

There is **no check valve fitted in the bore connected to the clutch,** this precludes the risk of residual line pressure which would tend to engage the clutch, or keep the ball release bearing in contact with the release levers.

The by-pass ports, which break into each bore, ensure that the systems are maintained full of fluid at all times and allow full compensation for expansion and contraction of fluid due to change of temperature.

They also serve to release additional fluid drawn into the cylinder through the small holes in the piston after a brake or clutch application. If this additional fluid is not released to the reservoir, due to the by-pass port being covered by the main cup, as a result of incorrect pedal adjustment, or to the hole being choked by foreign matter, pressure will build up in the systems and the brakes will drag, or the clutch tend to disengage.

To Remove Master Cylinder
1. Drain hydraulic system of operating fluid.
2. Remove the square panel under the dash, which forms the rear wall of the master cylinder pocket from inside the car. Remove also the rubber grommet, from the inside wall of the pocket, to facilitate the withdrawal of the rear master cylinder attachment bolt.
3. Disconnect the Bundy tubing from the connections at the rear of the master cylinder. Care must be exercised when removing the clutch Bundy tubing; this is connected first to an adapter and then to the cylinder body. It will be necessary to hold the adapter with one wrench, while loosening the Bundy tubing nut with a second. The connection for the brake operation is made direct to the master cylinder.
4. Withdraw the clevis pins from the lever push rod fulcrums by removing the split pins, plain washers and double coil spring washers.
5. Remove the nuts, lock and plain washers, from the master cylinder attachment bolts and withdraw the bolts, the rearmost one being passed through the aperture in the wall of the pocket into the car.
6. The master cylinder is now free to be lifted from its support bracket. Empty any fluid that may still be in the reservoir.

To Fit Master Cylinder
1. Ensure that the connection adapter is secure in the left-hand (clutch) outlet of the master cylinder.

2. Place the assembly in the master cylinder support bracket, connections to the rear, and secure at the front end, with the attachment bolt and washers, but leave the nut finger tight at this juncture.

3. The rear attachment bolt is fed in from inside the car, through the aperture in the pocket wall. This bolt passes through two adjustment brackets, one either side of the support bracket. With the washers in place screw on nut finger tight.

4. Connect the Bundy tubing to the master cylinder connections through the aperture at the rear of the master cylinder. The clutch operating pipe is fitted to the adapter on the left and the brake operating pipe, which is on the right, direct to the master cylinder.

5. Attach the piston rod fork ends to the pedals so that the heads of the clevis pins are nearest the center line of the master cylinder assembly. Secure clevis pins with new split pins after fitting double coil spring and plain washers.

6. Loosen the jam nuts of the adjusting brackets, at both sides of the support bracket, and turn the front nut in a clockwise direction to bring the master cylinder assembly forward to its fullest extent.

7. Secure master cylinder to support bracket by tightening nuts of securing bolts. Lock up jam nuts to the adjusting bracket.

8. Adjust pedal clearance.

9. Reprenish fluid in reservoir with clean Lockheed Brake Fluid. Bleed brakes. Bleed clutch.

10. Check the system for fluid leaks by applying firm pressure to the foot pedals and inspecting the line and connections for leaks.

11. Replace rubber grommet in wall of master cylinder pocket and the cover at the rear of the pocket.

Front Wheel Cylinders

The front wheel slave cylinders are mounted rigidly to the backing plates inside the brake drums and between the ends of the brake shoes. One cylinder is mounted at the front and the other cylinder at the rear of each brake plate and each cylinder operates one shoe only. They are connected by a bridge pipe.

A single piston in each cylinder acts on the leading tip of its respective shoe, while the trailing tip of the shoe finds a floating anchor by utilizing the closed end of the actuating cylinder of the other shoe as its abutment.

Between the piston and the leading tip of each shoe is a

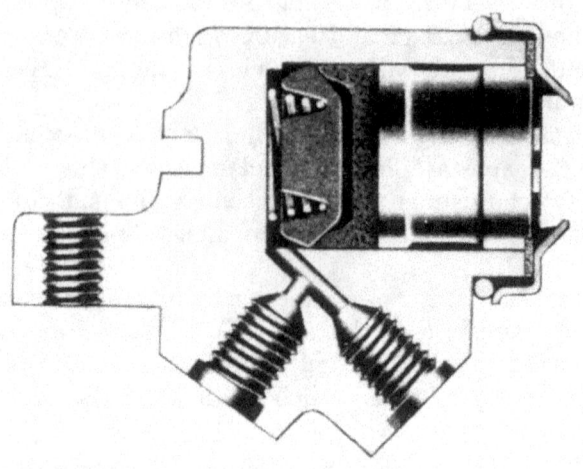

"Micram" adjuster which is located in a slot in the shoe.

Each front wheel cylinder consists of a body formed with a blind bore to accommodate a piston: A rubber cup, mounted in a cup filler, is loaded upon the piston by a spring which is located in the recess formed in the cup filler.

To Remove Front Wheel Cylinders
1. Jack up car, drain off hydraulic fluid, remove wheel, and brake drum.
2. Pull one of the brake shoes against the load of the pull-off springs away from its abutment on the wheel cylinders. Slide the micram mask off the piston cover of the operating piston. On releasing the tension of the pull-off springs the opposite brake shoe will fall away.
3. Remove the flexible hose.
4. Unscrew the bridge pipe tube nuts from the wheel cylinders and remove the bridge pipe.
5. Remove the fixing bolts and lock washers to withdraw wheel cylinders from back plate.

Rear Wheel Cylinder
The cylinder, which is fitted in an elongated slot in the rear brake plate, is free to slide in the slot between the tips of the brake shoes which are of the leading and trailing shoe type. The cylinder has a single piston operating on the tip of the leading shoe and this shoe abutts against a fixed anchor block at the bottom of the back plate the web of the shoe being free to slide in a slot in a block. The trailing shoe is located in a similar manner between the anchor and the closed end of the

cylinder and is free to slide and is therefore self centering.

The trailing shoes are operated by movement of the reaction of the leading shoe against the brake drum. A "Micram" adjuster is located in a slot in the top of the leading shoe.

The wheel cylinder contains a single piston, split in two, the inner piston being hydraulically operated while the outer piston is manually operated by the hand brake lever. A rubber cup mounted in the cup filler is loaded upon the inner piston by a spring. When operated hydraulically, the inner piston abuts against the outer piston leaving the handbrake lever undisturbed, and applies a thrust to the tip of the leading shoe through the dust cover, micram adjuster and mask. When operated manually, an inward movement of the hand brake lever brings the head of the contact lever into contact with the outer piston, thrusting it outwards against the leading shoe without disturbing the inner piston. A rubber boot is fitted to exclude water and foreign matter.

To Remove Rear Wheel Cylinder
1. Jack up rear of car. Remove road wheel and brake drum. Slacken off micram adjuster.
2. Drain off hydraulic fluid, disconnect handbrake cables and remove banjo bolt from banjo connection which is situated on the inner side of the brake plate.
3. Pull the trailing shoe against the load of the pull-off springs and away from its abutment at either end; on releasing tension of the pull-off springs the leading shoe will fall away. Collect the micram adjuster and mask.
4. Remove the rubber boot and the handbrake piston.
5. Swing the handbrake lever until the shoulder is clear of the back plate and slide the cylinder casting forward. Pivot the cylinder about its forward end and withdraw its rear end from the slot in the back plate. A rearward movement of the cylinder will now bring its forward end clear of the back plate.

Girling Brakes and Hydraulic Clutch — TR 3-4
(From Chassis No. TS.13101)

The brakes on the front wheels are the Girling Disc Brakes and on the rear are Girling HL.3 Drum Brakes. All four wheels are hydraulically operated by foot pedal operation, directly coupled to a CV master cylinder in which the hydraulic pressure is originated. A supply tank which provides fluid reserve for both brake and clutch systems is installed to allow for fluid replenishment.

An independent mechanical linkage, actuated by a hand lever

BRAKES

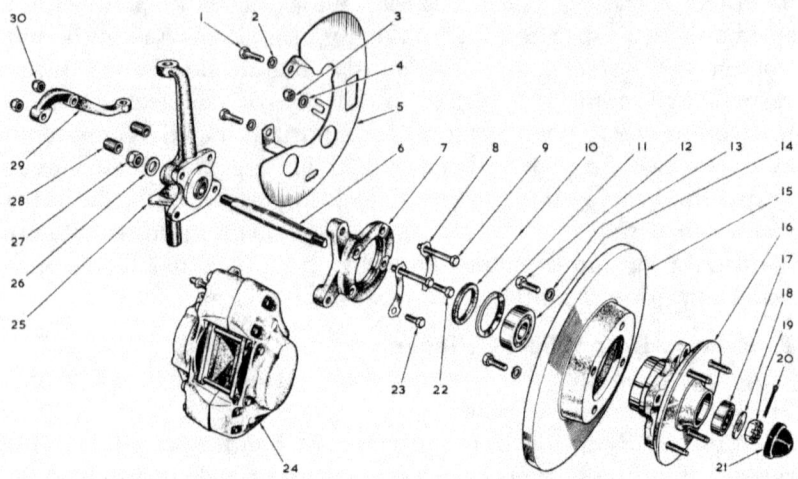

1	Bolt	16	Hub
2	Spring washer	17	Outer taper race
3	Nyloc nut	18	Washer
4	Plain washer	19	Slotted nut
5	Dust shield	20	Split pin
6	Stub axle	21	Hub cap
7	Caliper bracket	22	Bolt
8	Tab plate	23	Bolt
9	Bolt	24	Caliper unit
10	Felt seal	25	Vertical link
11	Seal retainer	26	Plain washer
12	Bolt	27	Nyloc nut
13	Spring washer	28	Distance pieces
14	Inner taper race	29	Steering arm
15	Disc	30	Nyloc nut

control, operates the rear brakes by levers attached to the wheel cylinder bodies, thus acting as a hand or parking brake.

Front Brakes

The front brakes are 11″ dia. Girling Disc Brakes, which are extremely simple in construction, consisting of the 11″ disc which is made from high quality cast iron and cast iron calipers mounted to a support bracket.

Due to the simplicity of these disc brakes the only normal servicing which will be carried out by the owner or garage will be the replacement of worn lining segments, seals and boots of the hydraulic caliper.

Lining Segment Replacement

Jack up the front of the car and remove road wheels. On the top of the caliper body are two setscrews which secure the segment retaining plates. The release of these will enable the retaining plates to be raised out of engagement with the casting and swung through an arc of 180°. The segments are then fully exposed and can be lifted out of the caliper.

Under no circumstances should attempts be made to reline

worn segments and these must be replaced by new parts.

In order to fit new segments the pistons in the caliper bore should be pushed to the bottom, and the new segments placed into position. When the segments are positioned correctly, the retaining plates should be replaced in their original position and the setscrews tightened down.

The replacement of segments is then complete and bleeding is unnecessary, but the foot pedal should be pumped until a solid resistance is felt.

Jack down the front of the car and road test.

To Replace the Rubber Seals

In order to replace the rubber "O" rings or seals it is necessary to remove the caliper assembly from the vehicle. The brake segments should be removed in the manner described above. Instead of pushing the pistons to the bottom of the bore withdraw them from the caliper body, taking great care not to damage the bores. The sealing rings may then be removed by inserting a blunt tool under the seals and prying out, taking care not to damage the locating grooves. Examine the bores and pistons carefully for any signs of abrasion or "scuffing." No attempt should be made to remove the end plug retainer, as this is screwed in tightly by **mechanical** means.

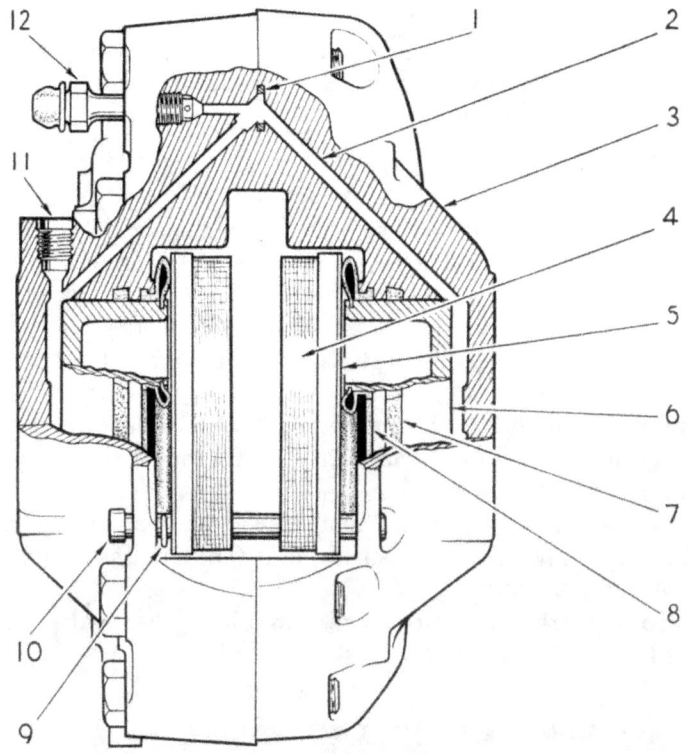

1 Rubber 'O' ring
2 Fluid transfer channels
3 Caliper body
4 Brake pad
5 Anti-squeal plate
6 Piston
7 Piston sealing ring
8 Dust cover
9 Retaining clip
10 Retaining pin
11 Flexible hose connection
12 Bleed nipple

It is important that in cleaning the components no gasoline, kerosene, solvent or mineral fluid of any kind should be used. Clean with alcohol and allow to vaporize, leaving the component clean and dry.

After cleaning and examining, lubricate the working surfaces of the bores and piston with clean genuine Girling Crimson Brake and Clutch Fluid.

Assembling

Fit new rubber seals into the grooves of caliper cylinder bore. Locate the rubber dust cover with the projecting lip into the groove provided which is the outer one of the cylinder bore.

Insert the piston, closed end first, into the bore, taking great care not to damage the polished surface. Push the piston right home and then engage the outer lip of the rubber boot into the groove of piston.

The replacement of the lining segments as described under the beading "Segment Replacement" will retain the pistons in position.

Refit the caliper assembly to the support bracket by means of the two securing bolts ensuring that the disc passes between the two lining segments.

Re-connect the pressure hose and bleed the brake, as described under "Bleeding the **System**."

Discs

To ensure that the brake functions at maximum efficiency a check should be made to see that the disc runs truly between the segments. The maximum run-out permissible on the disc is .004". (For instructions regarding wheel bearing settings refer to Front Suspension Section.) If excessive run-out is present this will cause the knocking back of the pistons which will possibly cause judder.

If it is found that the discs have been damaged in any way, which is extremely unlikely, it will be necessary to remove the discs from the car in order for them to be trued up. Under no circumstances should more than .060" be removed, with the finish to be 32 micro ins. maximum measured circumferentially and 50 micro ins. measured radially.

Rear Brakes

From the illustration it will be seen that they are of the drum type with a wheel cylinder and adjuster affixed to a backplate supporting the two shoes which are held in position by two return springs. The shoes, which are hydraulically operated by the Girling single acting wheel cylinder (incorporating lever handbrake mechanism), are not fixed but are allowed to slide and centralize. Lining wear is adjusted by a Girling wedge type mechanical adjuster common to both shoes. At the cylinder end, the leading shoe is located in a slot in the piston, while the trailing shoe rests in a slot formed in the cylinder body. At the adjuster end the shoe ends rest in slots in the adjuster links.

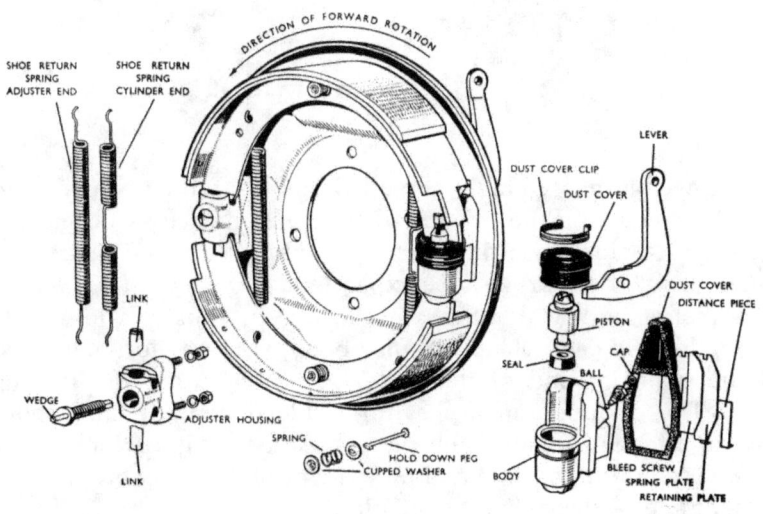

The shoes are supported by platforms formed in the backplate, these being held in position by two hold-down springs fitted on each shoe with a peg passing through a hole in the backplate.

The adjuster consists of an alloy housing with studs, which is spigoted and secured firmly to the inside of the backplate by nuts and spring washers.

The housing carries two opposed steel links, the outer end slotted to take the shoes, and the inclined inner faces bearing on inclined faces of the hardened steel wedge (the axis of which is at right angles to the links).

The wedge has a finely threaded spindle with a square end which projects on the outside of the backplate. By rotating the wedge in a clockwise direction the links are forced apart and the fulcrum of the brake shoe expanded.

A piston and seal moves in the highly finished bore of a light alloy die cast wheel cylinder body, while a slot, machined in the opposite end of the body, serves to carry the trailing shoe. The cylinder, incorporating a bleed screw with rubber cap, is attached to the back plate by spring clips which allow it to slide laterally. The handbrake lever pivots on, and projects at right angles through the back plate.

When the brake is applied, the piston under the influence of the hydraulic pressure moves the leading shoe and the body reacts by sliding on the backplate to operate the trailing shoe.

The handbrake lever is pivoted in the cylinder body and with it the trailing shoe.

Dismantling

If it is found necessary to remove a rear wheel cylinder, the following procedure should be followed:—

1. Jack up the vehicle, remove the wheels, and disconnect the rod from handbrake lever.
2. Remove the brake drum and shoes. Disconnect the pressure pipe union from the cylinder, and remove the rubber dust cover from rear of backplate.
3. By using a screwdriver, pry the retaining plate and spring plate apart, then tap the retaining plate from beneath the neck of the wheel cylinder.
4. Withdraw the handbrake lever from between the backplate and wheel cylinder.
5. Remove the spring plate and distance piece, and finally the wheel cylinder from the backplate.

Refitting the Rear Wheel Cylinder

Mount the wheel cylinder on to the backplate with the neck through the large slot. Replace the distance piece between cylinder neck and backplate, with the open end away from handbrake lever location. The two cranked lips must also be away from the backplate.

Insert the spring plate between the distance piece and backplate, also with open end away from handbrake lever location and the two cranked lips away from the backplate.

Replace handbrake lever. Locate the retaining plate between the distance piece and spring plate (open end towards the handbrake lever), tap into position until the two cranked tips of the spring plate locate in the retaining plate.

Fit the rubber dust cover. Attach the pressure pipe union to the cylinder and connection to the handbrake lever. Replace the shoes, brake drum, and bleed the system. Finally re-fit wheels.

Fitting Replacement Shoes

1. Jack up the car and remove road wheels and brake drums.
2. Remove the holding down springs by turning the washer under the peg head. Lift one of the shoes out of the slots in the adjuster link and wheel cylinder piston. Both shoes complete

with springs can then be removed. Place a rubber band round the wheel cylinder to keep piston in place.

3. Clean down the backplate, check wheel cylinders for leaks and freedom of motion.

4. Check adjusters for easy working and turn back (anti-clockwise) to full "off" position. Lubricate where necessary with Girling White Brake Grease.

5. Smear the shoe platforms and the operating and abutment ends of the new shoes with Girling White Brake Grease.

6. Fit the two new shoe return springs to the new shoes (with the shorter spring at the adjuster end) from shoe to shoe and between shoe web and backplate. Locate one shoe in the adjuster link and wheel cylinder piston slots, then pry over the opposite shoe into its relative position. Remove rubber band. Insert the hold down peg through hole in backplate, and replace spring and cupped washers smeared with Girling White Brake Grease.

7. Make sure drums are cleaned and free from grease, etc., then refit.

8. Adjust brakes.

9. Refit road wheels and jack down.

NOTE: The first shoe has the lining positioned towards the heel of the shoe and the second shoe towards the toe or operating end in both L.H. and R.H. brake assemblies.

Several hard applications of the pedal should be made to ensure all the parts are working satisfactorily and the shoes bedding to the drums, then the brakes should be tested in a quiet road before normal running is resumed.

Running Adjustments

The front disc brakes are entirely self-adjusting. The rear brakes are adjusted for lining wear at the brakes themselves, and on no account should any alteration be made to the hand brake cable for this purpose.

One common adjuster is provided for each brake assembly. Adjustment of both rear wheels is identical. Release the handbrake and jack up the car. Turn the square end of the adjuster on the outside of each rear brake backplate in a clockwise direction until a resistance is felt, then slacken back two clicks, when the drum should rotate freely.

Immediately after fitting replacement shoes it is advisable to slacken one further click to allow for possible lining expansion, reverting to normal adjustment **afterwards**.

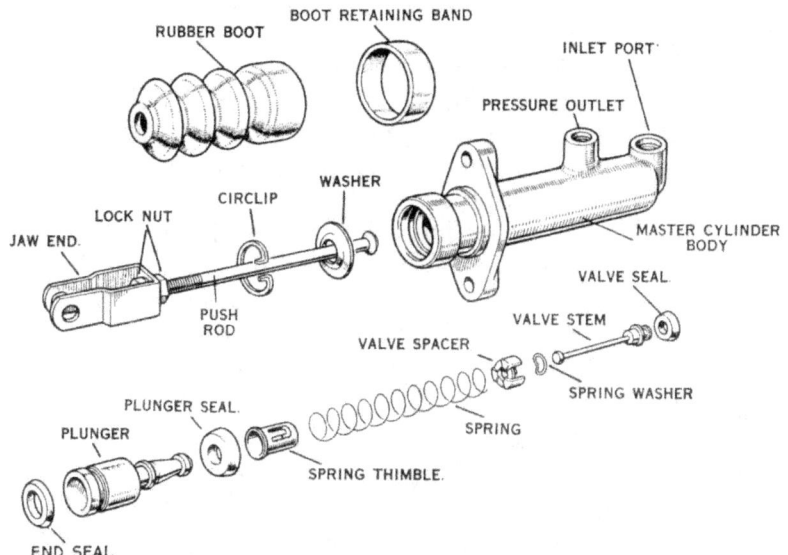

Hydraulic Clutch Operation

A slave cylinder mounted on the side of the clutch housing is mechanically connected to the clutch operating mechanism. This assembly, by reason of its hydraulic connection, is actuated by a Girling C.V. master cylinder to which the suspended clutch pedal is coupled.

When pressure on the clutch pedal is applied, the piston of the master cylinder displaces the fluid in the cylinder which in turn moves the piston of the slave cylinder, pushing against the lever of the clutch thrust race.

The CV Master Cylinder

This is the Girling CV Type, which consists of an alloy body with a polished finished bore. The inner assembly is made up of the push rod, dished washer, circlip, plunger and seal, plunger seal, spring thimble, plunger return spring, valve spacer, spring washer, valve stem and valve seal. The open end of the cylinder is protected by a rubber dust cover.

Dismantling

Disconnect the pressure and feed pipe unions from the cylinder and remove the securing bolts and clevis pin from jaw end. Pull back the rubber dust cover and remove the circlip with a pair of long nosed pliers. The push rod and dished washer can then be removed. When the push rod has been removed the plunger, with seal attached; will then be exposed. Remove the plunger assembly complete. The assembly can then be separated by lifting the thimble leaf over the shouldered end of the plunger. Ease the pressure seal off the plunger and remove back seal. Depress the plunger return spring allowing the valve stem to slide through the elongated hole of the thimble, thus releasing tension of spring.

Remove thimble, spring and valve complete. Detach the valve spacer, taking care of the spacer spring washer which is located under the valve head. Remove the seal from the valve head. Examine all parts, especially the seal, for wear or distortion, and replace with new parts where necessary.

Assembling

Replace the valve seal so that the flat side is correctly seated on the valve head. The spring washer should then be located with dome side against the underside of the valve head, and held in position by the valve spacer, the legs of which face towards the valve seal. Replace the plunger return spring centrally on the spacer, insert the thimble into the spring and depress until the valve stem engages through the elongated hole of the thimble, making sure the stem is correctly located in the center of the thimble. Check that the spring is still central on the spacer. Refit new plunger seal on to the plunger with flat of seal seated against the face of plunger, and a new back seal with lip of seal facing plunger seal. Insert the reduced end of plunger into the thimble until the thimble leaf engages under the shoulder of the plunger. Press home the thimble leaf.

Smear the assembly well with Girling brake and clutch fluid, and insert the assembly into the bore of the cylinder, valve end first, easing the plunger seal lips in the bore. Replace the push rod with the dished side of the washer under the spherical head into the cylinder, followed by the circlip which engages into groove machined in the cylinder body.

Replace the rubber dust cover, refit the cylinder to the chassis and bleed the system.

The Clutch Slave Cylinder

The slave cylinder is of simple construction, consisting of alloy body, piston with seal, piston stop, spring and bleed screw, the open end of the cylinder being protected by a rubber dust cover. The cylinder is mounted to the clutch housing by a flange and two bolts.

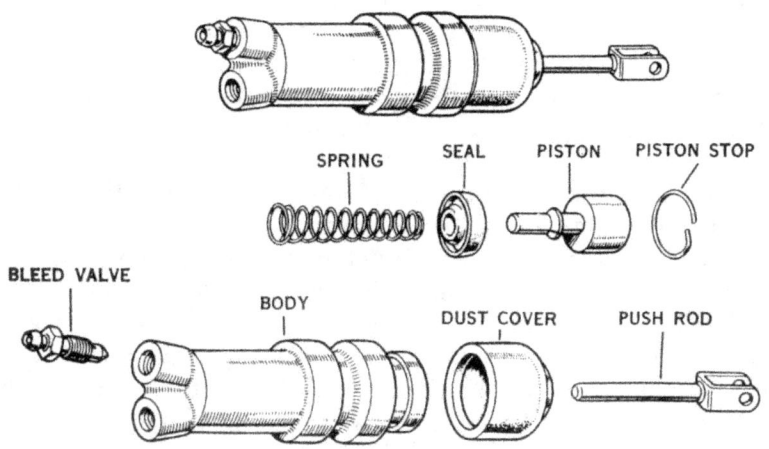

Bleeding

Remove the bleed screw dust cap, open the bleed screw approximately three-quarters turn and attach a tube, immersing the open end into a clean receptacle containing a little Girling Crimson Brake and Clutch Fluid. Fill the master cylinder reservoir with genuine Girling Crimson Brake and Clutch Fluid, and by using slow full strokes pump the pedal until the fluid entering the container is free from air bubbles. On a down stroke of the pedal, nip up the bleed screw, remove the bleed tube and replace the dust cap. After bleeding, top up the reservoir to its correct level of approximately three-quarters full.

General Maintenance

Replenishment of Hydraulic Fluid for both Brake and Clutch Systems

Inspect the reservoir at regular intervals and maintain at about three-quarters full by the addition of Girling Crimson Brade and Clutch Fluid.

Great care should be exercised when adding brake fluid to prevent dirt or foreign matter entering the system.

Important: Serious consequences may result from the use of incorrect fluids, and on no account should any but Girling Crimson Brake and Clutch Fluid be used. This fluid has been specially prepared and is unaffected by high temperature or freezing. **Never top up the system with any other fluid.**

Bleeding the Hydraulic System

With all the hydraulic connections secure and the reservoir topped up with fluid, remove the rubber cap from the L.H.

rear bleed nipple and fit the bleed tube over the bleed nipple, immersing the free end of the tube in a clean jar containing a little Girling Brake and Clutch Fluid.

Unscrew the bleed nipple about three-quarters of a turn and then operate the brake pedal with slow, full strokes until the fluid entering the jar is completely free of air bubbles.

Then during a down stroke of the brake pedal, tighten the bleed screw sufficiently to seat, remove bleed tube and replace the bleed nipple dust cap. **Under no circumstances must excessive force be used when tightening the bleed screw.**

This process must now be repeated for each bleed screw at each of the three remaining brakes **finishing at the wheel nearest the master cylinder.** Always keep a careful check on the reservoir during bleeding, since it is most important that a full level is maintained. Should air reach the master cylinder from the reservoir, the whole operation of bleeding must be repeated.

After bleeding, top up the reservoir to its correct level of approximately three-quarters full.

Never use fluid that has just been bled from a brake system for topping up the reservoir, since this fluid may be to some extent aerated.

Great cleanliness is essential when dealing with any part of the hydraulic system, and especially so where the brake fluid is concerned. Dirty fluid must never be added to the system.

General Advice On Hydraulic Components

The following precautions should be studied carefully.

Always exercise extreme cleanliness when dealing with any part of the hydraulic system.

Never handle rubber seals or internal hydraulic parts with greasy hands or greasy rags.

Always use Girling Crimson Brake and Clutch Fluid from sealed quart tins.

Never use fluid from a container that has been cleaned with gasoline, kerosene, solvent or trichlorethylene.

Never put dirty fluid into the reservoir, nor that which has been bled from the system.

Always use clean Girling Brake and Clutch Fluid or alcohol for cleaning internal parts of hydraulic system.

Never allow gasoline, kerosene, solvent or trichlorethylene to contact these parts.

Always examine all seals carefully when overhauling hydraulic cylinders and replace with genuine Girling spares, any which show the least sign of wear **or damage.**

Always take care not to scratch the highly finished surfaces of cylinder bores and pistons.

Always use WAKEFIELD/GIRLING Rubber Grease No. 3 (Red) for packing rubber boots, dust covers and lubricating parts likely to contact any rubber components.

Never use Girling White Brake Grease or other grease for this purpose.

Always replace all seals, hoses and gaskets with new ones if it is suspected that incorrect fluids have been used or the system contaminated with mineral oil or grease. Drain off the fluid, thoroughly wash all metal parts and flush out all pipes, etc., with alcohol or clean Girling Crimson Brake and Clutch Fluid.

Never use anything else for this purpose.

Always use a particular container (reserved for this purpose) for bleeding the system, and always maintain in a clean condition.

Always remember that your safety and the safety of others may depend on the observance of these precautions at all times.

TR 2-3 BODY

To Remove the Hood
1. Release the hood locks either side by cable or by turning the Dzuz fastener and leave the hood resting in this lower position.
2. Remove the four nuts and washers (two to each hinge) from under the dash inside the car.
3. With an operator each side of the car lift the hood squarely upwards.

To Fit the Hood
The fitting is the reversal of the removal. If the locks are cable operated the instructions on "Adjustment of Hood Locks" should be followed.

To Remove Front Apron
1. Open the hood by releasing the locks from inside the car, or cars after Commission No. TS.4229 fitted with Dzuz fasteners at the forward corners of the hood by use of the carriage key. Prop the hood open and disconnect battery.
2. Remove four bolts (two each side), which secure the top apron reenforcement bar to the "U" brackets, situated on top of the front fenders.
3. Disconnect the electrical wires at their snap connectors after suitably identifying them if the colors are not distinguishable.
4. If the car is earlier than Commission No. TR.4229, release the cable which connects the two locks from its clip. This clip is fitted at the center of and forward of the apron re-inforcement bar. On cars later than TS.4229 this instruction can be disregarded.
5. Remove the twelve bolts (six each side) which secure the outer edges of the apron to the fenders. These bolts are those which are fitted horizontally from inside the wheel arches. The other series of bolts, fitted vertically into the wheel arch, are **NOT** to be touched.
6. Remove the chassis frame to apron steady stay, at the apron end, by removal of the nut and bolt with lock washer.
7. Withdraw the bolt from the starting handle guide bracket. There is no necessity to remove the bracket itself.
8. The apron can now be removed by lifting the lower portion upward and forward to break the water seal and then lifting it bodily out of its brackets. The sealing beadings can now be removed.

To Fit Front Apron
The fitting is the reversal of its removal but care should be taken over the following points.
1. The sealing beading is adhered to the apron in such a manner that the hole is adjacent to the uppermost hole of the apron and the remaining slotted holes are adjacent to the lower holes.
2. The electrical wires are connected with regard to their color identifications and the wiring diagram as found in the Electrical Equipment Section or the special identifications if the colors are not distinguishable.
3. On completion of the fitting the hood must be lowered gently to ascertain that the lock plungers and locks align correctly.

Adjustment to Hood Locks
On cars prior to Commission No. TS.4229 the locks were cable operated. It is essential when the hood or front apron have been removed that the locks are checked for alignment and the operating cables are correctly set.
1. It must be positively determined that when the release knob is operated the release levers of the locks are pulled clear of the plunger apertures. This can be ascertained by an operator in the car and an observer at the locks. If the release lever is not fully clear the cable must be adjusted.
2. Plunger centers and apertures must be identical. Longtitudal positioning of the plungers can be approximated by positioning on the lock centers. First attempt at closing the hood should be done with gentle pressure and the locking mechanism released. Any fouling of the plungers can be easily felt and adjustments made.

To Remove Windscreen
1. Release the top
2. Remove windscreen wiper blades and arms.
3. Turn the windscreen stanchion securing screws 90° anti-clockwise. Although these screws are spring loaded it may be necessary to ease the head outwards to ensure that the bolts are quite free.
4. With operators each side of the car gently ease the windscreen assembly forward allowing the draft excluder to slide over the wiper blade spindles. The windscreen can be withdrawn and lifted from the car.

To Fit Windscreen
This is the reversal of the removal but the following points should be noted.

1. The stanchion guides should be greased to prevent corrosion.
2. After fitting the screen ensure that the draft excluder is in good condition and position correctly.
3. Fit the windscreen wiper arms and blades and test for correct arcuate movement.

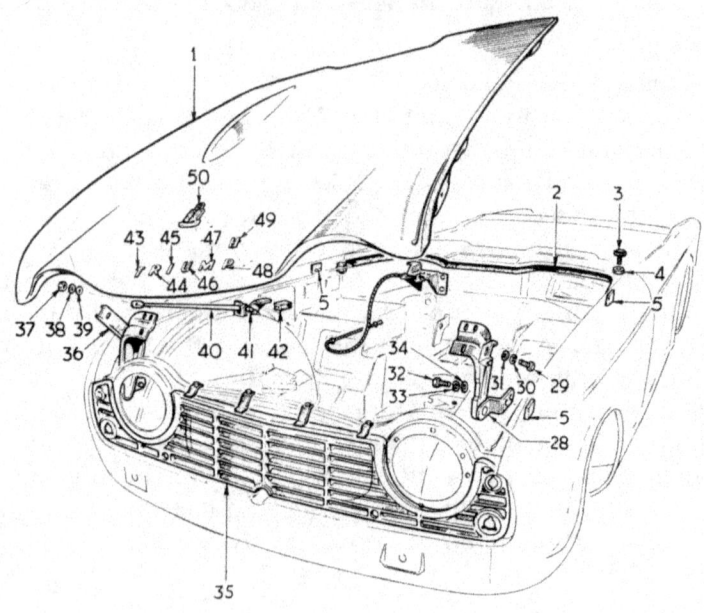

1	Bonnet	18	Bracket	35	Grille
2	Sealing rubber	19	Bolt	36	Bonnet hinge
3	Bonnet stop	20	Washer	37	Nut
4	Locknut	21	Washer	38	Washer
5	Rubber buffer	22	Lever	39	Washer
6	Bonnet catch (early models only)	23	Screw	40	Bonnet support stay
7	Bolt	24	Inner cable	41	Bonnet stay bracket
8	Washer	25	Outer cable	42	Rubber buffer
9	Washer	26	Grommet	43	'T'
10	Bonnet fastener assembly	27	Cable clip	44	'R'
11	Bolt	28	Bonnet hinge	45	'I'
12	Washer	29	Bolt	46	'U'
13	Washer	30	Washer	47	'M'
14	Spring retaining cup	31	Washer	48	'P'
15	Striker pin	32	Bolt	49	'H'
16	Spring	33	Washer	50	Medallion
17	Nut	34	Washer		

TR 4 BODY

To Remove Hood

Remove two bolts securing each hinge to the fender valance and lift the hood away. The hinges are secured to the hood with four bolts in each; the long bolt is used in the outer position.

To Refit

Refit the hinges to the hood and the hood to the body, tightening the bolts only sufficiently to prevent the hood from moving under its own weight.

Test the opening and closing action.

Elongated holes in the hood fixings permit limited adjustment in all directions.

An adjustable rubber buffer (3) fitted to rear corners of the engine compartment restricts unnecessary hood movement.

When correctly positioned, fully tighten all hinge securing bolts.

Hook Lock Adjustment

Slacken the clamping ferrule screw (23), push the hook lock control inside the car to within $1/8''$ of its fully in position, and re-tighten the screw.

Dovetail Adjustment

If the hood is loose at the catch plate, slacken off the locknut and turn the dovetail bolt in a clockwise direction until satisfactory adjustment is attained. Re-tighten locknut. Rectify excess dovetail spring pressure by turning the dovetail bolt counter-clockwise.

Front Grille

To Remove

1. Remove the parking and direction indicator lamps.
2. Remove both over-riders.
3. Remove grille (four screws in upper edge and four in lower edge).

To Refit

Reverse the above instructions and refer to the circuit diagram before re-connecting the lamps.

To Remove Windscreen

1. Pull off the no-draft welting from the screen pillars.

2. Remove three bolts (22) with cover plates (21), one nut (24) with washer (25) from the bottom of each screen pillar (11). These nuts are accessible under the facia.
3. Slacken bolts (16) and (17) which are accessible when the door is opened.
4. Lift out the windscreen assembly (11).
5. Remove the rubber weatherstrip (23) from the back of the windscreen assembly.

To Refit
1. Remove old sealing compound from the contacting surfaces of the windscreen weatherstrip and the scuttle panel.
2. Apply a fresh piece of Seal-a-strip along the underside of the rubber and refit the windscreen assembly.
3. There is provision for limited adjustment between the windscreen frame and door glass.
4. If adjustment is required, slacken the bolts (16), (17) and (20) on both sides of the car, raise both door glasses, and move the top of the windscreen to provide a uniform clearance between the glass and the windscreen. Re-tighten the bolts.
5. Seal the windscreen frame to the rubber with Seelastik.

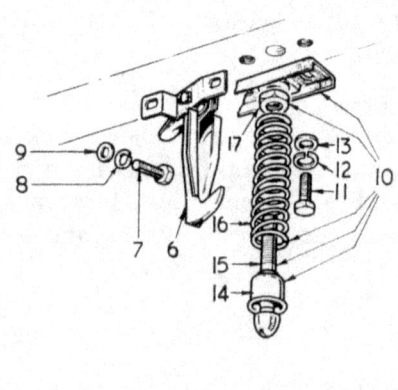

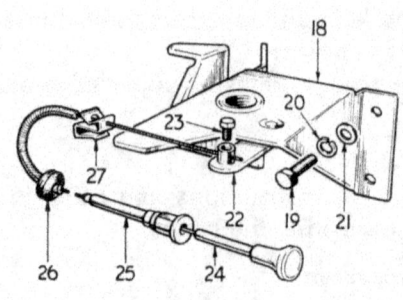

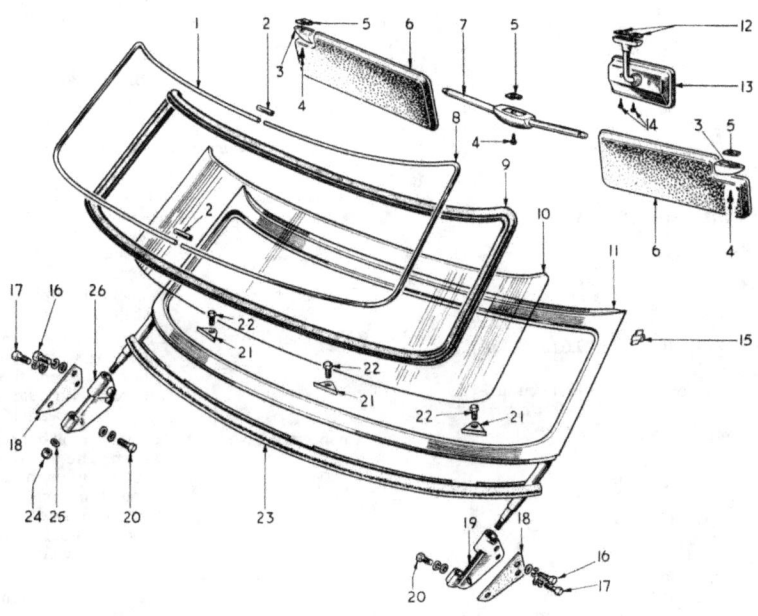

1	Moulding	8	Moulding	15	Bracket	22	Bolt
2	Cover plate	9	Rubber weatherstrip	16	Bolt	23	Seal
3	Mounting	10	Windscreen glass	17	Bolt	24	Nut
4	Screw	11	Frame	18	Packing piece	25	Washer
5	Spire fix	12	Packing piece	19	Mounting bracket	26	Mounting bracket
6	Visor	13	Mirror	20	Bolt		
7	Mounting	14	Screws	21	Cover plate		

GENERAL DATA

GENERAL DATA

Summaries of dimensions and tolerances, relative to various components are given at the commencement of the respective sections to which they refer. Whilst data given, in some instances, in this section appears elsewhere in the body of this manual, such information being frequently required, it is considered desirable that it should be summarised in this section for easy reference.

For the convenience of overseas readers, a table of metric equivalents is included in this section.

CHASSIS SPECIFICATION

Engine Details

Type	O.H.V. Push Rod Operated.
Bore of Cylinder	3.268″ (83 mm.)
Stroke of Crank	3.622″ (92 mm.)
Cubic Capacity (Swept Volume)	121.5 cu ins. (1,991 c.cs.)
Compression Ratio	8.5
Firing Order	1, 3, 4, 2
Compression Pressure (With three Sparking Plugs fitted and compression gauge in fourth cylinder engine warm, throttle set at tick over, using 20 SAE oil and operating the starter)	Average reading 120 lbs. per sq. in. (8.4 kgs. per sq. cm.)
Sparking Plug Make and Type	Champion No. L10S High speed work No. L11S.
Sparking Plug Reach	½″ (12.700 mm.)
Sparking Plug Gap	.032″ (.8 mm.)
Distributor	Lucas DM2 P.4
Distributor Break Gap	.015″ (.4 mm.)
Ignition Setting (Full Retard)	4° B.T.D.C. (Based on the use of fuel with a minimum Octane value of 80).
Vacuum Advance	Basic setting 4 divisions.
Inlet Rocker Clearance	Touring .010″ (.25 mm.) High Speed Motoring .013″ (.33 mm.)
Exhaust Rocker Clearance	Touring .012″ (.30 mm.) High Speed Motoring .013″ (.33 mm.)

The above measurements are based on a cold engine.

Crankshaft	Three journal molybdenum manganese steel stamping with integral balance weights.
Crankshaft Bearings	Vandervell bi-metal shell bearings.
Crankshaft Thrust	Four half semi-circular white metal faced washers fitted in pairs either side of the centre bearing.
Connecting Rods	60-ton molybdenum manganese steel stamping with big end caps offset to camshaft side. Floating gudgeon pin secured by circlips.
Connecting Rod Bearings, Big End	Lead indium bronze bearings.
Small End	Clevite Bush.
Pistons	Aluminium alloy split skirt compensating type, graded F. G or H.
Piston Rings	All fitted above gudgeon pin.
Compression Rings	Cast iron, .062″ wide.
Scraper Ring	Cast iron, .156″ wide.
Camshaft	Special cast iron with four bearings and silent contour symmetrical cams. Driven by Duplex chain.

GENERAL DATA

Camshaft Bearings	Front Bearing—cast iron sleeve ; 2nd, 3rd and 4th direct in crankcase. After Engine No. TS 9095E engines will be fitted with replaceable Vandervell shell bearings, See TR3 Supplement Engine Section "B".
Lubricating System	Wet Sump. Capacity 11 pints.
Oil Pump	Hobourn Eaton high capacity double eccentric rotor. Feed to main bearings, big end bearings and all camshaft bearings under pressure.
Oil Pressure	70 lbs. sq. in. at 2,000 r.p.m. (4.9 kg. sq. cm.)
Oil Cleaner	Purolator by-pass flow system with replaceable cartridge.
Carburettors	Twin S.U. H.4. Standard needles FV. For high speed motoring G.C. needles.
Valve Timing	With valve rocker clearance set at .015" (.38 mm.) Inlet Valve opens at 15° B.T.D.C. Exhaust Valve closes at 15° A.T.D.C. 15° is equivalent to .081" piston travel or 1.5" (3.81 cms.), measured round the flywheel adjacent to the starter teeth. Dims. on fan pulley = .72".
Cooling System	Thermostatically controlled.
Pressurised Radiator	Pressure release at 3¼—4¼ lbs.
Radiator Temperature	Normal running should not exceed 185°F. (85°C.).
Capacity of Cooling System	13 pints (7.4 litres).
With Heater	14 pints (8 litres).
Thermostat	Commences to open at 150°F. (70°C.). Fully open at 197°F. (92°C.).
Frost Precautions	With "Smith's Bluecol" anti-freeze mixture. Other brands as recommended by their manufacturers.

Degrees of Frost (Fahrenheit)	15°	25°	35°
Proportion	10%	15%	20%
Amount of "Bluecol" (Pints)	1.5	2.5	3

Piston Speed	2,850 ft./min. at 4,800 r.p.m. (This speed is equivalent to 100 m.p.h. in "Normal" top gear.)
Flywheel	Cast Iron with induction hardened shrunk-on steel starter ring gear.

Transmission

Clutch	Borg and Beck 9" single dry plate. Hydraulically operated. Ball bearing clutch throw out.
Gearbox	Four forward ratios and reverse. Synchromesh on 2nd, 3rd and top forward ratios. Silent helical gears. Oil filler combined with dipstick.

Ratios

Overdrive	Top	Top	3rd	2nd	1st	Rev.
Gearbox	.82	1.00	1.325	2.00	3.38	4.28
Overall	3.03	3.7	4.9	7.4	12.5	15.8

Rear Axle	Hypoid Bevel Gears. Taper roller bearings on differential and for Hypoid Pinion Shaft. Ball bearings for road wheels. Shim adjustment for Pinion and Crown Wheel adjustment.

GENERAL DATA

Rear Axle Ratio	......	3.7. (37T × 10T).
Wheels	......	Steel Disc Type with chrome nave plates (wire wheels optional extra.).
Suspension	......	Coil springs for independent front suspension with telescopic dampers. Wide semi-elliptic springs at rear, controlled by piston type dampers.
Brakes	......	Lockheed Hydraulic 10″ × 2¼″ front, 9″ × 1¾″ rear. (After Commission No. TS.5481 10″ × 2¼″ front and rear.) Two leading shoe type used on front wheels, leading and trailing shoe type on rear wheels. Alloy cast iron brake drums. Foot operation hydraulic on all four wheels. Hand operation mechanical on rear wheels only.
Steering	......	High Gear Cam and Lever type unit. Optional for use on right or left hand drive. 17″ (431 mm.) steering wheel with three spoke spring type.
Battery	......	12 volt, 51 amp. hour capacity, located under bonnet.
Performance Data		B.H.P. (Road Setting): 90 at 4,800 r.p.m. Maximum torque: 1,400 lb./ins. at 3,000 r.p.m., equivalent to 145 lbs./sq. ins. B.M.E.P. (See also Fig. 1).

Maximum Speeds
(Touring Trim)

Top Gear	110 m.p.h.	175 km.p.h.
3rd Gear	75	120
2nd Gear	45	75
1st Gear	25	40

Engine R.P.M. at	10 m.p.h.	10 km.p.h.
Top Gear	500	310
3rd Gear	660	410
2nd Gear	1,000	620
1st Gear	1,680	1,050
Rev. Gear	2,130	1,325

Acceleration Two Up

Gear	Speed	Time
Top	20—40 M.P.H. (32—64 Km.P.H.)	9 secs.
	30—50 M.P.H. (48—80 Km.P.H.)	9 secs.
Through Gears	0—50 M.P.H. (0—80 Km.P.H.)	8 secs.
	0—60 M.P.H. (0—96 Km.P.H.)	12 secs.

Fuel Consumption

Petrol	......	26—32 m.p.g. (10.87—8.83 litres per 100 km.).
Oil	......	3,000 m.p.g. (1,100 km. per litre.)

Car Dimensions

Wheelbase	7′ 4″	224 cms.
Track—Front	3′ 9″	114 cms.
Rear	3′ 9½″	116 cms.
Front wheel alignment	" Toe in " ⅛″.	
Ground clearance (under axle)	6″	15.2 cms.
Turning Circle (between Kerbs)	32′ 0″	9.75 metres

Overall Dimensions

Length	12′ 7″	384 cms.
Width	4′ 7½″	141 cms.
Height (unladen)		
Hood erect	4′ 2″	127 cms.
Top of Screen	3′ 10″	117 cms.
Hood down and Screen removed	3′ 4″	102 cms.
Luggage Space	See page 5 of this section.	

GENERAL DATA

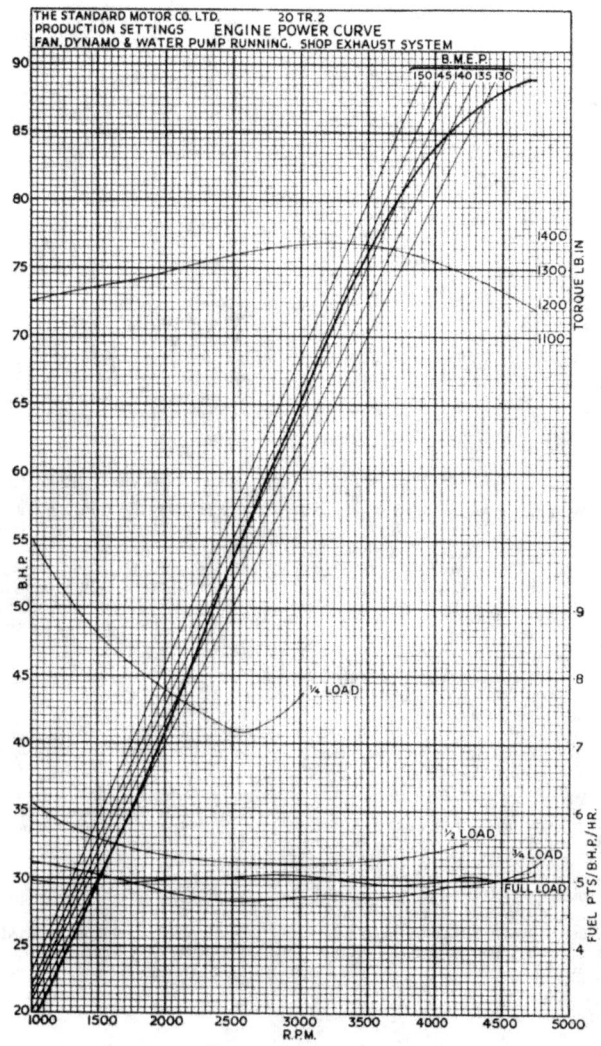

Fig. 1 Power Curve.

GENERAL DATA

Car Weight
Complete Car with Tools, Fuel and Water
    18 cwts. 3 qrs. 7 lbs. (955 kg.)
Shipping Weight
    17 cwts. 2 qrs. 21 lbs. (902 kg.)

Tyre Sizes and Pressure
Tyre Size .... 5.50″—15″.
Tyre Pressures
    Front ..... 22 lbs./sq. in. 1.55 kgsq./.cm.
    Rear ..... 24 lbs./sq. in. 1.7 kg./sq. cm.
Where cars are to be used for racing or special high testing it is desirable that the Dunlop Rubber Company be consulted for special tyres.

Water Capacity
Cooling System ..... 13 pints 7.4 litres
With Heater Fitted ..... 14 pints 8 litres

Oil Capacity
Engine—From Dry Drain and Refill ..... 11 pints 6.25 litres
    ..... 10 pints 5.7 litres
Gearbox ..... 1½ pints .85 litres
 ,, with Overdrive From Dry 3½ pints 2.0 litres
Rear Axle .... 1½ pints .85 litres

Petrol
Petrol Tank capacity ..... 12½ galls. 57 litres

Body Specification
Two seater open sports, all weather equipment. Detachable windscreen of Triplex safety glass. Provision for fitting aero screens.
Steel body rust-proofed.
Front wings, rear wings and complete front panel are bolted on detachable type.
Door hinged at front.

SPIRE SPEED NUTS

1. GENERAL NOTES

These speed nuts are being used in increasing numbers on our products at the present time in the place of nuts and lock washers, as, in many instances, they simplify manufacturing processes and speed up assembly work.

Although no particular skill is required in their application, an elementary knowledge of the correct way to fit them is necessary. It is not intended to refer to each type of speed nut in detail and, in any case, the types at present in use are likely to be increased as production proceeds and the desirability of their employment becomes apparent.

2. DESCRIPTION

Spire speed nuts provide a compensating thread lock. As the screw is tightened, the two arched prongs move inwards to engage and lock against the flanks of the screw thread. The prongs compensate for tolerance variations in the screw. A spring locking action is provided by compression of the arch in both prongs and base as the screw is tightened. The combined forces of the threaded lock and that provided by the spring prevent loosening due to vibration.

3. TIGHTENING TORQUES

Unlike normal threaded nuts, spire speed nuts do not require a great deal of torque when tightening the screw. The retention of the screw by the nut depends on spring tension alone. When tightening a screw into a speed nut, only sufficient torque should be used to produce the thread and spring lock shown in Fig. 3. Excessive

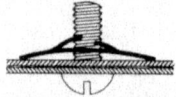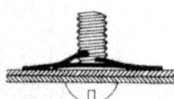

Fig. 3   Showing an Untightened Spire Nut on the left of the illustration and on the other side a fully tightened one.

torque will only distort the ends of the prongs and affect their spring tension and may even break them.
Spire speed nuts can be used indefinitely providing they have not been damaged by over-tightening.

GENERAL DATA

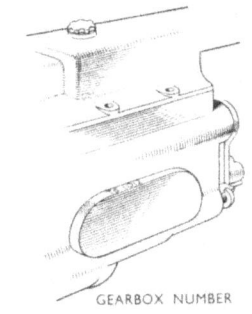
GEARBOX NUMBER

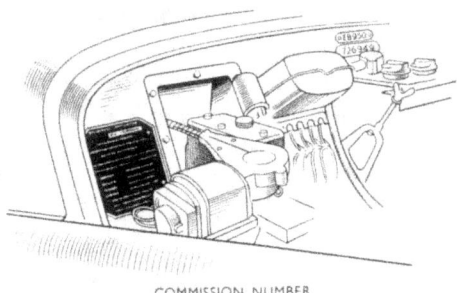
COMMISSION NUMBER

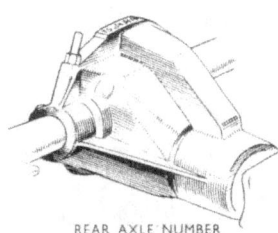
REAR AXLE NUMBER

RECONDITION PLATE

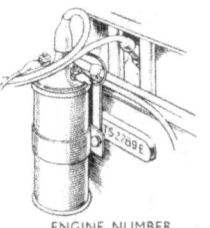
ENGINE NUMBER

Fig. 4   Commission Numbers.

4. **COMMISSION NUMBER** (Chassis Number)

   This number is found on a plate attached to the bulkhead under the bonnet at the right-hand side (see Fig. 4). It has the prefix letters "TS."

   NOTE: **It is important that this number is quoted when writing to the Company concerning the car and particularly when ordering spare parts.**

5. **BODY NUMBER**

   This number is stamped on an oval plate affixed in the centre of the bulkhead under the bonnet (see Fig. 4). It is a number with six numerals.

6. **ENGINE NUMBER**

   This number is stamped on a boss situated on the cylinder block casting below No. 3 plug (see Fig. 4). It has a prefix "TS" and a suffix letter "E."

   Factory Rebuilt Engines

   All factory rebuilt engines have the previous number erased and the new number stamped on a plate which is attached to the same boss (see Fig. 4).

   This plate also gives information as to the size of the crank pins and journals, also the date on which the unit was rebuilt. This number has a prefix "TS" and a suffix "FR."

7. **GEARBOX NUMBER**

   This number is stamped on the left-hand side of the box on the upper wall of the cast oval (see Fig. 4). This number has the prefix "TS."

8. **REAR AXLE NUMBER**

   This number is stamped on the upper rim of the flange to which the rear cover plate is attached (see Fig. 4). This number has the prefix "TS."

GENERAL DATA
RECOMMENDED LUBRICANTS
BRITISH ISLES

Component	Shell	Esso	Duckham's	Vacuum	Wakefield	B.P. Energol
ENGINE Summer	Shell X-100 30	Essolube 30	Duckham's NOL "Thirty"	Mobiloil A	Castrol XL	Energol S.A.E. 30
Winter	Shell X-100 20/20W	Essolube 20	Duckham's NOL "Twenty"	Mobiloil Arctic	Castrolite	Energol S.A.E. 20
Upper Cylinder Lubricant	Shell Donax U	Essomix	Duckham's Adcoids	Mobil Upperlube	Castrollo	Energol U.C.L.
GEARBOX	Shell X-100 30	Essolube 30	Duckham's NOL "Thirty"	Mobiloil A	Castrol XL	Energol S.A.E. 30
REAR AXLE **STEERING GEARBOX**	Shell Spirax 90 E.P.	Esso Expee Compound 90	Duckham's Hypoid 90	Mobilube G.X. 90	Castrol Hypoy	Energol EP S.A.E. 90
PROPELLER SHAFT JOINTS	Shell Spirax 140 E.P.	Esso Expee Compound 140	Duckham's NOL EPT 140	Mobilube G.X. 140	Castrol Hi-Press	Energol E.P. S.A.E. 140
FRONT WHEEL HUBS		Esso High Temperature Grease	Duckham's LB10	Mobilgrease No. 5	Castrolease W.B.	
REAR WHEEL HUBS and **ENGINE WATER PUMP** (Hand Gun)	Shell Retinax A	Esso Grease	Duckham's H.B.B.	Mobil Hub Grease	Castrolease Heavy	Energrease C3
CHASSIS. Grease Nipples (Hand or Pressure Gun)			Duckham's Laminoid Soft	Mobilgrease No. 4	Castrolease CL	
Oil Points (Oil Can) Body and Chassis	Shell X-100 20/20W	Essolube 20	Duckham's NOL "Twenty"	Mobil Handy Oil	Castrolite	Energol S.A.E. 20
REAR ROAD SPRINGS	Shell Donax P	Esso Penetrating Oil	Duckham's Laminoid Liquid	Mobil Spring Oil	Castrol Penetrating Oil	Energol Penetrating Oil
	ALTERNATIVELY USE REAR AXLE OR ENGINE OIL					
HANDBRAKE CABLES	Shell Retinax A	Esso Graphite Grease	Duckham's Keenol KG 16	Mobil Graphited Grease	Castrolease Brake Cable Grease	Energrease C3G
BRAKE RESERVOIR	GENUINE LOCKHEED HYDRAULIC BRAKE FLUID					

GENERAL DATA
RECOMMENDED LUBRICANTS
OVERSEAS COUNTRIES

Component		Duckham's	Vacuum	Wakefield	B.P. Energol	Shell	Esso	S.A.E.
ENGINE	Air Temp. °F. Over 70°	Duckham's NOL "Forty"	Mobiloil "AF"	Castrol XXL	Energol Motor Oil S.A.E. 40	Shell X-100 40	Essolube 40	40
	40° to 70°	Duckham's NOL "Thirty"	Mobiloil "A"	Castrol XL	Energol Motor Oil S.A.E. 30	Shell X-100 30	Essolube 30	30
	10° to 40°	Duckham's NOL "Twenty"	Mobiloil Arctic	Castrolite	Energol Motor Oil S.A.E. 20W	Shell X-100 20/20W	Essolube 20	20
	—10° to 10°	Duckham's NOL "Ten"	Mobiloil 10W	Castrol Z	Energol Motor Oil S.A.E. 10W	Shell X-100 10W	Essolube 10	10
	Below —10°	Duckham's NOL "Five"	Mobiloil 5W	Castrol ZZ	Energol Motor Oil S.A.E. 5W	Shell X-100 5W	Esso Extra Motor Oil "Zero"	5
	Upper Cylinder Lubricant	Duckham's Adcoids	Mobil Upperlube	Castrollo	Energol U.C.L.	Shell Donax U	Esso Upper Motor Lubricant	—
GEARBOX	Over 70°	Duckham's NOL "Fifty"	Mobiloil BB	Castrol XXL	Energol Motor Oil S.A.E. 50	Shell X-100 50	Essolube 50	50
	Over 10° to 70°	Duckham's NOL "Thirty"	Mobiloil A	Castrol XL	Energol Motor Oil S.A.E. 30	Shell X-100 30	Essolube 30	30
	Below 10°	Duckham's NOL "Twenty"	Mobiloil Arctic	Castrolite	Energol Motor Oil S.A.E. 20W	Shell X-100 20/20W	Essolube 20	20
STEERING GEARBOX	Over 10°	Duckham's Hypoid 90	Mobilube GX 90	Castrol Hypoy	Energol EP S.A.E. 90	Shell Spirax 90EP	Esso XP Compound 90	EP 90
REAR AXLE	Below 10°	Duckham's Hypoid 80	Mobilube GX 80	Castrol Hypoy 80	Energol EP S.A.E. 80	Shell Spirax 80EP	Esso XP Compound 80	EP 80
PROPELLER SHAFT JOINTS		Duckham's NOL EPT 140	Mobiloil GX 140	Castrol Hi-Press	Energol EP S.A.E. 140	Shell Spirax 140EP	Esso XP Compound 140	EP 140
FRONT WHEEL HUBS		Duckham's LB10		Castrolease W.B.			Esso Bearing Grease	—
REAR WHEEL HUBS and ENGINE WATER PUMP (Hand Gun)		Duckham's H.B.B.	Mobilgrease M.P.	Castrolease Heavy	Energrease C3	Shell Retinax A	Esso Chassis Grease	—
CHASSIS Grease Nipples (Hand or Pressure Gun)		Duckham's Laminoid Soft		Castrolease CL				
Oil Points (Oil Can) Body & Chassis		Duckham's NOL "Twenty"	Mobiloil Arctic	Castrolite	Energol Motor Oil S.A.E. 20W	Shell X-100 20/20W	Esso Handy Oil	20
REAR ROAD SPRINGS		Duckham's Laminoid Liquid	Mobilgrease M.P.	Castrol Penetrating Oil	Energol Penetrating Oil	Shell Donax P	Esso Penetrating Oil	—
		ALTERNATIVELY USE REAR AXLE OR ENGINE OIL						
HANDBRAKE CABLES		Duckham's Keenol KG3	Mobilgrease M.P.	Castrolease Brake Cable Grease	Energrease C3G	Shell Retinax A	Esso Spring Grease	—
BRAKE RESERVOIR		GENUINE LOCKHEED HYDRAULIC BRAKE FLUID						

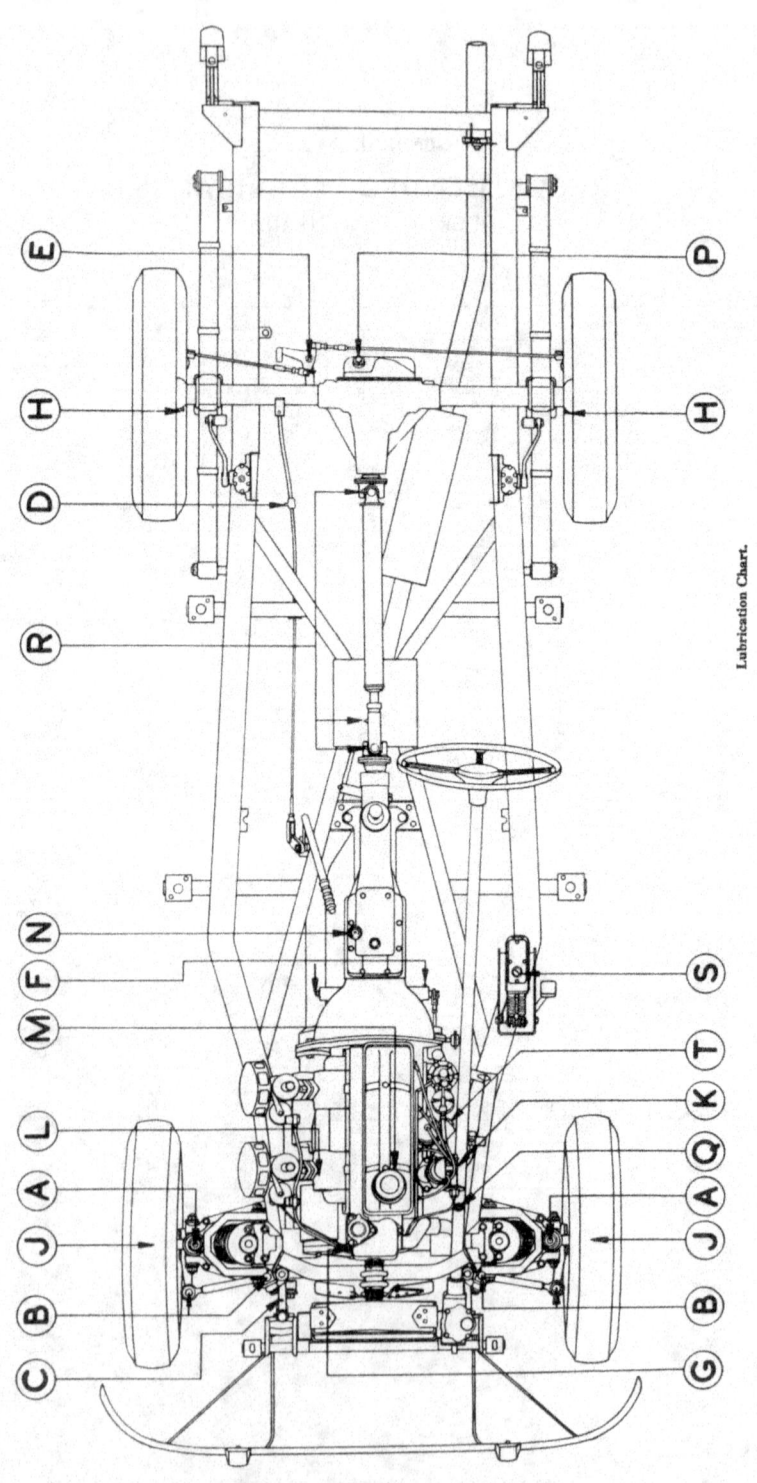

Lubrication Chart.

Ref.	ITEMS			DETAILS		Mileage Interval (Thousands of Miles)
A	Steering Swivels (4 nipples)			THREE OR FOUR STROKES	GREASE GUN	1
B	Steering	Outer Tie Rod Ball Joints (4 nipples)				1
C		Slave Drop Arm Pivot (1 nipple)				1
	Lower Wishbone Outer Bushes (4 nipples)					1
D	Handbrake	Cable (1 nipple)		FIVE STROKES		5
E		Compensator (2 nipples)				5
F	Clutch Shaft Bearings (2 nipples)					5
G	Engine Water Pump (1 nipple)					5
H	Hubs	Rear (2 nipples)				5
J		Front (2 nipples) Fitted up to Commission No. TS. 5348 only				5
K	Ignition Distributor			OIL AS RECOMMENDED	OIL CAN	5
	Handbrake Lever					5
	Carburettor Dashpots and Control Linkages					5
	Door Locks, Hinges, Bonnet Safety Catch, Boot and Spare Wheel Locks					5
L	Dynamo					10
M	Engine Sump		250 MILES	TOP UP OIL LEVEL		
				DRAIN & REFILL WITH NEW OIL		2½
	Oil Filler Cap			WASH		5
N	Gearbox			TOP UP OIL LEVEL		5
				DRAIN & REFILL WITH NEW OIL		10
P	Rear Axle					5
Q	Steering Gearbox			TOP UP OIL LEVEL		5
R	Propeller Shaft	Splines (1 nipple)		THREE OR FOUR STROKES WITH OIL GUN		5
		Universal Joints (2 nipples)				5
	Road Springs			CLEAN AND OIL		5
	Air Cleaners			OIL AS RECOMMENDED		5
S	Hydraulic Brake and Clutch Reservoir			TOP UP FLUID LEVEL		5
T	Oil Cleaner			RENEW CARTRIDGE		10

GENERAL DATA

NUT TIGHTENING TORQUES

Operation	Description	Detail No.	Specified Torque Range lb./ft.	Remarks
ENGINE				
CYLINDER HEAD	$\frac{7}{16}''$ UNF and UNC Stud	106960 / 106959	100—105	Tighten nuts with engine cold.
CONNECTING ROD CAPS	$\frac{5}{16}''$ UNF Bolt	105312	55—60	
MAIN BEARING CAPS	$\frac{1}{2}'' \times 13$ NC Setscrew	57121	85—90	
FLYWHEEL ATTACHMENT TO CRANKSHAFT	$\frac{3}{8}'' \times 24$ NF Setscrew	102065	42—46	
TIMING CHAIN WHEEL TO CAMSHAFT	$\frac{5}{16}'' \times 18$ NC Setscrew	56370	24—26	
MANIFOLD ATTACHMENT	$\frac{3}{8}''$ NC Stud	58688 / 102475 / 107055	22—24	
OIL PUMP ATTACHMENTS	$\frac{5}{16}'' \times 24$ UNF Stud	HN.2008	12—14	
REAR OIL SEAL ATTACHMENT	$\frac{1}{4}'' \times 20$ UNC Setscrew	UN.0755	8—10	
CLUTCH ATTACHMENT	$\frac{5}{16}'' \times 18$ UNC Setscrew	HU.0856	20	
ATTACHMENT OF END PLATES	$\frac{5}{16}'' \times 18$ UNC Bolt	HU.0856	14—16	Tapped into Aluminium
ATTACHMENT OF OIL FILTERS	$\frac{5}{16}'' \times 18 \times 24$ UNC Bolts / Cap Nut / Bolt	HB.0874 / HB.0882 / DN.3408 / HB.0856	18—20	
TIMING COVER	$\frac{5}{16}'' \times 18$ and 24 NC Setscrew	HU.0805 / HU.0857	14—16	
SUMP ATTACHMENT	$\frac{5}{16}'' \times 18$ NC Setscrew	100749	16—18	
PULLEY TO WATER PUMP SPINDLE	$\frac{5}{16}'' \times 24$ UNF Simmonds Nyloc Nut	TN.3208	16—18	
DYNAMO BRACKET TO BLOCK	$\frac{5}{16}'' \times 18$ UNC Setscrew	HU.0856	16—18	
DYNAMO TO BRACKET AND PEDESTAL	$\frac{5}{16}'' \times 24$ UNF Setscrew and Bolt	59115 / HU.0808	16—18	
ROCKER PEDESTAL	$\frac{3}{8}''$ NF and NC Stud	108205	24—26	
OIL GALLERY PLUGS	$\frac{7}{16}'' \times 14$ UNC / $\frac{3}{8}'' \times 16$ UNC	102785 / HU.0954	32—36 / 24—26	Tighten on to copper washer.
ATTACHMENT OF STARTER MOTOR	$\frac{3}{8}'' \times 24$ NF Bolt	NB.0915	26—28	
WATER PUMP ATTACHMENT	$\frac{3}{8}'' \times 16$ UNC Bolt / $\frac{3}{8}'' \times 16$ UNC Bolt	HB.0971 / HB.0968	26—28 / 26—28	
PETROL PUMP ATTACHMENT	$\frac{5}{16}''$ NF and NC Stud	31ST / 131C056	12—14	
THERMOSTAT ASSEMBLY TO CYLINDER HEAD	$\frac{5}{16}'' \times 18$ UNC Bolt / $\frac{5}{16}'' \times 18$ UNC Bolt	HB.0878 / HB.0866	16—18 / 16—18	
INLET TO EXHAUST MANIFOLD	$\frac{5}{16}'' \times 24$ UNF Stud	100419	12—14	
DYNAMO TO PEDESTAL FRONT	$\frac{5}{16}'' \times 24$ UNF Bolt	59115	16—18	
GEARBOX				
FRONT COVER TO GEARBOX	$\frac{5}{16}'' \times 18$ NC Setscrew	55771	14—16	
EXTENSION TO GEARBOX	$\frac{5}{16}'' \times 18$ UNC Bolt	HB.0866 / HB.0858	14—16	
TOP COVER TO GEARBOX	$\frac{5}{16}'' \times 18$ Bolts and Setscrews	HU.0851 / HB.0871 / HB.0873	14—16	
ATTACHMENT OF ENGINE TO GEARBOX	$\frac{5}{16}'' \times 18$ NC and NF Bolt and Stud	HB.0858 / 125C056	14—16	
REAR MOUNTING TO GEARBOX EXTENSION	$\frac{1}{4}'' \times 20$ UNF Bolt	HB.1112	50—55	

FRONT SUSPENSION				
BACK PLATE AND TIE ROD LEVERS TO VERTICAL LINKS	$\frac{1}{4}''$ × 24 UNF Setscrews and Bolts	HB.0925 HB.0922 HU.0905	24—26	
WHEEL STUDS AND NUTS	$\frac{7}{16}''$ NF	100869	45—55	
BALL PIN TO VERTICAL LINK	$\frac{1}{2}''$ × 20 UNF Nut—Slotted	2211 LN	55—65	To suit pin hole.
TOP WISHBONE TO FULCRUM PIN	$\frac{7}{16}''$ × 20 UNF Nut—Slotted	2210 LN	26—40	To suit pin hole.
SPRING PAN TO WISHBONE	$\frac{1}{4}''$ × 24 UNF Stud $\frac{1}{4}''$ × 24 UNF Bolt	107350 107351	26—28	
TIE ROD TO IDLER LEVER AND DROP-ARM	$\frac{1}{4}''$ × 24 UNF Simmonds Nyloc Nut	TN.3209	26—28	
TOP INNER FULCRUM PIN TO CHASSIS	$\frac{1}{4}''$ × 24 UNF Bolt $\frac{1}{4}''$ × 24 UNF Setscrew	HB.0913 HU.0908	26—28	
LOWER FULCRUM BRACKET TO CHASSIS	$\frac{3}{16}''$ × 24 UNF Bolt	HB.0805	16—18	
LOWER WISHBONE TO FULCRUM PIN	$\frac{7}{16}''$ × 20 UNF Nyloc Nut	TN.3210	26—28	
FRONT HUB TO STUB AXLE	$\frac{1}{2}''$ × 20 UNF Nut—Slotted	LN.2211	Tighten up and unscrew one flat.	
REAR AXLE				
BEARING CAPS TO HOUSING	$\frac{1}{4}''$ × 24 UNF Setscrew	100878	34—36	
HYPOID PINION FLANGE	$\frac{1}{2}''$ × 18 UNF	100892	85—100	To suit split pin holes.
CROWN WHEEL TO DIFFERENTIAL CASE	$\frac{5}{16}''$ × 24 UNF $\frac{3}{8}''$ × 24 UNF	107880 109735	22—24 35—40	Fitted from Commission No. TS.2181.
REAR COVER ATTACHMENT	$\frac{3}{16}''$ × 24 UNF Setscrew	HU.0805	16—18	
BACKING PLATE ATTACHMENT	$\frac{1}{4}''$ × 24 UNF Setscrew	HU.0908	26—28	
HUB TO AXLE SHAFT	$\frac{1}{2}''$ × 18 UNF Nut—Slotted	100892 112635	110—125 125—145	From axle No. TS.8039
REAR SUSPENSION				
SPRING FRONT END TO FRAME	$\frac{1}{4}''$ × 20 UNF Bolt	106251	28—30	
SPRING SHACKLE (NUT TO PIN)	$\frac{1}{4}''$ × 24 UNF Nut Shackle Pin	HN.2009 104953	26—28	
ROAD SPRING TO REAR AXLE	Clip Nyloc Nut $\frac{1}{4}''$ × 24 UNF	107688 YN.2909	28—30	
SHOCK ABSORBER TO FRAME BRACKET	$\frac{1}{4}''$ × 24 UNF Setscrew $\frac{1}{4}''$ × 24 UNF Nyloc Nut	HU.0908 TN.3209	26—28	

TR 4

GENERAL SPECIFICATION

Engine
Number of cylinders	4
Bore of cylinders	3·386″ 86 mm.
(Special Order)	3·268″ 83 mm.
Stroke of crankshaft	3·622″ 92 mm.
Piston area	36·0 sq. in. 232 sq. cm.
(Special Order)	33·5 sq. in. 216 sq. cm.
Cubic capacity	130·5 cu. in. 2138 c.c.
(Special Order)	121·5 cu. in. 1991 c.c.
Compression ratio	9 : 1
Valve rocker clearances—inlet and exhaust	0·010″ (cold) 0·254 mm.
Valve timing with valve rocker clearances set at 0·0165″ (0·42 mm.)	Inlet and exhaust valves to be equally open at T.D.C. on the exhaust stroke.

Performance Data (Engine)
Nett	100 B.H.P. at 4,600 r.p.m.
	Torque 1,520 lb in. at 3,350 r.p.m.
	(Equivalent to 147 lb/sq. in. B.M.E.P.)
(Special Order)	100 B.H.P. at 5,000 r.p.m.
	Torque 1,410 lb in. at 3,000 r.p.m.
	(Equivalent to 145 lb/sq. in. B.M.E.P.)
Piston speed at 100 m.p.h. (top gear)	2,850 ft/min. at 4,800 r.p.m. (3·7 : 1 axle).

Lubrication (Engine)
Type of pump	Hobourn-Eaton eccentric rotor.
Oil filter	Purolator ; A.C. Delco ; Tecalemit full flow (replaceable element).
Release pressure	70 lb/sq. in. 4·921 kg/sq. cm.

Ignition System
Contact breaker gap	0·015″ 0·4 mm.
Spark plugs—Type	Lodge CNY (Normal road use).
	„ HN (High speed touring).
	„ 2HN (Competition use).
	„ CN (Low octane fuel).
Gap	0·025″ 0·64 mm.
Firing order	1 : 3 : 4 : 2.
Ignition timing	4° B.T.D.C. (Basic setting).

Cooling System
Circulation	Pump.
Water pump type	Impeller — incorporating by-pass.
Temperature control	Thermostat.
	Opening temperature. 70°C (158°F)
	Fully open at 85°C (185°F)
Radiator	Pressurised—finned vertical flat tubes—extended header tank.
Filler cap	A.C. type.
— pressure	4 lb/sq. in. 0·28 kg/sq. cm.

Fuel System
Fuel tank	Non-pressure type mounted over rear axle.
Carburettors	Twin S.U. H6.
	Needle size — SM.
Air cleaners	Wire gauze type.
Fuel pump — type	A.C. mechanical with filter and sediment bowl.
— operating pressure	1¼ - 2¼ lb./sq. in.

Clutch
Type	Borg & Beck 9″ single dry plate.
Operation	Hydraulic.
Adjustment	Push rod at slave cylinder.

Gearbox
Type .. .. 4 forward speeds and reverse. Synchromesh on all forward gears.
Control .. .. Centre floor-mounted remote control.

Rear Axle
Type .. .. Hypoid bevel gears ; semi-floating axle shafts. Tapered roller bearings.
Ratio .. .. 3·7 or 4·1 : 1.

Gear Ratios

	Overdrive Top	Top	Overdrive 3rd	3rd	Overdrive 2nd	2nd	1st	Rev.
Gearbox Ratios ..	0·82	1·0	1·09	1·325	1·65	2·01	3·139	3·223

3·7 : 1 Axle

Overall Ratios ..	3·034	3·7	4·02	4·9	6·1	7·44	11·61	11·93

4·1 : 1 Axle

Overall Ratios ..	3·36	4·1	4·46	5·44	6·76	8·24	12·87	13·21

Brakes
System .. .. Girling hydraulic.
Front — Caliper disc.
Rear — Drum (leading and trailing shoes).
Adjustment .. .. Rear brakes only (1 adjuster each wheel).
Dimensions .. .. Rear shoes : 9" × 1¾" (22·86 × 4·45 cm.).

TYRE PRESSURE DATA

TYRE PRESSURES

OPERATING CONDITIONS	Goodyear Allweather Rib and Dunlop Gold Seal		Goodyear Allweather Rib Nylon and Dunlop Gold Seal Nylon		Goodyear Motorway Special and Dunlop Road Speed R.S.5		Goodyear D.F.S. (165—380) and Michelin (165/15X)	
	5·50/5·90-15		5·50/5·90-15		5·50/5·90-15		(165/15X)	
	Lbs. per sq. in.		Lbs. per sq. in.		Lbs. per sq. in.		Lbs. per sq. in.	
	Front	Rear	Front	Rear	Front	Rear	Front	Rear
Normal motoring with sustained speeds limited to 85 m.p.h.	20	24	20	24	20	24	24	32
Fast motoring on Motorways and similar roads with sustained speeds up to 100 m.p.h.	26	30	20	24	20	24	24	32
High speed tuning with speeds regularly in excess of 100 m.p.h.	Not recommended		26	30	20	24	24	32

Suspension
Front .. .. Independent suspension with wishbones top and bottom. Patented bottom bush and top ball joint swivels. Coil springs controlled by telescopic dampers. Taper roller hub bearings.
Rear .. .. Wide semi-elliptic springs, controlled by piston type dampers.

Steering
Type .. .. Rack and pinion unit. Telescopic steering column.
Caster angle .. .. 3°
Camber angle .. .. 2° Static laden.
King pin inclination .. .. .. 7°
Front wheel alignment .. .. .. Parallel to $\frac{1}{8}''$ (3·18 mm.) toe-in.
Parallel to $\frac{1}{16}''$ (1·59 mm.) toe-in if fitted with Goodyear D.F.S. or Michelin X tyres.
Turning circle .. .. 33' 0"   10 metres.

Chassis Data

	Imperial	Metric
Wheelbase	7' 4"	2·236 metres.
Track : Front (Disc wheels)	4' 1"	1·245 metres.
Rear (Disc wheels)	4' 0"	1·220 metres.
Front (Wire wheels)	4' 2"	1·270 metres.
Rear (Wire wheels)	4' 1"	1·245 metres.
Ground clearance (Static laden)	6"	15·24 cm.

Exterior Dimensions

Overall length	12' 10"	391 cm.
,, width	4' 9⅛"	146 cm.
,, height	4' 2"	127 cm.

Weight

Dry (excluding extra equipment)	2128 lb.	965 kg.
Complete (including fuel, oil, water and tools) ..	2240 lb.	1015 kg.

Capacities

	Imperial	U.S.	Metric
Engine — from dry	11 pints	13·2 pints	6·25 litres
Drain and refill	10 pints	12 pints	5·7 litres
Gearbox	1½ pints	1·8 pints	0·8 litres
With overdrive from dry	3½ pints	4·2 pints	2·0 litres
Drain and refill	2⅞ pints	3·3 pints	1·6 litres
Rear axle	1½ pints	1·8 pints	0·8 litres
Water capacity of cooling system	13 pints	15·7 pints	7·39 litres
With heater fitted	14 pints	16·8 pints	8·0 litres
Fuel capacity	11¾ galls.	14 galls.	53·5 litres

Electrical System
Battery .. .. 12 volt, 51 amps. hr.
Control box .. .. Model R.B.106-2.
Generator .. .. Model C40-1.

LOCATION OF COMMISSION AND UNIT NUMBERS

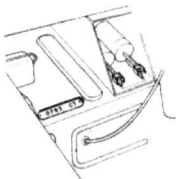

The Body Number is located on the R.H. side of the Scuttle Panel.

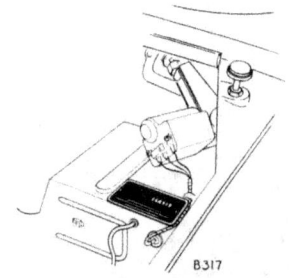

The Commission Number (Chassis Number) is located on the Scuttle Panel adjacent to the windscreen wiper motor and may be seen by lifting the bonnet.

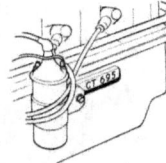

The Engine Serial Number is stamped on the L.H. side of the Cylinder Block.

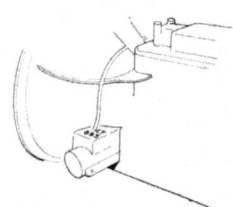

The Gearbox Serial Number is stamped on the L.H. side of the Clutch Housing.

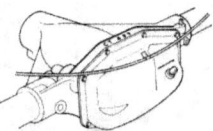

The Rear Axle Serial Number is stamped on the face of the Hypoid Housing Flange.

IMPORTANT

In all communications relating to Service or Spares, please quote the Commission Number (Chassis Number).

NUT TIGHTENING TORQUES

OPERATION	DESCRIPTION	SPECIFIED TORQUES lbs. ft.	Kgm.
ENGINE			
Cylinder Head	1/2" U.N.F. & B.N.C. Stud	100 - 105	13·826 - 14·520
Connecting Rod Caps	7/16" U.N.F. Bolt	55 - 60	7·604 - 8·293
Clutch Attachment	5/16" × 18 U.N.C. Setscrew	20	2·765
Camshaft Bearing to Block Front	5/16" N.C. Setscrew	16 - 18	2·212 - 2·489
Camshaft Bearing to Block Rear	5/16" U.N.F. Setscrew	12 - 14	1·659 - 1·936
Dynamo Bracket to Block	5/16" × 18 U.N.C. Setscrew	16 - 18	2·212 - 2·489
Dynamo to Bracket and Pedestal	5/16" × 24 U.N.F. Bolt	16 - 18	2·212 - 2·489
Distributor Mounting	1/4" N.F. & N.C. Stud	8 - 10	1·106 - 1·383
Dynamo Adjusting Link to Water Pump Body	5/16" U.N.C. Bolt	16 - 18	2·212 - 2·489
	5/16" U.N.C. Setscrew		
End Plate Attachment	5/16" × 18 U.N.C. Bolt	14 - 16	1·936 - 2·212
Engine Plate and Timing Cover Front ..	5/16" N.F. & U.N.C. Stud	12 - 14	1·659 - 1·936
Flywheel Attachment to Crankshaft	3/8" × 24 N.F. Setscrew	42 - 46	5·807 - 6·360
Fan Attachment	5/16" U.N.F. Bolt	16 - 18	2·212 - 2·489
Manifold Attachment	3/8" N.C. Stud	22 - 24	3·042 - 3·318
Manifold Inlet and Exhaust	5/16" × 24 U.N.F. Stud	12 - 14	1·659 - 1·936
Main Bearing Caps	1/2" U.N.C. Setscrew	85 - 90	11·752 - 12·443
Oil Pump Attachment	5/16" N.F. & N.C. Stud	12 - 14	1·659 - 1·936
Oil Seal Attachment (Rear)	1/4" × 20 U.N.C. Setscrew	8 - 10	1·106 - 1·383
Oil Filter Attachment	5/16" U.N.C. Bolts	22 - 24	3·042 - 3·318
	5/16" N.F. & N.C. Stud		
Oil Gallery Plugs	7/16" × 14 U.N.C. Setscrew	32 - 36	4·424 - 4·977
	3/8" × 16 U.N.C. Setscrew	24 - 26	3·318 - 3·595
Petrol Pump Attachment	5/16" N.F. & N.C. Stud	12 - 14	1·659 - 1·936
Pulley to Water Pump Spindle	5/16" 24 U.N.F. Simmonds Nyloc Nut	16 - 18	2·212 - 2·489
Pulley and Extension to Hub	1/4" U.N.F. Bolt	8 - 10	1·106 - 1·383
Rocker Cover	5/16" N.F. & N.C. Stud	2	0·276
Rocker Pedestal	3/8" U.N.F. & U.N.C. Stud	24 - 26	3·318 - 3·595
Sump Attachment	5/16" × 18 U.N.F. Setscrew	18 - 20	2·489 - 2·765
Starter Motor (Attachment)	3/8" × 24 N.F. Bolt	26 - 28	3·595 - 3·871
Timing Cover	5/16" × 18 & 24 N.C. Setscrew	14 - 16	1·936 - 2·212
Timing Chain Wheel to Camshaft	5/16" × 18 N.C. Setscrew	24 - 26	3·318 - 3·595
Thermostat Assembly to Cylinder Head ..	5/16" × 24 U.N.C. Bolts	16 - 18	2·212 - 2·489
Thermostat Housing	5/16" U.N.F.	12 - 14	1·659 - 1·936
Water Pump Attachment	3/8" × 16 U.N.C. Bolts	26 - 28	3·595 - 3·871
Water Pump Body	3/8" N.F. & N.C. Stud	26 - 28	3·595 - 3·871
Flywheel Ring Gear Attachment	5/16" U.N.F. × 1·25" Bolt	16 - 18	2·212 - 2·489
GEARBOX			
Extension to Gearbox	5/16" × 18 U.N.C. Bolt	14 - 16	1·936 - 2·212
	5/16" × 18 U.N.C. Setscrew	14 - 16	1·936 - 2·212
Gearbox to Engine Attachment	5/16" N.F. & N.C. Setscrew	8 - 10	1·106 - 1·383
Selector Fork Attachment	5/16" U.N.F. Taper Setscrew	8 - 10	1·106 - 1·383
Front Cover to Gearbox	5/16" × 18 N.C. Setscrew	14 - 16	1·936 - 2·212
Propeller Shaft Flange to Mainshaft	3/4" × 16 N.F. Slotted Nut	80 - 120	11·060 - 16·590
Top Cover to Gearbox	5/16" N.C. Setscrew	14 - 16	1·936 - 2·212
	5/16" U.N.C. Bolt	14 - 16	1·936 - 2·212
Mounting Rear to Gearbox Extension ..	1/2" × 20 U.N.F. Bolt	50 - 55	6·913 - 7·604
REAR AXLE			
Bearing Caps to Housing	3/8" × 24 Setscrew	34 - 36	4·701 - 4·977
Backing Plate Attachment	3/8" × 24 Setscrew	26 - 28	3·595 - 3·871
Crown Wheel to Differential Case	3/8" × 24 U.N.F.	35 - 40	4·839 - 5·530
Hypoid Pinion Flange	5/8" × 18 U.N.F.	85 - 100	11·752 - 13·826
Hub to Axle Shaft	5/8" × 18 U.N.F. Nut Slotted	125 - 145	17·282 - 20·047
Rear Cover Attachment	5/16" × 24 U.N.F. Setscrew	16 - 18	2·212 - 2·489

NUT TIGHTENING TORQUES—continued

OPERATION	DESCRIPTION	SPECIFIED TORQUES lbs. ft.	Kgm.
FRONT SUSPENSION			
Back Plate and Tie Rod Levers to Vertical Link	$\frac{3}{8}''$ × 24 U.N.F. Setscrew and Bolts	24 - 26	3·318 - 3·595
Ball Pin to Vertical Link	$\frac{1}{2}''$ × 20 U.N.F. Nut Slotted	55 - 65	7·604 - 8·987
Front Hub to Stub Axle	$\frac{3}{4}''$ × 20 U.N.F. Nut Slotted	See group 4	
Lower Fulcrum Bracket to Chassis	$\frac{5}{16}''$ × 24 U.N.F. Setscrew	16 - 18	2·212 - 2·489
Stub Axle to Vertical Link	$\frac{1}{2}''$ × 20 U.N.F. Stub Axle Thread	55 - 60	7·604 - 8·295
Lower Wishbone to Fulcrum Pin	$\frac{7}{16}''$ × 20 U.N.F. Nyloc Nut	26 - 28	3·595 - 3·871
Spring Pad to Wishbone	$\frac{3}{8}''$ × 24 U.N.F. Stud		
	$\frac{3}{8}''$ × 24 U.N.F. Bolt	26 - 28	3·595 - 3·871
Top Wishbone to Fulcrum Pin	$\frac{7}{16}''$ × 20 U.N.F. Nut Slotted	26 - 40	3·595 - 5·530
Top Inner Fulcrum Pin to Chassis	$\frac{3}{8}''$ × 24 U.N.F. Bolt		
	$\frac{3}{8}''$ × 24 U.N.F. Setscrew	26 - 28	3·595 - 3·871
Outer Tie Rod to Levers	$\frac{3}{8}''$ × 24 U.N.F. Simmonds Nyloc Nut	26 - 28	3·595 - 3·871
Lower Wishbones to Vertical Link Trunnion	$\frac{7}{16}''$ U.N.F. Slotted Nut	See group 4	
Hub Extension Studs for Wire Wheel Attachment	$\frac{7}{16}''$ N.F. Stud	65	8·987
Brake Disc Attachment	$\frac{3}{8}''$ N.F. Bolt	32 - 35	4·424 - 4·839
Caliper Attachment	$\frac{7}{16}''$ N.F. Bolt	50 - 55	6·913 - 7·604
Brake Pad Retaining Plate Bolts	$\frac{1}{4}''$ N.F. Bolt	5 - 6	0·691 - 0·830
REAR SUSPENSION			
Rear Road Spring	$\frac{3}{8}''$ Centre Bolt	30 - 35	4·148 - 4·839
Road Spring to Rear Axle	$\frac{3}{8}''$ × 24 U.N.F. Clip Nyloc Nut	28 - 30	3·871 - 4·148
Shock Absorber to Frame Bracket	$\frac{3}{8}''$ × 24 U.N.F. Setscrew		
	$\frac{3}{8}''$ × 24 U.N.F. Nyloc	26 - 28	3·595 - 3·871
Spring Shackle (Nut to Pin)	$\frac{3}{8}''$ × 24 U.N.F. Nut Shackle Pin	26 - 28	3·595 - 3·871
Spring Front End to Frame	$\frac{1}{2}''$ × 20 U.N.F. Bolt	28 - 30	3·871 - 4·148
CHASSIS			
Gearbox Mounting to Crossmember	$\frac{7}{16}''$ U.N.F. Studs	35 - 40	4·839 - 4·530
Gearbox Mounting Crossmember to Chassis	$\frac{3}{8}''$ U.N.F. × $\frac{3}{8}''$ Bolts	26 - 28	3·595 - 3·871
Body Mounting Extension to Chassis	$\frac{5}{16}''$ U.N.F. × $\frac{3}{8}''$ Bolts	18 - 20	2·489 - 2·765
Front Cross Tube to Suspension Turrets	$\frac{3}{8}''$ U.N.F. × $\frac{3}{4}''$ Bolts	26 - 28	3·595 - 3·871
STEERING UNIT			
Steering Unit to Chassis	$\frac{5}{16}''$ N.F. 'U' Bolts	12 - 14	1·659 - 1·936
Steering Column Coupling	$\frac{5}{16}''$ N.F. Bolts	12 - 14	1·659 - 1·936
Adaptor Column Coupling Unit	$\frac{1}{4}''$ N.F. Bolt	6 - 8	·8295 - 1·106
BODY COMPONENTS			
Seat to Runner Attachment	$\frac{1}{4}''$ U.N.F.	5 - 6	·6913 - ·8295
MISCELLANEOUS			
Wheel Studs and Nuts	$\frac{7}{16}''$ U.N.F.	45 - 55	6·221 - 7·604

RECOMMENDED LUBRICANTS—HOME MARKETS

Component		Mobil	Shell	Esso	B.P.	Castrol	Duckham's	Regent
ENGINE SUMP*		Mobiloil Arctic or Mobiloil Special	Shell X-100 20W or X-100 Multigrade 10W/30	Esso Extra Motor Oil 20W/30	Energol Motor Oil 20W or Visco Static	Castrolite	Duckham's Nol Twenty or Duckham's Q5500	Havoline 20/20W or Havoline Special 10W/30
UPPER CYLINDER LUBRICANT		Mobil Upperlube	Shell U.C.L.	Esso U.C.L.	Energol U.C.L.	Castrollo	Duckham's Adcoids	Regent U.C.L.
CARBURETTOR DASHPOTS	SUMMER	Mobiloil A	X-100 30	Esso Extra Motor Oil 30	Energol Motor Oil 30	Castrol XL	Nol "Thirty"	Havoline 30
	WINTER	Mobiloil Arctic	X-100 20W	Esso Extra Motor Oil 20W	Energol Motor Oil 20W	Castrolite	Nol "Twenty"	Havoline 20/20W
GEARBOX AND OVERDRIVE REAR AXLE		Mobilube GX.90	Shell Spirax 90 E.P.	Esso Gear Oil GP.90	Energol E.P. S.A.E. 90	Castrol Hypoy	Duckham's Hypoid 90	Universal Thuban 90
STEERING UNIT GREASE GUN		Mobilgrease M.P.	Shell Retinax A	Esso Multi-Purpose Grease H	Energrease L2	Castrolease L.M.	Duckham's LB.10	Marfak Multipurpose 2
OIL CAN		Mobil Handy Oil	Shell X-100 20W	Esso Handy Oil	Energol S.A.E. 20W	Everyman Oil	Duckham's General Purpose Oil	Havoline 20/20W
REAR ROAD SPRINGS		OLD REAR AXLE OR ENGINE OIL						
BRAKE CABLES		Mobilgrease M.P.	Shell Retinax A	Esso Multi-Purpose Grease H	Energrease L2	Castrolease Brake Cable Grease	Duckham's Keenol K.G.16	Marfak Multipurpose 2
CLUTCH AND BRAKE RESERVOIRS		CASTROL GIRLING BRAKE AND CLUTCH FLUID				WHERE THE PROPRIETARY BRAND IS NOT AVAILABLE, OTHER FLUIDS WHICH MEET THE S.A.E. 70 R.3 SPECIFICATION MAY BE USED.		

*Where circuit or other severe competitions are contemplated it is advisable to use oils of high viscosity in view of the increased temperature encountered.

ANTI-FREEZE SOLUTIONS	Mobil Permazone	—	Shell Anti-freeze	Esso Anti-freeze	B.P. Anti-freeze	—	Castrol Anti-freeze	Duckham's Anti-freeze	—	Smith's Bluecol

The grades listed are not in the order of preference

RECOMMENDED LUBRICANTS—OVERSEAS COUNTRIES

Component		Mobil	Shell	Esso	B.P.	Castrol	Duckham's	Caltex Texaco	S.A.E. & A.P.I. Designation
ENGINE* SUMP	Air Temp. °F. Over 70°	Mobiloil A.F.	X-100 Multigrade 20W/40 or X-100 40	Esso Extra Motor Oil 20W/40 or Esso Motor Oil 40	Energol Motor Oil 40	Castrol XXL	Duckham's Nol "Forty"	Havoline 40 or Havoline Special 20W/40	S.A.E. 40 M.M.
	40° to 70°	Mobiloil A	Shell X-100 30	Esso Motor Oil 30	Energol Motor Oil 30	Castrol XL	Duckham's Nol "Thirty"	Havoline 30	S.A.E. 30 M.M.
	10° to 40°	Mobiloil Arctic	Shell X-100 20W	Esso Motor Oil 20	Energol Motor Oil 20W	Castrolite	Duckham's Nol "Twenty"	Havoline 20/20W	S.A.E. 20W M.M.
	Below 10°	Mobiloil 10W	Shell X-100 10W	Esso Motor Oil 10W	Energol Motor Oil 10W	Castrol Z	Duckham's Nol "Ten"	Havoline 10W	S.A.E. 10W M.M.
		MOBILOIL SPECIAL	MULTIGRADE X-100 10W/30	ESSO EXTRA MOTOR OIL 10W/33	VISCO STATIC		Q20-50 Q5500	HAVOLINE SPECIAL 10W/30	
UPPER CYLINDER LUBRICANT		Mobil Upperlube	Shell Donax U	Esso Upper Motor Lubricant	Energol U.C.L.	Castrollo	Duckham's Adcoids	Upper Cylinder Lubricant	—
CARBURETTOR DASHPOTS		USE APPROPRIATE CURRENT SINGLE GRADE ENGINE OIL							
GEARBOX	Over 30°	Mobilube GX.90	Spirax 90 E.P.	Esso Gear Oil G.P.90	Energol E.P. S.A.E. 90	Castrol Hypoy	Duckham's Hypoid 90	Universal Thuban 90	G.L.4 Hypoid 90
REAR AXLE	Below 30°	Mobilube GX.80	Shell Spirax 80 E.P.	Esso Gear Oil G.P.80	Energol E.P. S.A.E. 80	Castrol Hypoy Light	Duckham's Hypoid 80	Universal Thuban 80	G.L.4 Hypoid 80
STEERING UNIT GREASE GUN		Mobilgrease M.P.	Shell Retinax A	Esso Multi-Purpose Grease H	Energrease L2	Castrolease L.M.	Duckham's L.B.10	Marfak Multipurpose 2	—
OIL CAN		Mobil Handy Oil	Shell X-100 20W	Handy Oil	Energol Motor Oil S.A.E. 20W	Everyman Oil	Duckham's General Purpose Oil	Home Lubricant	—
REAR ROAD SPRINGS		OLD REAR AXLE OR ENGINE OIL							
BRAKE CABLES		Mobilgrease M.P.	Shell Retinax A	Esso Multi-Purpose Grease H	Energrease L.2	Castrolease Brake Cable Grease	Duckham's Keenol KG 16	Marfak Multipurpose 2	—
CLUTCH AND BRAKE RESERVOIRS		CASTROL GIRLING BRAKE AND CLUTCH FLUID				WHERE THE PROPRIETARY BRAND IS NOT AVAILABLE OTHER FLUIDS WHICH MEET THE S.A.E.70 R3 SPECIFICATION MAY BE USED.			
ANTI-FREEZE SOLUTIONS		Mobil Permazone	Shell Anti-freeze	Esso Anti-freeze	B.P. Anti-frost	Castrol Anti-freeze	Duckham's Anti-freeze	—	Smith's Bluecol

* Where circuit or other severe competitions are contemplated it is advisable to use oils of high viscosity in view of the increased oil temperature encountered.

The grades listed are not in the order of preference

REAR AXLE

Parts and Description	Dimensions when new	Clearances when new	Remarks
Axle Ratio	3·7 or 4·1 : 1		
Track	4′ 0″		4′ 1″ with wire wheels.
Width between Spring Centres	2′ 11″		
Crown Wheel			
Number of Teeth	37 (41)		4·1 crown wheel is identified by two grooves on its periphery.
Locating Diameter	4·3750″/4·3760″	0·0010″/0·0030″	Diameter of location on carrier—4·373″/4·374″.
Maximum permissible Run-out	0·003″		When bolted to differential carrier.
Pinion			
Number of Teeth	10		4·1 pinion identified by two annular grooves on the splines.
Diameter of Journal—			
for Pinion Head Bearing	1·2506″/1·2511″		Bearing press-fit. Interference of —0·000″/0·0011″.
for Pinion Tail Bearing	1·0004″/1·0009″		Bearing light drive fit. Limits allow clearance of 0·0002″ to an interference of 0·0009″.
Spline Diameters—Maximum	0·9900″/0·9940″		
—Minimum	0·8460″/0·8475″		Driving flange locating diameter.
Thread Dimensions	⅞″—18 U.N.F.		
Axle Casing			
Internal Diameter for :			
Pinion Head Bearing Outer Ring	2·8578″/2·8588″		Ring is press fit in bore. Interference of 0·0005″/0·0021″.
Pinion Nose Bearing Outer Ring	2·4395″/2·4405″		Ring is press fit in bore. Interference of 0·0005″/0·0019″.
Differential Bearing Outer Rings	2·8445″/2·8455″		With bearing caps tightened, limits allow clearance of 0·0015″ to an interference of 0·0001″.
Width between Differential Bearing Outer Ring Abutments	7·2550″/7·2630″		
Maximum Spreading Load for entry of Assembled Differential Unit	3250 lbs.		Load applied between reaction points 30″ apart.
Axle Shafts			
Overall Length	26·31″		
Hub Bearing Journal Diameter	1·3135″/1·3140″		Bearing press fit on shaft. Interference of 0·0004″/0·0015″.
External Diameter of Serrations	1·0377″/1·0417″		
Number of Serrations	24		
Thread Dimensions	¾″ × 16 T.P.I. U.N.F.	Class 2A	
Keyway Width	0·2500″/0·2510″		
Driving Key Dimensions	1 $\frac{7}{16}$″ × ¼″ × ¼″		
Axle Shaft End Float	0·0040″/0·0060″		End float controlled by shim thickness between end of axle casing and brake backing plate. See remarks concerning "Thrust Button".
Hub Bearing Housing			
Internal Diameter for Bearing Outer Ring	2·7485″/2·7495″		Ring is press fit in housing. Interference of 0·0005″/0·0019″.

REAR AXLE — continued

Parts and Description	Dimensions when new	Clearances when new	Remarks
Pinion Setting Dimensions			
Distance from Head Bearing Abutment Face on Pinion to Centre of Crown Wheel Bearings	3·4375″		
Pinion Centre Line 'Offset' below Crown Wheel Centre Line	0·9990″/1·0010″		
Pinion Bearing Pre-load (without Oil Seal)	15/18 lb. ins.		Controlled by shim thickness between bearing spacer and nose bearing inner cone.
Backlash between Pinion and Crown Wheel	0·0040″/0·0060″		Controlled by shim thickness behind differential bearings.
Differential Unit			
Differential Sun Gear :			
Number of Teeth	16		
Journal Diameter	1·4985″/1·4993″	0·002″/0·004″	Clearance of Gear in gear carrier.
Number of Internal Serrations	24		
Internal Diameter	0·9750″/0·9790″		
Thrust Washer Thickness	0·0470″/0·0490″		
Planet Gear :			
Number of Teeth	10		
Internal Diameter	0·6250″/0·6265″	0·0008″/0·0028″	Clearance between gear and cross-pin.
Thrust Washer Thickness	0·0470″/0·0490″		
Cross-pin :			
Diameter	0·6237″/0·6242″	0·0003″/0·0020″	Clearance of pin in differential housing.
Length	4·19″		
Thrust Button :			
Length between Thrust Faces	1·3700″/1·3800″		Arrange hub bearing adjusting shims to permit the thrust button to assume a central position in relation to cross-pin.
Differential Casing :			
Diameter of Journal for Differential Bearings	1·5012″/1·5018″		Bearing press fit. Interference of 0·0006″/0·0018″.
Width of Case between Differential Bearing Abutments	5·3120″/5·3170″		
Dimension between Bearing Abutment and Crown Wheel Locating Face	1·5620″/1·5680″		
Internal Diameter for Differential Sun Gear Journals	1·5013″/1·5025″	0·002″/0·004″	Clearance of gear in gear carrier.
Width between Differential Side Gear Thrust Faces	2·3620″/2·3660″		
Diameter of Cross-pin Bore	0·6245″/0·6257″	0·0003″/0·0020″	Clearance of cross-pin in housing.
Differential Bearing Pre-Load (measured over both bearings)	0·0020″/0·0040″		Controlled by thickness of shims.
Hubs (Rear)			
Thread Dimensions for Withdrawal Purposes	1⅞″ × 8 T.P.I. S.A.E.		

Notes

STROMBERG CARBURETORS

Later TR 4s have been fitted with Stromberg carburetors in place of SUs. They are termed "CD" or "Constant Depression" type and are quite similar to the SU in principle, operating on the constant vacuum method of regulating fuel/air ratio. The choke and jet orifices vary with the degree of throttle opening and the speed of the engine.

The CD is a simple, compact and dustproof instrument with a concentric float chamber surrounding the jet orifice. This arrangement has certain advantages over the outrigged float chamber of the SU such as a steep flooding angle which insures good operation in hilly country and during hard cornering.

Three aluminum die castings are used in the CD: the main body, the suction chamber and float chamber. The air valve body and housing for the housing for the jet assembly are also light castings resulting an extremely light weight carburetor relative to bore size and air flow. A fast-idle setting is incorporated in the throttle to provide for increased engine speed during warm-up periods.

A description of the operation and adjustment of the CD follows. All numerals are references to callouts on the accompanying drawings.

PRINCIPLES OF OPERATION

Fuel enters the inlet 1. From here it passes into the float chamber via the needle 5, where flow is controlled by needle 8 and the twin expanded rubber floats on the common arm 7. As fuel level rises the floats lift and close the needle on its seat (by means of the float arm and tag) when correct level in the chamber has been attained. As the engine runs and fuel is drawn from the float chamber, the floats descend and again open the needle valve, thus maintaining a proper fuel supply at all times. (See " Float Level" for specifications)

Starting from Cold

When the choke control on the instrument panel is pulled out it operates the lever 6 at the side of the carburetor, this rotates the starter bar 20 to lift the air valve 18 in which is fitted the metering needle 29 from the jet orifice 19 to increase the area of the annulus between needle and orifice. In this manner the enriched mixture necessary to ensure cold starting is provided. Simultaneously, the cam on the lever 6 will open the throttle beyond the normal idle position according to the setting of the fast-idle stop screw 4 to provide the fast-idle speed when the motor is cold.

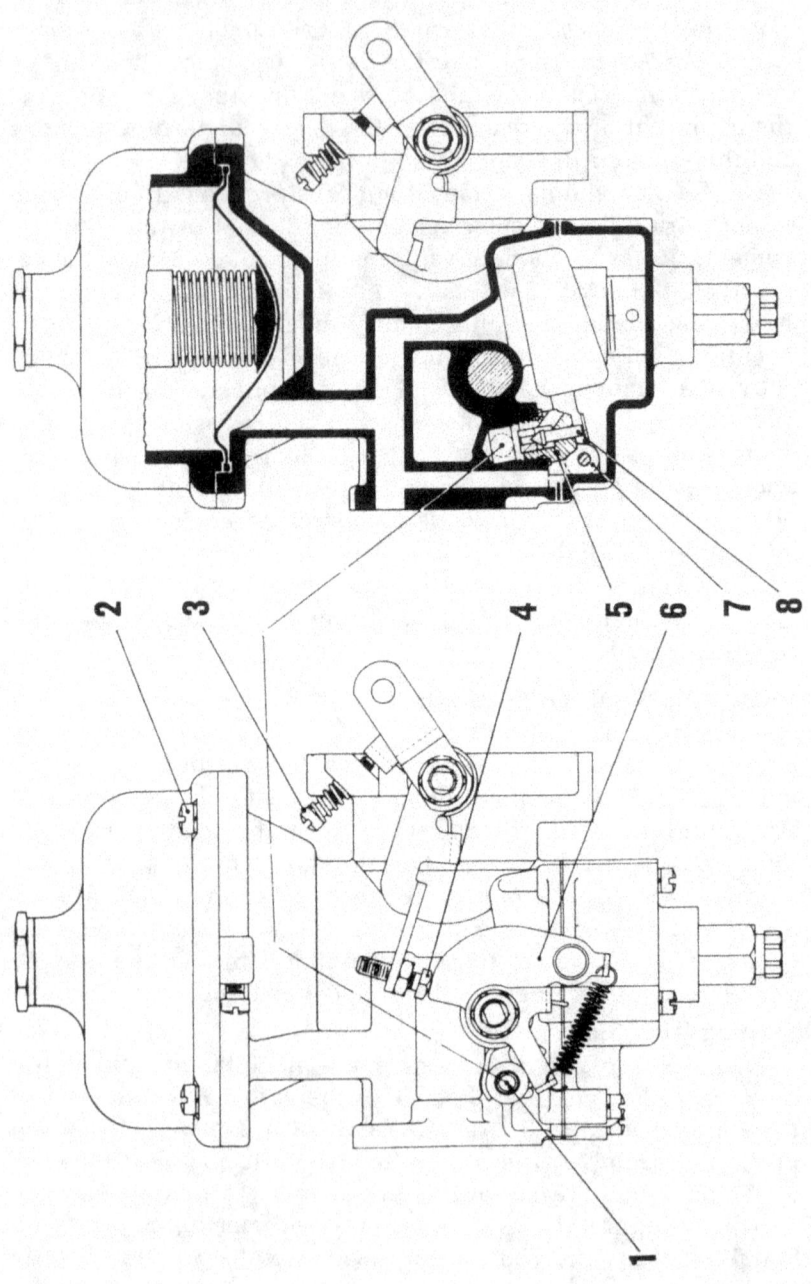

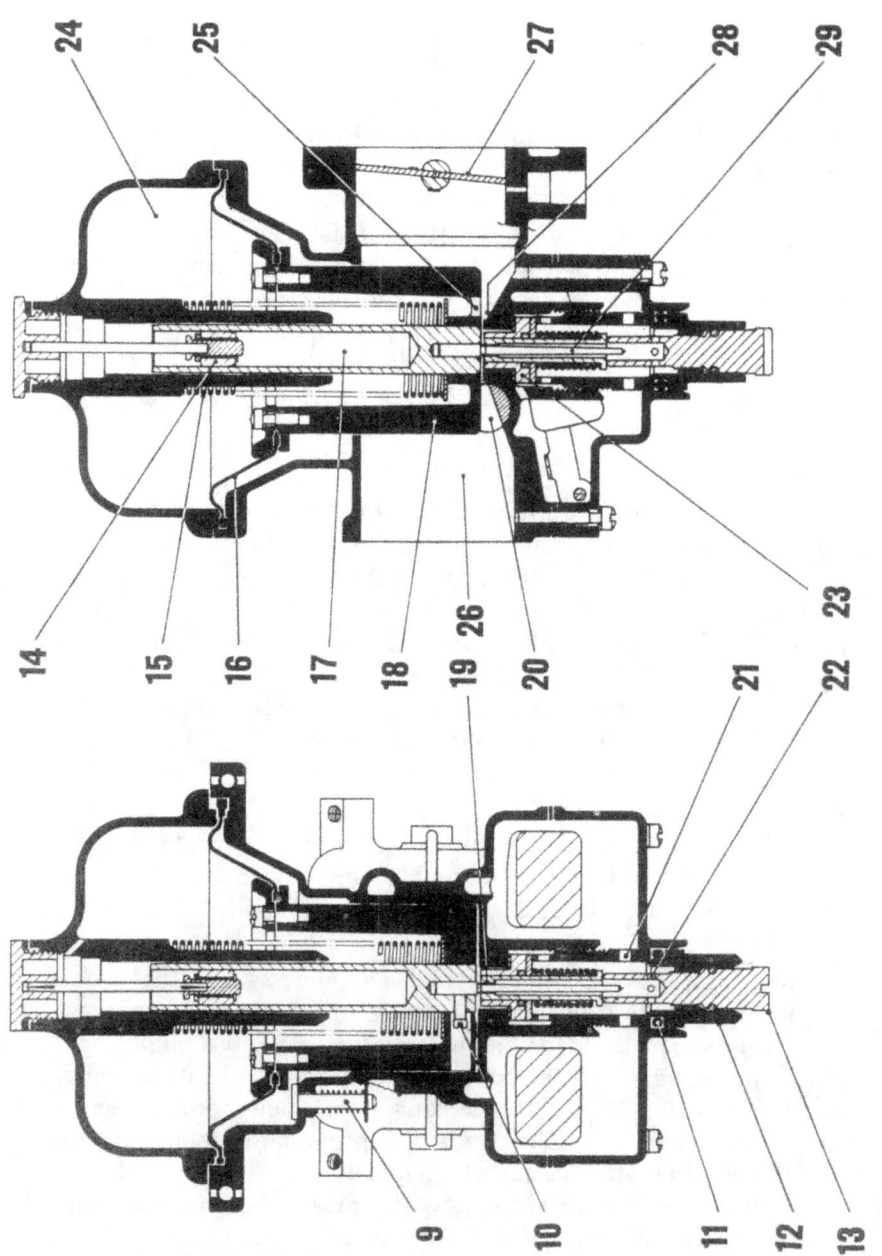

When the motor fires the increased depression will lift the air valve 18 to weaken the initial starting mixture and prevent the engine stalling through over richness.

While the choke remains in action the car may be driven away but the control knob should be released or pushed in gradually as the engine attains normal working temperature.

It will be appreciated that movement of the choke lever 6 will decrease progressively the extent of enrichment and degree of throttle opening for fast-idle to the point where the screw 4 is out of contact with the cam on the choke lever and the throttle is permitted to return to the normal idle position as determined by the setting of the throttle stop screw 3.

Note: The accelerator pedal should not be depressed when starting from cold.

Idling

There is no separate idling circuit in the Stromberg CD, and the fuel is provided by the jet orifice 19, the amount being controlled by the setting of the orifice adjusting screw 13 and the speed of idle by adjustment to the throttle stop screw 3 which limits the closure of the throttle when the foot is off the accelerator pedal.

Turning the orifice adjusting screw **clockwise** decreases the mixture strength; **anti-clockwise** will enrich.

Normal Running

With the opening of the butterfly throttle manifold depression is transferred (via a drilling 25 in the air valve) to the chamber 24 which is sealed from the main body by the diaphragm 16.

The pressure difference between chamber 24 and that existing in the bore 26 causes the air valve to lift, thus any increase in engine speed or load will enlarge the effective choke area since the air valve lift is proportional to the weight of air passing the throttle 27. By this means air velocity and pressure drop across the jet orifice remain approximately constant ensuring good fuel atomisation at all speeds.

As the air valve 18 rises it withdraws a tapered metering needle 29 held in the base of the air valve by the screw 10 from the jet orifice 19 so that fuel flow is increased relative to the greater air flow.

The metering needle is a variable and is machined to very close limits to provide a mixture ratio for all speeds and loads in line with engine requirements as determined by exhaustive tests on bench and road by specialists working in collaboration with the engine manufacturers.

Acceleration

At any point in the throttle range a temporarily richer mixture is needed at the moment the throttle is suddenly opened. To provide this, a dashpot or hydraulic damper is arranged inside the hollow guide rod 17 of the air valve.

The rod itself is filled with suitable oil to within a $1/4''$ of the end of the rod in which the damper 14 operates. When the throttle is opened, the immediate upward motion of the air valve is resisted by this plunger. For that short time the suction or depression at the jet orifice is increased and the mixture is enriched.

As a general rule the same grade of oil may be used in the dashpot to that which is used in the crankcase of the engine.

The downward movement of the air valve 18 is assisted by the coil spring 15.

Adjustments

Setting the Idle

Two adjustments are employed when regulating the idle speed and mixture, and the following procedure should be adopted in setting the throttle stop screw 3 which controls the speed, and jet adjusting screw 13 which determines the quality of air-fuel mixture entering the cylinders.

Remove the air cleaner and hold the air valve 18 down on to the bridge 28 in the throttle bore. Now screw up the jet adjustment screw 13 (a coin is ideal for this purpose) until the jet is felt to come into contact with the underside of the air valve. From this position turn down the jet adjusting screw three turns. This establishes an approximate jet position from which to work.

Run the engine until it is thoroughly warm, and obtain by means of the stop screw 3 an idle speed of some 600/650 r.p.m.

The idle mixture will be correct when the engine beat is smooth and regular, and by careful and gradual adjustment of the jet adjustment screw 13 the correct position will be determined.

As a check, lift the air valve a very small amount ($1/32''$) with a long thin screw-driver and listen to the effect on the engine. If the engine speed rises appreciably, the mixture is too rich and, conversely, if the engine stops, the mixture is too weak. Properly adjusted, the engine speed will either remain constant or fall slightly on lifting the air valve.

Adjusting and Synchronizing Twin Carburetor Installation

Loosen the clamping bolts on the throttle spindle couplings between the two instruments. Next unscrew the throttle stop screws to permit the throttles in each carburetor to close completely, then tighten the clamping bolts on the couplings between the spindles of the two carburetors.

Screw in the throttle stop screws 3 to the point where the end of the screw is just contacting the stop lever attached to each throttle spindle. From this point rotate the stop screw in each carburetor one complete turn to open the throttles an equal amount to provide a basis from which final speed of idle can be set.

Having reconnected the throttles and set each open an equal amount, regulate the jet adjusting screws 13 in the instruments as detailed under the heading "Setting the Idle" i.e. three turns down from the point where the jet orifice comes into contact with the base of the air valve 18.

When the engine is at normal temperature final adjustment to the jet adjusting screws and throttle stop screws can be effected. First set the stop screws to a suitable idle speed, turning each screw a similar amount. Finally the jet adjusting screws, turning each an equal amount until idling is even, as previously detailed.

If care is exercised in setting each throttle open the same extent then lifting each air valve in turn will give similar reaction as outlined under the instruction "Setting the Idle" and any final setting of the jet adjusting screw can be made to ensure idle speed remains constant or falls slightly on lifting the valve.

Note: Remember that the idle quality depends to a large extent upon the general engine condition and such points as tappet adjustment, spark plugs and ignition timing should be inspected if idling is not stable. It is also important to eliminate any leaks at manifold joints. There will come a time when the wear of throttle spindle and bearings in the carburetor will effect idle and it will be advisable to replace the spindle. Later, when a new spindle is not effective by reason of the degree of wear in bearings in the unit it will be necessary to fit a new carburetor.

Float Level

When correctly set and with the carburetor inverted the highest point of the floats should be approximately $\%_6''$ (14 to 15 m.m.) above the face of the main body with the fuel inlet needle on its seating.

Great care must be taken not to twist or distort the float arms, to ensure a constant fuel level.

Should it be necessary to reset the float level, this can be carried out by bending the tag which contacts the end of the needle 8. Care should be taken to maintain the tag at right angles to the needle in the closed position.

Note: An additional washer under the needle seating assembly will lower the level and is a simpler method of effecting a small change than bending the tag on the float.

Jet Centralization

The efficient operation of the carburetor depends on free movement of the air valve and needle in the jet orifice. In the Stromberg there is annular clearance around the orifice bush 23 which permits the lateral positioning of the bush and jet. Thus it may be clamped up in such a position that the metering needle 29 moves freely in the orifice 19.

When the carburetor leaves the factory the orifice bush is in the correct position and this can be checked by lifting the air valve by means of the spring loaded pin 9 and noting that the valve falls freely.

If for any reason, the jet assembly is removed, it must be re-centered.

Procedure

1. Lift the air valve 18 and tighten the jet assembly 12 fully.
2. Screw up the orifice adjuster until the top of the orifice 19 is just above the bridge 28.
3. Slacken off the whole jet assembly 12 approximately half-a-turn to release the orifice bush 23.
4. Allow the air valve 18 to fall; the needle will then enter the orifice and thus automatically centralize it. If necessary, assist the air valve drop by inserting a soft metal rod in the dashpot after unscrewing the damper.
5. Tighten the assembly 12 slowly, checking frequently that the needle remains free in the orifice. Check by raising the air valve approximately $1/4''$ and allowing it to fall freely. The piston should then stop firmly on the bridge.
6. Reset idle as outlined earlier.

Sticking of the air valve can be explained by dirt or carbon on the outside diameter of the air valve and the bore in which the air valve moves or if the metering needle is bent.

To remove the air valve assembly take off the top cover by undoing the screws 2 when the assembly with diaphragm can be lifted out of the main body.

The outside of the air valve and the bore can be wiped clean with a rag that is moistened with fuel or solvent but if the diaphragm is cleaned with gas it will expand and one will have to allow it to dry for a few minutes before it will fit on the bead and recess for the locating tab. Therefore, if it is necessary to clean the diaphragm it is best to use solvent.

In common with other products made from rubber compounds any contact of the diaphragm with volatile cleaners such as trichloroethylene should be avoided.

If examination of the needle indicates it is bent it should be replaced with a new one bearing the specified marking as detailed in the specification for the particular make and model of engine.

In replacing or fitting a new metering needle the shoulder must line up with the lower face of the air valve and the locking screw 10 tightened fully.

The needle is machined to very close limits and should be handled with care.

Air Valve/Diaphragm Assembly

A bead and locating tab is moulded to both the inner and outer radii of the diaphragm to ensure correct positioning of this item.

The diaphragm is secured to the air valve by a ring and screws with lockwashers and it is very necessary to ensure the bead is correctly located and the screws tightened fully.

Location for the bead and tab on the outer radii of the diaphragm is provided by a location channel at the top of the main body.

It is important that location beads and tabs are accurately positioned.

When refitting the suction chamber cover, place it accurately so that the screw holes line up with those in the main body, this will prevent any disturbance of the located diaphragm.

VelocePress "Autobooks" Service & Repair Manuals

Through our partnership with Brooklands Books Ltd, VelocePress is pleased to bring back these easy to read, concise repair manuals that have been out-of-print and unavailable for a number of years. The "Autobooks" series of manuals are guaranteed to become your close companion in the shop. We have included a sample listing, however, for the most up-to-date information please visit our website at **www.VelocePress.com**

- Alfa Romeo Giulia 1300, 1600, 1750, 2000 1962-1978 WSM
- Austin Healey Sprite, MG Midget 1958-1980 WSM
- BMW 1600 1966-1973 WSM
- Fiat 124 1966-1974 WSM
- Fiat 124 Sport 1966-1975 WSM
- Fiat 125, 125 Special 1967-1973 WSM
- Fiat 126 / 650 1972-1982 WSM
- Fiat 127, 900, 1050, 1971-81 W/S Manual
- Fiat 128 1969-1982 WSM
- Fiat 131 1975-1982 WSM
- Fiat 132 1972-1982 WSM
- Fiat 500 1957-1973 WSM
- Fiat 600 & Multipla 1955-1969 WSM
- Fiat 850 1964-1972 WSM
- Fiat 1100 & 1200 1957-1969 WSM
- Fiat 1300, 1500 1961-1967 WSM
- Jaguar E-Type 1961-1972 WSM
- Jaguar Mk 1, 2 1955-1969 WSM
- Jaguar S Type 420 1963-1968 WSM
- Jaguar XK 120, 140, 150 MK 7, 8, 9 1948-1961 WSM
- Land-Rover 1, 2 1948-1961 WSM
- Mercedes-Benz 190 1959-1968 WSM
- Mercedes-Benz 230 1963-1968 WSM
- Mercedes-Benz 250 1968-1972 WSM
- MG Midget TA-TF 1936-1955 WSM
- Mini 1959-1980 WSM
- Morris Minor 1952-1971 WSM
- Peugeot 404 1960-1975 WSM
- Porsche 911 1964-1969 WSM
- Porsche 911 1970-1977 WSM
- Renault 16 1965-1979 WSM
- Renault 8, 10 1100 1962-1971 WSM
- Rover 3500, 3500S 1968-1976 WSM
- Sunbeam Rapier, Alpine 1955-1965 WSM
- Triumph Spitfire, GT6, Vitesse 1962-1968 WSM
- Triumph TR2, TR3, TR3A 1952-1962 WSM
- Triumph TR4, TR4A 1961-1967 WSM
- Volkswagen Beetle 1968-77 WSM

VelocePress "Books & Manuals"

We have included a sample listing, however, for the most up-to-date information please visit our website at www.VelocePress.com

- FERRARI GUIDE TO PERFORMANCE
- IF HEMINGWAY HAD WRITTEN A RACING NOVEL
- OBERT'S FIAT GUIDE
- LE MANS 24
- FERRARI SERIAL NUMBERS PART I
- FERRARI SERIAL NUMBERS PART II
- MASERATI BROCHURES AND SALES LITERATURE
- FERRARI TUNING TIPS & MAINTENANCE TECHNIQUES
- ABARTH BUYERS GUIDE
- BMW ISETTA FACTORY WS MANUAL
- MASERATI OWNER'S HANDBOOK
- FERRARI BERLINETTA LUSSO
- FERRARI OWNER'S HANDBOOK
- FERRARI 250/GT SERVICE AND MAINTENANCE
- DIALED IN - THE JAN OPPERMAN STORY
- FERRARI BROCHURES & SALES LITERATURE 1946-1967
- FERRARI OPP, MAINTENANCE & SERVICE H/BOOKS 1948-1963
- PERFORMANCE TUNING THE SUNBEAM TIGER
- TRIUMPH MOTORCYCLES WS MANUAL 1937-1951
- TRIUMPH MOTORCYCLES FACTORY WS MANUAL 1945-1955
- TRIUMPH MOTORCYCLES (BOOK OF) WS MANUAL 1935-1939
- BMW M/CYCLES FACTORY WS MANUAL R26 R27 (1956-1967)
- BMW M/CYCLES FACTORY WSM R50 R50S R60 R69S (1955-1969)
- NORTON MOTORCYCLES FACTORY WS MANUAL 1957-1970
- NORTON MOTORCYCLES WS MANUAL 1932-1939
- FERRARI 308 SERIES BUYER'S AND OWNER'S GUIDE
- ARIEL MOTORCYCLES WS MANUAL 1933-1951
- VINCENT MOTORCYCLES MAINTENANCE AND REPAIR 1935-1955
- FERRARI SPYDER CALIFORNIA
- AUSTIN-HEALEY 6-CYLINDER MAINTENANCE & REPAIR
- HONDA MOTORCYCLES WSM 250-305 TWINS C/CS/CB SERIES
- PORSCHE 356 OWNERS WORKSHOP MANUAL 1948-1965
- PORSCHE 912 WORKSHOP MANUAL
- VOLVO 1944-1968 WS MANUAL ALL MODELS
- HONDA MOTORCYCLES MANUAL: 1960-1966 50cc TO 305cc
- DUCATI FACTORY WSM: 160cc, 250cc & 350cc OHC MODELS.
- ROYAL ENFIELD FACTORY WS MANUAL: 736cc INTERCEPTOR
- FERRARI BROCHURES AND SALES LITERATURE 1968-1989

———————www.VelocePress.com———————

www.ingramcontent.com/pod-product-compliance
Lightning Source LLC
Chambersburg PA
CBHW050135240426
43673CB00043B/1672